THE BARN OWL

Frontispiece The Barn Owl *Tyto alba alba* (photo: Roy France).

THE
BARN OWL

by

D. S. Bunn, A. B. Warburton and
R. D. S. Wilson

Illustrated by
IAN WILLIS

BUTEO BOOKS

Vermillion, South Dakota

598.97
B

ISBN 0–931130–09–3
Library of Congress Catalog Card Number 82–72126

Published in USA in 1982 by Buteo Books,
PO Box 481, Vermillion, South Dakota 57069 and
in Great Britain by T. & A. D. Poyser Ltd,
Town Head House, Calton, Waterhouse, Staffordshire, England

Text set in 10/11 pt Linotron Baskerville, printed by photolithography,
and bound in Great Britain at The Pitman Press, Bath

Contents

List of Photographs

List of Figures

List of Tables

Preface

Over the years it has become obvious to us that most of our relatives, friends and casual acquaintances have come to regard us as mentally deranged as a result of our long study of the Barn Owl: we are for ever being asked why we do it. Our only defence is to reply that there are many reasons, and because we realise that such an answer will satisfy nobody we have attempted to write this book in the hope that the reader will gain at least some inkling of the charisma of owl watching. We do lose inordinate amounts of sleep, we do get eaten alive by a varied assortment of biting flies, gnats, mosquitoes and midges, we are frequently exposed to the vagaries of the British climate, enduring a wide variety of conditions from freezing cold, torrential rain and dripping mist, to hot, muggy nights which make a night spent in a small hide a nightmare as the pounds drip off! We do spend long hours when absolutely nothing happens – *but*, at the end of the day we can turn for inspiration to Eric Hosking, that doyen of bird photographers who must surely be the model for all field naturalists. In his autobiography *An Eye for a Bird* he writes: 'In a lifetime of bird photography owls have brought me the greatest pleasure'. That, coming from a man who has been to so many marvellous places, has seen and photographed such a wide variety of species – and what is more, lost an eye to an owl – says it all, and makes further comment from us superfluous.

This monograph is the result of 19 years intensive study of the Barn Owl *Tyto alba* in various parts of north-west England, carried out between 1963 and 1982. As two of the authors were involved in the main fieldwork the observations represent the equivalent of 38 years work by a single observer.

Derek Bunn's studies took place in a remote, young conifer forest in the West Riding of Yorkshire (now Lancashire), in semi-suburban surroundings in east Lancashire, and in limestone pasture in south Westmorland (now Cumbria). Tony Warburton's work was based in south-west Cumbria in lowland farmland, a young mixed conifer plantation on fells surrounded by mature deciduous forest, and on dunes and wasteland near the sea. Thus, we have had the opportunity to study the bird in virtually all its habitats, and to compare its behaviour in each.

Since the bulk of our findings were concerned with northern birds we have been in constant touch with other observers throughout the country, and by utilising their data we hope that we have been able to produce a balanced picture of the Barn Owl in Britain as a whole, at the same time comparing this race's behaviour with that of sub-species in other parts of the world where appropriate.

·Due to a unique set of circumstances we have been able to supplement our observations of wild Barn Owls with those of birds watched at close quarters at A.B.W.'s home in Cumbria.

For the past ten years we have operated a breeding and nest-box scheme which has had as its main objective the release of young Barn Owls into the wild in suitable habitats. This has resulted in a very strong population of owls which live and breed in the immediate vicinity of the release area (including the garden) and these individuals have provided outstanding opportunities for close study of the year-long behaviour and inter-relationships of a viable population of Barn Owls.

It is now hard to believe that there was once a time when we felt it unlikely that enough would ever be learned of the Barn Owl's habits for a monograph to be contemplated. D.S.B. was fortunate in working in an area where the species was reasonably numerous, but none of his subjects used nesting sites where they could be profitably observed. A.B.W. on the other hand, was able to observe a pair at close quarters until one adult was shot. He then experienced great difficulty in finding other individuals, due to the extreme scarcity of the bird in the late 1960s in that part of Lakeland where he lived.

Whilst D.S.B. and A.B.W. were searching for subjects to observe, Robert Wilson was combing diligently through the literature for helpful references (a task which D.S.B. and A.B.W. found onerous, but which he, thankfully, seemed to enjoy!). In folklore the Barn Owl figures so prominently that in this respect his efforts were well rewarded and we hope that the chapter which resulted will enhance the appeal of our monograph. There were also many papers on the bird's diet, no doubt because of the ease with which the pellets of this species can be collected and analysed, but as regards behaviour there was almost nothing more detailed than that already contained in the better bird books.

Why then did we persevere with our plans to produce a monograph? The main reason was the very fact that so little was known about the species: due to most people's pre-occupation with sleeping at night, we were exploring untrodden ground and almost everything we observed was new and unrecorded – surely no field naturalist could wish for a better incentive to contribute something to science than this – or so we told our wives! Fortunately, as time passed, things changed for the better and there seemed less reason to be pessimistic. Whereas at first we took it for granted that the study of a nocturnal owl would be one of the most difficult undertakings in ornithology, we later had to revise this opinion, at least with regard to the Barn Owl. Most important, since all three of us are amateurs, our time was free when the birds were most active; this would not have been the case with a diurnal species. Secondly, the Barn Owl is basically sedentary when adult and, though some individuals gave us much difficulty in locating them, others either inhabited the same roost, or at most a handful of alternative sites, throughout the year and these could be readily discovered by a process of elimination. Later, as we shall describe, we found that Barn Owls are often easy to watch by torchlight and sometimes it was even unnecessary to use a hide when observing their general behaviour inside a building. Again, the fact that many of the Barn Owls in the area studied by D.S.B. and R.D.S.W. hunted in daylight throughout the entire year, was not known at first but, when the discovery was made and an excellent vantage point found, these two authors were able to make observations more rewarding than they had ever imagined possible.

We have no regrets about pooling our knowledge and collaborating in the production of this book. During most of the study A.B.W. worked alone, though he and D.S.B. were in constant touch. Only when it was realised that whoever proceeded to publish an account of Barn Owl behaviour would have to refer continually to the other's findings was it decided that the only sensible solution was to join forces. If either had relied on his own fieldwork this book could not have been published until a much later date. How well we agree with Donald Watson, who wrote in his excellent monograph, *The Hen Harrier* (1977): 'One of the rewards of a continuous study of one species is the realisation that the character of individuals differs widely and very little behaviour is predictable'. In no species is this more apparent than in the Barn Owl. It seems to delight in destroying all pre-conceived theories and 'facts' just when the observer is getting most confident that he understands his subject's every whim and facet of behaviour. It is this very unpredictability which lures the field-worker on in a bid to gain an insight into the mind of this most enigmatic of birds. In such circumstances, the opportunity to pool one's knowledge with the findings of another 'sufferer' is a god-send – and as we have found out – almost a necessity!

In acknowledging the help we have received from others we must first of all express our profound gratitude to those people who have allowed us to visit and carry out our observations on their land and premises; without these facilities this study could never have been contemplated. A.B.W. wishes to thank Mr J. Ashbrook, Mr J. R. Morris-Eyton, Mrs M. Walker, and in particular the Ministry of Defence for allowing him to carry out his Breeding and Release Scheme on their property. D.S.B. will be eternally grateful to Miss R. Edmundson and Mr & Mrs D. Lord, as well as to the Forestry Commission whose staff gave the project their full co-operation and support.

We would also like to thank those countless people who have willingly talked and corresponded with us, passing on their knowledge and experiences and thereby adding to the value of this book. Many of them are mentioned by name in the text but we wish to say a special thank-you to Derick Scott who has allowed us to draw freely from his voluminous notes on the species and to use whichever of his superb photographs we wanted. Dr D. W. Yalden of the Department of Zoology at Manchester University has helped us with a wide variety of problems during the course of the study and R.D.S.W. received valuable assistance from the staff of the Cambridge University Library, and from Miss Janet Varley who helped with the German translations. We must also acknowledge the help of the staff of the Royal Society for the Protection of Birds, in particular Neil Bowman and

Roger Lovegrove of the Wales Office, and the staff of the British Trust for Ornithology. We are particularly grateful to the latter organisation for permission to make use of their data on nest records, distribution and status. In this respect special mention must be made of the contribution of David Glue, who has kindly allowed us to draw on his analyses of Barn Owl diet and breeding behaviour, and of Robert Hudson who made invaluable suggestions for improving the original typescript. We are also indebted to Dr T. Clay, A. M. Hutson, F. G. A. M. Smit, K. H. Hyatt and S. Prudhoe, all of the British Museum (Natural History), for the information on parasites, and to Dr D. W. Snow of the Ornithology Department for his generous advice on a number of matters. Special thanks must go to Dr R. J. Kennedy, Tony Duckels and the others of the South-west Lancashire Ringing Group for keeping us informed of the progress of their Barn Owl nest-box study, allowing us to use their findings and sending us countless papers related to Barn Owl behaviour. D.S.B. also wishes to acknowledge the help of his good friend, the late Mr H. Clarke, who assisted with observations on several occasions when extra help was needed and who did much of the work in setting up and maintaining the nest-boxes in the forest study area. A.B.W., and indeed all of us, have to thank Messrs R. France, P. Hanson, D. Malpus and I. Marshall, who, after being invited to photograph various owls this author was studying, obtained some excellent shots, a few of which have been included here by way of illustration. Other valuable photographs have been donated by G. Himsworth, S. Lumley, A. Gate, W. Palfrey and E. J. & E. W. Ratcliffe, to all of whom we are greatly indebted. A.B.W. would also like to say a special thank-you to his long-suffering wife, Joan, for her continuing patience and encouragement during her years as an 'owl widow' while he carried out his research on the species.

Finally, in a last bid to justify our long obsession with the Barn Owl, let us quote Messrs Potter & Gillespie who wrote in 1925: 'The study of the Barn Owl is certain to furnish countless thrills, many a quickening of the pulse, and a greater appreciation of the economic value of this grotesque benefactor of mankind'. While remaining amazed that anyone could find such a beautiful creature 'grotesque', we heartily endorse their general sentiments.

D. S. BUNN
A. B. WARBURTON
R. D. S. WILSON

CHAPTER 1

Description and adaptations

CLASSIFICATION

The external characteristics of the order Strigiformes, which includes all the owls, are so well known as to render a description hardly necessary, and we believe an account of the internal structure would be exceeding the scope of this book. Most striking is the possession of a facial disk, though this is by no means so well developed in all species as in the Barn Owl. A sharp curved beak, a cere at its base and powerful needle-sharp claws that have earned the name of talons, are also constant throughout the order, while the fourth toe has much lateral movement so that it can be directed either forwards or backwards. There are eleven primaries, the eleventh (counting from the inside) being very small and hidden in the coverts. The eggs are white and laid in holes, or on the ground or in the old nests of other birds. The plumage is soft and loose and there is a special juvenile or *mesoptile* plumage, more fluffy than that of the adults, which succeeds the short (*protoptile*) down that the young possess on hatching.

Under the current generally accepted classification, essentially that given by Peters (1940), the order Strigiformes is divided into two families, each being further divided into two sub-families. The family Tytonidae is divided into the Tytoninae (Barn Owls and Grass Owls), all of the genus *Tyto*, and the Phodilinae (Bay Owls), both – there are only two species – of the genus *Phodilus*. The Phodilinae are said to be somewhat intermediate in structure between the Tytonidae and the major group of owls, the Strigidae, whose two sub-families, the Buboninae and the Striginae, contain numerous genera.*

The Strigidae have the inner toe much shorter than the middle toe; the

* Several authors (e.g. Ford 1967 and Norberg 1973) reject this separation which is based entirely upon the structure of the external ear.

inter-orbital septum (the bone dividing the two eye sockets) is thin; and the sternum (breast bone) possesses two deep incisions on either side. The Tytonidae have the inner and middle toes roughly the same length, the claw of the latter possessing a comb-like structure (Fig. 1a); the skull is proportionately longer, the inter-orbital septum is thick and the orbits relatively small; the sternum is fused to the furcula (wishbone) and has either one shallow incision or none; the facial disk is particularly well developed.

The members of the genus *Tyto* are characterised by their unusual colour pattern, by the long and almost equal eighth, ninth and tenth primaries, the tenth having the tips of the barbs all along their outer webs recurved and separated (Fig. 1b), and by the mesoptile (intermediate) plumage of the young being downy and quite unfeatherlike. The general appearance of the adults is rendered distinctly different from that of most Strigidae due to the long legs bearing only short feathers and the tibia being not so often hidden among the flank feathers; the tarsal joints are held close together and give Barn Owls a very characteristic knock-kneed appearance.

The classification described above is, however, far from being the last word on the taxonomy of the order. *The Handbook of British Birds* (Witherby et al 1943), for instance, adopts a classification under which the Barn Owls are only given separate sub-family rank, while, conversely, Professor C. G. Sibley of Cornell University, New York, has proposed the rather startling theory that they have a closer relationship with the falcons than with the other group of owls. He points out, in a lengthy paper published in 1960, that the systematists are continually faced with the problem of evolutionary convergence because structural and behavioural similarities may have arisen among unrelated groups by adaptation to exploit a particular ecological niche. Nor does he wholly accept the evidence for a relationship between groups sometimes provided by the presence of related species of feather-lice (Mallophaga) on *apparently* unrelated birds, since the parasites may have taken advantage only of a convergence in the feather structure. On the other hand, Sibley maintains that the molecular structure of the proteins characterising species is likely to be much more stable. This he studied by a method known as paper electrophoresis, using egg-whites, which is 'a process by which ions or other charged particles are caused to migrate in an electrical field. . . . The distance which a protein molecule moves on the horizontal axis is a function of its electrophoretic properties, i.e. net charge, size, shape, etc, and they identify the protein'. The results were studied by translating them into diagrammatic 'profiles' which could be compared with those of other species In some cases unexpected similarities or dissimilarities were noted which led to some proposed amendments to the currently accepted classification.

The phylogenetic (evolutionary) relationships between the higher groups of birds (that is the families and orders), have always been a difficult problem and a subject on which most ornithologists, including ourselves, are not qualified to comment. However, Professor Sibley's theory that the Barn Owl may be a 'nocturnal falcon' has not been accepted at the time of writing. The reviews of Vaurie (1960 and 1965) and of Voous (1960) made no changes to Peters' (1940) classification and neither does the checklist of owls of the world by Burton et al (1973). Everett (1977) follows Burton et al, but more positively considers *T. longimembris* as a sub-species of *T. capensis*.

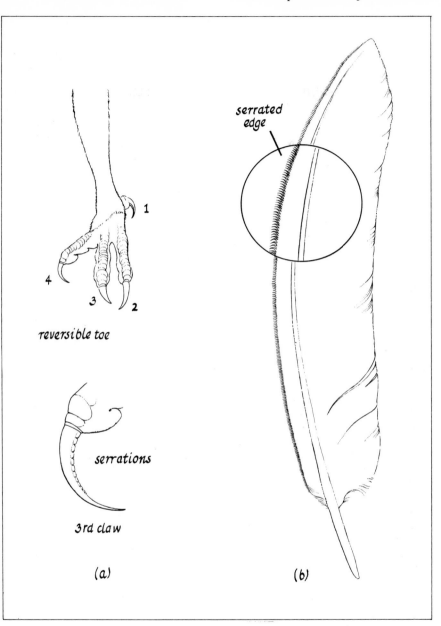

reversible toe

serrations

3rd claw

serrated edge

(a)

(b)

Fig. 1 Right foot and tenth primary feather of the Barn Owl (drawing by Ian Willis).

DESCRIPTION

At close quarters the coloration of *Tyto alba alba* is exquisite, yet on still closer examination the pattern can be seen to have been achieved very simply: with the exception of the primaries, secondaries and tail, every one of the feathers of the upperparts is buff with a distal alternate dark brown and greyish-white fleck and a varying amount of grey pencilling, most evident on the back and wing-coverts. The heaviness of these markings and size of the flecks varies individually, but is usually most marked in females. Likewise, the shade of buff varies, from a pale yellow to a rich reddish brown. Additionally, the extent of the buff and grey coloration varies; often in females the buff extends on to the breast. Conversely, in males the white underparts tend to extend on to the sides of the neck. A few dark flecks are usually present on the flanks.

The under wing-coverts are white with, perhaps, a few dark flecks and/or a little buff suffusion. Above, on their outer webs and along the inner webs near the shaft, the primaries and secondaries are buff with dark transverse bars and a varying degree of grey pencilling mainly at the tips; the bases of the feathers and the rest of their inner webs are white. Below, the buff coloration and barring is much fainter.

The tail feathers, of which there are twelve, are usually buff with dark bars and often some grey pencilling towards their tips; they are paler below. The central pair are the most strongly coloured, with the inner and outer webs evenly marked; the others are paler on their inner webs, the feathers becoming progressively whiter with fainter bars from the middle pair to the outer pair. A few individuals have been noted with entirely white tails.

The barring on both wings and tail is usually darkest in females, but again there is much individual variation, one light cock observed for many years having pure white primaries. Besides the ten long primaries and sixteen secondaries which are as described, there is a rudimentary eleventh primary only about 5·5 cm long, lying out of sequence above the second primary. It is white, sometimes tipped faint buff or with a dark distal streak.

The facial disk is white, usually with a patch of reddish brown in the corners of the eyes. The ends of the stiff feathers which form a ruff at the back of the disk may be either white, buff or buff with a blackish tip. The tendency is for the lower edge of the disk to be darkest, but some birds possess no coloured tips to the feathers.

The tibia and tarsus are feathered white, the feathers becoming progressively shorter and thinner towards the toes which bear only sparse white bristles.

This adult plumage is acquired while still in the nest, after the second down (which replaces the juvenile feathers of the Strigidae and most other birds for that matter).

The degree of variation in the plumage of this species was of enormous help in our studies. On the wing and at some distance from the observer, especially if he is watching from an elevated position, one Barn Owl may appear predominantly brown, while another will appear entirely white. The open wings of a lightly marked cock bird show so many light patches that the illusion of complete whiteness is very convincing, whereas a darker bird may appear very much like a Short-eared Owl in general colour. Thus, even at a distance, taking all factors into account it was usually possible to recognise our subjects individually when they were active in daylight.

The sexing of Barn Owls from the plumage alone can be very difficult. At the extremes there are cock birds which are very pale above and which show much white at the sides of the neck, while dark hens may not only show a lot of grey on the upperparts but a noticeable buff suffusion on the breast. However, it does not follow that a Barn Owl with much grey on the back will also have buff on the breast, more and larger spots and strong bars on the primaries: on the contrary each character appears to be independent of the rest. Thus, for identification purposes it is preferable to describe the female simply as 'darker generally'. In consequence we are at a loss to explain why certain experienced naturalists and aviculturists have stated that the possession of buff suffusions on the breast and facial disk are frequent characteristics of the *cock* when, in fact, they provide the best evidence, when they occur, that the bird is a hen (see Photo 14).

Occasionally, Barn Owls are observed in the field, and are sometimes 'obtained', in which the amount of buff greatly exceeds that normally possessed by ordinary dark individuals of *T. alba alba*. In these cases controversy may arise as to whether such birds are examples of the Dark-breasted Barn Owl *T. alba guttata* (Brehm) or merely unusually dark varieties of our own sub-species, many amateurs perhaps rashly ascribing them to the former. On close examination, however, few prove to be so generally dark as *T. alba guttata*, which is only a rare and spasmodic wanderer to this country. In deciding upon these questions it is helpful to take into account the number and location of the birds. If several have been reported, and particularly if they have been seen in the eastern half of England, then it is quite reasonable to suppose that they belong to the Dark-breasted form.

Usually the upper parts of *T. a. guttata* bear so much grey mottling that the buff coloration typical of the lighter form is all but completely obscured; also, the light and dark flecks are found even on the underparts. The white face of *T. a. alba* is normally absent, the reddish colour confined to the corners of the eyes in *alba*, extending to a greater or lesser degree all over the disk, the edges of which are also darker. The underparts are seldom white, but rather some shade of buff, with dark spots, larger and more numerous than in *alba*. Similarly, the wings and tail are darker and more heavily barred. The sexes are said to be alike (Witherby et al 1940). See Photo 30.

T. a. guttata is a slightly bigger bird than *alba*. Witherby et al give the following measurements: male, wing 275–305 mm, tail 115–125 mm, tarsus 55–62 mm, bill from base of feathers 25–30 mm (12 measured). Female, wing 270–295 mm. Baudvin (1975) gives the average weight of 32 unsexed French birds as 346 gm. Notwithstanding the above differences, Dr Snow of the Ornithology Section of the British Museum (Natural History) has confirmed (pers. comm.) that the two sub-species cannot always be separated, and this is not surprising in view of the fact that where they overlap in their distribution (see Fig. 2) they pair off randomly (Pile 1958, Baudvin loc. cit.).

There is one annual moult which lasts from about July to September or later but, judging from the cast feathers scattered about the roosts during August and September, most of the body moult takes place in those months. The primaries and secondaries are replaced slowly so as not to affect the flight and, indeed, from the little that is known, the moult of these feathers and the tail seems to be a complicated process. According to Snow (1967), the moult of the Barn Owl is different from that of most British owls, which shed the primaries from the inside (descendently). It begins with one or other of the middle primaries and then proceeds divergently to the outer and inner ends of the row. This pattern of moult was termed 'transilient' moult by Stresemann and Stresemann (1966) who found it to be variable and irregular in the Barn Owl and sometimes uneven in the two wings. The moult of the secondaries of British owls has not been studied in detail but it is believed that they are moulted in three groups with well separated feathers being lost simultaneously. The tail moult of the Barn Owl is much slower than in the other species and is irregular in sequence.

The subject is further complicated by personal observations of owls which apparently retained primaries (recognised by their dilapidated condition) for periods of up to three years. Piechocki (1961) also noted this in captive Barn Owls. It strikes us as rather remarkable that feathers, which are subjected to so much wear as the bird plunges repeatedly into thick vegetation after prey, are able to function satisfactorily for so long, especially as some cock birds have been observed to have become very dishevelled, and even to fly noisily when flapping hard, by the end of the breeding season. In one male a general lightening of the overall plumage was noted. This may have been due to fading caused by frequent wetting and drying through persistent hunting for the young, and/or exposure to sunlight during increased diurnal activity.

One may well wonder why the Barn Owl should be coloured so conspicuously when our other owls, including the Snowy Owl, all have a plumage designed to match their surroundings. However, the Barn Owl is far more of a hole-loving bird than the other British owls, not merely nesting in dark places but roosting preferably in the same sort of situations throughout the year. This might not only reduce the importance of a camouflaged colour pattern, but might make it advantageous to have a white body so that it can be seen by its mate and young. We have known Barn Owls nest in places where the amount of light entering at night must have been very small indeed so as to make it difficult for even an owl to see, the birds largely relying, we believe, on their kinaesthetic sense – just as we do when reaching for an unseen light-switch in a dark room. Some experiments with a family of owlets in a church steeple, described by Warham (1951), would appear to support this. At night these birds, which were evidently at least five weeks old at the time, were quite oblivious to waving movements of the author's hand outside the hide, though they become alarmed at once by any movement when a light was on. Unless the adults had better nocturnal vision, they must have found it difficult or impossible to see in these quarters during the darkest part of the night. Further evidence that Barn Owls rely on their kinaesthetic sense was provided by one of our cock birds which experienced a quite inordinate amount of difficulty in making its way to its nest when a few pieces of wood, which it normally had to negotiate, had been removed from in front of the nest.

Clearly, then, white coloration could help the owls to see each other in extreme darkness and Everett (1977) proposes the same theory; but it seems to us that the existence of sub-species with dark facial disks and underparts casts considerable doubt on its validity. An attempt to substantiate a quite different hypothesis, that the Barn Owl *is* coloured to match its *natural* surroundings, in particular the predominant type of rock in its habitat, failed, although possibly only because of the authors' lack of familiarity with the Barn Owl's surroundings and nesting (and roosting) habits throughout its range. It seems reasonable to assume, however, that the darker coloration of the female *T. alba alba* serves to render her less conspicuous on the nest.

A Barn Owl is approximately 30 cm long with a wing-span of around 85 cm. Witherby et al (1940) give the following measurements for *T. alba alba*: male wing 265–290 mm, tail 110–125 mm, tarsus 55–62 mm, bill from base of feathers 23–29 mm (25 British specimens measured), female wing 265–295 mm. The British Trust for Ornithology, at the time of writing, possesses only five records of weight and it is not known whether these concern healthy adult birds. However, Baudvin (1975) quotes the average weight of 63 unsexed examples of *T. a. alba* as 337 gm. Individuals vary in size considerably and, apart from a tendency for hens to be larger – about 50 gm heavier according to Baudvin – they are certainly stockier and in the field this is the more reliable guide to sex. Otteni et al (1972) state that the female can be identified during the incubation period by the presence of a brood patch (as Baudvin also mentions) and an enlarged reddened vent during the laying period. It seems reasonable to suppose that the eldest of any brood of owlets will make a bigger bird than the others, while the youngest, which may at times go short of food, is likely whether male or female to be somewhat undersized (see Chapter 5).

BARE PARTS

To complete the external description of the adult, the iris is very dark hazel, the whole eye appearing shiny black except on close examination. The cere, which is normally hidden beneath the wedge of bristles down the centre of the disk, is whitish flesh. The bill, which is straighter and directed more downwards than the bills of our other owls (the Strigidae), is whitish horn with perhaps some pinkish flesh colour towards the base. The toes vary from dark grey-brown to quite a bright shade of yellow, especially beneath (another useful means of individual recognition), and the claws are dark horn. The inner edge of the middle claw possesses a thin flange which narrows, sometimes abruptly, into the main claw about 6 mm from its tip (see Fig. 1a). In fully adult owls this flange is pectinated and is brought into action as a comb when the owl is scratching clean the edge of its facial disk or the bristles around the gape. The Tawny Owl also, and probably other species, often engage in bouts of disk-scratching but, though the flange is present, there are no serrations. Perhaps in the course of time our other owls will evolve similar refinements as have such widely differing species as the Cormorant, Heron, Nightjar and Black-tailed Godwit. Juvenile Barn Owls lack these serrations and, for that matter, the degree of development varies a good deal from adult to adult. The fourth or outer toe is remarkably mobile, but when relaxed takes a position mid-way between the front and back of the foot; the hind toe or hallux is also capable of some lateral movement. The reason for the arrangment of the toes will be explained later. The soles of the feet bear soft pads on which the scales are raised to form numerous tiny excrescences.

Day-to-day descriptions of the young Barn Owl are, we feel, best dealt with in the chapter on breeding (Chapter 5).

Although this book is largely concerned with the sub-species *Tyto alba alba* in the British Isles, no monograph would be complete without some mention of the world distribution of the remaining 35 sub-species. Similarly, a brief description of the other eight full species of the genus and the two species in the closely related genus *Phodilus* will, it is hoped, help the reader to gain a better understanding of the position of *T. alba* in the group as a whole.

As was mentioned at the beginning of this book, all members of the Tytonidae are characterised by the possession of a highly developed facial disk and small dark eyes as typified in *T. alba*. The purpose of the disk will be dealt with in detail later in this chapter and it is only referred to at this juncture to emphasise that it marks the order as primarily night hunting throughout its range. According to Grossman and Hamlet (1965) all the species of *Tyto* have voices akin to that of *T. alba*, being basically variations of the screech.

SUB-SPECIES

It is generally accepted that the Barn Owl *T. alba* is the most widespread land bird in the world and it is often described as 'cosmopolitan' – see Fig. 2. The range overlaps and supplements those of grass, brush, swamp and forest dwelling species of owl and shows a fair degree of adaptability to several variations of habitat. It is found in most tropical zones of the world and in temperate regions wherever the winter temperature does not fall too low. It usually avoids deserts and dense forests, as these are unsuitable habitats, and it is not found in any tundra region. It favours regions where the climate is tolerably dry and this is probably connected with its method of hunting, for as we have mentioned elsewhere, damp vegetation is a severe handicap to the bird. Because of its low resistance to cold it avoids areas such as Siberia, northern Russia, northern Canada, northern Scandinavia, Antarctica and high altitude countries such as Bhutan and Sikkim in the Himalayan Mountains.

Perhaps the most surprising feature about its world distribution is its virtual absence from New Zealand where the habitat would appear to be suitable for it to have spread successfully from the Australian regions. Its failure to do so is, perhaps, a further indication of its basically sedentary nature and usual aversion to crossing large expanses of water – though the periodic appearances in the British Isles of *T. a. guttata*, which crosses the North Sea from Europe, prove that shorter distances are not beyond its capabilities. Indeed in 1947, 1955 and 1960 the Australian Barn Owl *T. a. deliculata* did succeed in reaching New Zealand, for single individuals were observed in those years. It is also interesting to note that sub-fossil bones discovered in sand-dunes at Northland, New Zealand, in January 1966,

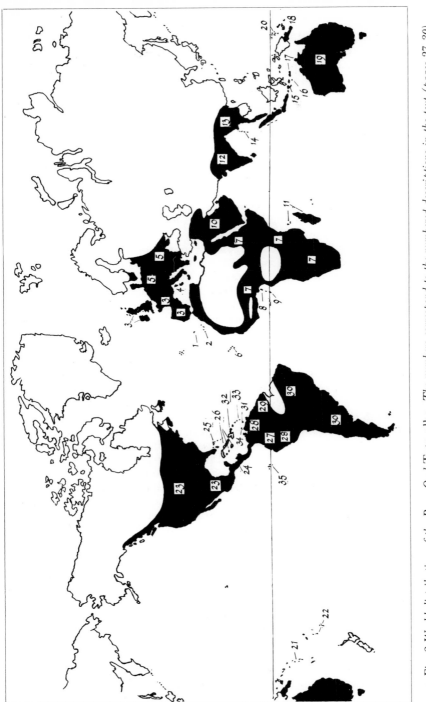

Fig. 2 World distribution of the Barn Owl Tyto alba. *The numbers correspond to the numbered descriptions in the text (pages 27–30).*

probably belonged to *T. a. deliculata*. It is probable, however, that most island forms were endemic when their habitats became separated from the mainland and that the characteristics which now make them distinct were evolved later; only those on islands very close to land seem likely to have arrived by their own powers of flight. The exception to this is the introduced Barn Owl of the Seychelles *T. a. affinis*.

Amongst the sub-species several differing colour phases occur. Though all have a basically similar plumage to that of our own race some birds are much darker and others much lighter, and in some parts light and dark phases occur in the same range. Both white-breasted and orange-breasted forms are to be found in North, Central and South America, the Caribbean Islands, the Galapagos Islands, Africa, the Comoro Islands and Madagascar, Sri Lanka, India, north Burma and Malaysia.

Orange-breasted individuals are generally darker above with a brownish facial disk and yellow-orange underparts, spotted with brown. In northern and eastern Europe a phase occurs which is dark in colour and has a reddish rust facial disk. This race, the previously mentioned *T. a. guttata*, overlaps with *T. a. alba* in eastern France, Belgium and Western Germany, and the two interbreed in these areas. Grey facial disks are characteristic of some dark-phase island birds such as those from Tortuga, Hispaniola and the Canary Islands. The former, as well as the Barn Owls from Central America and the Galapagos Islands, are barred rather than spotted on the underside. The white-breasted races are found in the Australian regions, most of the South Sea Islands, Arabia, Iraq, the desert regions of Palestine, the islands of Corsica and Sardinia and in southern and western Europe. In Corsica and Sardinia some individuals are almost pure white above and below.

The sub-species vary in size from 28–43 cm and, as with most life-forms, the larger races are to be found at the northern and southern limits of their ranges, with the smallest inhabiting the zones nearest the equator.

Before passing on to outline the distribution of each sub-species separately, the over-all distribution of the species will be described so that the reader may appreciate the wide range of the Barn Owl when taken as a whole.

It is found in Europe from southern Sweden and south-west Russia to the Mediterranean, Atlantic and North Sea coastlines. In North America it does not breed north of 45° latitude, which is roughly a line marked by Massachusetts, southern Ontario and Michigan, Iowa, Nebraska and northern California. However, it is regularly recorded as a visitor farther north up to 56° latitude. In South America it is only absent from the equatorial rain forests of the Amazon Basin and its range in the Americas includes the West Indies and the Galapagos Islands. It is found in many parts of Africa including Madagascar and the Comoro Islands, but is absent from the Sahara Desert region apart from the immediate area of Lake Chad and the Air Oasis. It is also missing from the forest zones including the equatorial rain forest of Zaire. The Canary Islands, Madeira and Cape Verde Islands have their own races. The range continues into India and Sri Lanka, Burma and the Malay Peninsula, the Andaman Islands in south-east Asia, Java and the associated small islands south of Borneo and Celebes, i.e. Bali, Lombok, Sumbawa, Flores, Sandalwood and Timor. It completes its distribution in Australia, New Guinea and the Pacific Islands.

It is unfortunate that apart from *T. a. alba*, *T. a. guttata*, *T. a. pratincola*, *T. a. hellmayri* and *T. a. affinis* (in the Seychelles) little or no detailed research has been carried out on the many sub-species, and there is little published data from which we have been able to draw information. In any case, space does not permit more than a few words about each race and we have therefore attempted to do no more than describe the individual distributions, including a little additional information wherever possible and appropriate. The order we use is that given by Peters (1940) in his *Check-list of the Birds of the World*, with the addition of one extra sub-species, *T. a. thomensis*, listed by Macworth Praed & Grant (1970). Burton et al (1973) do not include this sub-species, but agreement will probably never be reached as to whether certain races should be regarded as distinct.

(1)   *T. a. schmitzi* is the sub-species from the island of Madeira and is interesting because it eats more insects than the European race and shuns buildings at all seasons, breeding instead in crevices or holes in cliffs and rocks. In spite of this apparent independence from Man it is still killed by country people because of superstition, and in this respect it shares the fate of many other sub-species. It is said to be very nocturnal in habits and it is possible that this trait is a direct result of the persecution by Man.

(2)   *T. a. gracilirostris* is found in Fuertaventura and Lanzarote in the eastern Canary Islands.

(3)   *T. a. alba* is of course the main subject of this book and is found in the British Isles, Channel Isles, western and southern France, the Iberian Peninsula, the southern Alps in Switzerland, Italy south of the southern slopes of the Alps, countries adjoining the Mediterranean basin in Europe and North Africa and on the islands associated with the Mediterranean except Corsica and Sardinia. In North Africa its range extends from Morocco to Cyrenaica and south-westwards as far as the Spanish Sahara and northern Mauretania.

On the Coto Doñana Reserve in southern Spain it breeds in holes in Cork Oak *Quercus* sp. trees and shares this habitat with Little Owls and Jackdaws. It has been recorded at the Palacio within the reserve. In the Camargue region of France, Elm *Ulmus* sp., Poplar *Populus* sp. and Tamarisk *Tamarix* sp. grow into dense woods along old branches of the river Rhône, but around farmhouses the habitat becomes more parklike and is then colonised by a number of species associated with cultivated land, including the Barn Owl. As already mentioned, it inter-breeds with *T. a. guttata* where their ranges overlap in eastern France, Belgium and western Germany.

(4)   *T. a. ernesti* is the very light coloured race from Corsica and Sardinia.

(5)   *T. a. guttata*, the dark-coloured race which occasionally appears in Britain, is a native of southern Sweden, Denmark, the Netherlands, Germany, eastward through Poland to western Russia, southward to the Alps, Austria, Hungary, Bulgaria and the Crimea. It has been recorded as far north as Haapasaari Island in southern Finland (latitude 60°N) and Tromsya in northern Norway (69° 40′N). Its plumage has been described earlier in this chapter.

(6)   *T. a. detorta* inhabits Santiago and St Vincent in the Cape Verde Islands, off the coast of West Africa.

(7)   *T. a. affinis*, a large and comparatively powerful bird, is the race found in tropical Africa from Gambia, southern Sahara and the Sudan to Cape Province. It has also occurred as a migrant in North Africa. This is the race which was introduced to the Seychelle Islands with such disastrous results. In Africa it is more widespread than its near relations, the African Marsh Owl and Common Grass Owl, and has been recorded in the following National Parks and Reserves: Kenya – Marsabit Nature Reserve; Nairobi National Park (where it is an uncommon resident), Lake Nakuru National Park, Samburu-Isiolo Game Reserve (one record) and Tsavo National Park. Tanzania – Serengeti National Park. Uganda – Queen Elizabeth National Park.

The story of the introduction of this owl in the early 1950s to the Seychelles, which has been recounted in detail by Blackman (1965), makes fascinating and instructive reading, for it provides a good example of where the introduction of an alien predator has had quite unforeseen and unfortunate consequences for the indigenous fauna. In this instance the owl was brought in to control the rat population but, as it transpired, preyed mostly on birds and in particular on the Fairy Terns, one of the Islands' greatest ornithological attractions. See Photo 31.

(8)   *T. a. poensis* occurs on the island of Fernando Po (now Macias Nguema Biyoga) off the coast of Cameroon, West Africa.

(9)   *T. a. thomensis* is confined to the island of São Thomé in the Gulf of Guinea, West Africa.

(10)   *T. a. erlangeri* occurs in Saudi Arabia east to Muscat (Oman), extending north to Lebanon, Syria and Iraq, north-east into Iran and west into the Sinai peninsula and Cyprus.

(11)   *T. a. hypermetra* is confined to the Comoro Islands and the Malagasi Republic (formerly Madagascar). It differs from *T. a. affinis* only by its slightly larger size.

(12)   *T. a. stertens* from India, West and East Pakistan, Assam, Burma and Sri Lanka, is said by Pycraft (1910) to nest in deep burrows, but he does not give any reason why this behaviour should have evolved. The limits of the ranges of this race and *T. a. javanica* in Burma are unknown and the problem is accentuated by the similarity of the plumage.

(13)   *T. a. javanica* occurs in Burma, Thailand, Indo-China, southward over all of south-eastern Asia. In Malaya it is recorded as a rare visitor and has also now been added to the Chinese avifauna. It inhabits many islands in south-east Asia, including Java and Thousand, Lombok, Flores, Alor and Timor.

(14)   *T. a. de-roepstorffi*, an extremely rare race, is found only in the South Andaman Islands in the Indian Ocean.

(15)   *T. a. sumbaënsis* is confined to Sumba Island in Indonesia.

(16)   *T. a. everetti* is another island race, this time being confined to the island of Savu, 160 km west of Timor (Indonesia).

(17)   *T. a. kuehni* from Kisar Island is probably the race which occurs on the islands of the Lesser Sunda Chain from Flores to Timor. However, there is a possibility that this bird and *everetti* might be identical to *T. a. javanica* and certainly they are hard to distinguish from each other, the only apparent differences being the smaller size of *everetti*. It is also likely that these last five

races share a common ancestor because in the Pleistocene Age all these islands were joined to the mainland and formed a single land mass known as Sundaland.

(18)   *T. a meeki* is the bird of south-eastern New Guinea. It also occurs on Vulcan and Dampier Islands.

(19)   *T. a. deliculata* of Australia, Tasmania and the Solomon Islands is said by Burrows (in Kingsley et al 1885) to breed in hollow trees beside marshes in Australia.

(20)   *T. a. crassirostris* is found on Boaing Island in the Tanga Group, Bismarck Archipelago, east of New Guinea.

(21)   *T. a. interposita* is yet another island race and is found on the Santa Cruz Islands and the northern New Hebrides, both situated in the South Pacific and on Banks Island, off northern Queensland.

(22)   *T. a. lulu* is another South Pacific race from New Caledonia, the southern New Hebrides and the islands of Loyalty, Fiji, Tonga, Samoa and the Society Islands.

(23)   *T. a. pratincola* is the race from North and Central America, from northern California, Nebraska, southern Wisconsin, western New York and southern New England, south to Lower California and the Gulf States and through Mexico to eastern Guatemala and probably eastern Nicaragua. It is a vagrant to Cuba. Its plumage is extremely variable. According to Pycraft (1910) it breeds in deep burrows in Texas while Burrows (loc. cit.) elaborates further by stating that it tunnels into sand or clay banks and also nests in chinks and fissures of cliffs in California. Fisher (1893) quotes the only case known to him of this race breeding in the used nest of another bird – in this instance that of a crow. Pycraft (loc. cit.) mentions that in the southern states it may breed in the unused lofts of tobacco and sugar warehouses, as well as in hollow trees beside marshes in Pennsylvania. The habit of nesting in buildings seems to be more common in the east than in other parts of the United States. Eggs of this race have been found in almost every month of the year (Burrows loc. cit.). Fisher also states that except in the breeding season the Barn Owl may be considered more or less gregarious, with families of 7–10 individuals being found together regularly and colonies of fifty or more having been observed on occasions.

(24)   *T. a. guatemalae* continues the species' range southward into western Guatemala, Salvador, western Nicaragua, and Panama to the Canal Zone. Its plumage is quite distinct from that of *T. a. pratincola*.

(25)   *T. a. lucayana* inhabits the Bahama Islands, off Florida, USA, and is similar to *T. a. pratincola*.

(26)   *T. a. furcata* occurs on Cuba, Isle of Pines, Grand Cayman, Cayman Brac and Jamaica.

(27)   *T. a. subandeana* is found in the tropical zones of Colombia and Ecuador, and is very similar to the next race.

(28)   *T. a. contempta*, the darkest and smallest race, is an inhabitant of Colombia, Ecuador, Peru and Venezuela.

(29)   *T. a. hellmayri* is a nocturnal race from the Guianas south to the Amazon Valley. Its northern limit is Venezuela to the area where the range of *T. a. contempta* begins; its western limits in Brazil are not known.

For many years F. von Haverschmidt (pers. comm.) made observations on

this race in Surinam and found that it favoured the coastal zone where plantations cultivated by Man provide a suitable habitat akin to that favoured by *T. alba alba*. It also shares the habit of breeding in Man-made structures including old houses. It is found in the largest town of Paramaribo and breeds there. Females are usually larger and heavier than males. It takes a wide range of prey varying from insects and lizards to bats and rodents up to the size of hamsters, as well as small birds. Due to an abundance of prey and favourable weather conditions throughout the year, this race may breed in any month and normally rears two broods per 12-month period.

(30)   *T. a. tuidara* has its range from Brazil south of the Amazon to Chile (Valdivia) and Argentina (Tierra del Fuego).

(31)   *T. a. glaucops* inhabits the island of Tortuga and Hispaniola in the West Indies.

(32)   *T. a. nigrescens* inhabits the island of Dominica in the West Indies, but is little known.

(33)   *T. a. insularis* inhabits the southern Lesser Antilles (West Indies): St Lucia, St Vincent, Bequia, Carriacou, Union and Grenada. Both of the last two races favour high ground and share very dark coloration.

(34)   *T. a. bargei*, a very small race from the island of Curaçao, off the coast of Venezuela, is unlike any of the other local races and resembles a smaller version of the European Barn Owls.

(35)   *T. a. punctatissima*, from the Galapagos Archipelago, is amongst the smallest of the sub-species and is found only on James Island.

This completes our summary of the known sub-species although, as can be seen all too clearly, there is much scope for further study of the bird throughout its range. An example of the gaps which remain in our knowledge about even its distribution is provided by the status of the bird in the Azores. Bannerman & Bannerman (1966) wrote 'Barn Owls *T. alba* are reported to be absent as residents and on what evidence the white-breasted *T. alba alba* is said in *The Handbook* (II p 344) to *breed* in the Azores we have not been able to trace. The statement has been copied by other authors. There is, however, the possibility that a Barn Owl does occur as a vagrant. F. du Cane Godman (1870) wrote: "it is often met with in the eastern and central groups" and concluded that its range did not extend to the outer islands. He failed to find it himself. Ogilvie-Grant was also unlucky in 1903'. In conclusion the Bannermans felt that its occurrence, even as a vagrant, was doubtful. In their opinion any Barn Owl which might subsequently be discovered residing on these islands would prove to be an un-named sub-species.

OTHER SPECIES

The Common Grass Owl is found in southern Africa, parts of south-east Asia including India and the Philippines, Australia and New Guinea. Some taxonomists separate this bird into two species, each with distinctive plumage and geographical ranges. These are *T. capensis* inhabiting Damaraland and southern Angola, Malawi, Transvaal, Botswana, Natal and Cape Province, and ranging north to Zaire and Kenya; and the lighter phase *T. longimembris* from India, south-east China, north and east Australia, and south-east New Guinea, the Philippines and Celebes. *T. longimembris* has in fact been divided into several sub-species in different parts of its range.

It is a large bird of between 33 and 43 cm and, like most members of the genus, is mainly an inhabitant of open grasslands. Its behaviour is somewhat akin to that of the Short-eared Owl in that it spends much of its time on the ground and lays its eggs in a grassy hollow in open country. In appearance it resembles the Barn Owl but is slightly larger and darker above with longer, almost bare legs.

The Madagascar Grass Owl *T. soumagnei*, on the other hand, is found only in the dense evergreen forests of the north-east of the Malagasi Republic, and in this respect it differs from most other members of the genus. Like many forest-dwellers it is smaller than those species found in open habitats and measures only 25 cm in length. Its forest habitat has now almost disappeared due to clearance by Man, and like many species on this island its future is in the balance.

Two species occur on the island of Celebes, the first of which is the Celebes Barn Owl *T. rosenbergii*; the second is the Minahassa Barn Owl *T. inexpectata* which is only found in the northern peninsula of the island.

The Masked Owl *T. novaehollandiae* inhabits Tasmania, the forest regions of north-east, east and south Australia and part of New Guinea. Like the Common Grass Owl it has been divided into several sub-species. An interesting feature of this species is that females are much larger than males, thus enabling them to capture bigger prey such as Rabbits, Rat-kangaroos and Ring-tailed Opossums. The bird measures between 36 and 51 cm. It is said to be strictly nocturnal.

The Sooty Owl *T. tenebricosa* of Australia and New Guinea is an owl of dense forest and has the distinction of being the only species of *Tyto* which is completely lacking in yellow-orange colouring; it also has the largest eyes. The bird is 30–38 cm in length, the female being much larger than the male.

The New Britain Barn Owl *T. aurantia* occurs only on New Britain Island which lies to the east of New Guinea. This species is very similar to the Minahassa Barn Owl.

The forest-dwelling tropical members of the genus are generally considered to be rare birds, but in reality this may be due to the fact that little is known about their habits at the present time. Unless they are flushed by accident they are seldom encountered by casual observers, for their habitat of deep forest, wilderness grasslands and brush is not usually visited when the owls are active at night. They are therefore likely to remain enigmas until special efforts are made to study their behaviour and status.

The genus *Phodilus* comprises only the two Bay Owls and is closely related to *Tyto*, its members sharing the heart-shaped facial disk, serrated middle claw and general coloration. However, several small anatomical differences distinguish them from the typical Barn Owls, the most important being an incomplete facial disk above the eyes, an absence of operculi in front of the ears and a much weaker bill. The latter may perhaps indicate a more insectivorous diet than *Tyto*.

The Common Bay Owl *P. badius* is a forest-dweller from northern India through Indo-China to Malaysia. Five races have been named but apart from the nominate *P. b. badius* these races are regarded as rare with two of them being restricted to single islands. Indeed, *P. b. arixuthus* from Bunguran Island is known only from the original type specimen.

It is a small owl measuring some 25 cm in length and is said to be a very sluggish nocturnal species which spends the daytime roosting in tree holes. It takes a wide range of food including insects, birds, rodents, lizards and frogs, and lays only a small clutch of two to four white eggs. Its breeding biology appears to be closely akin to that of *Tyto*, the nest-site being hollows in trees. In the breeding season its call notes are said to resemble a mixture of those uttered by the Barn, Scops and wood owls, but at other times the call is said to be more of a typical owl-like single soft hoot.

The African Bay Owl *P. prigoginei*, known from only a single specimen collected in mountain forest in the eastern Congo, is apparently very similar in appearance, but is darker with a more compressed beak and smaller feet and claws.

PRE-HISTORY

Records of fossil Barn Owls, indeed of fossil owls in general, are remarkably scanty and for the following notes we have had to draw mainly upon the works of Brodkorb (1971) and Harrison and Walker (in Gooders et al 1970).

The present evidence suggests that the earliest members of the genus *Tyto* first appeared approximately 12 million years ago during the Miocene period. Their remains, like so many others of this period, were found in France, and since the 57 species of fossil birds discovered there included the first parrot and wood-hoopoe it would seem to suggest that France then had a tropical fauna akin to that of south-east Asia and Africa south of the Sahara.

T. ignota of the Middle Miocene (Helvetian) period was identified by the distal end of its right tarsometatarsus. *T. sancti-albani* and *T. edwardsi* both belong to the Upper Middle Miocene (Tortonian) period, the former leaving the distal portion of its tibiotarsus, proximal and distal ends of its tarsometatarsus, ungual phalanx, humerus and carpometacarpus, and the latter the distal portion of its right tibiotarsus.

A later fossil was the giant Barn Owl *T. ostologa* which was twice the size of any living species (making it in the region of 90 cm long) and inhabited the Caribbean. Its remains, comprising the proximal end of its left tarsometatarsus, were excavated from an Upper Pleistocene bat-guano cave in north-west Haiti. With the owl's remains were fossilised pellets which when analysed revealed the bones of large rodents which had formed its prey. It is thought that when great quantities of sea-water were locked in the continental ice-sheets during the Ice Age the Caribbean Islands were much larger than today and that many were connected, the implication being that both the giant owl and its rodent prey may have died out when their habitat shrank to its present size.

Also from the Upper Pleistocene (Wisconsin Age) was an owl from the Bahamas, *T. pollens*. This is known from a left femur as is *T. melitensis* from the Upper Pleistocene cavern deposits in Malta.

Two species are known from the Quaternary period – *T. cavatica* from

Puerto Rico, known from the proximal portion of its left tarsometatarsus, and *T. sauzieri* of Mauritius which left its humerus, tibiotarsi and tarsometatarsi.

T. alba itself dates from the Pleistocene period and its remains have been found in several prehistoric sites including, in England, those of the Celtic Iron Age lake village of Glastonbury in Somerset and the Roman site of Woodcutts in Cranborne Chase, Dorset. It has also been found in the top level of Edenvale Cave, Co. Clare, Ireland, and in the following other countries: Portugal, Spain, France, Monaco, Italy, Switzerland, Poland, Greece, Israel, the USA (California, Arizona, New Mexico, Texas and Florida), the Bahamas, Dominican Republic, Mexico (Nuevo León and Yucatán), Brazil and New Zealand.

SPECIALISATIONS

We have no wish to dwell in much detail on matters concerning anatomy and physiology but no monograph on the Barn Owl could afford to omit some account of the wonderful specialisations with which this bird is endowed for the efficient capture of its small mammal prey. We ourselves must rely entirely on the work of others for our information on the structure of the eyes and ears but hundreds of hours in the field make it possible for us to add some very relevant observations to the results and assumptions of the anatomists and laboratory workers.

The eyes of the Barn Owl are considerably smaller than those of most owls, yet we are led to believe from the many collective accounts of owls' vision that this species is no less well adapted than the others for seeing in the dark. From our observations of Barn and Tawny Owls we would seriously question any inference that the former's sight is as efficient as the latter's. Nevertheless, Curtis (1952) demonstrated irrefutably that the Barn Owl can see well enough to avoid objects placed in its flight path in light of exceedingly low intensity – such as would leave a man unable to perceive anything at all. Sparks and Soper (1970) interpret Curtis' results to mean that an owl (presumably a Barn Owl) can discern detail even on cloudy nights, while Payne (1971) deduces from Curtis' work that 'the visual threshold of owls is not low enough for an owl to see its prey under the conditions of poor illumination frequently encountered in the wild'. Whatever the case, before recording our own observations we must briefly describe the several specialisations that combine to make the sight of an owl so efficient in the dark.

First and most obvious is the large size of the eye, though this is not so marked in the present species. The cornea and lens are much enlarged also, and the latter is almost round (giving a short focal length) so that only a small image is focused on a retina that is quite near the front of the eye. This apparently results in very little light being lost, but the nerve cells themselves play at least an equal part in making use of what available light there is.

Of the two types of photo-receptive cells, rods and cones, the former, which are highly sensitive to light but not to colours, greatly predominate and are packed together in huge numbers. They contain a substance known as visual purple which is decomposed by light to produce minute electrical impulses. Groups of rods are connected to cells known as bi-polar cells and groups of these in turn are connected to ganglion cells whose axons transmit the combined impulses to the brain. This process, whereby numbers of light-sensitive cells join forces to produce a strong impulse in the brain, is known as summation and contrives to make the eye extremely sensitive to light at very low intensity, but it has one big disadvantage: the unique information acquired by each individual rod is lost when the impulses mix together in the bipolar and ganglion cells, with the result that only a single message reaches the brain from each group. Thus sensitivity to light is only gained at the expense of good colour vision and of visual acuity (ability to see detail). Owls can probably compensate the effects of summation to some extent by increasing the number of rods in the eye (the Tawny Owl is said to have 56,000 per sq mm) and perhaps the huge size of the eyes of some species facilitates the accommodation of such vast numbers.

We have said nothing so far of the other photo-receptive cells in the eye known as cones. Though lacking visual purple and being of little use in darkness, it is upon these that most keen-sighted diurnal vertebrates rely for their colour vision and visual acuity. They are normally gathered together to form a sensitive spot or *fovea* in the centre of the retina, though some birds have an extra sensitive spot at the back of the eye so that the brain can receive detailed information about areas in front of the head, when the eyes are used together in binocular vision, and at one side when an eye is functioning independently. Summation seldom occurs, each cone usually having its own bi-polar and ganglion cells so that the brain is able to form a detailed picture from information supplied by each cone individually.

It is hardly necessary to point out that it is a fallacy that owls cannot see in the daytime. On the contrary we may logically wonder, from our understanding of the workings of the rods and cones, whether owls can see rather better in daylight when their cones are able to function, albeit that these are limited in number. Certainly if the owl can see colour in the daytime it is highly probable that its visual acuity will be improved. We cannot do better here than draw the reader's attention to the extra detail distinguishable on a colour television screen when compared with a black-and-white set – the background of any country scene is alive with recognisable species of wild plants that might never be noticed on a monochrome picture.

However, at times even humans may find it worthwhile deliberately to use their rods at night. By looking straight at an object in the dark one is bringing the cones into action, as a result of which one can frequently discern nothing at all; by averting the gaze somewhat and looking to one side of the object it is often possible to see just a little of it. In doing this we are simply pointing some of our rod cells at the object and using our peripheral vision. We know also that, quite apart from the extra light admitted as a result of the immediate opening of our irises when we enter a dark room, a gradual increase of our sensitivity occurs as we become accustomed or 'adapted' to the change during the next few minutes.

A further specialisation towards improved sight, not concerned particularly with night vision and also shared by the diurnal birds of prey, is brought about by the ability not only of the lens but the cornea as well, to be adjusted very quickly by means of an unusually powerful muscle (Crampton's muscle) in order to keep a prey in sharp focus as the owl pounces down on it. This necessitates the development of strengthening plates (*scleral ossicles*) around the periphery of the cornea in order to protect the eye from being damaged by its own muscular activity. An eye which focuses well is said to have good accommodation.

Finally, the owl has virtually committed itself to binocular vision, seeing about 70% of its visual field through both eyes at once and having a total field of only about 110°. This enables it to judge distances more accurately when marking down prey, but places it at a definite disadvantage when keeping a look out for its own enemies, especially as the eyes are tubular in shape and too large and tightly fitted in the skull to make movement practicable. Certainly the great mobility of the neck, which can turn the head through 180° and in all directions, counteracts the small visual field to a large extent when the bird is active, but when dozing it is often possible to surprise an owl if a quiet enough approach is made. We do not think this disadvantage is emphasised enough in most books, probably because of little field experience by the authors. A 'normal' bird such as a pigeon has a total field of view of about 340°, enabling it to watch for the approach of danger from virtually any direction. Its binocular vision, on the other hand, is limited to about 20°.

The principle of binocular vision is that the two eyes, especially if they are wide apart as they are in owls, can view the same object from different angles and this enables the brain to calculate its distance very accurately. Owls, and many diurnal birds of prey too, supplement this method by another, the parallax method. They bob and weave their heads in a most comical manner in order to view an object from several different directions so that its position can be judged by observing the relative movement of the other things around it. The different species tend to have their own characteristic head-movement; for example, the Kestrel and Little Owl jerk or bob their heads sharply up and down a great deal whereas the Barn Owl's most characteristic head-movement is a lateral one. However, when really interested in something a Barn Owl will move its head in a most ludicrous manner, in all directions and sometimes with a circular motion, occasionally turning the head completely on a side so that one eye is positioned vertically above the other (see Plate 1). Newly fledged owlets move their heads so vigorously that they appear utterly ridiculous and one can only assume that they have the greatest difficulty in seeing properly at this stage. During observation in the dark these head movements provide a useful means of distinguishing large young from adults.

To complete the description of the eye, mention must be made of the nictitating membrane or third eyelid. This is possessed by all birds but, as it is normally transparent and its action very fast, it is seldom noticed. Its function in other birds is to sweep clean the front of the eye and no doubt in this it is more delicate and efficient than an ordinary eyelid. In owls, however, the nictitating membrane is opaque and particularly robust, and its action is more slow and deliberate. It comes as something of a surprise to find that when an owl is striking prey, feeding itself or tending its young, or is engaged in preening either itself or its mate, it does not use its eyes which are either closed or have the nictitating membrane drawn across them. In fact owls prefer to feel whatever they are touching, apparently using the bristles around the bill rather as many small mammals are said to use their vibrissae (whiskers). We can readily surmise that the large size and frontal position of the eyes has rendered them particularly susceptible to injury and has resulted in this frequent precautionary use of a specially toughened nictitating membrane. Nevertheless, owls do suffer injuries to their eyes occasionally. We may add that, as in humans, it is the upper eyelids of owls that perform the blinking movement, the lower lids only raising to close the eye when the bird is dozing.

During the last few pages we have been mostly extolling the virtues of the owl's eyesight but now it is time to see how this anatomical and physiological dissertation stands up in practice in the field. It was many years ago that one of us, while watching his first Barn Owl, discovered that if he stood still when he spotted the bird approaching him along some hedgerow, it would pass overhead at extremely close range without apparently noticing him. Years later, at the commencement of this study, the same author had an even greater surprise. A Barn Owl was in the habit of roosting on the edge of a fragment of ceiling in a derelict house. On one occasion when this author entered the building he heard a slight noise which indicated that the owl had gone into hiding at the back of the ceiling, as was often its custom. He therefore remained quiet for a few minutes and then gave an imitation of a Barn Owl's hiss. Immediately the owl came to the edge of the ceiling, looking around in all directions for the supposed intruder. Beneath, the observer kept absolutely still and at length the owl relaxed and began to doze above his head. After a minute or so he made a slight click with his fingernail, whereupon the owl looked down, saw him and dashed back into hiding. A week later a friend was taken to the house and was able to witness an identical performance.

Subsequently we have had many demonstrations of the Barn Owl's inability to recognise us at close quarters when we have been still and quiet. Once, one of us had a newly fledged owlet alight on his head while another stood just a few centimetres away staring into his face for several seconds before realising its (supposed) danger. This incident is similar to an experience by an assistant warden at the RSPB's Leighton Moss Reserve in North Lancashire. After watching a Barn Owl pounce on some small mammal the bird flew up and alighted on his head (Straton 1967)! Even this incident is not unparalleled, however, for we have heard of a Cheshire farmer who, whilst leaning against a fence post at dusk, had a Barn Owl rest on his head for a few moments. When one of the authors first began to watch Barn Owls at the nest he started by looking through a hole in the door of a large barn into an annexe where the birds were breeding. The adults, however, frequently came into the main barn where they preened and rested contentedly on the beams, though the observer was in full view below them. So long as he remained still and absolutely silent the owls failed to detect him. This accidental discovery enabled the author to watch another pair extremely closely, by simply bringing a chair into their barn and sitting down, torch in hand, to observe the birds in reasonable comfort. Without a hide vision is unrestricted and it is also much easier to move a chair than a hide to another position. In March and April, during their courtship, the adults occasionally passed or stood on the floor by the chair at a distance of about one metre.

Later, they visited the nest regularly without noticing him, at five or six metres, and the owlets when they fledged, often played under the chair and on the author's shoes. On one occasion a 67-day-old owlet perched on his left knee for a minute or more and then jumped across to his right knee, throwing grotesque shadows about the barn as it bobbed its head in front of his torch (Bunn 1976).

Mention of a torch prompts us to say that in our experience artificial light is ignored by Barn Owls, presumably because they have no reason to connect it with danger, though not surprisingly it will sometimes cause them to blink at first and half-close their eyes. However, confidence was shaken somewhat when on one occasion an attempt was made to watch a pair of owls earlier in the day than usual while the barn was still well lit by sunlight: both adults noticed the observer immediately they emerged from hiding, thus proving that they *can* see better in good light.

The above examples show undeniably that however quick a Barn Owl may be to detect movement on the part of an animal, without such movement its eyesight is often not keen enough to pick out and recognise an animal from its inanimate surroundings. We are quite certain that no other bird with which we have come into contact could be so fooled and we have no reason to suspect that the Tawny Owl, which frequently presented itself for comparative observations, is at all slow to recognise motionless humans.

One might be tempted to deduce from all this that prey is located entirely by the sense of hearing, but two of us spent many hours watching the hunting activities of an owl that was blind in one eye, and this bird had the greatest difficulty in catching prey (though it survived for at least fourteen months in this condition). If its ears alone were used in locating prey its efficiency ought not to have been impaired.

Turning now to the sense of hearing, we have to thank Roger Payne, working at Cornell University in the USA, for some truly amazing discoveries. In his initial description of the Barn Owl's auditory apparatus Payne brings to our attention some very interesting facts that are not generally appreciated. First of all he points out that the two flaps or operculi in front of the ears are positioned asymmetrically (see Fig. 3a). As the external ear-openings of owls vary considerably in complexity, it has been intimated (by Smith in Hosking & Newberry 1945) that the efficiency of the hearing of the different species can be guessed at from the degree of modification they have undergone. Therefore, since the squarish ear-openings of the Barn Owl are relatively small (though internally the ears are nearly as long as the skull), the species might not have been expected to have outstanding hearing when compared with such species as the Tawny Owl, Short-eared Owl, Long-eared Owl and Tengmalm's Owl which possess external openings that are enormous in size and asymmetrical in design. This may be the case, but Payne's discoveries and experiments raise the possibility that the Barn Owl's hearing is just as good as those species but that its efficiency has been achieved in a rather different way. Indeed, in view of the startling results of Payne's research, it seems impossible that the Barn Owl's hearing could be bettered.

Next it is pointed out that the facial disk of an owl is really made up of two enormous ear conches, *The Handbook*'s 'ruff' arising from a ridge of skin in which the feather sockets are grouped very densely, like the cells of a honeycomb, in order to make it as solid and impervious to sound as possible. The feathers of the ruff themselves are unusually constructed, with dense webbing and thick, flattened rachises (see Fig. 3b): the ruff is in fact a highly developed sound reflector. The two conches are separated between the eyes by a sharp wedge of white bristle-like feathers which cover up the buff-coloured feathers of the top of the head that extend down beneath it. The feathers within the ear conches are identical to the auricular feathers of any other bird and this is just what they are. They are quite the opposite in structure and purpose to the ruff feathers, being filamentous, devoid of barbules and readily permeable to any sound (see Fig. 3c).

We do not think this is the place to discuss the more complicated anatomy of the middle and inner ear – suffice it to say that there are definite differences from those of other birds which are designed to increase the acuity of hearing. The medulla of the brain (the part concerned with hearing) of a Barn Owl weighing 283·5 gm has been estimated to possess no less than 95,000 neurons; in comparison that of a Carrion Crow, weighing twice as much, had around 27,000 (Sparks & Soper 1970).

The experiments performed by Payne are highly technical and not easily understood by the layman. We must, therefore, choose carefully which facts to include in a book of this scope. Incidental to the experiments on the accuracy of the acoustic location of prey and the research into how this is achieved, are several extremely interesting observations on the behaviour and method of striking prey.

The main experiments at Cornell University were conducted in a light-proof room, 13 m long by 3·5 m wide, observations in darkness being made through an infra-red viewing device and by taking motion picture sequences with infra-red film. With the lights switched on in this room an owl would swoop at prey in a sure glide, feet carried under the tail, and was invariably successful in the final strike. In darkness, however, when the eyes could no longer play any part, the bird would flutter slowly down from its perch, legs dangling, and occasionally made mistakes – there were four misses in seventeen strikes during preliminary trials in a smaller room. It is possible that by flapping its wings and flying at about half the speed of a normal flight the owl was testing the resistance of the air so as to gain information on the proximity of the floor; on the other hand it may simply have been its way of ensuring against a possible high-speed collision with an unseen object. Uncertainty of the prey's exact distance may have been the reason why owls striking in absolute darkness also opened their talons sooner. It is significant, too, that owls which we have observed by torchlight at night in a large barn also flew cautiously in this way, with the body held at an angle to facilitate slow movement.

Payne began his experiments using mice with either a leaf attached to them or with leaves scattered on the floor of the room so that they would bump into them and cause the necessary tell-tale rustling noises. Photography disclosed that when striking moving prey, not only did an owl show great accuracy in complete darkness, but it was actually aware of the direction the mouse was travelling. This was shown by the fact that when the owl was approaching in the same direction that the mouse was moving, it always

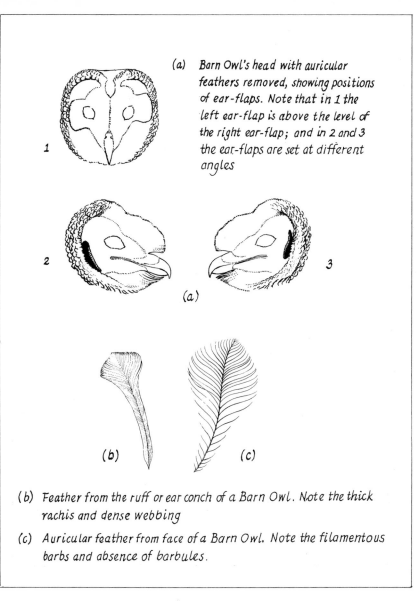

(a) Barn Owl's head with auricular feathers removed, showing positions of ear-flaps. Note that in 1 the left ear-flap is above the level of the right ear-flap; and in 2 and 3 the ear-flaps are set at different angles

(a)

(b) Feather from the ruff or ear conch of a Barn Owl. Note the thick rachis and dense webbing

(c) Auricular feather from face of a Barn Owl. Note the filamentous barbs and absence of barbules.

Fig. 3 The external auditory apparatus of the Barn Owl (after Payne 1971).

turned at right angles at the last moment so that the long axis of its two open talons, which together form roughly an oval shape, were aligned with the mouse's direction of travel, thus giving it the best possible chance of transfixing the prey with at least one claw. This probably explains the unusual mobility of the toes, for when grasping a cylindrical perch, such as a small branch, it is necessary for the outer toe to move from its lateral position to a more posterior one, or to a forward position for walking on a flat surface (see Fig. 1a).

Later, experiments were made using a loudspeaker hidden beneath a sand floor covering, through which rustling noises were played until the owl took wing; leaving the perch caused the speaker to switch off. By this means it was possible, by reference to the claw marks in the sand, to record the number of strikes that would have been successful had the loudspeaker been a mouse. This method also enabled Payne to discover that frequencies of above 8,500 cycles per second were essential for the owl to pin-point the sound source sufficiently accurately for a successful strike; when all frequencies above 5,000 cps were excluded the owl would not even attempt a strike and nor would it strike from a distance of more than about 7 m. Incidentally, the upper frequency limit of a Barn Owl's hearing is about 20,000 cps, which is similar to our own.

Payne also experimented by pulling a dead mouse with a leaf attached to it across the floor of the room. Giving the owl as little credit as possible, Payne calculated the angles of five of the birds worst misses, ignoring more than two hundred successful strikes. The results gave a mean miss of only 0·8° ± 0·5° in the horizontal plane and 0·5° ± 0·3° in the vertical plane. With the loudspeaker method the mean of twenty-three misses out of forty-four trials was 2·9° ± 2·0° in the horizontal plane and 2·5° ± 1·6° in the vertical plane. If the owl was given a further clue to the location of the sound-source by causing another leaf-rustle during its actual flight it was invariably successful.

An animal usually estimates the approximate direction of a sound-source by comparing the difference between the time of arrival of the sound at the two ears. The owl goes further, however, for their asymmetrical structure causes sounds of particular frquencies to reach each ear at different intensities. From the results of the 'three-dimensional sensitivity patterns', which Payne plotted by inserting a microphone into the ears of dead Barn Owls, he theorised that if an owl simply orientates its head so that the sound intensity is equal in both ears, it will be facing the source. In this respect the method of striking disclosed by the cine pictures is most interesting, for in both light and dark conditions the owl approached the supposed prey 'looking' straight at it. When about a metre from the target the owl would suddenly thrust the feet forward so that they almost touched the bill and then pull its head backwards out of the way. Thus the head, which had been on a collision course with the prey, was effectively replaced by the talons.

From exhaustive experiments with some other species of owls, including one species with asymmetrical and two with symmetrical ears, Payne suspects that only owls with asymmetrical ears are capable of catching prey in total darkness.

Finally there is the question of whether or not an owl deliberately moves its feather conches, as a dog moves its ears, in order to hear more precisely sounds coming from different directions. There is no doubt that the conches can be moved, more so in a Barn Owl than in other owls, for a resting bird folds back the ruff laterally, broadening and blunting the ridge down the centre and in fact giving the face an entirely different appearance. But no one to our knowledge has claimed to have noticed the disk of an owl changing shape in response to the various noises going on around it. Some authors (Stellbogen 1930, Heinroth & Heinroth 1958 and Sparks & Soper 1970) have stated that owls also move their ear-flaps, though this assumption seems to be based only on the presence of a series of specially well developed muscles attached to them, and again supportive observations appear to be entirely lacking. As owls can easily be tamed when young and therafter watched at extremely close range, it should not be too difficult to detect movements of the ear-flaps if these do occur. We have seen no evidence of this. Not surprisingly Payne found that any movement of the parts of the auditory apparatus changed the sensitivity patterns.

Payne's work can leave no doubt that the Barn Owl's hearing is something to be marvelled at and the present authors themselves have frequently had evidence of its acuity while watching from hides at a range of around 25 m. Even at this distance note-making is difficult, the slight clicking from some ball-point pens or the crinkling of paper being sufficient to attract the bird's attention – and unwrapping one's sandwiches in complete silence can be a major problem! It is not enough to approach a roost unseen, for frequently the bird will detect one's presence by sound alone. Having said this, however, we must take note that the conditions obtaining in Payne's experiments were very different from those encountered by a Barn Owl hunting prey in its natural habitats.

Just before beginning this study D.S.B. had been working with small mammals, and one point that he learned, which is pertinent here, is that a mouse or a shrew in its own territory is much more alert to danger than when in a strange place. A shrew, for instance, if put down outside its territory, can usually be re-caught with the hand alone without too much difficulty; but release one on familiar ground and it will disappear instantly. Similarly, when placed in a naturally set out cage, they move about slowly and uncertainly for an hour or more before normal behaviour returns. A second point is that the Short-tailed Vole, usually the staple diet of the Barn Owl in Britain, is by no means blind. Like many of our British mammals it has difficulty in separating a motionless predator from the general background, but any sudden movement is seen at once and causes an instantaneous retreat to safety. It should be appreciated, therefore, that while Payne's Barn Owls were handicapped by the darkness, so for the same and other reasons were the mice which in natural conditions must be very alert to the approach of the bird. If we then consider that a hunting owl has to contend with the distractions of noises from a multitude of sources – its own flight which is not quite as silent as one is usually led to believe (wing-beats are detectable on some of our tape-recordings made in buildings), bird-calls, aeroplanes, machinery and, perhaps worst of all, the wind rustling the trees and grass – most of which sounds are likely to be very much louder than any created by a small mammal, we will put into better perspective the difficulties faced by the owl if it relied solely upon its ears. That it does not was demonstrated by the owl, previously mentioned, that was blind in one eye. This bird had the greatest difficulty in catching prey; it not only hunted for much longer periods than is usual but covered a vast amount of ground, trespassing over four Barn Owl territories. Knight (1956) describes an interesting and relevant experiment with a tame Barn Owl that had been allowed to catch mice for itself in a dark building where it presumably had to rely on its ears alone. When an electric fan was switched on to drown the noises of the mice moving about on the floor the owl remained perched, seemingly unaware of their presence.

What are the sounds heard by the owls likely to be? In the case of voles almost certainly the chewing of the grass shoots on which they mainly feed. Such sounds are clearly audible to any human being with normal hearing and, since the vole is still while feeding, an owl should be able to locate it fairly easily. Indeed even a human could point with some confidence to its approximate position, though he could never catch it. Voles do make vocal noises quite often, too, but it is unlikely that owls rely on these as much as they must do on the squeaks of shrews. It is doubtful whether a feeding shrew makes sufficient noise, except perhaps when crunching up some particularly hard insect, for an owl to locate it acoustically, but these little animals are often quite noisy, especially in the breeding season. Then, their strident squeaks can be heard from far and wide as they chase about their territories. No owl – or competent naturalist – can fail to notice them. At other times shrews are less vocally inclined, but observations on captive animals disclose that when searching through thick vegetation they often utter a very quiet twittering note, the reason for which has not yet been discovered, though D.S.B. suspected echo-location. Whatever the purpose – and there must be one to mitigate against its disadvantageous advertisement to the shrew's enemies – owls may well be able to home in on such sounds.

The above account of the hearing of the Barn Owl leads us naturally to consider its flight, since the most frequently quoted characteristic is its silence, which is as much to permit the ears to pick up minute sounds as it is to ensure a quiet approach to its quarry. In the description which follows, it is assumed that the reader has acquired at least an elementary knowledge of the mechanics of bird flight, either from various specialised writings on the subject, or from other monographs which give good accounts of flight and cover the basic principles.*

* Notably *The Hawfinch* (Mountford 1957) and *Swifts in a Tower* (Lack 1956) – see References.

It is essential for the Barn Owl's hunting method that it should be able to fly slowly and gently. It must therefore have a very large wing area in relation to its weight (i.e. a low wing-loading) – and in this respect it would be hard to find a better example. The body is unexpectedly small beneath the soft feathers, averaging only 337 gm (Baudvin 1975), while the wings, which are very broad, have a span of around 85 cm and a total area of some 1,680 cm². Such a low wing-loading enables the bird to fly slowly without stalling and without the need for powerful wing-strokes which would create noise. The slower the bird can fly, the more thoroughly it can hunt the ground, and it is of interest to record here that the Short-eared Owl (which shared the habitat where R.D.S.W. and D.S.B. did the bulk of their research) hunts in precisely the same way as the Barn Owl except that it flies noticeably faster. Perhaps this is the reason why it is, apparently, less efficient in catching its vole prey. At times the Barn Owl looks almost fragile in flight, and certainly its wing muscles, which only contribute 10% of its weight, are small in comparison with those of powerful fliers such as the pigeon with wing muscles accounting for 30% of its weight. Nevertheless, a Barn Owl can show quite a turn of speed over short distances – D. Scott (pers. comm.) has clocked one at 50 mph (80 km/h) – and the bird can appear especially graceful when gliding and wheeling buoyantly in the teeth of a high wind. Its only difficulty in such conditions seems to be in maintaining the low height which is essential when hunting. However, Barn Owls do not invariably fly low – when crossing a valley or returning with prey from a long distance we have occasionally known one to travel at a height of 60–90 m, at least.

Returning to the mechanics of flight, broad wings, though they give plenty of lift, are not efficient aerofoils, and a square-ended wing increases turbulence and drag. Most birds with wings of this type overcome the problem by having emarginated primaries; the webbing is narrowed on one or both sides of the shaft for about half its length. As a result these feathers are separated from their neighbours when the wing is fully spread, so that the air flows smoothly from each feather as it does from the combined primaries of a fast, sharp-winged flier such as a swift or tern. Most owls, too, have emarginated feathers, involving in some cases the tenth to sixth primaries, but not so the Barn Owl. Instead, the tenth primaries (the eleventh in owls are very small and hidden beneath the coverts) are very long, almost or quite equalling the eighth and ninth. This produces a wing of greater length but with nothing to counteract any resultant drag. It seems possible that, having achieved the very slowest flight by these adaptations, 'streamlining' is less important, especially since the Barn Owl appears not to undertake definite migrations which would necessitate prolonged flight. It is perhaps relevant to mention here how much stronger and more capable the migratory Short-eared Owl appears on the wing in comparison with the present species, its prowess being occasionally well demonstrated by its successful attacks on such fast-flying birds as the small waders.

An examination of the upperside of the flight feathers of an owl reveals that much of the webbing possesses a velvet-like pile, this appearance being produced by the prolonged hair-like ends of the barbules. In addition the ends of the barbs along the leading edges of the tenth primaries, and on the emarginated portions of some of the other primaries, are to a greater or lesser extent prolonged and recurved so as to stand out separately from their neighbours like the teeth of a comb. The exact details vary among the species, but in the case of the Barn Owl only the tenth primaries have this feature (see Fig. 1b). The lack of serrations on the other primaries is of no consequence since their front edges do not meet the air-flow – the long tenth primaries alone have this task – for without separation by emargination each overlaps the other.

There can be little doubt that the velvety pile on the upper surfaces of the flight feathers and the comb-like fringes just described serve to smooth out and silence the flow of air over the wings. Again, there is probably some decrease of efficiency, the wings not cleaving the air quite so cleanly, but in a bird to which speed of flight is unimportant this would seem to be little disadvantage. Thorpe and Griffin (1962) state that the Barn Owl has eliminated ultra-sonic noise from its wing-beats – a point of significance when one takes into account the sensitivity of its prey species to such sounds. The tail is quite short and presumably plays relatively little part in the Barn Owl's flight.

Thus we have seen that the Barn Owl has many particular and remarkable adaptations to commend it to the ornithologist. We hope to show in the following chapters that its voice, behaviour and breeding biology are no less interesting.

CHAPTER 2

Voice

As might have been expected of so elusive a species, at the beginning of this study it quickly became apparent that little was known about the Barn Owl's way of life. True, it had been photographed at the nest often enough but, since in the birds' and the photographer's interests it is customary to wait until the young are a few weeks old before commencing operations, by which time the parents have ceased to spend much time at the nest, not a great deal of information could be gleaned from this source. In fact, apart from a few photographers' accounts of the late nesting stage, the 'intimate' behaviour of the Barn Owl did not appear to have been described in any detail. This neglect was particularly apparent in the lack of information concerning voice, for the majority of books make only brief mention of eerie screams, hisses and snores, with perhaps some reference to the twittering sounds that can be heard at closer quarters. Apart from a general acceptance that the snore is a food-call, no attempt seemed to have been made to classify and interpret the various notes.

Early in 1966, in order to remedy this, D.S.B. purchased a portable tape-recorder with an unattended running time of just over two hours. The machine was left before dusk in various buildings known to be frequented by owls and collected just before the tape ran out. The problem of noise from the motor present on the recordings was overcome by the use of a long extension lead for the microphone which enabled the machine to be positioned well away from it. This also allowed some attempt at monitoring and sometimes earphones were used so that a barn was effectively 'bugged'. However, monitoring of sound levels always proved difficult because it was impossible to forecast the intensity of a sudden call or the distance and direction of the bird uttering it. For the latter reason, especially, a parabolic reflector was not considered worthwhile and in practice it was better in most circumstances to use an ordinary non-directional microphone and to leave the record level at maximum so that nothing would be missed; it was only when the calling was fairly continuous, e.g. when recording the persistent snores of the hen or young, that monitoring could do much to improve the quality of the results.

Nevertheless, a fair collection of calls was soon preserved on tape and by listening to them repeatedly it was possible to commit them to memory. But their particular functions remained obscure and, as none of us had had much opportunity to observe Barn Owls at really close quarters, two zoo-bred owls were obtained in the hope that they would pair up and give some initial indication of the uses of the various call notes. As it eventually turned out, the 'pair' proved to be of two males, but fortunately they behaved much as a true pair and the information gained enabled tentative interpretations of most of the Barn Owl's vocabulary. These were later confirmed and expanded by observations on wild birds.

In the list given later in this chapter, seventeen separate *sound signals*, vocal and non-vocal, are defined. It is hoped that these represent the complete vocabulary of the Barn Owl but, despite the numerous hours spent observing the species, it would clearly be rash to assume that this is necessarily the case, for there may be calls used only in exceptional circumstances when the chances of an observer being present are remote. The literature has been searched for help in this respect and, indeed, we have frequently found descriptions of calls which could not easily be related to any in our own list. There is no doubt that this was due mostly to the difficulties of describing the vocalisations, but there are a few references to sounds that are worthy of special consideration.

Most interesting is the long controversial question of the Barn Owl's having a 'hoot'. No connection between 'hooting' and our 'wailing' was appreciated until one day a fellow naturalist who knew of D.S.B.'s work positively asserted that the Barn Owl does hoot because he had very recently *seen* one doing so. On describing his observation it was evident that two owls were behaving in a way which corresponded closely with the observations in which we had heard wailing. We believe, then, that our 'wailing' is the 'hoot' of the barn owl. Indeed, Aplin (1889) described it as 'a simple rather long "hooooo", the pitch dropping gradually, and the note having something of a *wailing* tone in it'. Additionally, however, the sustained defensive hisses of two brooding hens have been heard to progress into indisputable 'hoots' – see call 8.

Another note which has caused some doubt in our minds is the 'kewick call', mentioned by several writers and said to be not unlike that of the Tawny Owl. Warham (1951) fortunately describes the circumstances in which he heard a series of 'rather wheezy kewicks' and these are precisely such as one would expect to elicit the 'mobbing note', though we would not have thought it similar to the Tawny's kewick call.

This would appear to identify two 'mystery calls', but it must be confessed that some of the vocalisations described by Moffatt (1940), Trollope (1971) and various other workers have proved extremely difficult to relate to any of those described by us. It would, however, be undesirable to add these seemingly unrecorded notes to our list, as in all probability they are included already. One of the problems in studying the Barn Owl's voice is the difficulty of describing the calls satisfactorily, none of them being easily rendered in words, and it is therefore quite likely that we have failed to interpret the descriptions of these writers.

However, one note variously described as *get-get*, *kuk-uk-uk*, *kek-kek*, *git-git*, etc, may be an additional call. We ourselves have only heard it uttered by unseen flying birds in full darkness and, although on some occasions a Barn Owl was known to be in the vicinity, on others it was heard in places where, to the best of our knowledge, there were no Barn Owls. For this reason Bunn (1974) chose not to include the note in a paper on the voice of the Barn Owl. This resulted in three letters from people expressing surprise that he had not mentioned it. Witherby et al (1940) and Coward (1920) liken it to the flight-note of the Moorhen and we wonder whether, in fact, the Moorhen may be responsible, since this species seems to have a predilection for flying at night (Witherby et al and Coward). The Little Owl, too, has a flight-call *kit-kit-kit* which further confuses the issue, especially since it commonly shares the same habitat as the Barn Owl. The evidence provided by the many birdwatchers who believe the Barn Owl to be responsible for the call is very persuasive and every effort has been made to find proof, but without success – the bird was either unseen or seen only as a dim shape in the darkness. In just one case the observer believed he heard the call from a Barn Owl hunting in daylight, but we feel he too may have been mistaken. Though we may appear to be unreasonably cautious, we prefer not to accept this call until more positive evidence is available.

Another factor which hampered the classification of the Barn Owl's vocalisations was the way in which many of them vary and can grade into one another. It was at first hard to know which sounds were merely variations of one call and which were to be considered separate, with different functions. Sometimes these variations may be significant; for example, the harsh tone of the screech when a cock bird is attacking or has just driven off an intruder clearly indicates the bird's anger; but in other instances, such as the numerous variations of the hen's snore as she turns her head, moves about, stretches and preens, they are unimportant. Only complete familiarity with the species will enable the observer to solve these vocalisations correctly.

In addition to these not altogether unexpected variations, there is another type. When D.S.B. was maintaining daily observations on a pair throughout the breeding season he noticed that the hen's snore changed in character from day to day; it varied in tone, volume and periodicity. Similarly, the fledged young differed in their vocalisations at each vigil. On some evenings an owlet would do little more than snore, while on others it would continually utter a variety of chirruping and squeaking notes for no apparent reason.

In the list which follows we have allotted three paragraphs to each call roughly as follows: description, function and additional remarks. The calls have also been grouped descriptively so far as is possible, beginning with those most aptly termed screams, following these with the more hissing notes and then the chirruping, twittering and squeaking sounds. Finally there are two non-vocal sounds.

1. *The screech*
At its best only when given in flight: a loud drawn-out hissing scream with a marked gargling or tremulous effect (perhaps renderable as *shrrreeeeee*), of

about two seconds duration. The effort of the wing-beats is reflected in the call as in the speech of a person trying to talk while running. The full screech of the female usually has a different tone from that of the male and is not as perfectly delivered, tending to break off into a less tremulous scream.

The song of the Barn Owl in the recognised ornithological sense of the term: a declaration of territorial possession, an invitation to hen birds on the part of unmated cocks, a sexual stimulant between cock and hen and sometimes a contact call to the mate or young when some distance separates them.

Many variations. Frequently, as dusk falls, cock Barn Owls in particular give series of subdued screeches prior to emergence from the roost. If a hen is present she will often join in with similar screeches. Not all screeches are clear and tremulous – sometimes perched birds give hoarse non-tremulous versions and there is every gradation between the two. All forms of screech may vary from little more than a chirrup to a very loud scream. Occasionally two loud screeches are run together to produce a most bizarre sound, and during sexual chases the most strange-sounding screeches are heard. During and after encounters with intruding birds, not necessarily of the same species, the screech takes on a harsh tone, expressing anger, but apart from this no differences in the functions of any of the variations have been detected. The female's screech is generally more husky, this being increasingly evident the louder she calls.

2. *Purring*

In the cock, a continuous series of unusually mellow, subdued tremulous screeches; the hen's purring is distinctly higher pitched, held on a sustained note and not mellow.

An attracting or 'come over here' call to the mate. Used by the cock in courtship to invite the hen to join him at some possible nest-site, and used by the hen to call the cock to her at the nest or into some possible future nest-site when he arrives with prey.

Subdued screeches (No. 1) can grade imperceptibly into purring.

3. *Wailing*

Only heard on a few occasions. Noted as 'a lower pitched [than the screech] non-tremulous wail'. Has been likened to cats fighting.

On all occasions was uttered during aerial chases, together with much screeching. The two dashed to and fro for some time and this behaviour corresponded closely with records by other workers of what we believe to have been wailing in sexual chases.

It was suspected that the hen uttered the wails while the cock (the pursuer) did the screeching. Indeed wailing may simply be a development of the hen's less tremulous screech.

4. *The warning scream*

A loud, drawn-out, high-pitched scream or squeal, without a tremulous effect or hissing tone; almost always uttered in flight.

A typical alarm call: denotes fear and warns others.

May vary in volume, length and tone, but always easily recognisable. We believe the warning scream is sometimes thought to be the screech, as it is much more commonly heard in the daytime. It is frequently uttered at the sight of a human during diurnal hunting activities and rarely when flushed from the roost. As with most birds, the Barn Owl is particularly inclined to give the alarm when there are young ones present.

5. *The mobbing note*
An explosive yell, normally quite distinct from the warning scream.
Denotes a combination of fear and anger, directed at mammalian predators.
Depending on the emotion chiefly expressed it will differ from the warning scream to a lesser or greater extent. Usually heard from a perched bird that is screaming abuse at some ground predator. Newly fledged owlets are particularly inclined to use this call because they are less easily frightened than adults and will frequently direct it at humans.

6. *The anxiety call*
A plaintive but piercing whistle or scream. A 'toned-down' version of the warning scream given by a perched bird.
Expresses anxiety. Occasionally given by female when nest is endangered.
Seldom heard by the authors, the warning scream being more often uttered in this situation.

7. *The distress call*
A volley of loud screams.
Expresses distress or extreme fear.
Often a progression of the sustained defensive hiss (No. 8): if a hissing bird is approached closely or handled, by degrees the hiss will develop into this call. Used also in fighting.

8. *The sustained defensive hiss*
An incredibly loud and prolonged hiss repeated again and again, and often ending in a little squeaking whistle as the breath runs out. Bill appears closed, but is probably slightly parted.
To intimidate and frighten off enemies including aggressive members of its own species.
Varies considerably according to the provocation involved. The closer it is approached the louder and more screaming the hiss becomes and we have known this call, uttered by brooding hens, to develop into what could only be described as a shrill hoot. There is often a whistling or squeaking quality to the call, most evident at the end of a hiss as mentioned above. Typically uttered by cornered or captive birds but once heard directed at a motionless observer by a hen with young who suspected danger but was not sure of its identity. Heard more than once from well-fledged owlets that were suffering aggression from their parents.

9. *The brief defensive hiss*
A very short, quiet hiss which usually accompanies an active defensive display. Delivered with open bill.

Usually part of an intimidatory display (accompanying defensive posturing) to frighten off enemies (see Photos 2 and 25).

Often accompanied by tongue-clicking.

10.   *The courtship hiss*

A single hiss, sometimes with a whistling tendency, of greatly varying length and intensity.

Function obscure other than friendly recognition of mate and expression of excitement.

Uttered now and again when two birds are engaged in bouts of squeaking, chirruping and twittering, without any separate function that is readily apparent. The more drawn out hisses seem characteristic of the cock, but occur mainly outside the breeding season.

11.   *The snore*

A greatly varying hiss. May be short, long or very long, simply a hiss or with a marked rasping or wheezing quality, sometimes with a whistling tendency and at times with affinities to the screech or the sustained defensive hiss. The stable characteristic which clearly identifies it is that it is repeated usually in a most persistent manner. The voice of the hen can usually be recognised from that of the young by its throaty tone and shorter duration, but certainly not invariably. From about three weeks the snore of the young is characteristically wheezy and drawn out. The screech-like and very long drawn out hissing calls are delivered by owlets on the verge of independence when they seem almost to be exercising their voices. At this stage any activity among themselves, and of course the arrival of an adult with food, causes volleys of frenzied shrieks.

Not simply a food-call as is so often implied: basically a non-aggressive, self-advertisement call. As with the screech, the response depends on the circumstances: when uttered by the adults it strengthens the pair-bond and presumably serves to induce the sexual behaviour necessary for reproduction; when uttered by the young it acts as a constant reminder to the parents of their presence and, secondarily, ensures that they are fed; later it probably serves to suppress for a time the latent aggression of the adults. Snoring also functions incidentally – but importantly nevertheless – as a contact call, enabling the returning cock to locate the hen; it enables newly fledged owlets to find their way back to the nest by 'homing in' on the calls of the owlets still present and, at a later stage, keeps them in touch with one another as they explore around the nest-site.

Regular snoring is only heard from March to September and is essentially a female and juvenile characteristic. Nevertheless the cock also snores at times, but it is perhaps significant that with one pair which were closely observed throughout a twelve months' period the cock snored regularly only during the interval between the termination of breeding (when copulation ceased) and the end of September (when snoring stopped anyway) – a period when his 'masculinity' was probably at a minimum. Snoring *is* stimulated by hunger and not only do the hen and young snore more loudly and persistently when short of food, but we have witnessed both a captive and a wild cock expressing their hunger in this way. In ordinary snoring by the hen, if the cock is close-by her snores will be quiet and rapid; if very close and the two are engaging in courtship they will be muffled and uttered in quick succession with each breath; when some distance separates them a loud snore will be uttered every few seconds. Much of the variation in tone is only incidental to the movements of the bird's head, for snoring continues while the owl is preening and moving about. The snores of the newly hatched young are weak and infrequent, though if short of food they can be uttered quite persistently even at this stage. As the appetite develops the snore is heard more often, and after a fortnight it becomes very persistent during their accustomed feeding periods. At about this stage it starts to become more rasping and drawn out during excitement and soon it takes on these characteristics most of the time. It is then an extremely far-carrying sound and for a period of six or seven weeks the owlets scatter discretion to the wind and become anything but secretive.

Copulation is accompanied by frenzied snores on the part of the hen which should perhaps be described as a combination of snoring and purring.

12. *Chirrups, twitters and squeaks*

A varied mixture of notes, difficult to describe in further detail. Most characteristic is the cock's acknowledgement or self-advertising call to the hen – a combined little squeak and chirrup when he looks in her direction or approaches her; he also utters a more prolonged twittering version when he delivers food to the nest. Outside the breeding season, when the hen is no longer using the snore, she frequently greets the cock with tremulous squeaking notes. A more twittering version of the chirrup is heard characteristically from a bird that is being preened by its mate.

Basically excitement. More specifically they usually function as friendly recognition and attention-seeking notes which serve to preserve the pair-bond. Sudden louder twitters from the passive bird in mutual preening seem to indicate discomfort and perhaps serve to warn the active bird to be more gentle. They probably represent the adult form of chittering (see call 13).

Many variations but clear-cut differences, if they exist, are not readily apparent. Birds in close proximity frequently utter squeaking chirrups and twitters in friendly recognition and in courtship. The hen sometimes gives a 'rich' squeak which appears to be mid-way between a snore and a normal squeak. All the notes are used by both sexes, but some are more characteristic of one sex, as indicated above . We can only attribute chirrups heard from a captive Barn Owl defending food from a Snowy Owl, a cock bird pursued by an over-enthusiastic owlet and a captive struggling to escape from a cage, to excitement.

13. *Chittering*

A *series* of chittering (or twittering) notes. One newly hatched chick when calling loudly on being left by the hen, gave a whistle with each intake of breath. After the first week the call changes somewhat and becomes faster.

Expresses discomfort, attention-seeking; owlets use it when quarrelling and when touched.

Very characteristic of the owlets during the first month of life. Chicks call loudly with this note when the hen leaves them and also when exploring in the nest area. Once the hen finally ceases to remain with them the call is used much less frequently and when they begin to fly it is heard even less often, being replaced by the chirrups, twitters and squeaks of the adults from which it can no longer be positively distinguished.

14.   *The copulation note*
A repeated staccato squeaking, plaintive in tone and quite different from the ordinary squeaking notes.

Used by the cock during copulation.

Quite commonly heard in the first half of the breeding season due to the extreme frequency of copulation.

15.   *The food-offering call*
A highly distinctive, fast, chattering twitter.

Stimulates owlets to beg for food and, when used by the cock in food presentation, indicates his intentions.

Seldom used by the cock except when passing food to the hen in the early nesting period. Hen uses it on the nest from the day prior to the first egg hatching (probably she can hear the chick inside the shell) until the young can feed themselves without assistance. At first she utters the call a great deal not only when feeding the young but also when toying with the prey items strewn around the nest.

16.   *Tongue-clicking*
A clicking sound often accompanying defensive hissing.

Expresses excitement and often, more specifically, used to intimidate. Used also in courtship display. Well grown owlets tongue-click a great deal in excitement and aggression.

There has been controversy as to whether this sound, which is common to at least the British owls, is produced by snapping the beak, clicking the tongue or by vocal means. In the case of the Barn Owl each click is preceded by a protrusion of the tongue, the click being heard as the tongue is withdrawn and the bill closed. Observations on owlets in the nest, which are easier to watch closely, suggest that the closure of the bill is too gentle to create the sound and that it is actually produced by the movement of the back of the tongue in the muscular pharynx as the organ is withdrawn. Strangely, the tongue is usually protruded alternately from first one side of the bill and then the other.

17.   *Wing-clapping*
A single smacking sound, usually not at all loud and often followed by a quieter smack. D. Scott (pers. comm.) records a much louder version on rare occasions.

A form of display by the cock as he hovers momentarily in front of the hen in what we have termed the 'moth-flight'.

In its quieter form may be incidental to the strenuous type of wing-beat involved in hovering. In these cases the wings appear to touch either above or below the body, but D. Scott believes the loud wing-claps he witnessed were made on the upstroke. As owls in general clap the wings beneath the body this is quite at variance with what one would expect.

The owlets can use some of the calls of the adult while still in the nest. The two defensive hisses, the warning scream, the mobbing note and the food-offering call have all been recorded and on one occasion it was strongly suspected that a juvenile attempt at purring was being made by two-week-old owlets to call the hen back to the nest.

In addition to the vocalisations listed above there are other incidental sounds not to be confused with calls that have a definite function. When swallowing prey an owl will often give an odd chirp or two, and very characteristic is the cheeping sneeze of the well grown owlets (the adults sneeze without vocal accompaniment). Younger owlets frequently utter a drawn out, high-pitched whistling sound and a cock bird was once heard to make 'a very quiet vocal noise like a contented hen' while preening.

It is regretted that the above descriptions will not give the reader who has not heard the calls for himself a very good idea of their actual character, but the list does give an insight into the range of sound signals used – and therefore needed – by the species in the course of its daily life and breeding cycle. The chapters on behaviour and breeding should help the reader to appreciate better the situations in which many of the calls play their parts.

This completes the description of the Barn Owl: in the first chapter we dealt with the bird's appearance and the remarkable adaptations for its specialised way of life and, in the present chapter, we believe we have given a list that includes the whole repertoire of sound signals essential for the species' survival, enabling it to communicate alarm, to advertise its territory and attract a mate, to form and maintain the pair bond and to respond to the requirements of its young. In the next chapter we shall describe the behaviour of the Barn Owl, concentrating first on its general life-style and then, in Chapter 5, on that behaviour specifically associated with the breeding biology.

CHAPTER 3

General behaviour

GENERAL CHARACTERISTICS AND MANNERISMS

Before proceeding further we feel it is desirable to try to convey to the reader something of the 'personality' and 'temperament' of the species, for there must be few people who know the Barn Owl as more than a white shadow flitting silently out of a barn when disturbed, or as a typical owl-shaped bird sailing buoyantly along some hedgerow or ditch-side in its quest for prey. Even when resting and relaxed a Barn Owl does not disclose much about itself, except perhaps its extreme lethargy, and for the field-worker this characteristic is, infuriatingly, often the most striking! Of course, comparative inactivity is the rule among predators, for by feeding on food items rich in protein, they are able quickly to obtain sufficient nourishment to satisfy their immediate needs, whereas vegetarian species have to spend a large part of their lives contriving an endless meal.

Yet, even for a predator, the Barn Owl does seem to be an exceptionally inactive bird. A pair that one of us watched throughout one winter would, for long periods, perch motionless on one leg in their roosting barn, only occasionally breaking the monotony by ruffling their feathers or scratching their facial disks. Now and again they would preen, much as any other bird preens but paying an extraordinary amount of attention to the foot and leg that they were not standing on. In scratching, the toes were widely separated and one could distinctly see that it was the middle claw that was used, the serrations no doubt performing a combing action. This claw was cleaned regularly but much attention was also given to the short feathers on the leg itself. The oil gland was used a great deal and towards the end of the preening session the birds appeared to wipe the bill frequently on the upper surfaces of the wings behind the carpal joints, which were raised for the purpose; the eyes were rubbed in a similar action. Barn Owls shake themselves frequently, and a peculiar habit, also indulged in towards the end of the preening session, was a repeated shuffling of the wings, very reminiscent of a bird that has just bathed. Stretching was another frequent occurrence.

In one action the wings were flexed and raised so that the carpal joints were held over the lowered head, and in another the leg and wing on the same side were extended backwards while the bird balanced on the other leg. Incidently, a wet Barn Owl, if perched, will flap its wings vigorously so that it almost takes off and, like a gull, in flight will pause in mid-air to shake itself.

Throughout the winter, mutual preening took place regularly, the hen being the more attentive, approaching the cock with tremulous squeaks or whistles (Call 12) and preening him all over, but particularly about the face and back of the head and neck. The bird being groomed expressed its apparent pleasure by continuous twittering (another note included under Call 12), but now and again sudden louder twitters or chirrups seemed to indicate that its mate was being too rough! We do not class mutual preening (allo-preening) as true courtship, as even owlets engage in it: its main purpose is to maintain a friendly relationship and to preserve the pair-bond; it is probably of practical use, also, in keeping in good order those parts of the plumage that cannot be reached by the bird itself.

With the completion of preening the observer would wait hopefully for some more interesting activity, but almost always the bird or birds would begin to doze again, the cock giving a characteristic little side-to-side movement of the body, frequently noticed in other Barn Owls. We should mention here that we have used the term 'doze' rather than 'sleep' throughout this book since we have never known an adult bird sleep in the profound way characteristic of many mammals.

It would be two hours or more after darkness before these particular birds flew outside – and then only if the weather was fine! More usually the cock alone went out, making us wonder whether, despite the absence of courtship, the cock brought food to the hen all winter. However, since diurnally hunting cock birds have seldom been seen to take food to the roost outside the breeding season, we feel that this is unlikely to be a normal occurrence. To our knowledge, even during the breeding season that followed, these owls never emerged before dusk and, since they were observed on a great many occasions, they could truly be regarded as totally nocturnal which seems to be unusual for British Barn Owls. D. Scott (pers. comm.) once knew an even more lethargic pair which bred in a drying shed of a disused brickworks. The shed was infested with Brown Rats and House Mice and there was every indication that the birds rarely left the building, for neither Scott nor the caretaker ever saw them outside and their pellets contained nothing but rats and mice, all of which they had seemingly caught indoors.

Perched on a beam, fence-post or wall, resting or preening, the Barn Owl gives the impression that it moves about very little on its feet and somehow inclines one to suppose that it would be very awkward when doing so. On the contrary, however, it is not at all awkward and moves about in a distinctly parrot-like fashion with the body held almost horizontally. It is also a remarkable jumper and can spring about 60 cm without using its wings. It can run fast, too, though this is more a feature of flightless individuals such as birds that have suffered wing injuries, and well-grown owlets that have not yet developed their flight feathers.

Another point worth mentioning is that a relaxed Barn Owl does not display the long legs quoted as characteristic of the Tytonidae: the plumage is loose, covering all but the lower tarsus and toes, and the owl, especially the female, looks quite plump.

In the realms of conjecture, one of our captive Barn Owls had the peculiar habit of peering intently at the roof of their shed and then flying up to it as though there was a possible exit there. This odd behaviour was dismissed at the time as being a rather senseless attempt to escape, but later it was found that the female of the pair described earlier not uncommonly did the same, although this bird sometimes managed to squeeze itself on to one of the rafters just beneath the roof-slates. Possibly the captive bird was expressing a need to find a high retreat where it would feel safe. Another activity that we cannot account for is the fact that in hot weather Barn Owls frequently stamp their feet rapidly as though suffering some discomfort.

Barn Owls are very much creatures of habit. Not only do they tend to roost in the same place and take the same routes when hunting, but they almost always leave a building via the same exit hole. Often the hole chosen is not the most obvious one, a small opening being preferred to a much larger one. Re-entry is performed in the same individual manner by particular birds, one perhaps pausing in the entrance, another swooping straight inside. In our studies we have found such individual traits invaluable in identifying our subjects in the field.

In its disposition the Barn Owl creates something of an anomaly. In many of its remote haunts, in deserted farms on high ground for instance, it is exceedingly wary and nervous, and yet in other circumstances it can accustom itself to the busy life of the farmyard and learn to ignore the sound of humans working in the near vicinity.

There are few, if any, genuine records of Barn Owls attacking Man, but they will protest vigorously when a nest with young is examined, screaming loudly with Call 4. Generally speaking – and this is also noticeable with captives – they are much bolder at night and, if suspicious of the presence of some enemy, will sometimes come closer to ascertain its identity. On several occasions Barn Owls that have noticed some movement on our part while we were hiding amongst thick tree cover, have flown towards us and hovered silently overhead until, suspicions confirmed, they have flown off with a piercing scream (Call 4).

This warning scream is probably the most familiar call of the Barn Owl, for it is commonly uttered even in daylight when an owl encounters a human being while hunting. Many people mistake it for the true screech of the species (Call 1). On occasion we have been subjected to a whole series of screams from an unseen owl flying around our heads, and one male in the forest study area even used to circle screaming when flushed from his roosting barn in the daytime, hence he was named 'The Screamer' by one of the foresters! By far the most remarkable incident took place when one of us entered a barn where an owl was roosting and made some quiet hissing sounds in order to entice the bird out – a ploy which often works. Not only did it emerge from its hiding place, but it began fluttering to and fro in front of the observer, uttering volleys of piercing screams, perhaps more correctly interpreted as a combination of Calls 4 and 5. The bird could still be heard screaming from inside the barn when the observer had left and walked some 100 m away.

Although individuals differ markedly in their characters and dispositions, the Barn Owl as a species is, above all, a very nervous creature, flinching at every unexpected sound or movement, however harmless. At times it will jump right off its feet when startled by some loud noise or close-passing bird. In captivity, even hand-reared owls that have been quite tame have a strong tendency to become completely wild when adult – a neurotic disposition which contrasts markedly with that of the almost placid Tawny Owl.

ROOSTING

The roosting habits of the Barn Owl tend to attract an unusual amount of attention, probably because this is how many people encounter it. We, as mainly diurnal creatures, are active when the owl is resting and this obviously increases the chances of it being found at its roost. This point is worth making because there must be many familiar diurnal species with equally interesting roosting habits about which we are completely ignorant. How many of us could say where our garden Robins and Blackbirds roost each night for instance?

For roosting, the Barn Owl definitely prefers better shelter than its frequent neighbour, the Tawny Owl, and this difference in behaviour is most marked in captive birds. In our experience a Barn Owl nearly always establishes itself in one favoured site – often that subsequently used for breeding. Here it roosts regularly, and if the site happens to be in a building (which it usually is in our parts of north-west England), not only is the same perch habitually used, but usually precisely *the same part* of a chosen beam, etc. This is clearly indicated by the pellets and droppings beneath, and traces of fluff adhering round about. These are the signs to be searched for when looking for proof of occupancy at possible Barn Owl sites. It is likely, of course, that other suitable roosts will exist in the bird's territory (which, as we will see later, probably extends for at least a kilometre in any direction), but these seem only to be used after the bird has been disturbed or when the adults have well-grown young in the nest. Intending fieldworkers should note that a single flushing is sometimes enough to cause certain individuals to move away from the site and great care should be taken to keep disturbance to a minimum. Wherever possible we only enter a roosting site after we have seen the occupants leaving to hunt.

There is a tendency for a roosting Barn Owl to be fairly well hidden. For instance, it will often select a rafter that is close to the roof of the building so that it occupies the small space between the timber and slates. Alternatively, it may squeeze itself into a hole in the wall or the gap between the inner and outer layers of bricks of the wall, where buildings are constructed this way. Another site is the space to be found in many barns between the top of the wall and the slates, and popular positions for both roosting and breeding are the tops of what remains of the ceilings of derelict houses, and the dark tunnels formed among loosely arranged bales of hay.

Barn Owls do, however, roost in the open more than we, at least, first supposed. Nevertheless, such outdoor roosts, when discovered, are usually impressive in their seclusion, unlike those of the Tawny Owl which are often quite exposed. The most frequently recorded tree roosts are in spruce *Picea* sp., pines *Pinus* sp. and Holly *Ilex aquifolium*, where the dense evergreen foliage gives good cover at all times of the year, but we know of one large Oak tree *Quercus petraea* that has been used as a roost from time to time, and a roost in an Alder *Alnus glutinosa* that was thickly clad in Honeysuckle *Lonicera periclymenum*. An interesting site recorded by Ash (1954) was on low stumps among high reeds, where two Barn Owls were found roosting. Oakes (1953) quotes a record by T. S. Williams of a Barn Owl roosting throughout the winter of 1925/26 in a large Gorse bush *Ulex* sp. in open country; he expressed the opinion (which we share) that owls found at 'open' roosts are mostly juveniles. Coward (1920) records roosting beneath an overhanging bank, but this does not surprise us for such sites are sometimes used for nesting by both *Tyto alba alba* and *T. a. pratincola*. Nor is the Barn Owl averse to spending lengthy periods on the ground, for we have seen it alight and remain down, evidently dozing in the manner of a Short-eared Owl.

Relevant to the subject of tree roosts are the occasional reports of luminous or 'ghost' owls. Sightings of apparently phosphorescent Barn Owls have elicited several notes in the ornithological journals and, improbable though these claims may seem, there can be no doubt that such phenomena have occurred. The most satisfactory explanation is that Barn Owls must occasionally roost in hollow trees where luminous bacteria or the common fungus *Armillaria mellea* (Honey Fungus), which is also sometimes luminous, are saprophytic on the rotten wood inside. Fine particles of the decaying wood, covered with bacteria or fungus, adhere to the plumage and a 'ghost' owl is created.

REACTIONS TO DANGER

When disturbed at an indoor roost a Barn Owl reacts in a variety of ways. Most simply it flies out, frequently using an exit on the opposite side of the building so that its departure is unobserved. A remarkable example of this method of escaping detection was exhibited by the male of a pair with young observed in 1969. There was a hayfield behind the nesting barn and the male, which hunted diurnally, would have been in full view of anyone working in the hayfield when he entered or left the building via a hole in the gable end. When haymaking began he still entered at the gable end, but astonishingly he began to leave via a cat-hole in the bottom of one of the doors at the front of the building, thus keeping the building between himself and the workers in the field as he flew away. It is impossible to tell whether or not this was a thought-out response by the owl, but the implication is there. Often the owl will fly a long way before alighting after disturbance and we have noticed that in windy conditions it sometimes allows itself to be swept away downwind, irrespective of its normal direction of flight and territory, so as to facilitate the quickest possible getaway.

As an alternative to hasty departure, the owl may remain where it is in the hope of being overlooked. Its behaviour on these occasions is interesting. When dozing it assumes a relaxed posture, standing on one leg with the body at an angle of about 60° or less, the wings held in what we may call the 'normal' position for want of a better word, the head facing forward and the eyes closed. (It should be noted that a healthy owl never turns its head round to tuck its bill into the scapulars as has been stated and actually illustrated in one popular owl book!) Any slight noise will cause the bird to open its eyes and look towards the source. At the first hint of danger the bird lowers its other leg, draws itself upright and holds its wings very close to the body, almost wrapping them round itself. In this way the white underparts are partly concealed and the owl rendered less conspicuous. The eyes, which may have been opened at first, almost close now so that they do not attract attention – eyes are always the weak link in an animal's camouflage, hence many species having stripes through them to break up their outline.

It is worth mentioning here that the nocturnal Tawny Owl and Long-eared Owl behave in exactly the same way at the approach of a human, whereas the diurnal owls such as the Little Owl and Short-eared Owl seem to open the eyes wide and stare at the 'enemy' fixedly. When a Tawny Owl is seen looking down from its daytime roost through almost closed eyelids, it is often assumed that this is its way of limiting the amount of light entering the eyes; and this explanation seems obvious and reasonable until it is discovered that when relaxed a Tawny Owl fully opens or completely closes its eyes like a Barn Owl, only drawing the lids together to peep through narrow slits when it is aware of danger. We must conclude, therefore, that owls do this in an attempt to make themselves less conspicuous – the difference between tame and wild individuals of the same species is most marked in this respect.

It is surprising how often a perched Barn Owl can escape detection when a building is entered. One would expect that its light coloration would catch the eye, but this is not so. On numerous occasions we have looked cautiously through the door of a barn and scrutinised the beams without seeing anything. Then, when we have entered on the assumption that the building was unoccupied, an owl has suddenly flown from a beam where it must have been in full view all the time.

A third reaction to danger is for the bird actively to hide itself, flying to some crevice or dark place as soon as it becomes aware of the observer's approach. Understandably, perhaps, such behaviour is more characteristic of the female because her reaction is almost invariably to 'lie low' when first disturbed at the nest. On these occasions some individuals may 'sit' very tightly indeed, as was admirably demonstrated by a remarkable experience of two of the authors in January 1972. Accompanied by a friend they entered a small barn in order to clean out a nesting box that had been used for several years. The cock owl had flown out as they approached and, as there was no sign of the hen, they supposed her to be absent. However, when their companion had been busy reaching into the box to clear it of debris for at least two minutes, the hen Barn Owl suddenly dashed out from the space alongside, between the top of the wall and the slates, almost hitting him in the face. Had the others not been looking on, he would have been convinced that the bird had come out of the box.

This sort of behaviour must occasionally lead to Barn Owls being cornered by their enemies and the species has developed two extremely bizarre and elaborate defensive displays to cope with such a situation. In one (see Photo 2) the bird sways from side to side, standing first on one foot and then the other. The wings are lowered, the tail spread and the feathers fluffed up. The head is moved in a most odd fashion, being lowered and swayed from side to side, while the bird continues to glare at the source of its fear, and emits quiet puffing sounds (Call 9) with open bill. These are often accompanied by 'beak-snapping' (really tongue-clicking). Every ten seconds or so the bird looks down and shakes the head quite rapidly in a seemingly ludicrous manner. It then looks up and continues the display as before, the whole performance appearing as an unending cycle of head-swaying punctuated by head-shaking. Since the eyes are off the enemy in head-shaking, it is difficult to see the benefit of this action, as one might expect a hesitant foe to seize the opportunity to attack, but one must assume that such an elaborate display could only have evolved if it had advantage for the bird. Perhaps the contrast between the starkly white face alternating with the much darker back of the head, is enough to deter most natural enemies. The almost black eyes will also serve to highlight the face when it is raised. Occasionally during the display a Barn Owl will make a sudden lunge forward that is most disconcerting to the observer, but it is only bluff. One of us has seen this ruse used successfully by a captive bird to dispossess a Tawny Owl of a dead pigeon.

The other defensive display does not involve posturing. On the contrary, the bird tends to cower as far from the enemy as possible, tongue-clicking and giving vent to powerful and fiercesome hisses (Call 8), these being delivered with the bill closed or nearly so. The nearer the bird is approached the louder the hisses, and ultimately they may be better described as screams (Call 7). Which of the two displays is used seems to depend more on the individual bird than on the circumstances, and many owls employ a combination of both.

A third display, which we have seen only in captive semi-tame adults and by fledged owlets when threatening each other, is probably more aggressive than defensive. In this the owl opens its wings wide and spreads and raises the tail, glaring, puffing and tongue-clicking (see Photo 25).

When actually attacked, or if approached too closely, the owl responds by raising its talons and leaning backwards. From this position it will strike upwards with lightning speed, the claws sinking deeply and painfully into the flesh of an incautious hand.

If picked up, the Barn Owl often behaves in yet another way, closing (or appearing to close) the eyes and lying quite prostrate as though asleep – or dead – i.e. 'playing possum'.

CHANGES OF DISK SHAPE

There is a distinct difference between the shape of the facial disk of an inactive owl and one that is alert; this difference is highly significant when considering the auditory apparatus of the bird. When dozing the ruff feathers are depressed backwards laterally giving the face its peculiar heart-shaped appearance. The feathers of the wedge between the eyes and down the centre of the face are relaxed so that the wedge becomes broad and rounded, perhaps even obscuring the field of vision somewhat, since the eyes seem deeply embedded in the feathers. When active the disk is much rounder and the wedge sharp-edged, the ruff being held forward with the feathers of the wedge pressed strongly together. Since the disk is used as a 'sound receiver' it is hard to avoid the conclusion that having relaxed the facial feathers while resting, the bird has 'switched off'. However, one would expect a dozing Barn Owl to be vulnerable to enemies and therefore in need of all its senses at such a time. That the ears are still superbly efficient, even without the aid of the disk, is eminently demonstrated to any observer who has tried to creep up on a resting bird in an attempt to catch it unawares! It is more likely that the disk comes into play as an aid to *directional* hearing rather than as an 'early-warning' system.

A further demonstration of the mobility of the disk is seen when the owl is feeding. Then, the lower part of the ruff is moved backwards so that the bill pokes out from the face like that of a hawk, giving it a most untypical appearance.

TERRITORY

It is obviously a difficult task to try to map the territory of a primarily nocturnal species and one whose territory must be measured in kilometres rather than metres. Nevertheless, two of us have been fortunate to have worked in an area which, although not typical, gave us the opportunity to overlook virtually the whole of two Barn Owl hunting territories and parts of the hunting territories of a further six birds. This was in a young coniferous forest in the West Riding of Yorkshire (now part of Lancashire), where a valley newly planted with small trees could be surveyed from a high vantage point. Fig. 4 shows this study area with the territory boundaries drawn in as they were in 1969. It will be seen that they tend to coincide with 'natural' features, e.g. streams and the edges of plots. The dotted areas represent the very young plantations which were the most productive prey-wise, while the shaded parts represent areas where the trees were too large and impenetrable for hunting and the owls' activities were confined to the rides separating the plots. (The rides, however, provided hunting territories that were far superior to those in more usual habitats.) Unmarked areas represent agricultural land outside the forest, grazed by sheep and cattle. Territories A, B and C were known reasonably accurately, while territory D may have been even more extensive than is indicated, though parts on the agricultural land in the north of this territory were probably only temporarily attractive during hay-making operations when prey became exposed. Territory E was imperfectly known. The solid circles represent the buildings used for roosting.

Many of the owls hunted in daylight – hence the success of the study – and some hundreds of hours were spent observing with one or more owls in view. Territories B, C, D and E were held by pairs and territory A by a single male. The birds could be recognised at a distance quite easily when hunting diurnally. The male from territory D was exceptionally white, small in body,

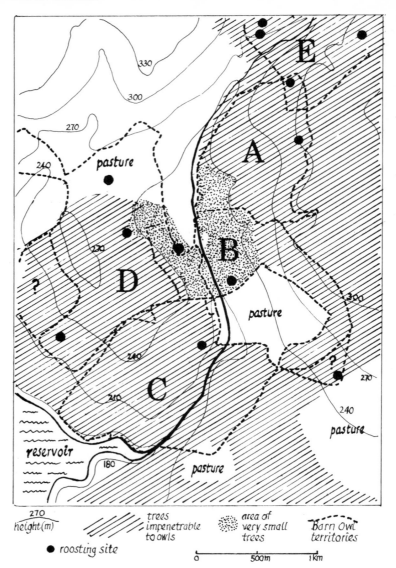

Fig. 4 Sketch map showing the hunting territories of five Barn Owls in an area of young coniferous forest in north-west England.

but with long wings and a very graceful sailing flight. Its 1969 mate had dark wings with contrasting white patches at the sides of the neck. This bird disappeared in 1970, but the male found another female in 1971, a huge dark bird. The unpaired male in territory A also showed more white than is usual, but was a large bird with a laboured flapping flight, most uncharacteristic of a Barn Owl. Perhaps for this reason it habitually hunted by 'post-hopping', that is by watching for prey from fence posts and walls. It never engaged in prolonged flights and at best would only make a brief sortie over the young plantation, lasting a few seconds. The male from territory E was similarly coloured, but by contrast had a very graceful buoyant flight; its mate was not seen hunting. The male from territory B was also mainly nocturnal and was seldom seen in daylight outside the breeding season. However, it was often observed when feeding young and could be distinguished by its average coloration and fast flight. Its mate was also of average coloration for her sex, but was a slow flier with characteristic, gentle wing-beats and her dark feet were noticeable. She was very diurnal and often hunted near the vantage point, so close views of her were commonplace. The male of the pair from territory C was a very large bird, bigger than his mate and almost as dark in colour with bright yellow feet. He was a most energetic hunter and displayed a deep wing-action in contrast to that of his mate which was shallow. All these points, combined with the fact that their activities were restricted to certain areas, made it a simple matter, using binoculars, to identify all the Barn Owls regularly seen.

The map shows that in such a habitat the Barn Owl seems to require quite a small territory for a predator, 2·5 km^2 being apparently quite adequate even when the vole population is at a low ebb as it was in 1969. However, in grazed farmland the productive areas from the owl's point of view will be confined to the hedgerows, streamsides, borders of woods and copses, and to the buildings themselves. In this habitat, therefore, the owls will be obliged to fly a great deal farther from the roost in order to cover the same amount of favourable hunting ground. In such circumstances the territory size will probably be doubled at least. At the extreme in this respect, Dr L. S. Garrad (pers. comm.), of the Manx Museum in the Isle of Man, suspects that the Manx owls sometimes even fly to the mainland to hunt – a distance of over 30 km – because the remains of voles, which do not occur on the island, have occasionally been found in their pellets. We find it hard to believe that a Barn Owl will deliberately 'commute' to feed on the mainland and would suggest that those owls which egest pellets containing voles might be newly arrived immigrants. Another alternative is the possibility that voles might exist on the island in small numbers – a challenge here for the Manx naturalists perhaps! Territories on arable land, where small mammals become season- ably abundant in fields of corn, probably fall mid-way between young forests and grazed farmland in summer, but will presumably have to be extended in winter.

A final consideration is that the territories in our particular forest may have been smaller than normal because of intra-specific competition. The area attracted a population of Barn Owls far higher than is usual these days but we were surprised when, in 1968, two pairs began breeding in nest-boxes in barns less than 800 m apart. However, there are a number of records of Barn Owls nesting in the same building (e.g. Callion 1973, Baudvin 1975). Indeed, at times it seems that the species is not particularly territorial, several having been seen roosting in close proximity. It is tempting to explain away such aggregations as family parties, but the number of birds involved precludes this. Smith and Marti (1976) quote several instances of communal roosting and nesting on the part of *T. a. pratincola* in the USA.

DEFENCE OF TERRITORY

Animals that hold territories must be prepared to defend them. In the Barn Owl, as with a great many other birds, the most common form of territorial defence is the *song*. The screech may hardly seem deserving of such a description, but song it is in the ornithological sense of the word, being both a means of attracting the opposite sex, while at the same time proclaiming the male's ownership of the territory.

When male Barn Owls first become active at dusk they usually advertise their possession of the roost by repeatedly uttering subdued screeches, and it is very typical of cock birds and some hens to utter a loud screech as they fly off and as they return. In addition they may indulge in a *song-flight* immediately they emerge, flying steadily over their territories, repeatedly changing direction and screeching every few seconds. These territorial flights are quite brief and often the bird returns to the roost after two or three minutes and lapses into inactivity again.

Moffat (1940) quoted evidence to suggest that Barn Owls in Ireland are more vocally inclined in some localities than others. Although the hoarse screams of the hen which Moffat heard uttered every four seconds were undoubtedly what we have termed snores, we too have noticed a similar variation with regard to the true screech, for in the forest study area the owls called far more frequently than elsewhere. This is not really surprising, for since the song is the main means of defending the territory from other members of its own species, it is only to be expected that in areas with high populations of owls the screech will be used more often than in those with isolated pairs. Territorial strife must be a constant feature of their daily lives in such circumstances and the same appears to apply to the Tawny Owl which was even more noisy in the forest than is usual elsewhere.

Occasionally, brief fights and angry chases by Barn Owls do occur. Most commonly the territory owner flies straight at the intruder and the two then rise rapidly, almost vertically, breast to breast, before the latter makes off, sometimes hotly pursued by the resident bird. We have never been close enough to observe exactly what happens in these steep ascents, but we suspect that its purpose is to present their talons to each other, one attacking and the other defending itself. In such scuffles the aggressor screeches loudly.

On a few occasions while observing daylight hunting we have seen a Barn Owl wander into another's territory and be chased off by the resident bird. On most occasions, however, they seem to take little notice of one another. This could sometimes be due to the narrow field of vision of an owl, enabling an intruder to pass unnoticed and, certainly, from what we know of a Barn Owl's sight, there is little likelihood of the intruder being detected while perched some distance away. On more than one occasion we have seen the intruder escape its pursuer by throwing itself beneath thick conifers or by diving behind a wall and alighting on the ground.

PERMANENCE OF TERRITORY

How faithful are Barn Owls to their territories? This has been a vexed question for us and we confess to having had some differences of view. On the one hand, all the known adults in the forest study area remained in their territories during the four years they were under regular observation; conversely, in other areas Barn Owls have apparently disappeared from their territories after breeding, only to reappear in the following spring. Bearing in mind the resident behaviour of the forest birds, and of proved residents in other British habitats, we suspect that these apparent migrants have only changed their roosts within the territory and reverted to their more nocturnal habits. There is no doubt that the onset of the moult and decline in breeding condition causes Barn Owls to become less active, less vocal, and thus more elusive.

Barn Owls are past masters in the art of secrecy, 'lying low' and remaining undetected even when their roosts are visited. Many seldom emerge before real darkness, and this is an obvious reason why few people are familiar with them. We do, however, accept that there are occasions when some Barn Owls will desert their territories; for example, when a habitat changes and becomes unsuitable, as happened at one of our Cumbrian sites when a rise in the water-table flooded part of the land, covering some of the owls' much favoured hunting ground. Excessive and continued disturbance also causes birds to abandon their territory (particularly if they are not feeding young at the time) and we cannot stress this fact enough. Neil Bowman (pers. comm.) found that in central Wales, owls occupying territories on high ground move to lower altitudes with the advent of severe winter weather, presumably due to the lack of food, whereas the lowland population remains sedentary. Yet, after heavy snow in the forest study area in November 1965, an adult female was found dead on the floor of a barn, presumably having succumbed because it *failed* to leave the territory – another example of the singular habits of individual Barn Owls!

Our own observations suggest that male and female Barn Owls are equally sedentary in the British Isles, yet some populations of *T. a. pratincola* have been found to be migratory in North America (see Chapter 6). Some pairs we have studied in Britain have remained together throughout the year, though courtship outside the breeding season was confined to mutual preening. Two unattached cocks stayed in their territories for three years, one then securing a mate and the other continuing single throughout the study period. A hen held her territory all winter until joined by a cock in February, and another, whose mate had disappeared, remained in the territory until she succumbed during a period of heavy snow.

However, by no means all pairs continue to roost together and in some cases little has been seen of the hen for long periods. Here again we found evidence that the females do not really desert the territories, for evening watches outside one cock's roosting barn revealed that he was sometimes visited by a hen, or went out and returned in company with one. When this happened much excited courtship took place, suggesting that they were still paired and pleased to see each other again – if we may be a little anthropomorphic!

There is one way in which the territory may be changed, slowly, without really contradicting what has been said so far. This is by its gradual extension in one direction and abandonment in another, so that over a period of time the birds come to occupy entirely new ground. We have known such an occurrence in Cumbria and have witnessed a similar change in the forest study area, the cause of which may be surmised as follows. The cock from territory E at one time hunted regularly in the young plantation in territory A. In April 1969, however, a new male arrived and one encounter between these two birds was actually seen. For a time both males hunted the same area, but by the end of the summer of 1969 the newcomer seemed to have gained dominance, for although the territory E male bred successfully that year it was not seen again in territory A, working instead the areas farther north.

HUNTING — TIMES

Apart from brief glimpses of owls flushed from their roosts, most observations of Barn Owls are made when they are in search of prey. The times of hunting vary greatly between individuals and we are somewhat at a loss to account for this. The exceptionally good observation sites in our forest study area gave two of us excellent opportunities to study their behaviour. About a dozen Barn Owls were present in that part of the forest and the daytime habits of nine of these were known well or fairly well. Table 1 gives the average times of diurnal emergence in respect of eight birds during the non-breeding seasons, 1969–71. However, we emphasise that these owls emerged diurnally only to hunt. Nevertheless, this was interesting in itself and also helped us to map some of the territories and to observe the relationships with other species of birds.

Of these nine owls (six males and three females), eight (five males and the three females) were regular diurnal hunters. They would begin to appear in the late afternoons (in winter) or early evenings (in summer) an hour or more before sunset, and would hunt either until they caught prey or for about forty-five minutes, after which they seemed to lose enthusiasm, perhaps because they were tired. Sometimes, when a capture was made, the prey would be eaten on the spot or taken to a nearby fence post or some sheltered bank at the edge of the taller trees to be eaten; then, after resting a few moments, the owl would fly directly back to its roost. Alternatively, some birds would lapse into inactivity and doze on a post or wall till dark, when they could no longer be observed. Silent though they were by day, as dusk fell their screeches could be heard from here and there as they advertised their territorial rights to the rest of the Barn Owl population.

Once we came to appreciate the regularity with which some Barn Owls hunted in the afternoons and evenings before dark, it occurred to us that since they chose to hunt in daylight there should be another emergence in the early mornings. Dawn watches nicely confirmed this (see Table 2), even to the extent of showing that a song-flight often preceded the hunting foray. Thus, as one would expect, the activity pattern was reversed. One of our vigils demonstrated this perfectly. As the first light of day began to appear the cock emerged and performed a noisy song-flight over the territory; three minutes later he returned with a screech and entered the barn; further subdued screeches were heard from within and then all went quiet. Twenty-six minutes later, by which time it was no longer dark, he emerged again, without a sound this time, to hunt over the nearby plantation; eleven minutes later he returned silently, entered the barn and evidently commenced to roost as there was no further activity.

Although these Barn Owls usually emerged at the times given, they might occasionally be seen at any time of the day. The impression has been gained

---

TABLE 1: *Diurnal hunting activities between September and March of eight Barn Owls in a young coniferous forest in Lancashire (formerly the West Riding of Yorkshire). The data under-estimates their diurnal activities because at times it was clear that they had hunted before the observer's arrival. Daylight = up to 15 minutes after sunset*

	Sept	Oct	Nov	Dec	Jan	Feb	March
OWL A (male): Observed 5.3.69 to 16.10.71							
Av. no. mins before sunset when first seen	42		33	92		93	73
Number of occasions owl seen in daylight	4		5	4		2	9
*Number of occasions owl not seen in daylight	10	7	8	1	3	2	5
OWL B (female): Observed 5.3.69 to 16.10.71							
Av. no. mins before sunset when first seen	49	58	69	87	54	36	89
Number of occasions owl seen in daylight	12	6	8	4	1	1	5
*Number of occasions owl not seen in daylight	3	1	6	3	3	3	13
OWL C (male): Observed 2.2.69 to 4.3.72							
Av. no. mins before sunset when first seen	42	45	77	78	79	128	99
Number of occasions owl seen in daylight	10	6	8	2	4	6	13
OWL D (male): Observed 12.1.68 to 5.3.72							
Av. no. mins before sunset when first seen	18	103	59		29	103	92
Number of occasions owl seen in daylight	1	5	7		4	1	9
OWL E (? female): Observed 30.11.69 to 28.12.69							
Av. no. mins before sunset when first seen			58	84			
Number of occasions owl seen in daylight			1	6			
OWL F (female): Observed 23.3.69 to 14.3.70							
Av. no. of mins before sunset when first seen			84				88
Number of occasions owl seen in daylight			1				5
OWL G (female): Observed 6.12.69 to 8.3.70							
Av. no. mins before sunset when first seen				44		169	268
Number of occasions owl seen in daylight				5		1	1
OWL H (male): Observed 19.3.69 to 9.11.69							
Av. no. mins before sunset when first seen		40	121				78
Number of occasions owl seen in daylight		1	1				6

*In these cases the territory was so well overlooked that it is probable that when the birds were not seen they were not active.

TABLE 2: *Activities of five Barn Owls* Tyto alba *during three dawn watches in a young coniferous forest in the West Riding of Yorkshire, December 1969 (from Bunn 1971)*

Date	Time	Mins from sunrise	Observations
6th	08.35	−37	Took up station; sky clear, and light enough for me to be fairly certain there were no owls hunting
	08.50	−22	A appeared and began hunting
	08.58	−14	B appeared in the window of her barn
	09.04	−8	B began hunting
	09.14	+2	B flew back into the barn
	09.25	+13	A resting on wall, having finished hunting
	09.50	+38	Left vantage point
25th	09.00	−27	Took up station; C hunting already
	09.15	−12	D now hunting (soon disappeared from view)
	09.25	−2	A now hunting
	09.37	+10	B now hunting
	09.50	+23	B returned to her roost
	10.30	+63	Left vantage point; C and A still present
26th	08.20	−68	Took up station; weather very clear and ideal for sighting the owls, but none could be seen
	09.10	−18	A and B now hunting
	09.30	+2	C seen briefly
	09.40	+12	B finished hunting and returned to her barn; A had just disappeared, presumably having finished hunting
	09.54	+26	D appeared, hunting below his barn
	10.24	+56	D no longer visible
	10.30	+62	B emerged again and appeared to make two captures
	11.05	+97	B returned to her barn
	11.25	+117	C now hunting purposefully
	11.35	+127	E appeared, diving into the grass quite near me
	11.47	+139	E still present, having been rather inactive, now resting on a post; A reappeared as I left

by some workers (e.g. Hosking & Newberry 1945) that the species can foresee unfavourable weather and will emerge earlier than usual in order to avoid it. Because of these statements particular note was taken of emergence times and subsequent weather conditions, but a consistent correlation could not be demonstrated. In the forest, only continuous rain kept them in the barns; in showery weather they would simply alight until the rain stopped.

As we have seen, the majority of the forest Barn Owls hunted diurnally throughout the year, but what happens in other areas? In response to a request for information on diurnal sightings of Barn Owls (Bunn 1971) letters were received from various parts of England, from which it was evident that some birdwatchers were very surprised to see the bird in daylight while others regarded it as nothing unusual. It seems, therefore, that there are Barn Owls all over the country that habitually hunt by day, but others that are almost or entirely nocturnal; the proportions we do not know. We originally assumed that the Barn Owl is a primarily nocturnal species that will hunt in daylight when it is either short of food, as in severe winter weather, or when the demand is increased, as when feeding young; this being strongly supported by instances in which Barn Owls that had hunted regularly in daylight for their young became completely nocturnal as soon as the latter had become independent. However, our subsequent discovery that many of the forest Barn Owls hunted in daylight regularly throughout the year completely shattered this idea.

Why there should be such differences in behaviour we do not know. It has been stated (Davis 1933) that the Short-tailed Vole has peaks of activity during the hour after sunrise and the hour after sunset (it remains reasonably light after sunset for a further forty minutes). Since this species of rodent was by far the most important food item of the forest Barn Owls, it ought to have been advantageous for the owls to hunt at the times when the voles were most active and this was probably what happened in the case of the diurnal hunters, for we frequently noticed the nibbling sounds from feeding voles well *before* sunset, at about the time the owls began to emerge. However, if this is the answer it is rather strange that some of the forest birds were mainly nocturnal outside the breeding season and even more strange that one Barn Owl, the hen in territory B, after hunting diurnally for at least two years, suddenly became quite nocturnal like her mate. Moreover, the Short-tailed Vole is the most important prey species virtually everywhere on the mainland of Britain.

Another theory which may be more tenable than the original one, since it explains both these anomalies, may be propounded as follows:

1.   Most Barn Owls have no objection to being abroad in daylight in the absence of mobbing and other disturbances.

2.   As the Short-tailed Vole's two peaks of activity are largely in daylight, when the Barn Owl's vision is better than at night (see Chapter 1), it is doubly advantageous for the bird to hunt at these times in areas where the vole forms the main prey species.

3.   Severe mobbing (principally by corvids and gulls) and/or human disturbance has an inhibitory effect on daytime emergence.

The above is supported by four observations:

(a)   Corvids in the forest study area, where voles comprised 70% (numerically) of the diet, were scarce in the early years and mobbing was minimal.

(b)   After the hen from territory B had become nocturnal it was discovered that a Pheasant feeder had been placed by its barn and that this was attracting an almost constant if small number of Magpies, Jackdaws and Carrion Crows which would doubtless have harrassed the owl whenever it ventured forth in daylight.

(c)   The one entirely nocturnal pair we have watched lived on an inhabited farm near a town. Apart from numerous corvids, they would have continually encountered humans (of which they were no less frightened than other Barn Owls) had they emerged in daylight.

(d)   A captive Barn Owl that dashed out of its shed whenever D.S.B. entered, would, on being swooped upon and screamed at by Magpies and passing gulls, re-enter despite D.S.B.'s presence, suggesting that its fear of these birds was even greater than its fear of humans. It must be stated that this owl had never lived in the wild, but neither was it at all tame.

One would not expect every Barn Owl to respond in the same way, of course; depending on their individual temperaments some will be bolder in emerging than others, but if one can accept the three generalisations stated above one may reasonably assume the following:

1.   That with minimal mobbing owls will *tend* to hunt regularly throughout the year at the best times for catching prey, even if this is in daylight;

2.   that if some mobbing by large birds is almost inevitable diurnal activity will be confined to those occasions when hunting is more urgent (i.e. in adverse winter weather and the breeding season), *this applying to the majority of Barn Owls*; and

3.   that a minority which suffer very severe harrassing will never emerge in daylight. (In fact the nocturnal pair referred to in (c) above spent much time hiding behind bales of hay, etc, because people frequently entered their barn, and it was for this reason, perhaps, that they only emerged under cover of darkness.)

Undoubtedly many more observations on Barn Owls – and the species which share their territories and mob them – are necessary before this theory should be accepted. We suggest it here because no other satisfactory explanation seems to have been put forward – perhaps one of our readers will be stimulated to take up the problem!

We have spoken at some length about 'nocturnal' and 'diurnal' individuals but these, of course, are misleading terms and refer only to the feeding habits at dusk and dawn; that is, whether or not the owl emerges a little before dusk or a little after, and just before dawn or just after. In other words, it has been established that a feed usually takes place at around dusk and again around dawn, but nothing has been said of any other feeds that may occur during the night. Outside the breeding season one is not likely to find the answer very readily, but observations at nests have disclosed that feeds take place usually up to about 0200 hours, but seldom afterwards until dawn. This is comparable with the lull in activity which is evident during the afternoon in the case of diurnal bird species and we are inclined to believe, therefore, that throughout the year many Barn Owls have three fairly distinct feeds during the twenty-four hours – one at dusk or in the late afternoon, one very approximately about midnight and a third at dawn, the night feed being the most variable. Hosking & Newberry (1945) noticed a change in the prey species brought to a nest they were studying at a Norfolk farm as the night progressed – from Short-tailed Voles at dusk to Brown Rats later in the night. They believed this to be due to the parents' being less active later on, capturing the prey as they sat about the farm buildings. We fully support this theory, having found Barn Owls to be relatively inactive at night, within the breeding season and outside it, suggesting that they make no determined effort to find prey but wait quietly on a suitable perch for some unwary victim to appear.

HUNTING — METHODS

As we have said, the forest vantage point gave two of us excellent opportunities to study the hunting behaviour and full advantage was taken. The habitat did dictate to a certain extent the method employed but basically it is similar in all areas. The Barn Owl is endowed with long, broad wings to enable it to hunt by flying slowly and gently, with scarcely a sound, over likely areas for prey. Through binoculars one can see the turning of the head as the bird peers (*and listens*) intently into the grass, and sometimes one can even discern that the owl is following the progress of some small mammal. At close quarters the flight is perhaps a little higher than it appears at a distance, frequently being around 1·5 to 4·5 m, but the bird rises and falls continually, at times barely clearing the ground. It pauses, jinks sideways, hovers, retraces its 'steps', and thus responds to the tell-tale movements of its prey. Frequently it drops down into the vegetation, few such pounces being exactly alike. According to the circumstances, it may dive forward, drop straight down with wings raised, throw itself sideways or appear to perform a somersault in the air to change its motion of flight by ninety degrees. On occasions we have seen it give a powerful wing-beat to add impetus to the strike.

Upon hitting the ground it lies where it falls, grasping at the prey with the feet and steadying itself by spreading its wings over the grass. There is no possibility of seeing what actually happens at the last moment of the strike so we must again fall back on Payne's cine films (see Chapter 1). These disclose that, having established the prey's exact location, the owl flies straight at it, at the last moment withdrawing the head, swinging the feet forward into the position the head formerly occupied and closing the eyes, presumably as a safety precaution. At the very last moment, when the owl is so near the victim that the camera never actually recorded it, the talons are spread widely to grasp the prey. In total darkness the talons are opened earlier than this and the camera was able to record them widely spread before the impact. It may be that when flying blind an owl is uncertain of the prey's (and ground's) exact distance and so opens the talons sooner to be sure of having them ready in time. However, occasions in nature when an owl cannot see the ground must be virtually non-existent.

If unsuccessful in its pounce the bird may wait a moment for some tell-tale movement in the grass and, on hearing and re-locating the prey, will spring at it like a cat, striking again. As we have already said, Barn Owls are extraordinarily agile on their feet, running fast, sometimes with a peculiar skipping action, and it is not unusual to see short chases occurring on the ground following an unsuccessful strike. If, however, the quarry gives no further clue as to its whereabouts the owl quickly rises and continues as before.

In the forest, several of the owls concentrated their hunting on the most productive areas, that is, on the newly planted plots where the trees were too small to hinder them. There, they were free to exploit every part of the ground and in windless conditions would fly to and fro in all directions. Generally, however, there was some wind and the owls would hunt by beating slowly into it until the end of the plot or territory was reached; they would then fly back fast downwind to begin again. In the rest of the forest the owls could not hunt in this way and had, of necessity, to follow the rides. The same applies in habitats where the grass is grazed. Small mammal prey found there are generally confined to the edges of fields, woods, copses, stream-banks and buildings, etc, and consequently the owl's hunting is mainly limited to those areas.

It is very evident when watching Barn Owls in such circumstances that they are creatures of habit, for a bird will take the same direction on leaving its roost and follow a favoured route time after time: one must conclude that they are aware of the best hunting grounds in their territories and the easiest areas to work in the prevailing conditions. The direction of the wind must greatly affect an owl's hunting, since it obviously will not take a route where the wind would be directly behind it, making progress too fast to hear the sounds produced by its prey.

The above account suggests that the Barn Owl hunts by prolonged flight over likely small mammal habitats, and in the case of most individuals this is true, at least when they are reasonably hungry. Many birds, however, when not so hungry hunt in a less energetic way which we have dubbed 'post-hopping'. They also practise this method when, after hunting unsuccessfully for half-an-hour or more, they appear to become tired, but a minority post-hop by preference most of the time. In post-hopping a bird flies from perch to perch, frequently along a line of fence posts, pausing for a minute or so on each to scrutinise the ground below. This, in fact, is the method normally employed by the Tawny Owl (Photos 19 and 20).

A third method, observed by M. Jones (pers. comm.) and D. Scott (pers. comm.) is a Kestrel-like hovering, though at the usual low altitude. All Barn Owls hover at times, some more than others, but these two ornithologists observed individuals that hovered repeatedly, only advancing a few metres between each pause.

So far we have no reason to believe that Barn Owls ever hunt in pairs co-operatively. Occasionally we have seen two flying together, but always this has been a case of one bird following the other for a short-distance in courtship.

A belief to which we cannot subscribe is that Barn Owls sometimes use the screech when hunting, either to flush the prey or to frighten it into immobility. We need not trouble to discuss here what effect the screech might have on a vole or shrew, for we are confident that this note is only directed at other owls. As we have said, it is quite normal for Barn Owls to screech as they fly over their territories at night and if this were part of their hunting technique it would surely be heard also by day; yet in hundreds of hours spent observing Barn Owls hunting in daylight we have never once heard one screech. Indeed, it is most unusual for a Barn Owl to use this call at all during the day except in territorial encounters with birds of its own species.

Incidentally, some observers have expressed surprise at the Barn Owl's nocturnal screeching because they assume its prey will take cover and the owl will ruin its own hunting prospects. In reality this is not the case because, quite apart from the fact that the hunting territory is so extensive, small mammals seem not to be frightened of sounds coming from more than a few metres away.

A method that *is* employed occasionally is for an owl to flap its wings against bushes in which small birds are roosting. One of us observed two Barn Owls separately using this method, one flapping against gorse bushes *Ulex* sp., where Linnets roosted, in November; and the other beating at Hawthorns *Crataegus monogyna*, which held a massed Starling roost, in December.

Lastly, Barn Owls differ widely in their characteristics of flight when hunting. Basically, they all appear beautifully buoyant, the wings beating gently and the flapping flight punctuated by graceful glides. However, the length of the wings seems to vary a good deal and the wing strokes may be characteristically shallow or deep. Some hover more than others – as long as a minute has been recorded – and the degree of buoyancy varies individually. Examples of these variations are given in Chapter 3. Of possible significance is the fact that two of the male Barn Owls in our forest study area had noticeably deeper wing-beats than their mates. Two other cock birds also had characteristically deep wing-beats, but their mates were not observed well enough to see how they flew. This data is too meagre to permit any conclusions, but it is just possible that the sexes have different wing-beat characteristics.

HUNTING EFFICIENCY

Those who have watched Barn Owls closely, especially at the nest, are likely to have been impressed by the sheer efficiency of the bird. The frequency with which prey is sometimes brought in is almost unbelievable and has caused at least one birdwatcher (Warham 1951) to wonder whether there was some cache nearby that the owl was drawing on. He aptly describes the visits of the parents to this nest as 'more reminiscent of the activities of a pair of warblers than those of an owl' and adequately supports this statement by an impressive record of one night's feed. We quote below some outstanding records that we have obtained and there was certainly no cache in these cases because the birds could be seen hunting.

26.6.67   Both parents hunted on this occasion which followed two evenings of torrential rain. Feeds occurred at 19.36, 19.50, 19.58, 19.59, 20.07, 20.14, 20.15, 20.24, 20.29, 20.38, 20.43, 20.48, 20.55, 20.59, 21.05, 21.20, and 21.32 (TOTAL: 17 items).

15.7.67   On this fine sunny evening the following activities involved the cock alone:
   20.39   Began hunting.
   20.49   Returned with prey.
   20.49½ Departed.
   20.51½ Returned with prey.
   20.52   Departed.

20.58 Returned with prey.
? Missed its departure.
21.00 Returned with prey.
21.00½ Departed.
21.06 Returned with prey.
21.06½ Departed.
21.13 Returned with prey.
21.14 Departed.
21.22 Returned with prey.
21.22½ Departed.
21.28 Returned with prey.
? Missed its departure.
21.34 Returned with prey.
21.35 Re-emerged from barn and alighted on wall.
21.36 Departed.
21.39 Returned with prey.
21.39½ Departed.
21.42 Returned with prey.
TOTAL: 11 items

19.7.67   During this vigil one observer watched the arrival of the parents from a hide while another watched their hunting activities from a high vantage point.

19.54 Cock flew off to hunt.
19.58 Returned with prey.
20.02 Hen returned with prey.
20.04 Cock and hen departed.
20.10 Hen returned with prey.
20.11 Cock returned with prey. Hen departed.
20.14 Cock departed.
20.19 Hen returned with prey.
20.22 Cock returned with prey. Hen departed.
20.28 Hen returned with prey.
20.29 Hen departed.
20.34 Cock departed.
20.46 Hen returned with prey.
20.47 Hen departed.
20.50 Cock returned with prey.
20.52 Cock departed.
21.09 Cock returned with prey.
TOTALS: Cock 5 items, hen 5 items.

Most Barn Owls, when feeding well-grown young, hunt energetically by continuous flight; that is, they seldom alight between pounces and, having brought prey to the nest, they leave within a minute or two to hunt again until the requisite amount of food is obtained. A good example of this was observed on 15th May 1971, when a cock bird was seen to catch nine prey items, probably Short-tailed Voles, between 17.15 and 18.10 (55 minutes), eating the eighth itself. It was completely undeterred by several brief showers that occurred during the hunting foray. There are, nevertheless, individuals which hunt more slowly over a longer period and the cock of one pair (described earlier in this chapter) would often take an hour or more to bring in each item, though this is quite exceptional.

In the forest, where Barn Owls could be watched hunting for voles along with Short-eared Owls and Kestrels, one could not fail to be impressed by the greater efficiency of the Barn Owl, although, unfortunately, this was not quantified and therefore remains a subjective opinion. The Kestrel, of course, hunts in an entirely different way and takes a wider variety of prey including small birds and insects, but it is a little surprising that the other owl should be any less adept. Its ears are highly asymmetrical, denoting the keenest sense of hearing, and its method of hunting is identical, except for the speed of flight: it fairly skims along and we have the impression that it moves too fast over this type of terrain to scrutinise the ground adequately. No doubt its added speed would place it at an advantage over the Barn Owl in open habitats such as saltmarshes and this might well explain why small birds, including even the fast-flying waders, at times figure quite largely in its diet (Glue 1970a, 1972 and 1977).

Not surprisingly the Barn Owl's hunting is affected by the weather, but it is almost incredible how efficient they can be in adverse conditions, such as high wind, when they often succeed in taking prey within five or ten minutes.

METHOD OF KILLING

Undoubtedly the only instinctive method Barn Owls have of killing prey is by gripping with their feet and increasing pressure in response to further movement; we have many times observed captive birds repeatedly clutching and releasing dead prey in apparent killing practice, and owlets will frequently play with inanimate objects such as stones and pieces of wood in such a manner. In one barn, the owlets liked to play at gripping a piece of hose-pipe which would have been about the same thickness as a mouse's body. In most cases the pressure exerted should be enough to cause instantaneous death whether the claws transfix the prey or not, but various writers have mentioned other sophistications which may have been developed by some birds individually. In one of these, employed when an owl is tackling large prey, for example Brown Rats, the owl repeatedly seizes the animal by the nose with the bill and jerks the head backwards, so dislocating the neck. Another method, described by Maxwell Knight (1956), is for the owl to bite through the skull as soon as the animal is gripped with the foot, and he felt sure that a captive owl that had lived in the wild was doing just this; also that a younger captive that had never hunted for itself, after at first only clutching prey to death, later added the coup de grâce of the older bird to its technique. J. G. Goldsmith (pers. comm.) has found this to be the normal method of killing; a second 'tweek' with the bill being applied to the other end of the body within a second or two if it still moves. Moon (1940) suggested that skull biting is an individual trait and stated that it had not occurred with Barn Owl prey examined by him. Kolbe (1946) and Reed (1897), respectively, found skull damage in mammalian prey taken by *T. a. affinis* and *T. a. pratincola*. Captive birds, when given dead prey, have made sudden movements of the head beneath the body as though to deliver a bite and, before eating the victim, they frequently nipped it a good deal. It may be that these actions represented the rudiments of a coup de grâce which, in the wild, might have been developed as the birds' experience grew. Usually, observations in the field are too distant to enlighten one about the method of killing, but occasionally we have seen a bird that has just made a capture appear to seize and wrench at the prey in its talons. On several occasions, one cock bird was seen deliberately to crush the skull of a small mammal before presenting it to the hen.

Intrinsic with the subsequent dealing with prey is the phenomenon known as mantling, which is very characteristic of owls and birds of prey generally. The body is held horizontally over the victim and the wings lowered as though to shield it from any competitor that might rob it of its prize. Indeed, this appears to be the purpose of the action, for an owl that is not mantling will immediately do so if approached by another owl.

EATING OF PREY

Barn Owls more than other owls seem disposed to swallow their prey whole. Even sixteen-day-old owlets can do this with small voles, an accomplishment which greatly facilitates their feeding. The actual swallowing of a mouse-sized mammal is achieved in the following way: after toying and nipping at the prey the owl picks it up deliberately in the bill and manoeuvres it into a head-first position, often with the assistance of one foot. It then repeatedly opens the bill and jerks its own head forward to seize the animal farther along the body until it can be swallowed. If the prey is around maximum swallowing size the sequence is reversed once it has become lodged well inside the bill, the head jerking backwards and the bill and pharynx opening so that the momentum carries it into the oesophagus, leaving the owl looking rather uncomfortable for a while! Birds, however, always seem to be decapitated and the body eaten piecemeal, the tearing of strong flesh being aided by skilful twists of the bill as the owl stands on the carcase with both feet; the head is sometimes rejected. Some attempt is also made to remove the larger feathers, the plucking movements being extremely vigorous. After the meal the bill is rubbed clean on some convenient object.

CARRYING OF PREY

When bringing in prey a Barn Owl almost always carries it in one foot all the way. On alighting, very typically it pauses in the entrance and then transfers the victim to the bill before flying inside. Notwithstanding this, some birds regularly transfer prey to the bill in flight – and indeed will on occasions pass the food from bill to claw and vice versa more than once. Rarely the victim, particularly if it is small, will be carried all the way in the bill and D. Scott (pers. comm.) knew of a cock bird that habitually carried prey by this method. When held in the bill small mammals are normally gripped by the scruff of the neck.

Owls, like parrots, are often said to use one foot more than the other.* It is

* In parrots this is true.

sometimes stated that the bird is left-'handed' (e.g. Fisher 1951), so for a time at a nest in the forest study area a record was kept of which foot was used, either to stand upon (as resting owls usually tuck one leg into the feathers) or to carry prey. The results showed more variation than was expected: the left foot was employed 4 times for standing upon and 30 times for carrying prey, while the right foot was employed twice for standing and 25 times for carrying prey. Similar note was taken at a nest in Cumbria, resulting in the same conclusion that there is little truth in the statement. It is, incidentally, often very difficult to ascertain which foot a resting owl is standing upon as the leg used takes a central position for balancing purposes.

BEHAVIOUR WITH OTHER SPECIES

The commonest inter-specific behaviour witnessed when watching birds of prey is the phenomenon of *mobbing*. To list all the kinds of birds we have seen mobbing Barn Owls would be pointless, for it seems that almost any species will do so on occasions. Nevertheless, the Barn Owl – and we believe other owls – suffers less from mobbing by small passerines than does the Tawny Owl, and sometimes its presence seems to cause reactions more of fear than aggression among small birds. A probable explanation is that the Tawny's fat, large-headed appearance elicits the maximum mobbing response, while the more slimly built species are less provocative. We cannot recall a single instance when a resting Barn Owl has attracted a veritable swarm of small passerines such as commonly pester the Tawny Owl. Usually all one hears are a few thin alarm notes from one or two small birds in the vicinity.

The Barn Owl, like the Tawny Owl (but unlike the Short-eared Owl), never seems to turn on avian tormentors during mobbing. The only signs of aggression witnessed by us have been under unusual circumstances. On one occasion a cock Barn Owl, which had a nest in an old house shared by numerous Jackdaws which often mobbed it, was badly frightened when it spotted the author concerned inside the house. When it returned fifteen minutes later it began circling the building and suddenly made a dive at one of the Jackdaws perched on the roof, causing it to fly off in alarm. A Jackdaw was also the species involved in another incident. This, a hand-reared individual, was at liberty and was in the habit of roosting on top of one of A.B.W.'s aviaries at night. A wild cock Barn Owl which had bred in the garden (but now had independent young) suddenly deviated from its course to swoop at the roosting Jackdaw. The attack was not followed through and the impression gained was one of play rather than real hostility. Since these are the only occasions in a great many hours spent watching Barn Owls that we have witnessed an attack on another species, we feel that the first incident was probably an example of displacement activity and the second a mild response to the presence of a corvid near its nest-site.

Most mobbing suffered by the Barn Owl occurs when it is in flight: passing gulls may stoop at it, Curlews and Lapwings will chase it off their territories, and sometimes it is surrounded by twittering flocks of hirundines. The Barn Owl suffers more serious mobbing, however, from corvids and diurnal birds of prey. In such encounters the owl reacts either by beating a hasty retreat to the nearest barn or by alighting; its tormentors then usually lose interest.

The Kestrel is perhaps the most persistent and dangerous aggressor, for while hovering over the owl's territory it can readily watch all the actions of its competitor below. Time and again a Kestrel will stoop at an owl, making life very difficult for it, and we always wondered whether the Barn Owl that was blind in one eye (mentioned in Chapter 1) received the injury from a Kestrel, for it suffered a great deal of mobbing from one of these birds. The owl is at a big disadvantage because it must hunt below the falcon and is much slower on the wing. Its restricted field of vision also often prevents it from detecting the Kestrel's approach, though fortunately for the owl, the Kestrel frequently advertises its intentions by excited calling.

In the forest these encounters were regularly observed and it was not at all unusual for an owl to break off from hunting to take refuge among the trees. Only twice have we seen these two species actually come to grips. In one instance a hen bird was being continually swooped upon by a Kestrel as she hunted for her brood, doing her best to stay out of trouble by returning to the nest under the cover of a line of trees which led to the barn. When she re-emerged the Kestrel attacked again and there was a skirmish in the air. A brief glimpse was had of the owl flying behind a screen of trees with the Kestrel hanging below it, but when the owl re-appeared a few seconds later the Kestrel had vanished. The distance was too great to see what had taken place, but it was assumed that as the Kestrel stooped the owl had struck at it in self-defence and the two had become locked together momentarily. That the incident had shaken the owl was obvious, for it did not re-appear again. In the second incident, a hen bird returning with prey was seized by the wing by a Kestrel, the two tumbling earthwards and disappearing from view. Nevertheless a few moments later the owl arrived at the nest none the worse and still holding its prey.

A further incident was witnessed at much closer range by Everett (1968). A Kestrel swooped at a Barn Owl which was carrying prey. It passed below the owl, rolled on its back and seized the prey in both talons. The owl was flapping along about a metre above the ground and for a few seconds it flew on, losing height, carrying the vole and the upside-down Kestrel with one foot. Then the wildly flapping Kestrel broke loose with the prey and flew off. An even more exciting account of a Kestrel robbing a Barn Owl was described by Dunn (1979): 'F. Oates and I saw a male Kestrel sitting on the apex of a chicken coop in the centre of a small field. It was uttering a very excited chatter: "*kee-kee-kee*", repeated two or three times. Suddenly, a Barn Owl flew out of the coop carrying a small rodent and towards an old barn. The Kestrel gave chase and attacked the owl from behind; it grabbed the rodent and appeared to be "back-pedalling" frantically, trying to take it from the owl. The latter continued flying, dragging behind it the Kestrel, which was still hanging on to the rodent when the owl disappeared into the barn. Neither bird was seen for half an hour: then we saw the Kestrel preening in the top of a tree. In the afternoon, we revisited the area and again saw the Barn Owl quartering the same field, at times only 4 m from us. It dropped into the grass twice, but did not appear to catch anything; on a third occasion it caught a large rodent and mantled it in the grass. Within seconds, the Kestrel arrived, apparently from nowhere, and landed on the owl's back. The two rolled over in the grass, fighting for the prey; the falcon managed to take this and flew off over the valley. The Barn Owl lay in the grass for about a minute, with its beak open and wings spread, and then resumed hunting. When it next caught a small rodent, it swallowed it almost immediately.'

Despite the above, probably due to the shortage of sites the two species often frequent the same buildings. There were several examples of this in the forest study area and Fellowes (1967) describes a situation where the two were nesting only 2 m apart and shared the same entrance. Apparently they would not have been able to see one another while at their respective nests, but when the Barn Owls left or entered the building, they would have had to pass within half a metre of the Kestrels' eggs.

On another occasion one of the authors witnessed a pair of Carrion Crows mobbing a Barn Owl in a field. It is doubtful whether any damage was done, but the encounter looked quite serious to the observer, for every time the owl attempted to fly away the crows harrassed it so closely that it was immediately forced to the ground again. At length the owl took off and dashed into a barn two or three hundred metres away. Dickson (1972) also saw a Carrion Crow twice clutch the back of a hunting Barn Owl with its feet, forcing it to the ground. Other predators that have been seen to attack Barn Owls are Hen Harriers, Short-eared Owls and Tawny Owls; the latter is dealt with in Chapter 7 when discussing its effect as a competitor. One of us also saw a male Peregrine stoop on a Barn Owl which reacted by diving under a bush.

The Barn Owl's reactions towards mammalian species vary according to the reactions to be expected from the animals concerned. Foxes and domestic cats are mobbed with Call 5, which we have named the mobbing note for this reason; and families of fledged owlets, which are bolder than the adults, will gather about a Fox and scream abuse at it. Likewise, human beings are often mobbed by young owls, whereas the sight of a Man by an adult would elicit a warning scream and a hasty departure.

A large dog is evidently considered less of a threat, for A.B.W.'s collie accompanied him on many vigils and either attracted no attention whatsoever or was only watched with mild interest. Rabbits and Brown Hares are normally completely ignored by adult Barn Owls, although D. Scott (pers. comm.) once observed a Barn Owl repeatedly diving at a Hare which zig-zagged frantically, not knowing which way to turn to avoid its tormentor. There can be no question of the owl trying to catch the Hare for food, for this species is far too powerful a creature.

That young Barn Owls are less aware of which species represent danger and which are harmless was demonstrated to us several times when a family of fledged owlets frequently mobbed a Hare that was in the habit of feeding in front of the derelict farmhouse they were inhabiting. An amusing incident occurred one evening when the cock, which always ignored the Hare, arrived with prey. One of the owlets was mobbing it, and the adult, assuming that some predator was in the vicinity, became extremely nervous and hesitated on the roof for several minutes, passing the prey from foot to bill and vice versa, not daring to feed the young.

We have not observed the response to the presence of Stoats and Weasels, predatory species that arouse great anxiety among many small birds. Their significance as enemies of the Barn Owl is discussed in Chapter 7.

DRINKING, BATHING AND SUNBATHING

Surprising though it may seem after all our years of fieldwork with this species, we have never observed wild Barn Owls engaged in any of the above activities. However, it would be dangerous to draw too many conclusions from this for negative results prove nothing. Captive Barn Owls we have had drank little or not at all, unlike one Tawny Owl which drank frequently. That some Barn Owls certainly do drink in captivity is shown by Smith & Richmond (1972), who include a table which shows that the bird used in their experiments drank water at least three times in twelve hours on one occasion when it was being observed continuously. In drinking an owl behaves very much as other birds, except pigeons, immersing the bill and then raising and tilting up the head to allow the water to run down the throat. Because of the paucity of observations of wild Barn Owls drinking, we believe that it is unlikely that many bother to do so. Probably they obtain all the water they need from the flesh of their prey.

In captive Barn Owls, bathing is very much an individual habit – one will take a bath every day and appear to thoroughly enjoy itself (if birds can experience such feelings), while others show obvious repulsion at the prospect of getting wet at all. In between these birds are some which will bathe at intervals of a few days. Many captive birds of various species over-indulge in bathing because they have nothing else to do and we would not expect wild Barn Owls to bathe every day, nor even very frequently. During our intensive studies of individual pairs we only occasionally saw a Barn Owl return to its barn on a dry night with its feathers bedraggled as though it had had a bath. Even then the most likely explanation is that they had become wet from the dew on the grass into which they would have stooped many times while searching for prey. The only eye-witness account of a wild Barn Owl bathing seems to be that of J. G. Goldsmith (pers. comm.) who once flushed one from a stream where it was bathing on a very hot sunny afternoon. Wet owls, incidentally, carry their wings low with the primaries spread slightly, perhaps to facilitate drying.

If it happens at all, sun-bathing must naturally occur in the daytime, and consequently it seems highly unlikely that it is anything but a rare occurrence. Indeed, in our aviaries the Barn Owls invariably hide away in bright sunlight, unlike the Tawny Owls which sun-bathe with every appearance of enjoyment. A case of a Barn Owl sun-bathing (Bentham 1962) is therefore of great interest: 'The bird was lying on a small sunny patch of ground beneath a large tree. One wing was raised, fully exposing that side of the body to the warmth of the sunshine'. D. Scott (pers. comm.), during many years of watching Long-eared Owls, saw similar behaviour on a small number of occasions and two of our Tawny Owls – one living free – were seen to spread their wings in the sun on a few occasions: perhaps it is more a case of wild owls being too wary to be caught in the act.

CHAPTER 4

Food

In contrast to the subjects of the last two chapters, innumerable studies on the diet of the Barn Owl have resulted in a wealth of literature on this subject – no doubt due to the ease with which pellets can be collected and analysed compared with the difficulties inherent in studying the general behaviour of a primarily nocturnal bird – and an entire book could be devoted to pellet analyses and the conclusions drawn therefrom. Before proceeding further it will be appropriate to say a few words about pellets themselves.

PELLETS

Many people have the misconception that birds of prey are the only group to produce pellets, but over 300 species of birds have been found to do so. Pellets are the indigestible remains of the food eaten by birds which, instead of being excreted with the other waste materials, are regurgitated through the mouth as a compact mass. Most consists of hard objects of little nutritional value and in the case of the owls the contents comprise such items as bones, claws, teeth, bird's beaks and the chitinous remains of insects, all wrapped in fur and feathers. Owls need to eject pellets as they have a low acid content in their stomachs, and bones cannot be broken down like the rest of their food. Smith & Richmond (1972) showed that the pellet is formed by the muscular action of the gizzard during digestion, the freshly formed pellet passing from the gizzard into the proventriculus after digestion is completed. Here it remains until it is regurgitated.

The pellets of owls and most diurnal birds of prey have distinctive characterisics which make them relatively easy to identify, none more so than the Barn Owl. Glossy black when fresh, they remain smooth and dark in colour even when dry; they are also much less friable than those of other owls. Average measurements have been given as 45 mm × 26 mm (Glue 1967), but Buxton & Lockley (1950) showed how variable pellets can be when they gave maximum measurements of 110 mm × 50 mm circumference. In contrast to this, Barn Owls may produce small roundish pellets about the size of large marbles which often contain little but fur. These may well be residual remains of prey already ejected in a previous pellet when subsequent hunting has been unsuccessful.

A bird that is about to eject a pellet looks decidedly miserable and listless, and even if offered food will not eat it until the pellet has been disgorged. To accomplish this the owl lowers its head a little and shakes it from side to side; after a moment the pellet appears between the parted mandibles and is dropped. If it does not appear quickly the bird can often be seen repeatedly opening and closing its mouth, as if inducing the pellet to move up the oesophagus.

Pellet analyses

The majority of pellet analyses have been carried out in Western Europe and North America, but fortunately enough work has been done in other countries to enable us to gain a clear insight into the food habits of the species throughout much of its range, e.g., Africa (Kolbe 1946, Coetzee 1962, Hanney 1963, Heim de Balsac 1965, Wilson 1970, Laurie 1971), Austria (Bauer 1956), Canada (Doersken 1969), Iraq (Nader 1969), Italy (Moltoni 1937, Lovari 1974, Lovari et al 1976), Malaysia (Medway & Yong 1970), Portugal (Buckley 1976), Spain (Herrera 1973 & 1974), Surinam (Haverschmidt 1962) and Switzerland (Zelenka & Pricam 1974).

Our own observations and those of many other workers prove quite conclusively that the Barn Owl has no food preferences as such, apart from a distinct disinterest in invertebrates; it simply feeds on those animals which are small enough to be easily killed and are susceptible to capture in the course of its chosen method of hunting. In other words, as Ticehurst (1935) aptly put it, 'opportunity makes the meal'. Being adapted to hunt by continuous flight, the Barn Owl is certain to take any small mammals which frequent open habitats such as coarse grassland, farmland, young forestry plantations and marshes. Prominent amongst these are the Rodentia, particularly voles of the sub-family Microtinae typified by the Short-tailed Vole, Common Vole and Pine Vole in Europe, and the Meadow 'Mouse' and Pine Vole in north and eastern America. Lovari (1974) sums up the importance of these animals when he states: 'on the whole, Microtinae seem to be a basic food source for Barn Owls in most countries and habitat types, even if the species preyed upon vary accordingly'.

The Microtinae are of course widespread in temperate and sub-arctic regions of the Northern Hemisphere, but do not occur south of Guatemala in America, or northern Burma and the Himalayas in Asia. In Africa only one species, *Microtus mustersi*, is found, and in the generally dry habitats of this continent gerbils of the genera *Gerbillus*, *Tatera* and *Pachyuromys*, and the Multimammate Mouse, replace Microtinae as the primary prey species. In western America the Pocket Gopher and the Pocket Mouse predominate.

With the exception of Australia and the southern half of South America, shrews of the family Soricidae have a world-wide distribution and are also taken in large numbers by Barn Owls, despite the fact that they are distasteful to many carnivorous mammals. Although they are separated into two distinct groups – the red-toothed shrews of Europe, northern Asia and North America, and the white-toothed shrews of the Mediterranean region, Africa and southern Asia – there is little difference in behaviour and both groups are equally common prey items wherever they occur.

Many workers have found that the numbers of secondary prey species taken are inversely proportional to the numbers of Microtinae captured by the owl. By far the commonest example of this is when Soricidae form the main alternative to Microtinae, but other variations include Microtinae and Murinae (*Apodemus* spp.) in France (Heim de Balsac & Beaufort 1966) and Italy (Contoli 1975, Lovari et al 1976), and even between members of the Microtinae themselves, i.e. *Microtus* and *Pitymys*. In all these groups the correlation has been linked with the relative proportions of woodland and open areas in the owls' territories.

The Microtinae/Soricidae relationship is the typical pattern of most British pellet analyses, the number of Common Shrews in the samples rising and falling in direct correlation with the numbers of Short-tailed Voles taken. A good example of this is given by Webster (1973) who analysed 679 pellets from south Westmorland (now Cumbria) – see Fig. 5. Short-tailed Voles and Common Shrews formed almost 90% of the prey weight in this sample, with Wood Mice and Pygmy Shrews as the main secondary items. A similar picture is described in Michigan, U.S.A., by Wallace (1948), the species in this instance being the Meadow Mouse and the Short-tailed Shrew.

Ticehurst (1935) concluded that the Barn Owl's diet differed according to locality, the relative numbers of food items in the pellet samples being a true reflection on the actual abundance of the prey species in the area hunted over. Glue (1974), on the other hand, analysed the diet of 188 Barn Owls throughout Britain and Ireland – a total of 47,865 vertebrate prey items – and while agreeing that the diet varied from region to region, he considered that the importance of Short-tailed Voles in the diet depended more upon the habitat and its physical characteristics than on actual prey numbers. Hanney (1962) reached a similar conclusion during his work in Nyasaland (now Malawi), showing that, although this country has a wide spectrum of small mammals, the number of minor prey species taken by the owls was not necessarily a true reflection of their abundance in the two areas from which the pellets were collected.

Some knowledge of the habitats, behaviour and populations of small mammals is essential for a reasonable understanding of the relative vulnerability of the different species. It must also be appreciated that trapping results may not necessarily provide an accurate estimate of the relative populations. For example, because of their energetic foraging activities, Common Shrews soon encounter Longworth traps and so are caught much more readily than the comparatively inactive Short-tailed Voles, thereby invalidating the results. A factor which could affect the seasonal vulnerability of shrews is their noisy behaviour in spring and early summer when numbers of individuals often become highly excited, darting to and fro and squeaking loudly in some form of sexual and/or territorial behaviour.

It should be no surprise that the Short-tailed Vole and Common Shrew are the two main prey species in mainland Britain, for they are the two most abundant species in the open habitats over which the Barn Owl normally hunts. The Wood Mouse and Bank Vole, though both are common, would not be expected to occur so frequently in the diet, being woodland and hedgerow species and therefore not so vulnerable to predation by the Barn Owl; also the former is very agile. Similarly, the House Mouse is not a regular denizen of the open fields, though one would expect them to be caught within buildings more often than apparently they are in this country. Strangely, the pair observed for twelve months from inside a Lancashire barn (described at the beginning of Chapter 3) were never seen to attempt to catch the House Mice in it. Brown Rats on the other hand are less confined to buildings, and young animals form an important part of the diet in some areas; full-grown rats would be a dangerous proposition for the Barn Owl. Water Voles are likewise common in many Barn Owl territories and young ones are taken; perhaps the aquatic habitat may explain why they figure less often in significant numbers. The Pygmy Shrew shares much the same habitat as the Common Shrew but is seldom caught in such large numbers. This may be due to its small size and quick reactions – a difficult target for the owl. It also appears to be less numerous than its congener. Relative scarcity may also be the reason why the Bank Vole never figures so importantly in the diet as our most abundant rodent, the Wood Mouse.

It is when there is a dearth of Short-tailed Voles that the other species listed above increase in importance. Glue (1967) quotes an example of this at Eling, Hampshire, where the numbers of Short-tailed Voles declined markedly during the summer of 1965. Working on Ticehurst's hypothesis, this should have heralded an immediate increase in the incidence of the commonest secondary prey species in the pellets, that is, Wood Mouse and Common Shrew. Instead the number of Wood Mice dropped from 18% to 9% of the prey weight in the following winter months, and the Common Shrew dropped from 7% to 2%. The owls, no doubt responding to the disappearance of their main food item, had changed their hunting grounds to a mixed farmland area where Brown Rats were abundant in the hedge-banks and corn-ricks. This animal became the principal prey of the owls through-out the period, rising from 15% in the summer of 1965 to 41% the following winter. Despite the increased intake by the owls, there was no evidence to suggest an increase in the numbers of Brown Rats in the area.

As can be seen from Figure 5, Webster (loc. cit.) found a very marked seasonal change in numerical importance of the Short-tailed Vole and Common Shrew in the Barn Owl's diet, vole numbers being highest in autumn and winter and the shrew being the reverse with highest numbers in spring and summer. However, one must not regard this as typical. For instance, Glue found little evidence of seasonal variation in the diet of a pair of Barn Owls at Nursling, Hampshire, Short-tailed Voles constantly forming the main prey item of between 74% and 89% prey-weight. This anomaly can probably be explained by differences between the two habitats. Webster's study area consisted of meadows grazed by dairy cattle and sheep, with a larger area of poorly drained, rush-covered land and some limestone grassland. None of these are optimum habitats for voles which prefer large open areas of coarse grassland – of which there were over 28 hectares at

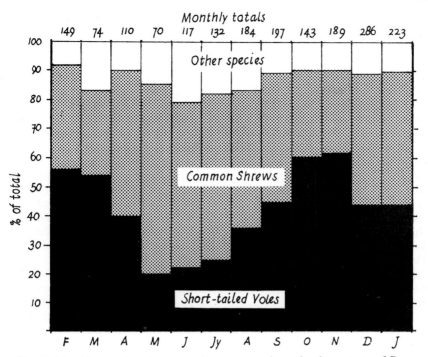

Fig. 5 *Monthly variation in mammalian prey as shown by the contents of Barn Owl pellets (after Webster 1973).*

Nursling as well as lengths of railway embankments which are also favoured by voles. It would seem that, although Webster's breeding site itself held a strong attraction to the owls, the hunting territory could only provide good numbers of voles in autumn and winter, that is, after the vole breeding season, whereas Glue's area held a strong enough vole population to enable the owls to feed primarily upon them throughout the year.

On one point we must disagree with Webster. A drop in the number of pellets collected in the spring months was attributed by him to the owls leaving the home territory to hunt elsewhere due to the shortage of voles. However, this pair had also been studied by one of the authors and we would venture to suggest that the decrease in pellets was actually due to the hen owl spending virtually all of her time in the nest-site prior to laying her eggs. This is normal behaviour at this time of the year and, since she would egest most of her pellets on the inaccessible ceiling where the nest was situated, they would not be found. All or most of the pellets collected from the floor would therefore be from the cock bird only which, at that stage of the breeding season, would be providing the hen with all of her food. There is, however, no reason to suggest that Webster's findings are not perfectly valid with respect to the prey ratios.

It seems obvious from this that the characteristics of the habitat do have a bearing, not only on what mammalian prey is available to the owl, but also on their actual numbers throughout the year. Variations in altitude, exposure, average climate and vegetational cover, ensure that few areas are likely to be exactly alike.

In his classic study of the Tawny Owl, Southern (1954) found 'very emphatic seasonal fluctuations' in the relative importance of its mammalian prey species and concluded that these were related to changes in the vegetational cover, large prey being taken more commonly in the summer months when the smaller species were hidden by dense undergrowth. Because of the differing habitats exploited by the two owl species, Webster felt that this is unlikely to be the case with the Barn Owl due to its predilection for grassland, where seasonal changes in vegetation cover are less marked than in woodland. We would agree with this viewpoint, particularly since it has been shown that in good weather conditions the owl is capable of capturing prey by hearing alone. Even in winter, voles tend to remain under the cover of the decaying field-layer of dead grasses and herbs, and it seems unlikely that any slight increase in vulnerability would be enough to explain the marked changes in prey composition which have taken place in some cases. Against this, Simon Starkie (pers. comm.) has told us of a male Barn Owl which was in the habit of hunting nightly over rough grassland in his extensive grounds in Cumbria. No change in this behaviour occurred until the grass became tall, whereupon the owl ceased to be a regular visitor and paid only sporadic visits to these favoured hunting grounds. It is, of course, possible that the owl had found a more profitable area which it was temporarily exploiting – a habit not infrequently observed by the authors and akin to the case described by Glue at Eling – but the change in hunting grounds might equally well have been linked with the length of the grass. Mention must also be made at this juncture of the suggestion by both Webster and Southern that haymaking activities might increase the vulnerability of Short-tailed Voles. Indeed, in the second year of Webster's study the 'winter pattern', that is, an increase in vole intake, occurred in August, a month earlier than in the previous year and may have been linked with an area of grassland being cut as hay in July. Massey (1971) also noted that Short-tailed Voles were taken most frequently in the winter months, before becoming scarce again in April and May when the ground cover was beginning to grow.

From the foregoing, it will be seen that in most cases, no matter what theme one pursues regarding the diet of the Barn Owl, the one constant factor that recurs time and time again is the presence or absence of a Microtine vole species as the main prey item. Depending upon the state of the vole population in an area at any given time, the make-up of the owl's diet can vary enormously within the limits of prey size, vulnerability and availability, and the life-style of the owl is affected in various degrees according to these factors. Unlike the case of the minor prey species, there appears to be a distinct correlation between the actual numbers of voles present in an area and those taken by the owls.

When a vole population undergoes one of its periodic 'crashes', it means that difficult times are in store for any resident owls unless one or more of the minor prey species is present in above average numbers. In this context, it would be wrong to interpret the rise in Common Shrew numbers in Webster's sample as increases in the actual shrew population, for it must be appreciated that a Common Shrew weighs barely half as much as a Short-tailed Vole. Thus, for every vole normally captured, the owls have to take two shrews to make up for the loss of bulk caused by the vole decline. This is another reason why pellet samples are unreliable as a means of assessing small mammal populations.

Although we have emphasised the part played by Short-tailed Voles and Common Shrews, it should not be thought that the minor prey species are of no importance. On the contrary, in some instances they become of primary importance, and this has usually been correlated with the type of habitat over which the owl has been hunting. Heim de Balsac & Beaufort (1966) in France and Lovari et al (1976) in Italy found that in the wooded areas of these countries the Wood Mouse was the main prey species, while Herrera (1973), working in south-west Spain, showed that in his area the House Mouse and *Rattus* spp. represented no less than 90% of the diet in lowland damp grassland and 78% in cultivated areas. In the high ground worked by Man (e.g. Olive groves), the House Mouse still made up over 60% of the diet, but as the habitat became more mountainous and changed to more natural woodland, without any cultivation, the House Mouse population declined and the Wood Mouse increased markedly. In the latter habitat, rats became scarce and formed only a negligible part of the diet.

The importance of the House Mouse in south-west Spain is noteworthy in itself. This species is rarely a significant feature of Barn Owl diets elsewhere, although exceptions do occur. For example a sample of pellets from Philo, Illinois, USA, contained 42% House Mice (Cahn & Kemp 1930). The reason for the virtual absence of House Mice from most pellet samples lies in the dependence of this species on occupied human habitations which are often inaccessible to the owls. Where this mammal does feature prominently, the suggestion is of an atypical free-living population in open countryside (Glue 1974, Lovari et al 1976), though often these areas are in the close proximity of villages or other Man-inhabited buildings. There can be little doubt that it is the life-style of this mouse in Spain which decreed its relative importance in Herrera's sample, for on the Iberian Peninsula a free-living (and therefore vulnerable) form occurs and Buckley (1976) found it to be by far the most important prey item of the Portuguese Barn Owls studied by him. They formed 52% of the total prey-weight, with only the Mediterranean Pine Vole (15%), the Wood Mouse (10%) and the White-toothed Shrew (9%) of significant secondary importance.

The situation is much the same for *Rattus* spp; in only a few cases do these animals form a very high percentage of the prey weight (Medway & Yong 1970, Herrera 1974).

No voles or Common Shrews exist in Ireland or the Isle of Man and Barn Owls there have, of necessity, to prey upon other mammal species. Fairley (1966) analysed pellet samples from two Barn Owls in Co. Down, Northern Ireland, and found that Wood Mice (51%) and Brown Rats (30%) were the main prey items by weight, with House Mice (15%) and Pygmy Shrews (2%) being taken in smaller quantities. Significantly, these four species are the only small mammals which are widely distributed in Ireland. Glue

(1970b) found a similar picture for Wood Mice (53%), but in his sample the Brown Rat increased to 40%, with Pygmy Shrews (6%) forming the only other appreciable prey item, House Mice being unimportant at less than 1%. Glue also analysed a sample of pellets from Braddon, Isle of Man, and showed that there the Brown Rat assumes even greater importance as the principal prey species (59%). As in Ireland, the Wood Mouse (28%) is the only other small mammal to be a significant prey item, the House Mouse (4%) and Pygmy Shrew (1%) being taken by Manx owls in even smaller numbers than in Ireland. Perhaps to compensate for this, birds (8%) were taken more frequently than in Ireland (1%). A side-effect of this dependence on Brown Rats is that it is highly unlikely that the Manx Barn Owl population will ever expand, due to the limited food potential of the island. Moreover, the Manx government has in recent years conducted a campaign to eradicate the rat by using Warfarin, and evidence has come to light that the Barn Owl population has declined due both to the reduction in their main prey item as well as the possible effects of eating poisoned rats.

Yet another good example of the Barn Owl's opportunism as a hunter is that of the birds which are present on Skomer Island, Pembrokeshire, South Wales, in some years. On this well-known sea-bird reserve only five mammals are endemic – the Rabbit, Wood Mouse, Common Shrew, Pygmy Shrew and the race of the mainland Bank Vole, the Skomer Vole. Analysing pellets found in an outbuilding in September 1967, Brown & Twigg (1971) showed that the resident Barn Owls habitually took the four smallest mammals, but totally ignored the multitudinous Rabbits, even small ones probably being too difficult for the Barn Owl to tackle. The lack of Short-tailed Voles in the analysis confirmed that the birds survived adequately on this limited selection of prey and apparently had no need to visit the nearby mainland to augment their diet. This confirmed the findings of Buxton & Lockley (1950) who collected pellets from a Skomer roost in January, April and May 1947. Skomer Voles formed 62% prey-weight, Common Shrews 30%, Wood Mice 5% and Pygmy Shrews 3%. The significant point is that the Skomer Vole, despite being a race of the woodland-haunting Bank Vole, has become adapted to the open habitat of the island and consequently forms a far greater proportion of the owls' diet than would be the case with the mainland vole.

Before leaving mammalian prey we must consider the larger species which are commonly available, and the bats.

Moles are abundant in Britain, but Glue (1974) found them in only 14% of the diets analysed by him – not surprising in view of their strictly subterranean habits. They formed less than 1% of the total prey weight, although in one case in Lincolnshire 40 animals, in 1,850 prey items, formed 8% of the prey-weight. When they *are* taken it is mainly in the summer months between May and August, and Glue feels that these may be young animals dispersing in search of unoccupied territories. In any case, from observations in our aviaries we have formed the conclusion that Barn Owls (as well as other medium-sized birds of prey such as Short-eared Owls and Kestrels) have difficulty in breaking open the tough skin of this animal. Even when they succeed they give the impression that they find the flesh distasteful and they rarely eat much.

Rabbits must be readily available to many Barn Owls, but even a young animal would probably be rather too much for an owl to kill easily and Glue found them in only 3% of the diets.

Of the mustelids, Weasels are sometimes caught, although rarely. Stoats, on the other hand, have not been recorded so far as we know. This is hardly surprising since the Stoat is well known for its ferocity and we know of cases where *they* have preyed upon Barn Owls (see Chapter 7).

We know of no instances of hares *Lepus* spp. and only one of squirrels *Sciurus* spp. featuring as prey in Britain. Again, this probably reflects the strength and size of these animals. Although squirrels mostly frequent unsuitable habitats for Barn Owls hunting in Britain, this does not apply in North America, for instance, with respect to such species as the ground squirrels *Citellus* spp., and the Eastern and Western Chipmunks. The only case known to us was recorded by Fitch (1947) who found a single young ground squirrel *Citellus beecheyi* in his Californian sample. Amongst the more unusual mammalian prey items taken have been a domestic kitten and a young Guinea-pig, but both of these were isolated cases.

Instances of specialisation in bat-hunting have been recorded. Bauer (1956), for example, found no less than 55·3% of the diet of some Barn Owls in Austria to consist of these animals. Three species were identified, the vast majority being the Mouse-eared Bat. From identification of those species found in other pellet samples it seems that the general rule for other prey applies to this Order too, i.e. availability and vulnerability determining which species are taken. For instance, in Britain the four species identified by Glue were the Natterer's, Long-eared, Pipistrelle and Noctule, all among the most widely distributed and abundant members of the Vespertilionidae in the British Isles, and all roosting and breeding in hollow trees and buildings – sites likely to be inhabited by the Barn Owl. Ruprecht (1979) found the same correlation in the results of 1,030 Barn Owl pellet collections in Poland: 41·5% contained the remains of 20 of the 21 species of bats found in that country. Broadly speaking, taking into account the relative scarcity of some species, the species present in greatest numbers were those most likely to share the roosting habitat with the owls. Haverschmidt (1962) recorded 34 bats of three species out of a total of 465 vertebrates taken in Surinam, and Neil Bowman (pers. comm.) found two specimens of the Greater Horseshoe Bat with a single Whiskered Bat in his mid-Wales sample.

So far we have made no mention of birds in the diet of the Barn Owl, but they are, of course, a regular feature in many pellet analyses as a minor prey item. As with mammals, the species taken depends upon its size and behaviour, but within these limits the Barn Owl is capable of capturing a wide variety. In Britain the House Sparrow and Starling are the most frequent bird prey, and it is interesting to note that Boyd & Shriner (1954) found the same two species to be the commonest avian prey of Barn Owls roosting in the centre of a city in Massachusetts, USA. However, any species of comparable size will be taken readily should the opportunity arise, and Glue found they formed 2% of the prey-weight in the pellet samples he analysed in his British study. In practice, of course, the opportunity to capture birds seldom arises, for in the daytime small birds are much too alert to be taken unawares by a comparatively slow-moving owl. As we have mentioned in Chapter 3, some Barn Owls will beat against bushes to disturb and catch roosting birds and in most cases where birds are taken in above average numbers it is communally roosting species that are involved, e.g. House Sparrow (Sage 1962), Red-winged Blackbird, forming 16% of the prey in 157 pellets from Ohio, North America (Carpenter & Fall 1967), and Spotless Starling in Spain (Fernandez Cruz & Garcia 1971). On the RSPB's Leighton Moss Reserve in north Lancashire, a Barn Owl joined the Sparrowhawks in the winter of 1966/67 to feed very largely on the Starlings which came to roost 'en masse' in the Phragmites reeds each night. Even more remarkable, D. Scott (1979) knew of a Barn Owl that occasionally brought juvenile and adult Moorhens to its nest. We envy him his observations of the cock winging his way homeward with such a burden – a feat one would think impossible. Among the more unusual avian prey recorded are: young Rook, Corncrake, Dunlin, Common Snipe (the head and beak forming a remarkable pellet), Woodcock, Wood Pigeon and Lapwing.

There is strong evidence that birds are taken most frequently when the regular mammalian prey becomes scarce and it is unlikely to be coincidence that in Ireland and the Isle of Man, where Short-tailed Voles and Common Shrews are absent, birds are taken in higher numbers than in any other area of Britain. It should therefore come as no surprise to learn that in certain circumstances some Barn Owls will specialise on birds as primary prey. This is true of the Mediterranean population – particularly that in Mediterranean areas of North Africa – which is forced to take more non-mammalian prey than Barn Owls in temperate countries, due to the decrease in small mammal species in the Mediterranean region (Herrera 1974). In one Moroccan locality birds formed 88% of the total vertebrate prey (Brosset 1956), while an even more remarkable case was that of some Tunisian Barn Owls which had a 100% bird diet (Heim de Balsac & Maysaud 1962).

Herrera has shown that Mediterranean Barn Owls actually take less prey-weight (average 19·57 g) per prey item than do temperate birds (average 23·60 g per item). They are therefore forced to eat a greater diversity of food items of lesser food value than small mammals, and there is no doubt a correlation between this and the availability of food. In view of this it is interesting to note that southern Spain has a smaller Barn Owl population than elsewhere on the Iberian Peninsula.

A similar case where Barn Owls are forced to feed upon birds because of a lack (in this case a complete lack) of mammalian prey, is on the West African islands of Razo and Brancu (Heim de Balsac 1965). In the absence of mammals the resident Barn Owls largely support themselves by feeding upon birds, in particular sea-birds, and concern has been expressed about the possible effect this might have upon the rare Razo Short-toed Lark. The Seychelle Islands are another area where Barn Owls are having a serious effect upon rare birds. Introduced from Africa in 1949, the Cape Barn Owl *T. alba affinis* was intended to provide a biological control on the abundant rats which were causing havoc amongst the coconut plantations. Unfortunately the owls found the endemic sea-birds easier to catch, with the tame and trusting Fairy Tern suffering more than most. As a result the hoped for saviour of the coconut plantations now has a price upon its head and efforts are being made to eradicate the Barn Owl from the Seychelles as a whole.

A contradiction to what has been said in the foregoing is provided by Errington (1932) who stated that in Wisconsin, North America, the Barn Owl seemed unable to change from a mammalian diet to an avian one, and therefore perished in the midst of an abundance of winter birds. This is at complete variance with our experiences with *T. alba alba*. In the hard winter and deep snow of 1981/82 our Cumbrian population of Barn Owls quickly exploited the flocks of foraging Chaffinches and Skylarks on barley stubble, at least four birds hunting throughout the daytime period when this source of food was readily available.

Reptiles are taken in much smaller numbers than amphibians and this is presumably a reflection of the relative behaviour of the two groups. A typical example of the ratio of reptiles and amphibians taken is provided by Haverschmidt (1962) who recorded only one reptile (unidentified) compared with 60 individuals of the frog *Leptodactylus ocellatus* preyed upon by the Barn Owl *T. a. hellmayri* in Surinam.

The fast-moving diurnal Lacertid lizards are the usual reptiles found in pellets, and while Herrera (1973) feels that for south-west Spain their presence in the prey sample might indicate hitherto unknown nocturnal behaviour by the lizards, it could be due to some diurnal activity by the owls, although this was not recorded in the study area. The lizards taken include the Spanish Sand Lizard, Green Lizard and Wall Lizard. Snakes are rarely taken, but Fitch (1947) records a Gopher Snake being taken in California, as well as three skink species and a 'Fence Lizard'. Reptiles form the only other alternative to birds for the Razo and Brancu Barn Owls mentioned earlier. Glue makes no reference to snakes being taken in Britain, only Lacertid lizards appearing in his pellet samples.

Unlike the reptiles, it is because of their nocturnal emergence that amphibians, particularly frogs and toads, become vulnerable to the owls. They are slow-moving, frequently available in large numbers (during the breeding season), and often noisy. Consequently they are present in the diet of many Barn Owls hunting over habitats which suit this group, i.e. damp pastures, marshes and water edges. We know of no case where Barn Owls have specialised in taking amphibians, even for a short period. Our own observations suggest that when frogs are offered to owlets by the adults they are rejected.

One item we have never had the good fortune to see captured is fish and we must confess that for a long time we doubted the validity of such records. However, it is impossible to ignore such observations as those of Charles Waterton (in Stanley 1838) who saw a Barn Owl drop perpendicularly into the water and rise with a fish in its talons which it carried to the nest. This observation took place long before dark and there can be no doubt as to its accuracy. Similarly, our friend Derick Scott (pers. comm.) also witnessed a Barn Owl catch a good-sized Roach from the River Anholme, in Lincoln-shire, in the first light of a September day. Other species recorded are Perch, Brown Trout, Rudd and a small Carp. The Rev M. A. Mathew (in Butler et al 1897) mentions a tame Barn Owl in his possession that was very fond of small Trout which it invariably bolted tail first. Experiments we have carried out with captive owls confirm that they are not averse to eating fish if it is available. Nevertheless, we feel that it is quite exceptional for fish to be taken in the wild and it is significant that Glue found no trace of them in his samples.

Before leaving the subject of the variety of prey taken by the Barn Owl we must consider the invertebrates, for these usually figure in most analyses to some extent. On this occasion we can definitely state that the Barn Owl does show intentional discrimination – in largely ignoring them. In comparison with such species as the Tawny Owl and Little Owl, the Barn Owl takes only a minute proportion of invertebrate prey, even when it is available in quantity. The first two species take moths and beetles, especially the dor beetles *Geotrupes* spp. and ground beetles *Carabus* spp., and they often specialise in taking large earthworms *Lumbricus* spp., many of their young being reared on a diet containing a large percentage of this item. Our captive Barn Owls, on the other hand, will consistently ignore such fare, even when they are exceptionally hungry, and in those instances where we have seen invertebrates taken the owls have always been newly-fledged juveniles in the process of learning the arts of hunting. At these times even such ludicrously insignificant species as craneflies (Tipulidae), spiders (Arachnida), Common Earwigs *Forficula auricularia* and moths (Lepidoptera) have been seen to be caught and eaten. Glue found beetle (Coleoptera) remains in 20% of his samples, 342 individuals being calculated from thorax, head, leg and elytra counts. Where they could be placed into family groups they comprised 74 Geotrupidae (dor beetles), 28 Carabidae (ground beetles), 26 Scarabacidae (chafers), 10 Staphylinidae (rove beetles), 4 Lucanidae (stag beetles) and 2 Dytiscidae (true water beetles). Eighty large dung beetles *Caratophyus typhoeus* also occurred in the 60 pellets analysed by Buxton & Lockley (1950) on Skomer Island, particularly in the April and May following the hard winter of 1946/47 when the small mammal population was unusually low. Earthworms were found in only three of Glue's samples, and the Common Earwig once, as was *Ligia oceanica*, a coastal isopod taken on one of our study areas near Millom, Cumbria.

One of the most impressive studies which gives proof of the Barn Owl's deliberate avoidance of invertebrate prey is that of Lovari (1974), who studied the diet of four raptors – the Barn Owl, Little Owl, Buzzard and Kestrel – in the Siena district of central Italy. Gizzard contents were examined over three years and it was found that the Little Owl, Buzzard and Kestrel all took insects as their staple diet during the autumn and winter months, as against birds and small mammals during the spring and summer. Lovari considered that this might be due to the high availability of arthropods in the Mediterranean region during autumn and winter. The Barn Owl, on the other hand, though hunting in the same area as the other species, continued to take mammals as its main prey, and although two Barn Owls had taken many Orthoptera, including the bush-cricket *Decticus albifrons* in the autumn months, there was not a single case of insects in the winter diet.

Herrera also found that, in his area of south-west Spain, invertebrates were mostly taken in the autumn and early winter months. However, even at these times their proportion in biomass was not great, the maximum being 3·5% from one locality where the principle prey, the House Mouse, was scarce during the period of the survey.

TABLE 3a: *Numbers and percentages of prey species found in 200 pellets produced by a pair of Barn Owls and their three young on a Nottinghamshire farm in 1970. (Courtesy: D. Scott, analysis by M. Johnson)*

Species	Number	% by nos.	% by weight
Short-tailed Vole	318	40·7	40·9
Bank Vole	21	2·7	2·7
Water Vole	2	0·3	1·3
Brown Rat	35	4·5	22·5
House Mouse	13	1·7	1·7
Wood Mouse	32	4·1	4·1
Harvest Mouse	5	0·6	0·2
Rabbit (young)	1	0·1	1·3
Common Shrew	261	33·4	16·8
Pygmy Shrew	29	3·7	0·8
Water Shrew	3	0·4	0·3
Mole	2	0·3	1·3
Noctule Bat	1	0·1	0·1
Pipistrelle Bat	1	0·1	0·0
Weasel	1	0·1	0·6
Birds	41	5·2	5·3
Invertebrates	16	2·0	0·1
Average number of prey items per pellet:	3.9		

TABLE 3b: *Numbers and percentages of prey species found in 600 pellets collected from 30 Barn Owl roosts in Lincolnshire during the winter of 1967/68. (Courtesy: D. Scott, analysis by M. Johnson)*

Species	Numbers	% by nos.	% by weight
Short-tailed Vole	1240	46·8	44·0
Bank Vole	171	6·5	6·1
Water Vole	34	1·3	6·0
Brown Rat	91	3·4	16·1
House Mouse	30	1·1	1·1
Wood Mouse	269	10·1	9·5
Harvest Mouse	31	1·2	<0·1
Rabbit (young)	2	<0·1	<0·1
Common Shrew	539	20·3	9·6
Pygmy Shrew	76	2·9	<0·1
Water Shrew	15	<0·1	<0·1
Mole	2	<0·1	<0·1
Whiskered Bat	1	<0·1	<0·1
Birds	149	5·6	5·3
Average number of prey items per pellet: 4·5			

TABLE 4: *Percentage of prey species found in 135 pellets collected in Gisburn Forest, Lancashire. (Analysis by D. Glue)*

Sample 1	Species	% by nos.	% by weight
44 pellets	Short-tailed Vole	69	84
	Common Shrew	23	14
	Pygmy Shrew	8	2
Sample 2			
35 pellets	Short-tailed Vole	69	82
	Common Shrew	28	17
	Pygmy Shrew	2	<1
	Water Shrew	1	<1
Sample 3			
56 pellets	Short-tailed Vole	73	88
	Common Shrew	15	9
	Pygmy Shrew	13	3

Several authors have found that large grasshoppers sometimes feature as the main invertebrate prey and this is perhaps to be expected considering the Barn Owl's predilection for grassland. Otteni et al (1972) found grasshoppers in 2·6% of their pellets from Texas, USA, and these suddenly increased to 10·4% for no apparent reason in 1971. Probably the owls were exploiting a temporary abundance of grasshoppers, for there was no such dependence upon them when mice 'crashed' in 1968; birds on the other hand were taken more frequently. Lovari et al (1976) also mention large grasshoppers of the genera *Decticus* and *Ephigger* as the main invertebrate prey in Central Italy.

Having discussed the various prey items at some length, we now summarise the Barn Owl's diet in Britain in the following tables.

Tables 3a and 3b are excellent examples of typical British analyses and are noteworthy for the wide variety of prey taken. The analyses were made by M. Johnson of Lincoln Museum and we are greatly indebted to Derick Scott for putting these data at our disposal.

In comparison with these two examples, in Table 4 we give the percentages of prey species taken by a Barn Owl in our forest study area in the West Riding of Yorkshire (now Lancashire). Here the habitat was ideal for a large population of Short-tailed Voles and these greatly outnumbered all other species in the pellets. Moreover, the uniform habitat offered very little variety of species. Although Table 3 shows fine examples of the Barn Owl's wide spectrum of prey species, they are not really what we would expect to find in our northern study areas; the Harvest Mouse, for instance, would be absent and the Brown Rat would not hold such a prominent position. Because of this, and to give some idea of the variation in different areas of Britain, we can do no better than to show Glue's table for the whole of the British Isles (Table 5).

TABLE 5: *Regional analysis of 188 Barn Owl pellet samples by prey weight, collected in Britain and Ireland between 1960–1971. Results expressed as percentage of total prey weight. (After Glue 1974)*

Region and no. of prey units	Short-tailed Vole	Common Shrew	Wood Mouse	Bank Vole	Brown Rat	House Mouse	Others
South-west England (8074 p.u.)	59	14	13	6	1	<1	7
South-east England (6721 p.u.)	54	11	12	3	11	1	8
Eastern England (9329 p.u.)	40	10	8	4	28	3	7
Midlands (4200 p.u.)	50	16	11	7	7	<1	9
Northern England (3575 p.u.)	60	19	8	3	2	<1	8
Wales (3918 p.u.)	56	17	10	5	6	<1	6
Scotland (5962 p.u.)	56	21	12	3	2	<1	6
Ireland & Isle of Man (2045 p.u.)	—	—	57	—	31	7	5
Combined Regional Analysis (43,824 p.u.)	50	14	13	4	11	1	7

The pellet samples were collected from a widespread geographical distribution and from numerous habitats, i.e. young forestry plantations, scrub, upland pasture, arable and mixed farmland, parkland, open mature woodland, waste ground, wet rough grassland, marsh and saltmarsh.

DAILY FOOD INTAKE

In view of the enormous amount of work done on pellets the reader could be forgiven for assuming that it is an easy matter to assess the daily food intake of an owl. In practice nothing could be further from the truth and the account that follows, of the research that has been undertaken in order to ascertain how many pellets are produced per 24 hours, will give some insight into the problems involved.

Contrary to former belief, pellet ejection is a conscious action, not a reflex one. This means that within reason a pellet can be regurgitated at will in response to certain stimuli. Observations on captive birds indicate that provided food has been eaten some hours beforehand, a pellet is frequently produced whenever the owl believes that another meal is imminent. Some workers have stimulated owls by actually offering them another food item, while others have induced pellet egestion by allowing the owl to see a live vole outside its cage (Reed 1897, Guérin 1928, Chitty 1938, Smith & Richmond 1972). Even more remarkable, the latter workers also noted that there was an increase in free hydrochloric acid in the stomach of their owl half-an-hour after they entered the room in which the bird was kept, the obvious interpretation being that this individual had learned to associate them with the provision of food – the equivalent of human mouth watering! This helps to explain the almost instantaneous production of pellets which invariably greets A.B.W. when he arrives at his aviaries with the food-bucket in order to feed the Barn and Tawny Owls – he has often taken advantage of this in order to show the manner of pellet ejection to visitors. Reed found that sometimes his owls' anticipation was so great that in their desire to get a further meal they regurgitated pellets containing half-digested meat. Conversely, it should be noted that Armitage (1968) discovered that Long-eared Owls could retain the pellet if no food was in prospect. This probably helps assuage the pangs of hunger and we have no reason to believe that this does not also occur with the Barn Owl. Chitty suggests that hunger determines the length of time that a pellet is retained by the owl, but it seems more likely to be a case of the owls lacking the proper stimulus (i.e. available food) to induce pellet egestion. These last remarks should not be construed as meaning that pellets cannot be produced without the stimulus of an imminent meal.

Smith and Richmond did a useful experiment to determine what effect an excess of readily available prey had upon their Barn Owl's rate of pellet ejection – very pertinent when one is considering Barn Owl food intake during times of vole 'plagues', etc. To achieve this they fed the bird on prey items of known weight, then placed a wire cage containing additional live prey where the owl could see it. The bird was observed from outside the room and was given another weighed meal as soon as it regurgitated a pellet. This was continued throughout the night and day with various weights of prey being offered up to a level where the owl simply killed and stored it. This indicated when the owl had taken its optimum prey weight. They found that when the owl was aware that another meal was possible there was no difference between day and night feeds in pellet ejection time; nor was there any variation caused by differing prey-weights. The minimum time in which the owl could normally produce a pellet was 6·5 hours after its last meal, though a few pellets were recovered in less time under unusual circumstances. The normal pattern was for the bird to continue eating available prey until the critical 6·5-hour pause occurred. After that time one large pellet was produced, containing the remains of all the prey items eaten in the period before the pause. This could be many hours after the first meal was taken. It was found that mice, swallowed at intervals of less than 6 hours, delayed pellet egestion until the last item was digested, and this confirms the findings of Guérin (1928). As Smith and Richmond rightly point out, this delaying effect is limited by the bird's food capacity, and it is virtually certain that pellets containing many individual mammals represent a period of continuous feeding where the prey is taken at intervals of less than the critical 6·5-hour period needed to enable digestion to take place.

It must be remembered that in the experiments quoted above, the owl was constantly aware that food was available when it needed it, and because of this we must be cautious of interpreting the results as being typical of wild birds. Nevertheless, the discovery of 6·5 hours as the minimum period before

1 The long flexible neck of the Barn Owl is ably demonstrated by this eight-week-old hand-reared owlet (photo: G. Himsworth).

2 Hand-reared Barn Owlet giving defensive display (photo: G. Himsworth).

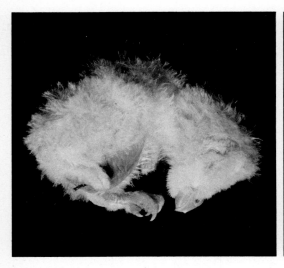

3   Owlet at 9 hours (photo: Ian Marshall).   4   Owlet at 7 days (photo: Ian Marshall).

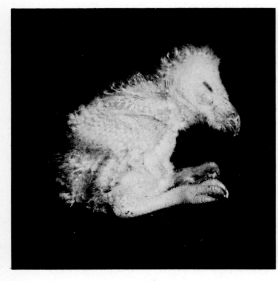

5   Owlet at 14 days (photo: Ian Marshall).   6   Owlet at 21 days (photo: Ian Marshall).

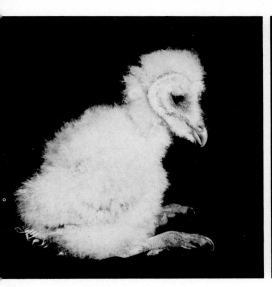

7 Owlet at 28 days (photo: Ian Marshall).   8 Owlet at 35 days (photo. Ian Marshall).

9   Young Barn Owl at 42 days (photo: Ian Marshall). See also Photo 10 overleaf.

10 Young Barn Owl at 56 days (photo: D. Malpus).

11 Young Barn Owl engaging in wing-flapping exercises (photo: D. Malpus).

12 Two newly-fledged owls giving vigorous food-begging display when a parent returns with prey (photo: W. Palfrey).

13 Female Barn Owl brings a Short-tailed Vole to her young in the cavity between ceiling and floorboards of a derelict house (photo: P. Hanson).

14 Male Barn Owl by its nest. Note the light-coloured secondaries and sides of the neck which often enable the sexes to be distinguished (photo: P. Hanson).

15 Adult Barn Owl with common Shrew (photo: Derick Scott).

16 Young Barn Owls 'stare in rapt concentration at the favoured entry points' (page 131). The female has a Mole (photo: Derick Scott).

17 Two young Barn Owls await the return of an adult with prey (photo: Derick Scott).

pellets can be egested is of paramount importance to any food study, as is the inhibiting effect of small, regular intakes of food. Both these factors presumably apply no matter what circumstances prevail. Other workers have found that where no further supply of potential food is visible (as would be the case in the wild), other considerations come into play. For instance the time interval, before pellet egestion, increases with the amount of prey-weight eaten (Chitty 1938, Collins & LeCroy in Marti 1974), and this gives credence to statements that the time interval is greater after the night feed (1600–2400 hours) than the day feed (0600–1400 hours). This would not be surprising since the former is the time of peak activity by both the owl and its principal prey species, so that, given normal circumstances, this will be the main feeding period and result in the greatest intake of prey weight – presumably the digestive system of the owl will need a greater length of time to deal with the larger amount of food consumed. The actual length of time varied, but could be more than double that involved after a small meal. Another of Chitty's findings was the rather surprising one that although prey weight affected pellet egestion times, the percentage of roughage contained in the prey did not, thus suggesting that nutritional food content is of greater significance than actual bulk when it comes to pellet formation and egestion, the time taken by the enzymes to break down the food being the factor which causes the variation in egestion periods.

Most workers (e.g. Glue 1967, Massey 1971, Zelenka & Pricam 1974) follow the findings of Guérin (1928) who studied captive and wild Barn Owls in France. His conclusion was that although a maximum of four pellets in 24 hours could be obtained in exceptional circumstances (thus confirming Smith & Richmond's figures for the minimum egestion period), the usual number is two. These consist of a small 'pelote nocturne' dropped on the hunting grounds before a second meal is taken, and a 'pelote diurne' which represents the morning meal and is dropped at the day roost. The latter was therefore believed by most workers to be the one they collected at the owl roost and used in their analyses. According to this theory, these pellets would represent approximately half of the bird's daily food intake, the rest of the material being lost due to the non-recovery of the 'pelote nocturne'.

As we have seen, it is folly to interpret Guérin's conclusions too literally, for so many factors exist which affect egestion that one can never assume that the owl under observation is behaving 'normally' – particularly when the study is being carried out on captive birds. Owlets, for instance, usually eat smaller meals than the adults but feed more frequently, particularly when there is a surplus of prey at the nest. Consequently, they tend to produce more pellets than the adults, averaging three per day in studies we have made. Southern also showed that young Tawny Owls would sometimes produce several pellets from a single meal, so presumably this could also be the case with Barn Owlets, though we have never known this ourselves. Wallace (1948) and Marti (1973) both formed the opinion that the American Barn Owl *T. a. pratincola* averaged less than two pellets per day, a conclusion two of the present authors reached independently in their separate studies of *T. a. alba*. However, in all of these cases the work was done mainly with captive birds, which are probably unreliable as guides to wild behaviour. Although it has often been postulated that captive birds will eat less than their wild counterparts (due to the latter having to expend more energy to obtain food), it usually seems to be forgotten that many captive creatures over-eat when food is freely available! The individual traits of the owl under observation obviously colour the findings of the researcher – and this applies equally to wild as well as captive birds.

The captive owls we studied were fed mainly on dead, day-old domestic fowl chicks and the daily intake was two – in one pair less than two – per adult bird. If three were given, the surplus chick was either cached or ignored. However, the birds varied in their feeding behaviour: some would eat two chicks one after another, in which case a single pellet resulted, while others would eat one chick immediately and the other after casting a pellet in the morning hours. This would result in a second pellet during the daytime period, that is, the 'pelote diurne' of Guérin. Wallace (loc. cit.) made observations on three captive Barn Owls (one an owlet) and obtained differing results for each one! Like us he found that owls, particularly nestlings, having eaten their fill would not eat again until they had regurgitated the pellet-forming materials – a trait which makes the night-feeding of a brood of hand-reared owlets a harrowing experience!

Several observers, including Wallace, when attempting to assess pellet production and food intake, make the mistake of believing that only during the long, dark nights of winter can a Barn Owl have enough time to catch and eat a large meal, form a 'pelote nocturne' before daylight, and then go out to hunt for a second, pre-dawn meal to enable a 'pelote diurne' to be produced. They argue that after daylight has arrived it is too late for the owl to hunt, whereas we have proved that for *T. a. alba* at least, daylight hunting is a regular occurrence in some areas (Bunn 1971).

A final argument against the reliability of Guérin's hypothesis is that it pre-supposes that the birds remain away from the daytime roost all night, only returning with the arrival of daylight. In fact, the majority of Barn Owls we have studied had the habit of emerging just before sunset, hunting for about an hour and then returning to the daytime roost, either to digest their meal if hunting had been successful, or to rest prior to trying again soon after midnight. A second rest period would follow this last activity and, depending on how the night's hunting had gone, either a third food foray would take place (presumably after ejecting the 'pelote nocturne' at the roost), or the birds would simply 'sit about' in the vicinity of the roost before retiring for the daytime hours. If feeding had been bad or the birds had been kept at the roost by inclement weather (either of which would affect pellet egestion), it was not unusual for them to remain out hunting until late in the morning. Thus the contents of pellets collected at the roost are useful only as a guide to the species taken as prey, not as a reliable assessment of overall food intake.

In the same context, the counting of *numbers* of prey species found in each pellet is equally worthless as an assessment of their food value, because of the differing weights of the species concerned. For this reason most workers now rely on Southern's method of regarding the prey species as so many 'prey units'. Prey units are derived from their average body-weights, taking as standard a 20 g animal and awarding it a prey unit of 1·0. This gives a far better indication of each species' importance in the diet and enables one to hazard a guess as to the daily food requirements in the wild. Because of its

TABLE 6: *Average live weight of Barn Owl food species and their relative prey units*

Species	Average weight (g)		Prey unit
	Southern	Yalden	
Mole	100	70	5·0
Common Shrew	10	8	0·5
Pygmy Shrew	4		0·2
Water Shrew	15	12	0·75
Natterer's Bat	8		0·4
Noctule Bat	28		1·4
Pipistrelle Bat	5		0·25
Long-eared Bat	7		0·35
Weasel	100		5·0
Rabbit	200		10·0
Harvest Mouse	6	5	0·3
Wood Mouse	20	18	1·0
House Mouse	20	12	1·0
Dormouse	30	20	1·5
Brown Rat	100	60	5·0
Bank Vole	20	16	1·0
Water Vole	100		5·0
Short-tailed Vole	20	21	1·0
Common Frog	20		1·0
Common Toad	20		1·0
Birds	10–100		0·5–5·0

wide use we have followed Southern's method in this book, but would draw attention to Yalden (1977) who suggests slightly different weights in some instances.

Yalden's figures are probably more reliable than Southern's, so Table 6 gives Southern's interpretation and Yalden's amendments where applicable.

It should be emphasised that no matter what method is used, errors are bound to occur due to the variation in age and weight of the prey. For instance, there is a vast difference between the weight of a juvenile rat (about 100 g), and a full-grown specimen, which can weigh as much as 500 g (Glue 1967). In the above table both they and the Water Vole, as well as Rabbits, are assessed as juveniles, for these predominate in the majority of cases where they feature in the diet.

Let us now try to answer the thorny question of how much a Barn Owl eats in an average twenty-four hour period. As we have seen, it is useless to attempt this by collecting pellets and counting their contents, as the birds may well have ejected some pellets away from the roost. It is equally pointless to count the average *number* of prey species per pellet and multiply the answer by two (assuming two pellets a day), for clearly the contents can range from a single item to a great many, depending on what the owls have caught. It is by no means unusual to find pellets containing a single animal, and if the prey has been a well-grown rat this might well represent the owl's full daily intake. If, on the other hand, the pellet contains only a low prey weight (a single shrew or vole for instance) this is usually indicative of unsuccessful hunting, and in such circumstances the bird would probably attempt to capture further prey before roosting for the day. To give some idea of the variation which can occur, we have records of one pellet containing the skulls of twelve Pygmy Shrews and another with the skulls of thirteen Common Shrews (both, incidentally, from Webster's site in south Westmorland). These are not as remarkable as they might seem at first glance; a perusal of Table 6 shows that a Common Shrew is only approximately half the weight of a Short-tailed Vole, and a Pygmy Shrew one-fifth. These pellets would therefore be roughly equivalent to pellets containing two-and-a-half and six-and-a-half voles respectively. What *is* significant is when a pellet is found containing high numbers of Short-tailed Voles or their counterpart. One found by us contained seven voles which, on the premise that this represents an entire meal, gives a figure of approximately 140 g. Similarly, a remarkable pellet from the New Forest, Hampshire, contained individuals of six different species, namely, Short-tailed Vole, Bank Vole, Common Shrew, Water Shrew, Wood Mouse and Mole, suggesting a total of 185 g. We would venture to suggest that in this case the contents represented the total food taken for that day. We base this on the fact that the two day-old chicks eaten by our captives each average 37·3 g, giving a daily intake of only about 75 g – which suggests that British Barn Owls in the wild consume about twice the weight of food as captives.

That Barn Owls are capable of eating much larger quantities is apparently proved by a story told of Lord Lilford when he was a schoolboy. He is said to have fed a half-grown Barn Owl on nine mice one after the other, all of which it swallowed. Three hours later the bird took four more, making a total of thirteen mice consumed in this single meal! If the food items were indeed mice, this means that the owl took in approximately 260 g prey-weight – which seems an excessively high figure. Possibly the bird was simply a greedy individual which behaved atypically due to its confinement, but there is another possibility: the old naturalists had the habit of calling shrews 'shrew-mice', and if the animals given to the owl were Common Shrews this would give us a more reasonable figure of approximately 130 g. A significant factor here is the observation of Konishi (1973) that his owls (three *T. a. pratincola*) would cease to strike more prey after eating two mice. Unfortunately, he does not tell us how long it was before the birds began to hunt successfully again, nor what the daily total of mice taken was. Zelenka & Pricam (loc. cit.) state that their owls (*T. a. alba* and *T. a. guttata*) averaged seven (5–9) small mammals per day, i.e. about 140 g. Collins & LeCroy (in Marti 1974) give a figure of eight, i.e. about 160 g, for *T. a. pratincola*, while Guérin, by assumption, suggested six, i.e. about 120 g, for *T. a. alba*. Both Evans & Emlen (1947) and Marti (1974) estimated the intake of *T. a. pratincola* on the basis of two pellets per day, as per Guérin. They suggest figures of 150 g and 110 g respectively, but make no allowance for the size of the owl nor time of the year. The last point is an important one as Marti and

Chitty (1938) each found. They discovered that their owls ate more in cold weather, suggesting a high metabolic rate caused by the Barn Owl's low body-fat content. This probably explains Bauer's findings that Mediterranean Barn Owls take less prey-weight daily than do those from temperate regions.

From these various results, and ignoring such observations as those of Lord Lilford which are based on maximum performance rather than average intake, we conclude that in normal circumstances most Barn Owls have a daily intake of between 100–150 g and, strangely, this seems to apply to races of such vastly differing body-weights as *T. a. alba* (av. 337 g), *T. a. guttata* (av. 356 g) and *T. a. pratincola* (542–661 g). It is a great pity that so many of these findings are based on the intake of captive birds, for as we have pointed out, there is always an element of doubt with observations so made. However, our own observations of Barn Owls in the wild suggest that for *T. a. alba* at least, a daily intake of seven to eight vole-sized animals would be about average.

OTHER USES OF PELLETS

Heim de Balsac (1965), Glue (1970b) and Herrera (1973) all comment on the usefulness of pellets in obtaining a quick sample of the small mammal fauna of an area where little is known of their distribution, and one of us had the exciting experience of recording the Dormouse in a pellet from a Cumbrian study area. Thanks to the expertise of Dr Derek Yalden, and the vigilance of his wife Pat, this unusual item of prey was spotted in a sample where it could not possibly have been anticipated. This Dormouse proved to be 160 km farther north of the only previous post-war record of the species in northern England and resulted in the discovery of a viable population of these animals in what is possibly their only Lakeland haunt.

Another, somewhat unexpected, benefit of pellet analysis is the discovery of numbered bird-rings in the pellets. Though a rare occurrence when compared with the usual recovery circumstances – much less than 1% according to Glue & Morgan (1977) – rings are well worth searching for, especially as many avian prey items would otherwise be difficult or impossible to identify. Previously unrecorded prey species have been found for some birds of prey by this means.

FOOD STORAGE

First let it be said that we have no proof that wild Barn Owls ever store food outside the breeding season, but in view of the following observations we certainly do not discount the possibility.

The strongest indication of regular food storage is the way in which captive Barn Owls, Short-eared Owls, Little Owls and Tawny Owls carefully secrete uneaten food in some dark corner. Tawny Owls are particularly fastidious about this and one we kept, after leaving the remains of an uneaten prey item in some hiding place, would suddenly go back to it a few seconds later as if to ascertain that it was still there, then back away from it as though to implant its location on its memory. Afterwards it would only return when it became hungry again. Short-eared Owls, too, return and eat cached food in captivity and one of us has watched this species caching freshly caught prey in grass tussocks on the Ribble saltmarshes. In this respect these species differ from the Barn Owls and Little Owls we have kept, which seem to leave stockpiled food items untouched.

In June 1967 one of us discovered a freshly killed Short-tailed Vole and a Meadow Pipit lying side by side on an inside window-sill of an old house in which an unmated cock bird was roosting. At the time it was assumed that the owl was probably simply satisfying its instinct to bring in prey during that period of the year, and even if this was not the case they could have been brought in for courtship purposes as there was always the possibility that an unattached hen was in the vicinity. More convincingly, however, prey items were discovered at the roost of a hen bird, suspected to be unmated, in December; three days later they were gone, presumably eaten by the owl. Kaufman (1973) confirmed that in captivity *T. a. pratincola* would kill all live mice offered to it, then cache any that it could not eat immediately. Wallace (1948) further confirmed that this subspecies stockpiles prey in the wild; but in this case he records huge numbers of surplus animals, namely 80 mice in one instance and a staggering 189 in another! On these occasions, however, the activity was linked with feeding the young and would only appear to have been a gross exaggeration of the normal foraging behaviour by the adults, in particular the cock.

Against the contention of food storage outside the breeding season is the fact that Barn Owls almost always eat prey where it is caught or on some nearby perch. Once their hunger is satisfied they return to the roost or begin to doze where they are: they do not engage in further hunting and take their next capture to the roost as would be expected if food storage was habitual. There is also the fact that Konishi's owls would not strike at live prey once they had consumed two mice, and this surely casts doubt on the validity of food storage in the wild.

USEFULNESS OF THE BARN OWL

The reader may have noticed that so far in this book we have made no mention of the beneficial role of the Barn Owl. This is no chance omission; almost every reference to the bird in literature stresses how beneficial it is and the desirability of encouraging it on this account, but there are two separate reasons why, regrettably, we must question the amount of emphasis attached to such statements.

In the first place it is a gross mistake to categorise the Barn Owl's prey species into those that are 'harmful' and those that are 'beneficial' to Man, as is often done so glibly. Let us consider a few British species in the order of frequency that they tend to be preyed upon. First there is the Short-tailed Vole which, as we have seen, can be regarded as the staple diet in most territories. In the main this rodent leads a blameless life, feeding harmlessly enough on young shoots and the succulent bases of long grass stems, while sheltering under the thick tussocks that usually form in the absence of grazing. Therefore, by preference they inhabit patches of uncultivated land where they can do little or no damage, and their effect on a hay crop must surely be negligible. Even in our forest study area, where the voles exist in ideal conditions and fluctuate in the manner for which they are famous, the Forestry Commission have found them quite innocuous. It is only when population peaks coincide with the establishment of fresh plantations, and during the local 'plagues' that occur in Britain on rare occasions, that the vole becomes economically harmful due to its habit of ring-barking and of branch-stripping young trees.

Second in importance to the Short-tailed Vole is the Common Shrew. It would be futile to try to assess the usefulness or otherwise of shrews, for these little animals eat an enormous variety of invertebrates which are themselves difficult to categorise, as well as a good deal more vegetable matter than is usually appreciated.

The Wood Mouse and Bank Vole, though pests at times in gardens and horticultural nurseries, feed mostly on the seeds, fruits, shoots and roots of wild plants and consequently cannot really be considered as serious economic problems.

House Mice and Brown Rats are, however, undoubtedly formidable pests to mankind and any predator that can help reduce their numbers must certainly be classed as beneficial. However, with the progress of science, and population studies in particular, a change of thinking has taken place concerning predator/prey relationships. This has resulted in a re-assessment of the true role of each and it is now known that instead of exerting a natural control on the prey species as was formerly believed, it is more a case of the predators being controlled by the current level of the populations of their prey species. In fact the relationships are more complex than this, but without going into further detail it will suffice to say that neither the Barn Owl nor any other predator is likely to have any controlling effect upon the numbers of our small mammals: the population of Short-tailed Voles in the forest study area, for instance, fluctuated in its characteristic cycles despite an abundance of predators of many species, including Kestrels, Barn Owls, Tawny Owls, Short-eared Owls, Foxes, Stoats and Weasels. We are prepared to concede that a pair of breeding Barn Owls will thin out the numbers of small mammals in the immediate vicinity of their roost, but that is all.

CHAPTER 5

Breeding

The problems inherent in the study of a shy and mainly nocturnal species such as the Barn Owl are daunting to say the least, and we have often had cause to question our sanity in attempting such a task. For one thing the number of useful observations one is able to make, casually, is limited and the most frequent views are of distant birds quartering their hunting grounds in search of prey, or of perched, inactive individuals at or near the roost. Though not without interest, such observations provide only a brief insight into the behaviour of the species, and a closer approach is necessary if one is to become more deeply acquainted with one's subject. It is with the onset of the breeding season that this becomes practicable, for not only do the birds become more active, vocal, and easier to locate, but the observer is able to work from the cover of a hide and to watch the more intimate details of the owl's life as long as certain rules are adhered to (see Appendix 3, Watching the Barn Owl).

THE BREEDING SEASON

During our study we have defined the breeding season as that period when serious courtship occurs and when either eggs or young are present. In our experience the end of the breeding season is usually heralded by the onset of the annual moult, and once this becomes apparent it can be reasonably assumed that one or both of the pair has lost condition and that further breeding activity is unlikely. When a second brood is produced the moult of the body feathers is either postponed or dispensed with altogether, depending on how late in the year the adults are freed from their parental duties. Unfortunately there appears to be no data on the way the moult proceeds in those races which breed continuously throughout the year.

The length of time a Barn Owl takes to hatch and rear its young to full independence is extraordinary, for a newly laid egg will not produce an independent owl in less than fourteen weeks. Add this to the several weeks during which the birds engaged in pre-nesting behaviour and the fact that the youngest of a brood of five will be at least eight days behind the eldest, and one can appreciate the remarkable amount of time devoted to breeding. The British Barn Owl *T. a. alba* is often quoted as breeding in every month of the year except January (e.g. Prestt in Gooders et al 1969, Fitter et al 1969, Prestt & Wagstaffe in Burton et al 1973); yet our own fieldwork and searches through the literature have failed to reveal any first-hand evidence of a clutch being started in Britain in January, September, October, November or December, so presumably these records refer only to the *presence* of eggs or young, and will in most cases mean that the observer has found owlets in the later stages of development.

The case is not so simple with other races, for it has been shown that many of these will breed throughout the year where conditions and prey availability make this possible. Thus *T. a. affinis* has been recorded as rearing four broods in Rhodesia, with the eggs of the second and third broods being laid while the young of the previous broods were still in the nest (Wilson 1970). *T. a. hellmayri* breeds throughout the year in Surinam, the main breeding season being from August–December, with second broods being started in January and some nests being found in the period March–May (Haverschmidt 1962). The picture with the American Barn Owl *T. a. pratincola* is even more complicated. In the north-eastern States it breeds throughout the year (Henny 1969), whereas Wallace (1948) states that in New York the Christmas Census workers could normally depend on finding unfledged young at some site or other. In Michigan it may breed almost continuously during peak years of the *Microtus* cycle, downy young having been recorded in the nest in every month of the year. However, when its staple prey is scarce it slows down, or may even miss a breeding season altogether. We should also mention that captive British Barn Owls of the race *T. a. alba* do not breed continually even when over-abundant food is offered. This seems to indicate that prey abundance is not the only factor affecting the breeding season – weather conditions and time of year also play a part.

In contrast to north-east America the breeding season is very short in California, i.e. January–June, with 50% of clutches being started between 9th March and 16th April (Bent 1938). F. Gallup (in Stewart 1952) pointed out that this correlates with the rainy season when vegetation is lush and prey plentiful. Such a short breeding season naturally precludes second broods and indicates the great variation which can occur amongst individual races in different parts of their range.

The data contained in 291 British Trust for Ornithology nest record cards covering England, Wales and Scotland during the period 1942–75 reveal no evidence of a connection between the dates of laying and the geographical location of British nests; Fig. 6 summarises the laying period as shown by these cards (after Glue, in prep.).

As can be seen, in Britain the months of April, May and June account for 92·4% of nests, the mean laying date being 9th May. There is, of course, a very good reason for this: the stage at which the young from these nests are most demanding in their food requirements coincides with the rodent population peak in July and August. This ensures that a regular, easily

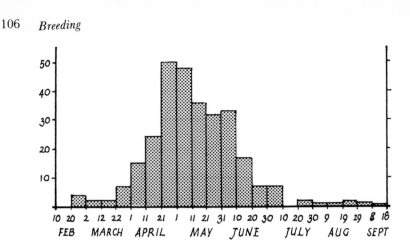

Fig. 6 Dates of first eggs at 291 Barn Owl nests in Britain (after Glue, in prep.).

captured supply of prey is available, created by the relative abundance of young, inexperienced – and hence less alert – animals.

We suspect that it is nests begun during the later months of the breeding season (i.e. in July and August), many of which are probably replacement clutches, that give rise to most of the reports of so-called second broods. The young from such nests will still be at and around the nest sites in November and December, and anyone unfamiliar with the Barn Owl's breeding biology could be forgiven for assuming that they are the progeny of second broods. However, as we shall see later, second broods are a rather rare occurrence in Britain. There may be many reasons for genuine first clutches being delayed until so late in the season. Disturbance at the nest site, when no alternative suitable breeding place exists in the territory; temporary shortage of prey due to bad weather; and conditions which adversely affect the habitat and result in the hen obtaining insufficient food to stimulate laying, seem the most obvious and likely.

COURTSHIP

As we mentioned in Chapter 3, some pairs remain at the nest site throughout the year, roosting together and indulging in activities which maintain the pair-bond – mostly mutual preening and conversational chirruping and squeaking. However, other pairs carry on a looser association whereby both stay in the breeding territory but occupy different roosts. In our experience the latter is the commoner occurrence. They pay periodic visits to each other and also meet during their nightly excursions, maintaining the pair-bond in this way. Sometimes one of the pair apparently deserts the breeding territory (or dies), leaving the other bird alone. It is not only the cock which remains as territory-holder, for we have known of instances where the hen stayed as sole occupier of the breeding territory during the winter. Other pairs move away from the nest site together, usually after disturbance, and occupy a new roost in another part of the territory. They may even change the extent of the territory itself, taking in new ground if this is unoccupied by other Barn Owls, and abandoning once favoured haunts. In such cases the pair may still return to the traditional nest site at the onset of the breeding season, usually in early March, as the attachment to this is very strong and it is the focal point of any territory.

It is by no means unusual for Barn Owl pairs to use the same nest site for up to twenty or thirty years and there are several records, which seem reasonably acceptable, of up to seventy years. Ringing data and our own experiences show that when one of the pair succumbs the remaining bird may stay until it is joined by another mate, which sometimes takes place in the season that the former partner was lost (Baudvin 1975). This may still occur even when mates disappear in successive years, with the result that the site continues to be occupied. Several instances were recorded by Baudvin where both partners had changed in two years. In those areas of Europe where *T. a. alba* and *T. a. guttata* are both to be found (i.e. eastern France and western Germany) the choice of a partner of the other race is a matter of chance and many intermediate forms result.

Certain sites seem to have a special attraction for Barn Owls and are re-occupied by itinerant birds when they are found to be vacant due to the death or departure of the original birds. Since the species is by preference sedentary, a pair which leaves its winter roosts and returns to a breeding site in spring normally includes at least one of the previous season's breeders; but despite all these variations in the behaviour of wintering birds, it is rare for a breeding territory to be deserted by both birds, unless some unfavourable change takes place within the habitat.

If conditions are suitable, true courtship may begin in late February. One of the first indications is an increase in the number of daylight sightings of normally nocturnal cock birds as they hunt for prey to present to their mates. The frequent screeching song flights of the cocks as they patrol their territories at dusk and after dark, are another sure sign of courtship activity, serving both to repel neighbouring cocks and to attract the opposite sex. It is by no means unusual to see the pairs associating together at night, and they begin to indulge in the sexual chases which are such a feature of Barn Owl courtship. In these, the cock persistently follows the hen wherever she goes, the two turning, twisting and weaving in a most intricate manner, often at great speed. Occasionally the cock follows the hen in a more leisurely manner, flying approximately two to six metres above and a little to the rear of her. Although silent chases do occur, the birds usually screech frequently during these activities, the hen's broken, more screaming voice being readily distinguishable from the pure 'pea-whistle' screech of the cock. Her indescribable utterances at these times may properly be classed as our wailing – see Chapter 2, Call 3.

Two other display flights are performed by the cock in courtship. In one of these, which we have termed the *moth flight*, the cock hovers in front of the perched hen at the level of her head, retaining this position with legs dangling for a period of up to five seconds. In all the cases observed by us the cock faced the hen, so exposing his white underparts and underwings. On several occasions wing-clapping has been heard during this display but, as was explained in Chapter 2, we are not altogether convinced that this is a deliberate part of the performance because we have sometimes seen captive birds clap their wings together involuntarily while flapping hard in a confined space. In our observations the wing-clapping of the Barn Owl could not be compared with the more familiar loud wing-clapping displays of the Long-eared and Short-eared Owls: the cock Barn Owl merely produced a double flipping noise, the first sound being louder than the second, and although the claps were clearly audible they were only moderately loud. On one occasion a single wing-clap was heard during a suspected aggressive display when two owls mounted in the air facing each other, and it is perhaps significant that in such a performance the wing action would be particularly strenuous as during the moth flight. However, that such wing-clapping – whether true display or unintentional – is a rare element of Barn Owl behaviour is illustrated by the experiences of D. Scott who, in fifteen years, worked through seven complete nest cycles and spent from two to eight weeks at nests of five other pairs. He informs us that during all this time he only observed wing-clapping on four occasions, and two of these were by the same bird. Contrary to our own experiences he describes the wing-clapping on one occasion as being 'such a clatter that it was audible at fifty yards'.

Although two of our own observations were made in the early part of the year, most of the cases of wing-clapping known and reported to us have occurred when the owls had young in the nest. One such observation by Scott is reproduced in full because of its exceptional interest: 'The nest was twelve feet up in the side of a haystack. The hen was brooding very small young and the display took place fifteen minutes before dark. The cock appeared and pitched on to a branch of the tall hawthorn tree behind and to the left of the hide. He had a vole in his beak and sat for five minutes being mobbed by a cock Blackbird and a pair of Robins. The cock then flew into the nest-hole and deposited the prey. He flew out immediately and alighted on the same branch. A moment later the hen left the nest and flew to the top of the stack where she began to sway and vibrate her wings, her face pointing upwards towards her mate whose elevation was slightly higher. The cock suddenly launched himself from his perch, paused in mid-air, lifted his wings high above his head and smacked them together. He then flew to the hen's side and copulated'.

We are also grateful to J. G. Goldsmith for informing us of a quite different method of wing-clapping to that we have described. He writes: 'I have but a single observation of "wing-clapping", at Caistor St Edmund's, Norfolk, where one was crossing over an area of woods, with pasture in the middle which was occasionally hunted and which contained a tree in which they nested one year. It flew higher than I have previously seen one fly (about 45–50 m) and performed a spiralling circular flight with exaggerated clapping wing beats, before rising again and continuing over the next piece of woodland.'

The Barn Owl is not the only species for which a *moth flight* has been recorded. Mountfort (1957), in his monograph of the Hawfinch, refers to the moth flight performed by that species and describes it as a 'queer, fluttering flight, but with shallow wing-beats'. It has also been noted in the Serin and occasionally in the Chaffinch, while Conder (in Mountfort) refers to the Goldfinch performing such a display.

The second type of aerial display seen at this time we have termed the *in-and-out flight*. In this the cock repeatedly flies in and out of the nest site in order to entice the hen into it: he flies out, circles around screeching, then swoops back inside. His calling from within usually has the desired effect of attracting the hen to him, but if this fails he may resort to a song flight. Occasionally, when highly excited, the cock will indulge in an *in-and-out flight* when the hen is already at the nest site; his excitement infects her and she responds by uttering courtship notes. Barn Owls frequently fly in and out of buildings during normal activity, but in the display just described the flight and wing action are much faster than usual. When the nest site is a tree-hole the cock's display takes the form of a fast flight around the tree with frequent calling; courtship then takes place when he alights at the side of the hen or enters the hole. *In-and-out flights* have also been recorded in the Redstart, Pied Flycatcher and Little Owl. In these species, all hole nesters, it is similarly used by the cock to attract the hen to the nest site.

Unpaired birds are even more vocal and in March 1968 one cock Barn Owl was observed screeching regularly every few seconds while perched at the entrance hole of a barn it inhabited. This bird was visited from time to time by at least one unattached hen and once, in the darkness, a hen, recognisable as such by her different screech, was heard to leave him and fly to another screeching cock about 1 km away. On one occasion when early courtship was observed the hen was far from enthusiastic about the cock's close attentions and adopted a threatening posture, crouching down with wings slightly raised and spread, and 'glowering' at the cock.

In March and April the cock begins to utter his loud territorial screeches with greater regularity at and around the nest site and loud screeching duets occur with some pairs. This increase in screeching by the cock indicates his return to breeding condition and in our experience in Lakeland this stage is usually reached some six weeks before egg-laying begins. The cock continues to strengthen the pair-bond by soliciting his mate's attentions, interesting her in a suitable nest site and finally bringing her into laying condition by presenting her with a plentiful supply of food.

A peculiar change now comes over the hen: she reverts to juvenile behaviour (not unlike courting *Homo sapiens*!) and commences to snore repeatedly, standing about like an owlet awaiting the return of a feeding adult. This change has been noted at around five weeks before egg-laying and is a useful guide to when eggs could be expected. As stated in Chapter 2, the hen's snore is normally less drawn out than that of the fledged young, but it is unmistakably the same note, every bit as persistent and with the same function: i.e. to stimulate the cock into bringing food and to solicit his attentions generally. Thus, each sex stimulates the other.

By comparison, apart from his territorial screechings, the cock is very quiet, only uttering occasional chirrups as he glances towards her, though strangely he sometimes snores too. Copulation occurs frequently, usually at possible nest sites, but not necessarily at the site which is finally chosen. The birds spend considerable time exploring other likely places before making up their minds and the cock often takes the initiative in this exploratory behaviour.

Having found an attractive site he will crouch down, scratching with his feet and poking about with his beak. This is similar to the behaviour found in other species, particularly among waders, where the cocks make token nest-scrapes and try to attract the hens to them. Strangely we have also noted it in unfledged owlets at around two months of age, indicating its innate origins.

Sometimes the cock Barn Owl will call the hen to him by purring (Call 2), at the same time moving about the nest site stamping his feet. Though this may form a slight depression for the eggs, it is more symbolic (ritualised, in ornithological language) than functional; copulation almost always follows. The hen is often sufficiently interested to join the cock without any invitation and the two crouch and shuffle about the site with lowered wings, the hen snoring and sometimes tongue-clicking. We have no record of the hen scratching out a nest-hollow.

Copulation occurs every few minutes whenever the birds are active at this stage, in many instances without prior display. The hen simply begins to snore more quickly and quietly and lowers her body, whereupon the cock mounts, balancing with widely spread wings and by holding her nape feathers in his bill, uttering a special staccato squeaking note (Call 14) reserved for the occasion; some cocks also utter a few snores. The cock's copulatory movements have a somewhat mammalian character, for every two or three seconds he makes convulsive thrusts accompanied by bursts of louder squeaks. Meanwhile the hen's snores increase in volume until at the moment of cloacal contact they are often quite frenzied. The act is quite lengthy, lasting from ten to twenty seconds, and upon completion certain cocks habitually give one or two loud screeches; such individuals may also screech as a preliminary to copulation. At times the cock mounts without any invitation from the hen whatsoever, but she seems to welcome his attentions none the less. Upon dismounting, the cock often begins to doze while the hen preens him, concentrating on his underparts and head. Strangely, the cock will sometimes crouch in front of the hen before copulation, as if inviting her to mount, and it is perhaps relevant to mention that it is by no means unusual, when two cocks are kept together in captivity without a hen, for one of the birds to assume a passive, female role.

Copulation, however, is not in itself sufficient to induce the hen to lay: as already mentioned, she must also obtain a surfeit of food. Our aviary birds are deliberately given large amounts of food and February clutches are by no means unusual. The date for the first egg of one pair in the years 1973–79 were: 19th March, 28th February, 14th February, 19th February, 25th February, 27th February and 25th February – a remarkably consistent record and dates which were early enough to allow them to produce two broods annually in six of these years and three in one year (1976). In the wild, however, the hen's requirements have to be met almost entirely by the cock because of her tendency to remain at the nest-site at this time. He is only able to do this satisfactorily if he can catch sufficient prey, and bad weather or a shortage of prey will prevent nesting activities from proceeding further. This may well explain the delay that normally occurs between the commencement of courtship and the actual production of eggs, for normally in February, March and even early April the cock cannot bring in sufficient food to trigger off laying without expending an inordinate amount of energy.

Eventually, at around one month before the laying of the first egg, the cock is able to bring in enough food and to do so regularly.

Although food presentation sometimes occurs without prior display the cock normally arrives with a self-advertising chirrup. On hearing this the hen commences an excited snoring and then changes to her characteristic high-pitched purr. If she is perched on a beam away from a possible nest site she will often fly to some dark place before starting to purr, in order to call the cock to her. The cock then approaches, uttering little twittering chirrups or the food-offering call (Call 15), and offers her the prey. She takes it and then, holding it in her bill, crouches down to invite the cock to mount. He does so immediately and copulation occurs. When the act is completed the hen eats the prey unless her hunger has already been satisfied, in which case it may be left at the nest – or courtship-site. Such a performance can be expected to occur two or three times every evening and in his enthusiasm the cock often brings in far more prey than the hen can dispose of, the unwanted offerings eventually rotting where they lie. In the dry atmosphere of a barn the prey may sometimes mummify and thus provide lasting evidence of the owls' activities. This behaviour is similar to that of the Hen Harrier, for the late Eddie Balfour noted that copulation followed almost every food presentation by the cock of this species until the sexual urge was subordinated by that of brooding (in Watson 1977).

Tongue-clicking, bill-fencing and cheek-rubbing are regular and important features of Barn Owl courtship and they are extremely common amongst the owlets once they become active. In this behaviour the two birds run towards each other with lowered heads. They touch bills and make rapid fencing movements which are momentarily concentrated on the bill area before becoming wider to take in the face as well; tongue-clicks, twitters and snores are uttered at the same time. After intensive study of this behaviour, both in adults and owlets, we believe that it represents a form of *ritualised feeding*. The circumstances in which it occurs – courtship, intense excitement and the greeting of incoming owls – are all occasions when latent aggression can spring to the surface, and this appeasement gesture undoubtedly serves to reduce that possibility.

Cheek-rubbing often develops into mutual preening and this activity is a frequent occurrence between mated pairs at all times of the year. In one pair it was the hen (as with domestic pigeons) that usually took the active part in mutual preening, the smaller cock snuggling up to his mate and almost creeping under her in an apparently servile manner. Cock Barn Owls, in general, frequently give this impression of inferiority when in the company of their larger, more robustly built mates, especially when the hens utter their immensely powerful hoarse screeches, but the cocks too can be impressive when in noisy pursuit of rival males that have invaded their territories.

As the weeks pass the pair show increasing interest in one particular nest site and the hen begins to spend a lot of time there, sometimes accompanied by the cock. She becomes so tied to it, in fact, that she is occasionally reluctant to leave even in the face of extreme disturbance, and this can delude the observer into thinking that she is already incubating. As a consequence of all this time spent at the nest, pellets begin to accumulate and their fragmented remains help to form a soft base for the eggs to lie on when they are laid. Sometimes, however, the hen will unexpectedly lay her eggs in a site to which she has previously paid little attention.

Before leaving the subject of courtship behaviour we feel obliged to mention a display described by Hosking & Smith (1943) which has been re-quoted in several books. The incident occurred on 3rd June in a Norfolk barn where the observers were carrying out photography at a nest containing four young, the largest of which was 13 days old. The cock entered the barn followed closely by the hen; neither of the birds brought in prey. After the cock had paid a fleeting visit to the nest he joined the hen on a beam, the two perching side by side about 30 cm apart facing the observers: 'There followed a certain amount of beak-snapping, presumably by both birds, and then the cock slowly extended his head and neck upwards until the latter was fully extended, when the neck and throat feathers were puffed up to a remarkable degree. His beak was wide open and his head thrown well backwards. He then proceeded to sway his head from side to side and then to roll it round in curious snake-like motions. Meanwhile the hen bird swayed in sympathy and emitted a snoring note, well described by the Handbook's phrase "a purring chirrup". She then moved sideways toward the cock, who lowered his head and both birds proceeded to rub "cheeks" together. This appeared to involve the use of the feathers at the edge of the facial discs. The two birds then clicked their bills one against the other, and then the cock seized the female's neck widely in his bill and swayed her from side to side, the hen meanwhile purring intermittently. After this both birds stood quietly together for a moment and then left to commence hunting. This display took about ten minutes to complete'.

This account has puzzled us for some time because, despite all our observations taken over many years, neither we nor D. Scott, who has also witnessed Barn Owl courtship on numerous occasions, have ever observed owls extend their necks and wave their heads with wide open beak in the manner described – unless about to eject a pellet. The seizing of the hen's neck feathers can perhaps be explained as an abortive attempt at copulation, but the posturing with thickened neck and open bill is most difficult to reconcile with any courtship activity known to us. It must be concluded, therefore, if this behaviour was not a prelude to pellet egestion, that Hosking and Smith were fortunate in seeing a display not hitherto recorded.

NEST SITES

As its name suggests, the Barn Owl is often associated with man-made structures such as barns, derelict houses, ruins, outhouses and even occupied premises, where quiet and secluded nest sites are available. However, in some areas, especially in the Midlands and in the south and east of England, holes in trees also figure prominently. Where it occupies man-made structures the attraction is the site and not the presence of Man as is sometimes implied, the owl nesting *despite* human presence rather than because of it. It is interesting to compare our Table 7 figures, based on an analysis of 186 nests, with those of Blaker (1933) who analysed no less than 915 records obtained in 1932 alone – a reflection of the relative abundance of the Barn Owl in Blaker's day perhaps.

TABLE 7: *Relative importance of various Barn Owl nest sites in Britain*

A. *Bunn, Warburton and Wilson*	%
Barns (including indoor haystacks and owl boxes in barns)	33·32
Hollow trees	31·72
Old houses	12·90
Outbuildings	10·22
Cliffs	3·23
Holes in walls, etc	2·69
Thatched roofs	1·61
Inhabited houses	1·61
Haystacks in the open	1·08
Dovecotes	0·54
Granaries	0·54
Disused hop kilns	0·54

B. *Blaker*	
In holes in hollow trees, chiefly Oak and Elm, but including also Beech, Ash, Willow, Sycamore, Walnut, Apple, Horse Chestnut, Spanish Chestnut and Scots Fir	42·96
In barns, outhouses and farm buildings, on rafters, piles of hay, in boxes and baskets	33·66
In holes in walls, ruins, church towers, chimneys, roofs of houses	13·22
In owl boxes and dovecotes, with and without doves as well	6·01
In holes in rocks, in cliffs, quarries, mines, etc	2·84
In trees, but not in holes, chiefly Yew	1·31

Although our site descriptions differ somewhat from those of Blaker, it can be seen that the Barn Owl is by no means confined to barns; in fact hollow trees are equally or more important, and *The Atlas of Breeding Birds in Britain and Ireland* states that 39% of nests recorded on 282 nest record cards were situated in old trees, though these were isolated rather than in dense woodland. In the north-west of England, where the main part of our fieldwork has taken place, hollow trees are rarely used as nest sites because trees with suitable cavities are far from common. Table 8 gives details of 221 tree nest-sites recorded on BTO nest record cards, and Table 9 the nest position of 140 of these (after Glue, in prep.).

As can be seen, large decaying trees are of great importance and the recent loss of English Elms *Ulmus procera* in Britain due to Dutch Elm Disease, is

TABLE 8: *Tree nest sites of 221 Barn Owls* Tyto alba. *(After Glue, in prep.)*

	No. of nests	Height of nest (m)					not known	Average nest height (m)
		0·3–1·5	1·8–3·0	3·4–6·1	6·4–9·1	9·4–125·2		
Elm *Ulmus*	69	1	11	33	19	4	1	5·4
Oak *Quercus*	53	1	16	26	5	0	5	4·2
Ash *Fraxinus excelsior*	37	3	11	20	1	0	1	3·7
Tree spp. (unidentified)	37	1	11	19	3	0	3	3·7
*Other spp.	25	1	4	16	2	0	2	4·8
TOTALS	221	7	53	114	30	5	12	4·6

*Other species: Lime *Tilia cordata* 7, Beech *Fagus sylvatica* 6, Willow *Salix* 2, Poplar *Populus* 2, Sycamore *Acer pseudoplatanus* 2, Walnut *Juglans regia* 2, Alder *Alnus glutinosa* 1, Scots Pine *Pinus sylvestris* 1, Horse Chestnut *Aesculus hippocastanum* 1, Yew *Taxus baccata* 1.

certain to have a serious effect on Barn Owl numbers where this tree was the dominant species in open countryside (mainly the Midlands, East Anglia and the South-west).

It is of interest that some of Blaker's tree nests were said to be in woods. Although no details are given, we are inclined to suspect that they were actually on the edges of woodland, for the Barn Owl rarely ventures far into trees unless there are rides along which it can fly.

It will also be noticed that church towers figure in Blaker's list, but are absent in that of the authors. In the past this site was frequently adopted and in the Netherlands led to its being known as the Church Owl (*Tyto alba guttata* being the sub-species involved); the fact that overgrown churchyards were likely to be well populated by small mammals was no doubt an added

TABLE 9: *Position of nest in 140 trees occupied by Barn Owls* Tyto alba. *(After Glue, in prep.)*

Position of nest	No of nests	%
Main trunk – cleft or cavity	70	50·0
Snapped-off trunk or decaying stump – vertical chamber	27	19·3
Pollarded tree – cavity or branch cluster	21	15·0
Large hollow branch – split or cavity	14	10·0
Wooden nest-box	6	4·3
Tree bole – hollow near ground	2	1·4
TOTALS	140	100·0

attraction. The decline of this nest site can probably be linked with the increasing numbers of such species as the Jackdaw, Feral Pigeon, Starling and House Sparrow, for these, too, are partial to nesting in church towers and in the interests of hygiene are frequently kept out by blocking up the access points with chicken wire. This, of course, also effectively excludes the Barn Owl.

Of some interest is Blaker's remark that dovecotes were often taken over by owls irrespective of whether or not they were occupied. It is very likely that this often brought the wrath of the owner down upon them – though we have heard of one understanding farmer who found alternative accommodation for his fantail pigeons when their cote was adopted by a pair of Barn Owls!

When using deserted houses, a favourite position for the nest is in the open space between two joists of a ceiling. In the case of a groundfloor ceiling the owls can frequently find a cavity between what remains of the ceiling and the floorboards immediately above it, while in the case of an upstairs room there will be a suitable crevice for them between the ceiling and the roof slates. Recesses in chimneys are also commonly used. Should such enclosed sites be unavailable, however, Barn Owls are not averse to nesting unhidden between the joists supporting a groundfloor ceiling, where the floorboards above have been removed, or even openly on the floor. In North America few suitable ruins exist and such nest sites are uncommon. Significantly, the habit of nesting in buildings is more frequent in the highly populated East than elsewhere in North America, which suggests that it is more a case of lack of opportunity rather than differing behaviour in *T. a. pratincola* that dictates the choice of nest site in that country.

The authors have noticed that hay seems to be attractive to Barn Owls, both as nest sites and as cover at roosts, because the birds can hide amongst the bales. Where farms possess several barns it is usually found that the one containing hay also holds the owls, and sometimes this is strikingly illustrated as the birds move from barn to barn according to the amount of hay present. Sadly, this liking for hay often works against them, for they tend to nest amongst the bales with the result that when these are removed the eggs are inadvertently destroyed. Often a farmer is completely unaware of the owls' presence and sometimes the owlets come to grief in the same way. It may be, however, that hay also has a survival value for the species in hard winter weather, both for its insulating properties and as a harbour for prey.

Unfortunately, modern prefabricated barns are of little use to owls because they often have neither access points nor nest sites – a far cry from the days when some barns were specially provided with owl windows. We feel certain that this is one of the main factors in the recent decline of the species and D. Scott (pers. comm.) believes that for this reason the proportion of hollow trees used as nest sites, as opposed to buildings, has been increasing for some time in his study area – in Lincolnshire and Nottinghamshire.

For a variety of reasons we are of the opinion that the Barn Owl was once a cliff-dweller, and a scrutiny of Table 7 reveals that most of the present-day man-made sites can be interpreted as no more than facsimiles of cliff-ledges, crevices and caves. This is not unique to the Barn Owl and can be equally said of such species as the Kestrel, Jackdaw, Swallow, Swift and House

Martin. The Swallow in particular *must* have been a denizen of caves in the past, for no other natural site could provide the sort of situation it needs in which to build its nest. In Britain, some Barn Owls still nest on cliffs, especially sea cliffs in Wales and Scotland; Macpherson (1892) mentions pairs which nested in clefts in the red sandstone cliffs above the River Eden in Westmorland and Coombes (1933) quotes instances of owls breeding in remote cliffs in the Lake District at heights between 300 m and 450 m. Stokoe (1962) records the species breeding in rocky gullies and crags up to 370 m in the Lakeland fells while Dr D. A. Ratcliffe informs us that during his Peregrine survey he found Barn Owls occupying probable nest sites in rock crevices close to falcon eyries in south-west Scotland in April 1951, 1964 and 1972; and that in August 1950 he discovered a nest containing two young in a secluded tree-grown rocky glen in Roxburghshire.

The North American Barn Owl *T. a. pratincola*, particularly in the western States and Mexico, frequently nests in the sides of gullies, and although many natural cavities exist it has been found that the Barn Owl will sometimes excavate a hole when necessary, using its feet to scratch out a tunnel over a metre long, ending in an elliptical chamber measuring about 60 cm (Behle 1941, Martin 1973).

We list below some of the more unusual nest sites known to us personally and others communicated to us by reliable fellow naturalists or documented in the literature:

(a)   In the depression where a tree forked into two stout branches from the main trunk (2 cases).

(b)   In the old nests of other birds, e.g. a Woodpigeon's nest in an Ivy-covered tree (S. Craig, pers. comm.); two Carrion Crows' nests, one in a tall Hawthorn and another in the top of a Pine tree (D. Scott, pers. comm.), and in the case of *T. a. affinis*, the nest of a Hammerhead Stork in Africa (Kolbe 1946).

(c)   In the large open chimney of a house – for two seasons despite the fact that the chimney was in constant use (Henwood 1954)!

(d)   In a large hollow at the foot of the trunk of an old Oak in Derbyshire (Kirkman & Jourdain 1938).

(e)   On the spiral stone steps of an old well 9 m below ground level (J. Nuttall, pers. comm.).

(f)   Under tree roots on the Isle of Islay; and in a hole in the ground on the same island (both records given to us by C. G. Booth).

(g)   In the banks of the River Mite in Cumbria, the site being an abandoned Otter holt.

Several other species share a liking for similar nest sites to the Barn Owl and sometimes there is competition. Kestrels are frequently found nesting in close proximity to Barn Owls and when this occurs the unfortunate owls if caught out in the daylight hours, are usually subjected to extremely vicious and persistent attacks. The ferocity of such attacks varies from Kestrel to Kestrel but, surprisingly, when inside the buildings they seem to ignore each other and both species usually manage to rear their young successfully. In one case the nests were little more than a metre apart, yet both survived. Similarly, a Little Owl was successful only two metres from a Barn Owl nest

TABLE 10: *Altitudinal distribution of 390 Barn Owl* Tyto alba *nests in Britain. (After Glue, in prep.)*

Altitude in metres (feet)	No. of nests	%
0–61 (0–200)	212	54·3
61–122 (201–400)	83	21·3
122–183 (401–600)	60	15·4
183–244 (601–800)	23	5·9
244–305 (801–1000)	9	2·3
305–381 (1001–1250)	3	0·8
TOTALS	390	100·0

in which a healthy brood was reared. Jackdaws are commonly found nesting in the same building as Barn Owls and in such cases the hen owl must be continually on her guard, for of course corvids are by no means the safest of neighbours where eggs or young birds are concerned. It is in these circumstances that the importance of the hen's continual presence at the nest in the early stages can be fully appreciated; by the time she begins to leave it to hunt for food the owlets have grown and are much less vulnerable. Of the nest histories examined, one nest was predated by Jackdaws and another by Ravens (one of the cliff nests).

In one case where Kestrels and Barn Owls were in direct competition for a nest site in Norfolk there was an interesting sequence of events. The birds were nesting in an old cattle shed which had been used by the owls for several years, the nest site being a ledge approximately 2·5 m above the floor. In mid-May an inspection was made and three young Kestrels were found huddled together directly below the ledge. On the ledge were four young owls – and some broken eggs of the Kestrel. It would appear that the Kestrels had intended to nest on the ledge until the Barn Owls evicted them. The Kestrels must then have set up home below and eventually the young Kestrels and owlets were seen on the wing after being successfully reared.

Glue (in prep.) has produced tables showing regional distribution of 571 BTO nest record cards on a county basis and the numbers of nests found in each. He has also quantified the breeding habitats of 422 Barn Owls in Britain as listed by these cards. After careful consideration we have avoided the temptation to quote these data as we feel that they reflect observer coverage rather than a true picture of Barn Owl breeding habitats. What *is* shown is the Barn Owl's ability to breed in virtually any habitat apart from urban areas, *provided suitable nest sites are available*. Table 10, however, shows that altitude *is* important and reveals that the Barn Owl, although highly adaptable, is basically a lowland bird.

THE EGGS

The eggs of the Barn Owl are white, without gloss, and are less rounded and more elliptical than those of most other owls; the clutch quickly becomes discoloured in the grimy conditions of the nest. They are smaller than might be expected: *The Handbook* gives the average size of 100 British *T. a. alba* eggs as 39·74 × 31·57 mm, maximum sizes 45·0 × 33·4 mm and 39·0 × 33·5 mm, minimum sizes 36·2 × 31·2 mm and 42·5 × 29·1 mm. Size varies slightly amongst the sub-species and Haverschmidt (1962) gives an average size of 41·3 × 33·6 mm for 18 *T.a. hellmayri* eggs. For comparison the average size of a hundred eggs of the Tawny Owl in Britain, quoted in *The Handbook*, was 46·69 × 39·06 mm.

Barn Owls make no attempt at nest building but, as was mentioned earlier, the pre-nesting behaviour of the adults, in which they spend much time at the future nest site, tends to produce a layer of fragmented pellets which incidentally gives a reasonably soft bed for the eggs. Wallace (1948) suggests that these pellets are deliberately chewed to form nest material but this does not appear to have been witnessed. The debris further accumulates as breeding continues and by the time the owlets leave the nest a thick layer has formed.

It is in this debris that a small moth lives out its life cycle, the same moth that is the curse of housewives and is known in the vernacular as the 'clothes moth'. In fact several species have been recorded in pellet samples but the most usual is *Monopsis rusticella*. The larvae of these moths are easily recognised by their off-white bodies and brown heads. It has been suggested that the nests of owls, etc, are the original home of this domestic pest, so pellet analysts beware! The debris also provides a home for many other creatures including a whole variety of mite species (*Acarina*), and occasionally one finds a parasitic Nematode worm that has been regurgitated with a pellet.

The eggs are usually laid at two- to three-day intervals, but Kirkman & Jourdain (1938) record cases where they have been laid in pairs with about a week between each pair; the gap between two of a pair is not stated. We have no experience of this but have known of a few cases where the interval between eggs exceeded three days and Pickwell (1948) quotes a seven day gap between two *T.a. pratincola* owlets in a clutch of six; the rest of the clutch showed the normal two-day intervals.

Because the hen begins to incubate immediately the first egg is laid, the young hatch at corresponding intervals and this causes a great discrepancy in their size – so great in fact that the effect is startling when first seen. It is difficult to conceive that the youngest of the brood can possibly survive when its appearance is compared with that of the first-hatched, for when unusually large broods are involved there can be over two weeks' difference in their ages.

CLUTCH SIZE

The size of the clutch is extremely variable, every number from two to eleven having been recorded. Lack (1947) states that the clutch size of owls increases with latitude, but this is certainly not the case with the Barn Owl, the decisive factor in this species being the availability of prey, a factor which Lack also mentions as pertinent. Clutches of five are the more common in

TABLE 11: *Clutch sizes of 178 Barn Owl* T. a. alba *nests in Britain. (After Glue, in prep.)*

No. of eggs	1	2	3	4	5	6	7	8	9	10
No. of nests	0	10	18	53	60	20	12	3	2	0
Expressed as %	0	5·6	10·1	29·8	33·7	11·2	6·7	1·7	1·1	0

Average clutch size = 4·68

Britain, and Table 11 gives the size of the clutches as a percentage of a sample analysed by D. E. Glue (in prep.) from BTO nest-record cards and British Museum records.

There is no evidence that young hens lay smaller clutches than mature birds and Barn Owls of either sex are capable of breeding at under twelve months of age. This latter ability was confirmed when a captive pair owned by a correspondent, J. Trollope, produced seven eggs; the cock bird was only nine months old at the time and the hen but six months. Breeding at under 12 months of age has also been noted in *T.a. guttata* (Schneider 1937), and Stewart (1952) records one case of *T.a. pratincola* breeding 10 months after being ringed as a nestling. However, the most conclusive proof of the hen's fecundity was obtained from one of our own birds ringed as a nestling in 1971 which in 1972 laid a total of 16 eggs in three unsuccessful clutches. The failure of this bird may well indicate that as with many other first-time breeders (both avian and mammalian), although normal numbers of young are produced, fewer are reared successfully than is the case with older, more experienced pairs. Not only will the female's behaviour at the nest affect the outcome, but also the parents' ability to catch ample prey to rear the brood should they hatch. Replacement clutches occur fairly frequently when a previous clutch has failed, and the first egg may be laid as quickly as six days after the first clutch has been abandoned.

The mistake is sometimes made of assessing the full clutch size from the number of young present in the nest. However, a comparison of Table 11 and Table 12 shows how unreliable such estimates are likely to be (Glue, in prep.).

TABLE 12: *Brood sizes in 109 Barn Owl* T. a. alba *nests in Britain. (After Glue, in prep.)*

Brood size	1	2	3	4	5	6	7
No. of nests	8	37	32	23	8	1	0
Expressed as %	7·3	33·9	29·4	21·1	7·3	0·9	0

Average brood size = 2·96

INCUBATION

The Handbook gives the incubation period of the Barn Owl as 32–34 days (information supplied by R. H. Brown). However, Hosking & Newberry (1945) were surprised to record a period of only 30 days in one case. Kirkman & Jourdain (1938) give 30–31 days and D. Scott (pers. comm.) has three records of 30 days and one of 29 days. Thus we are faced with a reported incubation period varying from 29–34 days. Is this an accurate picture?

The solving of such a seemingly simple problem is apt to appear easier than it is. In order to know the date of laying the hen must be flushed from the nest every day (at the stage when she is most likely to desert), subjecting her to undue pressure, especially as the Barn Owl is inclined to be an extremely 'tight' sitter. And there will be additional disturbance after the fourth week of incubation in order to ascertain the hatching date. Even these drastic measures do not give an entirely accurate answer unless the time of day of laying and hatching is known. Without it there may conceivably be a final error of as much as two days, and it is probably this time-lapse which has produced such a wide disparity of records. In the light of this disturbance factor and the associated high risk of desertion (Otteni et al (1972) found 23% of nests were deserted after observer disturbance during incubation) it is little wonder that field-workers with any regard for their subjects are loath to attempt a detailed check, and both Baudvin (1975) and ourselves have found this a hindrance in assessing the incubation period with accuracy. However, by examining a nest whenever the hen left to defecate we were able to secure a record as accurate as it is possible to obtain with wild birds, of 31 days. We have several other observations that suggest the incubation period to be 30–31 days and this is confirmed by many accurate records we have obtained from captive birds. There may, however, be occasional variations outside these limits. The picture appears to be the same amongst other races of the Barn Owl, for Wilson (1970) gives 31 days for *T.a. affinis* in Rhodesia, both Wallace (1948) and Nice (1954) about 30 days for *T.a. pratincola* in America, and Honer (1963) 30 days for *T.a. guttata* in the Netherlands.

At some nests which we have studied it was noticeable that the persistent snoring of the hens became quieter when the first eggs were laid. The cocks, too, appeared more subdued; and with one captive male, the preliminary screeching that it had indulged in before copulation, was dispensed with, as was the post-copulatory screech, although copulation continued.

Once incubation commences, the hen leaves the nest only at long intervals of about eight hours and this inactivity increases her weight. This is only temporary and, as might be expected, the extra weight is quickly lost as soon as she starts to hunt actively again. When the hen does leave the nest she dashes about, no doubt relieving pent up energy. She often preens her ruffled plumage and, most important of all, defecates before returning to the nest after five to ten minutes. The droppings of an incubating hen are copious and provide a useful clue that the eggs have been laid. The large brood-patch in the feathers of the underparts can sometimes be seen quite clearly when the hen is off the nest at this stage, particularly when she is perched at a higher level than the observer. It is generally accepted that only the hen Barn Owl incubates but in 1972 we made a remarkable observation that casts some doubt about this. The first egg of a second brood had been laid two days previously, but the hen had left the nest and joined the cock on a favourite perch. One of the owlets from the first brood then flew to the cock who immediately dropped down to the nest. He began to nuzzle the egg with either his beak or the wedge of feathers down the centre of the disk and then carefully pushed it under him, showing every intention of settling down to incubate. Unfortunately, at this moment the hen came down beside him and before he could lower his body further she pushed him aside and sat on the egg. We had a further surprise in 1973 when a captive male was seen incubating on no less than six occasions, on two of which both cock and hen were sitting side by side, each with two eggs under it. After the first ten days this was not observed again. Baudvin (1975), who worked at nests where some pairs comprised mixed *T.a. alba* and *T.a. guttata*, which enabled positive recognition of the individuals, also mentions that the cock sometimes incubates for a brief time and he records a cock covering the owlets on one occasion. Merrian (1896) observed a Barn Owl *T.a. pratincola* actually relieve its incubating mate at a tree cavity nest site in southern California, so there can be little doubt from all these reports that some cocks will incubate on occasions. However, that this is abnormal behaviour is shown by the fact that, unlike the hen, the cock does not develop a brood-patch.

It has already been mentioned that the hen sits quite tightly even before the eggs are laid and this pattern continues throughout incubation. Indeed by the time the eggs are due to hatch she will sometimes prove almost impossible to flush and may be caught if the observer is unscrupulous enough to do this. Nevertheless, such tight-sitting must save many a nest from discovery; though it is a surprising feature when one considers how readily Barn Owls desert their roosts outside the breeding season, after even a minimum amount of human disturbance. However, it should not be assumed that the hen's behaviour indicates that she is unaffected by the close proximity of danger; on the contrary, by staying on the nest she subjects herself to far more stress than if she were to leave at once.

Hens that have been flushed in the early stages of incubation tend to fly off silently and leave the vicinity, but later, when the eggs are near to hatching, their parental fervour increases and they are more likely to sit nearby uttering agitated warning screams. Once this stage is reached, and during much of the subsequent nest history, the same call is used a great deal by anxious hens and may sometimes change to the mobbing note or anxiety call. The cock is much less vocal and often leaves silently without warning the hen of the imminent danger. The probable reason for this is to avoid drawing attention to the nest site. Similarly it has been noted that Barn Owls often use an entrance to the nest site other than the obvious one to human eyes.

When the cock leaves to go hunting the hen stops snoring and waits silently until she hears the quiet chirrups (or occasionally subdued screeches) that announce his return. Some cocks will call long before they arrive with prey and when working in a hide we have often been alerted by the hen's response although we have heard nothing. The hen's response is the begging snore, or sometimes purring, to encourage him to bring in the prey he is normally carrying. However, with courtship over the cock's ardour abates somewhat and he brings only enough food during incubation for the hen's immediate needs, and it is unusual to find uneaten prey in the nest at this stage.

The hen changes her position frequently while incubating and sometimes rises slightly and turns the eggs by reaching beneath her body with her bill and the wedge of facial bristles. Her restlessness increases as hatching time draws near and the owlet begins to call from inside the first-laid egg. If the observer is working from a hide at close quarters he will be able to hear her uttering a soft twittering note in response. Though somewhat anthropomorphic, perhaps, it is impossible to associate this call with anything other than maternal affection, for the contented tone of it is unmistakable. It is in fact a soft version of the food-offering call which the hen uses constantly when the owlets hatch and she is offering them food.

In our experience, even when the clutch is complete, copulation continues at all nests where there is room for the cock to mount. Before he leaves for his first hunting trip of the evening he commonly pays a social call to the incubating hen and where copulation is possible it sometimes takes place at this time; certainly it occurs regularly whenever he returns with prey.

BROOD SIZE AND FLEDGING SUCCESS

BTO nest-record cards show conclusively that it is rare for more than four young to be reared successfully in Britain.

In Table 13 David Glue (in prep.) illustrates the outcome of 115 completed clutches and it can be clearly seen that there is a noticeable drop in the number of broods which achieve 100% fledging success when the clutch exceeds three eggs, and this drop becomes severe in clutches of five or over. Indeed, in only one case did the owls succeed in rearing more than five young, while no less than 27% of clutches failed completely.

TABLE 13: *Outcome of 115 completed clutches of Barn Owl* Tyto alba *in Britain. (After Glue, in prep.)*

Clutch size	Number of clutches	Failed to hatch or fledge	Brood size (No. successfully leaving nest)							100% fledged
			1	2	3	4	5	6	7	
1	0	0	**0**	0	0	0	0	0	0	0
2	3	0	2	**1**	0	0	0	0	0	33·3
3	12	4	1	3	**4**	0	0	0	0	33·3
4	36	6	4	7	9	**10**	0	0	0	27·8
5	40	12	4	5	8	6	**5**	0	0	12·5
6	15	6	0	1	1	2	4	**1**	0	6·7
7	6	1	0	1	0	3	1	0	**0**	0
8	2	1	0	0	0	1	0	0	0	0
9	1	1	0	0	0	0	0	0	0	0
TOTALS	115	31	11	18	22	22	10	1	0	

TABLE 14: *Fledging success during 4 years of Barn Owl breeding on Côte d'Or, France. (Mixed* T. a. alba *and* T. a. guttata.*) (After Baudvin 1975)*

Year	State of M. arvalis population	No. of nests	No. of young reared to ringing age	Average no. of young per nest
1971	high	36	22 known	(results not known) for 13 nests
1972	peak population	157	572	3·6
1973	'crash' year	6	11	1·8
1974*	high peak	258	1161	4·5

*Larger area surveyed than in 1972

As might be expected, fledging success is closely linked with prey abundance and this is an important factor in the survival of owlets. Baudvin (loc. cit.) felt that weather conditions might affect the numbers of young reared but of course both these factors are interwoven in most years and should not be considered in isolation. Otteni et al (1972) suggest that an increase or decrease in the population of a *single* prey species has no immediate effect on Barn Owl nesting density or success, but that the productivity of the Barn Owl population is greatly reduced when the *overall* small mammal population decreases in availability to a point where the owls depend on birds for 32% or more of their food. However, contrary to Otteni's hypothesis, the effect of a prey 'crash' will depend on the extent to which the individual owls rely on a single species as prey. Where alternative small mammals are readily available the owls will undoubtedly take them (see Chapter 4), but in the case of Barn Owls dependent upon *Microtus* the effect of a 'crash' can be catastrophic in both the number of nests and the number of young reared. Baudvin, for instance, found enormous differences in the four years of his study on the Côte d'Or. It goes without saying that the variations were entirely linked with the relative numbers of voles during the years in question – see Table 14.

Similarly, Otteni et al, working with *T.a. pratincola* in southern Texas, found that their birds reared 1·5 times more young per pair in years of prey abundance than in years of limited prey populations. There were 12·2 breeding pairs in their study area between 1965 and 1970 until the small mammal population declined after the severe winter of 1969/70. In 1970, 12 pairs attempted to breed but reared markedly fewer fledged young (92% down on 1969). The only owlets to fledge were fed 91% on Red-winged Blackbirds, while two young abandoned at five weeks old were being fed 72% on blackbirds. An even lower rodent population was recorded in the winter and spring of 1970/71 and in 1971 only five pairs bred, a 58% drop on 1970. Completed clutches were 50% lower. Fred N. Gallup (in Henny 1969) found that brood sizes in southern California were highly variable, ranging from 4·71 in 1951 to 2·75 in 1961. All these cases reflect the typically erratic pattern of Barn Owl breeding biology.

Baudvin showed that in France the young from large broods had just as much chance of fledging successfully as those from smaller broods. Their nest-weight was virtually the same and prey left at the nest was just as abundant in large broods as small – a logical conclusion given the above facts.

THE OWLETS

Before describing the development of the young it must be pointed out that there is some variation between broods and also among individuals of the same brood. Development is directly related to the amount of food received, which in turn is dependent on such factors as prey densities, local weather conditions and the enthusiasm of the adults in hunting. Also, we have noted that owlets in open nests develop faster than those in confined spaces (i.e. holes in trees and walls, etc) where room for exercise is severely limited.

The time taken for a young Barn Owl to break clear of the egg is quite short: in most cases the first hole appears in the egg in the evening and the chick hatches in the early hours of the next morning. We have also recorded afternoon hatching. On the day before hatching the owlet can be heard calling lustily from inside the egg and it is to this stimulus that the hen owl responds with the quiet food-offering call already described. The strength of the hen's maternal instinct is beautifully illustrated by Dr Paul Bühler (1970) who observed a hand-reared hen actually helping the owlets to hatch by breaking off fragments of shell with her beak and removing shreds of membrane and larger pieces of shell from the young birds. After the owlet had fought free she plucked off the remains of the embryonic sac and other remaining material and nibbled the young bird clean. Small pieces of shell and the embryonic sac were swallowed immediately, but larger pieces of shell were either left at the nest or held in one foot, broken up and eaten. The magnificent photographs he took of this remarkable event are unique and we greatly envy him his good fortune in witnessing such interesting behaviour at close quarters. Hatching help has also been recorded in the Falconiformes (Accipiterinae), Gruiformes (Gruidae and Rallidae), Charidriformes (Recurvirostridae), Passeriformes (Corvidae and Mimidae), and as well as Tytonidae in the Strigiformes, probably the Striginae. It has sometimes appeared to us that the cock, too, is aware of the imminent hatching of the young, for at some nests we have noticed a definite increase in activity on his part at this juncture.

The newly hatched owlet weighs about 20 g in the case of *T.a. alba* (Pickwell (1948) recorded 17·9–21·2 g for *T.a. pratincola*) and can only be described as ugly. Large-headed, pot-bellied, weak-legged and only 50 mm long, it lies helplessly on the nest debris unable to raise itself. Its eyes are firmly closed, making bulbous lumps on the head and, though it is moderately clad in short, greyish-white down on its upperparts, the pink skin can be clearly seen. There are bare patches on the sides of the neck and back of the tarsus, though the front of the tarsus and toes are covered. The ivory-coloured bill bears the egg-tooth, used to break through the shell, and surprisingly this appendage does not normally scale off until the second down begins to appear at around 14 days (16 days for *T.a. pratincola* (Stewart 1952)). It is interesting to note that Hosking & Newberry (1945) record Short-eared Owls losing the egg-tooth at nine days, but of course this bird's development is much faster generally than that of the Barn Owl. Most other groups of birds shed the egg-tooth between the second and third day, but a long retention period seems to be the rule amongst owl species.

As soon as it is dry the owlet is capable of uttering faint snores. It also chitters complainingly if the hen is flushed from the nest, but as soon as she returns it feels the benefit of her warmth and falls silent again. We have never seen a newly hatched owlet fed and, since it is unusual to find prey lying in the nest at this stage, it seems probable that it does not need to eat until the second day.

The adults vary in their behaviour when dealing with the fragments of hatched egg shell. These are normally in two sections consisting of the separated halves and in most cases are pushed into the corners of the nest cavity, or to the periphery of the nest hollow where corners do not exist. However, a cock bird was once seen to leave the nest with what appeared to be a section of shell in his bill, and Trollope (1971) records a captive cock removing egg shells and broken eggs. At another nest we studied, the egg shells were simply dropped from the nest entrance and were found littered almost immediately beneath the nest itself. As this nest was inside a ruined farmhouse the shells clearly gave away its position and thus contradicted the supposed advantage of egg shell removal to avoid attention being drawn to the site. The egg shells were also removed or eaten at a nest at Great Harwood, Lancashire, as there was no trace of them in the nest site itself (a metal trunk) nor in the near vicinity. Infertile eggs normally remain in the nest until they are broken by the movements of the growing young or become buried in the accumulating debris. We have known several instances in which an unhatched egg was found intact in the nest after the owlets had flown.

By the second day the owlet is already larger and stronger. It begins to utter occasional begging snores and the chittering note is perceptively louder. The next owlet due to hatch cheeps in reply from inside the egg and this probably encourages the older chick to remain close to the clutch, so ensuring that it receives the benefit of the hen's warmth. The asynchronous hatching places the first owlet, and to a lesser degree the next to hatch, in an unusual position. In other nidicolous species, where most of the young hatch simultaneously, they are attracted by each other's warmth and movements, and naturally huddle together in the centre of the nest. Nidifugous young, on the other hand, are able to see and move to their parents whenever they wish to receive their attentions. But for the first of the Barn Owl chicks neither mechanism is possible and, since it is capable of moving about the nest to a limited extent, it may become separated from the eggs. Should this occur and the owlet be unable to find them again it will die from neglect, for the hen will ignore it even when it is only a few centimetres from the eggs. Such behaviour is in stark contrast to the motherly concern of Bühler's hen and is difficult to explain. Once, a 3-day-old owlet was found in this plight and on the very brink of death when it was only 23 cm from the incubating hen. It had somehow reached the outer limit of the nest area and had obviously been there for some time because it was very chilled and stiff and showed little sign of life. If the author concerned had not been able to warm its body in his hands before replacing it, it would certainly have succumbed within a very short time. It is remarkable, though far from unique in the bird world, that the hen will do nothing to help her young when such an incident occurs. Even when the owlets are much older a similar situation can arise: in the rush for food it sometimes happens that an owlet is dislodged from a high nest site when even if it survives the fall it will die from starvation and exposure despite its calls, for the adults concentrate their attentions wholly upon the young in the nest. Such accidents may be responsible for some of the reports of supposed cannibalism where an owlet has disappeared mysteriously and cannot be accounted for.

That the calling of an unhatched owlet can serve as a homing device to its future nest-mates is illustrated by an observation at one nest in which a disturbed hen left hurriedly and dislodged two chicks aged one and three days. They had been displaced approximately 25 cm from the three eggs and chittered plaintively. One of the unhatched young then began to reply whereupon both owlets started to make their way back to the nest – albeit laboriously – despite the fact that they were completely blind. *Owlet 1* was obviously stronger than *Owlet 2*, for its legs were developing and were thicker than those of the younger bird. It managed to creep to within 15 cm of the clutch before resting, and ultimately, after a protracted struggle, *Owlet 2* also reached this position and huddled up to its nest-mate. After a short rest the owlets again began to move and finally succeeded in making their way back to the eggs. The question arises, how did the displaced owlets distinguish between their sibling's call and that of the unhatched owlet which was in the position they wanted to reach? Possibly they 'homed-in' on the more contented note of the unhatched owlet as against the distress note they themselves were uttering.

By the third day (when the oldest owlet is two days old) the cock is evidently aware of his increased commitments because the first surplus prey offerings begin to appear at the nest. Large awkward items, such as birds and Brown Rats, are normally decapitated before being brought in, but the majority of the prey species are small – mainly Short-tailed Voles and Common Shrews in most British habitats. Of interest is the possibility that the cocks lack the instinct to break up food for the owlets because in the authors' experience this is done solely by the hens, though cocks will decapitate and partially pluck birds. At one nest it was observed that even at 22 days an owlet was incapable of dismembering a Starling brought in by the cock and tried in vain to swallow it whole. The cock did not help and all the owlets had to wait for the return of the hen before they could obtain food. One is forced to conclude that if some disaster befalls the female and the male is left in sole charge, the owlets will only be reared successfully if they are old enough to swallow their food whole, even if he does not desert them. It is interesting to note that Donald Watson (1977) discusses exactly the same situation in his monograph on the Hen Harrier while MacNally (1970) and Brown (1976) make the same comment regarding Golden Eagles and Sparrowhawks, respectively.

Throughout the period when the owlets' eyes remain closed the hen Barn Owl feeds them in a manner completely different from that of a diurnal bird of prey, and also from the way they are fed at a later stage of development. She straddles the chicks from the rear and lowers her head over them to offer dangling strips of meat, the close proximity of the adult's body guiding the young birds and enabling them to locate the proffered food long before their eyes begin to function. This is borne out by the fact that hand-reared owlets, when offered food from in front in their early weeks, will ignore it; but when one touches the bristles at the base of the beak after first dangling the meat over their heads, they take it instantly. This behaviour is probably shared by owls generally, for Hosking & Newberry (1945) include a photograph of a Short-eared Owl feeding its young in exactly this manner and they also record the Long-eared Owl and Tawny Owl using the same method. It is probable, too, that the Little Owl shares this behaviour, for hand-reared owlets of this species also will gape only when food is dangled over their heads and brushed against their facial bristles.

Copulation still continues at some nests, although the duration varies. For instance, two pairs stopped copulating eight days after the first egg hatched, while another was still doing so when the eldest owlet was 29 days old.

Once the eggs hatch, the hen usually stops her incessant snoring and only snores as the cock approaches with prey. It is interesting to speculate whether such behaviour coincides with the stage when the owlets themselves begin to call, for by snoring the owlets continue, and take over, the job of stimulating the cock to bring in food. It seems likely that there is some connection, because at a nest where the owlets stopped snoring with their usual vigour, the hen recommenced calling. After two or three days of severe gales another hungry hen began to snore raucously in unison with the owlets. The pressure now on the cock can be gauged from the behaviour of one hen which continued to snore demandingly after her hardworking mate had brought in six prey items in under thirty-five minutes!

At most nests with young, the cock commences to hunt in the early evening and can be seen carrying prey towards the nest site. Typically he flies back very directly and purposefully with the prey in one foot, and repetition of this behaviour is a sure sign of a family of owlets. The brooding hen behaves in much the same way as during incubation and only leaves the nest to defecate. However, at one nest in a derelict house, when the eldest owlet was only two days old, the cock arrived with repeated screeching calls and the hen responded by flying out to meet him. A great deal of screeching then ensued from both birds before the hen returned to the nest. She then began to utter repeated, subdued screeches which had a raucous quality quite distinct from the usual begging snores; the cock responded with similar calls and came into the house. The hen immediately began to utter a note which sounded like a combination of the purr and the begging snore, and at this the cock became highly excited and gave frenzied screeches as he entered the nest-hole. Quickly, amidst tremendous noise, copulation took place, with foot-stamping also being heard. Afterwards the hen's snores became shorter and quieter while the cock uttered a few quiet chirrups. The cock then left with a loud territorial screech and his mate lapsed into silence. The departing screeches of the cock are another variable factor, for some cocks hardly ever call in this way whereas others rarely leave silently once darkness falls. Whatever the situation, with one notable exception we have found the cocks far less inclined to use the screech after the first week of the owlets' hatching, and it is not normally heard again with regularity until courtship is renewed, usually in the eldest owlet's seventh week.

Despite what has been said about the mortality among small owlets, the hen Barn Owl is a most assiduous parent. She tends the young constantly, again and again uttering the soft food offering call (Call 15) as she encourages them to take food. This call clearly excites them and they respond with begging snores. To initiate a feed the hen pulls a tiny piece of flesh from the prey and offers it to any snoring owlet; should one show interest she will continue to feed it until it falls quiet. Her patience is a revelation as she repeatedly passes the morsels of food to the young birds – even when to the human observer it is obvious that they are satiated. As a result of her persistence such feeding sessions can be surprisingly lengthy and one hen took seventy minutes to dispose of a single Common Shrew! It is interesting to note that in the early days of the owlets' lives the hen continues to feed them throughout the daylight hours, and a captive hen was observed to feed a two-day-old chick at intervals of approximately one hour throughout the 24-hour period. Since virtually no roughage is given at this early age there was no pause for pellet egestion.

The comparative cleanliness of the nest during the first two weeks is striking, for although prey items are regularly found lying about the site and further pellets accumulate, there is usually no sign of adult or owlet faeces in the debris. Close observations have revealed that the hen is responsible for this nest hygiene; she cleans the immediate nest area by eating any faeces she finds and in this she displays remarkable thoroughness. Such behaviour is apparently shared by the Short-eared Owl because Hosking & Newberry (1945) have recorded a hen of this species cleaning its nest in like manner. Surprisingly, D. Scott (pers. comm.) has not observed the hen Long-eared Owl doing this, but of course the owlets of this species fledge at around three weeks against the seven to eight weeks of the Barn Owl, so the need for nest hygiene is less acute. Another possibility is that the Long-eared Owl droppings are voided over the edge of the nest or drop through the bottom. In the Barn Owl such cleanliness is essential because, in common with other birds of prey, the faeces are very liquid and characteristically contain much white fluid, the counterpart of urine in mammals. Consequently, if the droppings were allowed to remain, the young birds would soon become soiled and encrusted with them. Even solitary adults are careful when voiding their faeces and will not soil a crevice or hole in which they are roosting. When sitting on a beam they step backwards with raised wings and tail to defecate over the edge.

The hen continues to clean the nest until she begins to join the cock in hunting for the growing brood, usually when the youngest owlet is around ten days old. At this stage the onus for nest hygiene is transferred to the owlets themselves. They accomplish this by backing out of the nest until either they reach the outer rim of the nest hollow or their rear-ends touch an obstruction; they then wave their tails in the air and defecate. Soon the nest acquires a thoroughly 'whitewashed' appearance at its perimeter, but the important part, the centre where the owlets rest, remains clean. At some nests, as soon as the last owlet had hatched all the young left the centre of the nest and retreated to the darkest part of the cavity. Defecation then took place at the entrance and a thick layer of droppings quickly accumulated. Not surprisingly such behaviour causes the nest to become malodorous after a month or so and, with the addition of dead prey items, forms an attraction to numerous flies.

When the owlets are too young to move to the edge of the nest they already waggle their tail stumps prior to defecation and this alerts the hen who then cleans up the droppings from the bottom of the nest. The behaviour is similar to that of passerine chicks, with the difference that the adult passerine collects a faecal-sac (the faeces are conveniently wrapped in mucus) directly from the cloaca before it reaches the floor of the nest. Despite all this adaptive behaviour, however, some nests unavoidably become fouled due to their location. For instance, one of us studied a nest which was situated in a metal trunk. Inevitably, though the owlets defecated along the sides of their container, they could not avoid soiling the interior. As a result, by day 44 the nest was wet with faeces and their tail feathers had become very dirty.

As the owlets begin to grow there is a marked tendency for the amount of snoring to increase. The number of prey items brought to the nest also increases. Should food be slow in arriving, the older owlets, even at a week old, will nibble at the nest debris and their nest-mates as if searching for morsels to eat. At ten days they have been seen flapping their stumpy wings and using them when moving about the nest.

The eyes remain tightly shut for approximately 12 days, but then begin to open for short periods after first becoming visible as small slits. For a while after opening they retain the blue, blind-looking appearance of the eyes of many young creatures, but the owlets can apparently see through them immediately, for they begin to hiss and give feeble tongue-clicks when disturbed.

Tiny quills become visible at around 13 days and these quickly open to form the long second (mesoptyle) down. This is far denser than the first down and is pure white instead of dull greyish-white – not creamy buff as stated by Witherby et al (1943), Fisher (1951) and countless other authors who have repeated the earlier statement over the years. The reason for the long, second down is readily apparent. In the first place the young bird has outgrown its hatchling (protoptile) plumage. This first down is quite thick and adequate initially, but as the body grows and fills out, patches of bare skin become visible and rapidly enlarge until the original down filaments scarcely cover the body at all. At 10 to 13 days, just before the second down appears, the young owlet is exceptionally ugly, its body largely bare with only wisps of the first down which do little to improve its appearance. Secondly, the hen ceases brooding altogether when the eldest is about three to four weeks old (and the youngest usually about 13 to 20 days), so it is important that at least the majority of owlets have an adequate warm covering by this time. Those without their second down are able to obtain sufficient heat by snuggling against and under their older nest-mates, thus enabling them to survive the cold nights when the hen is absent.

Brooding ceases gradually, the hen tending to stand over the owlets rather than brood them. At one nest, when the eldest and youngest were 22 and 10 days old respectively, the returning hen stood near the nest watching them for about five minutes. After this she went to the owlets and attempted to brood them by walking backwards on to them. However, two or three of the family were much too big for this and she eventually satisfied herself by crouching down by the side of them. By this means the younger members could have crept beneath her if they had needed her warmth. The two largest owlets could be seen standing upright on either side of her. Further evidence of the decline of her brooding drive was provided on this occasion by the way she left the nest at the slightest suspicion of danger. When the eldest and youngest were 25 and 13 days old the visiting hen only stood by them, feathers fluffed up and wings drooping a little. By the next vigil, four days later, the hen was no longer visiting the young except to feed them.

It is usually suggested that the reason for staggered hatching, with its resultant discrepancy in size, is to enable the larger owlets, in the event of food shortage, to eat their smaller nest-mates and so survive at their expense; or alternatively, to ensure that the smallest owlets die first and leave what food is available for the few remaining. However, as we shall illustrate in the section on cannibalism, the picture is not as simple as that and we must look for other possible reasons for its occurrence.

When the hen begins to leave the nest she starts to take an active part in the search for food, though she is not usually as energetic or regular in this as the cock. However, the variation between different hens is marked, some scarcely helping at all and others bringing in more than the cock.

The snoring of the young is now as loud as that of the hen and has a rasping tone to it. At one nest, when the hen left the owlets for a few moments, it was suspected that they tried to call her back with an attempt at purring, and certainly they are capable of uttering a number of adult notes at this stage – see Chapter 2 and Appendix 2. When bringing in prey the parents can often be separated by the fact that the cock utters twittering chirrups while the hen snores or remains silent.

Although the owlets can usually be heard snoring until well after dusk, we have been surprised to note that the adults do not always respond to this feeding stimulus. Despite the fact that they are raising a brood, the parents keep to the basic pattern of hunting, with a period of high activity just prior to and after dusk, followed by a quiet period until around midnight, with a final burst at dawn. Many times we have watched adults go back to the roost after the first bout of activity despite the fact that the owlets were still snoring stridently in the nest. Could it be that the adults have learned from experience that it is a waste of energy to hunt outside the main periods of prey activity?

By now, with the youngest of the family over a fortnight old, the owlets are capable of swallowing prey whole and their appearance changes rapidly as the primary quills grow and the facial disk takes shape. Later, at four weeks, the tail too begins to develop and the iris turns brown as in the adults. At open sites the eldest owlet may come to the edge of the nest to look around.

When a little over a month old the owlets start to wander about if the nest site permits, peering around with their typically exaggerated head movements. They bob up and down comically and move their heads in rapid circular motions, displaying intense curiosity in their surroundings. They soon learn the routes used by the adults when they bring in prey and stare in rapt concentration at the favoured entry points (Photo 16). When an adult arrives the owlets often retreat into the nest again, but if several are hungry at the same time they will pack together and jostle for attention without retreating. The adults do not spend much time at the nest at this stage and normally leave immediately the prey is passed over.

The snores of the hungry owlets are now very loud indeed and can often be heard from a considerable distance in the evenings. From the general tone the observer can often gain an insight into what has happened during his absence. If hunting has been poor, or if the adults have been slow in going out to hunt, the persistent raucous snores of the hungry owlets soon leave him in no doubt about the fact. Conversely, if the owlets have been well fed they will be comparatively quiet, though usually one or other of the brood has been unlucky and continues to call. It is apparent that they become accustomed to the main hunting times of their parents, for snoring commences just before the beginning of the evening activity and becomes desultory throughout the quieter periods. It is comparatively rare for all the owlets to snore loudly at the same time and usually one finds that an odd individual, or perhaps two, is making most of the noise.

Like many nestlings the young owls are considerably heavier than the adults in the later stages of growth. Baudvin (1975) shows that in *T. a. alba* the daily weight increase is a phenomenal 12 g between the 6th and 15th day of life, dropping to 8 g at 16–25 days and halving to 4 g from 26–30 days. His maximum weight was of a 30-day-old owlet at 475 g. Two weighed by us at 34 and 36 days old were both found to be 453·6 g compared with the 337 g of an average adult. Two hand-reared, and no doubt overfed, owlets actually reached 539 g and 567 g at 33 and 35 days old respectively. From Baudvin's and our own findings we conclude that from around one month old the weight of owlets drops until they reach the flying stage at around 2 months of age. By then much of the surplus body fat has been lost, and by the time they become independent they weigh only a little more than the adults, averaging about 340 g in *T. a. alba*. We have no evidence to suggest that this weight loss is the result of a *deliberate* decrease in feeding rate by the adults as the young near fledging time – as occurs with some raptors such as the Kestrel, Merlin and Marsh Hawk. The growth rate, however, does vary from brood to brood and depends almost entirely upon the amount of food which is brought for the owlets. The weight also drops after defecation and pellet egestion and this should be borne in mind when studying this aspect.

The basic pattern described above also applies to *T. a. pratincola* – and probably all other races of *T. alba*, allowing for the variations in weight among these sub-species. For instance, the grossly overweight owlets weighing 530 g and 567 g at 33 and 35 days old would be typical of *T. a. pratincola* owlets at that age, this race being considerably larger than the British bird.

When examined, owlets show extraordinarily contrasting behaviour. At 14 days they crouch motionless with a mild show of defensive hissing and tongue-clicking, but if approached too closely at around 26 days an owlet will roll on to its back, though in our experience it usually fails to strike or grip with the feet when given the opportunity. By 35 days this attitude has changed and although they tend to stay very quiet until the observer moves away, a few individuals will, if provoked, strike with their talons, though without doing much damage. At 43 days some owlets will use their claws viciously and effectively, while others are content to lie prostrate with their eyes closed as if feigning death. We found one such individual completely ineffective in its defence at 44 days, for it only bit feebly when held in the hand. Three days later, however, it was biting aggressively and hard. As owlets at 43 days are quite capable of defending themselves, the behaviour of two caught for examination at 60 and 58 days was rather surprising. They lay passively, using neither beak nor talons, and even failed to utter defensive hisses or tongue-clicks. However, it may be that they would have been more aggressive towards a natural predator.

At the majority of nests the relationship between the owlets is very good and serious disagreements are rare. Mild bickering does occur at times, particularly when they are acutely hungry during periods of bad weather, but it normally involves only defensive hissing and tongue-clicking. Nevertheless, it does seem that certain individuals tend to be bad-tempered irrespective of food supply and such owlets do occasionally cause outbreaks of aggression. One such 56-day-old bird was seen to attack two of its nest-mates ferociously in a fit of pique when it missed a feed by the cock. It pecked at one of them violently and screamed loudly and angrily (possibly a juvenile mobbing note) before knocking it to the floor below. It then flew to another owlet, attacking it in a very determined manner. Fortunately at that moment the cock again returned with prey, whereupon the angry owlet charged at him and snatched the food, gulping it down greedily while at the same time uttering ill-tempered raucous snores. Such viciousness by the young is rare and we believe that the aggression sometimes aroused is tempered by the ritualised feeding display already mentioned.

As we have noted earlier, several factors influence the moment when an owlet leaves the nest site for the first time. The first to go is almost always the eldest bird and, depending on the site characteristics, it will venture from the nest to explore at between five and eight weeks of age. At one nest the hen brought in prey just after *Owlet 1* had left the nest for the first time. The owlet tongue-clicked at her, probably in excitement, and the hen responded with a loud threat call (Call 5). Perhaps she had been taken by surprise and, not recognising her own young, had mistaken it for an intruder, but we suspect from our observations that, once she ceases to brood, the hen gradually develops a 'love-hate' relationship with the owlets which intensifies until she (rather than the cock) finally drives them off. More evidence of this will appear later. However, the owlets' juvenile behaviour placates her at this stage and averts aggression. Once the eldest owlet has made the first move the others quickly follow, copying its example, and this often results in the younger ones leaving at a less advanced stage.

Excursions from the nest are only brief at first and the owlets frequently run back to it or their nest-mates as if seeking reassurance. When approached in this way an owlet (frequently one remaining in the nest) snores loudly and crouches, at the same time turning its white facial disk upwards. Often it flaps its wings and in effect adopts the typical stance of an owlet in the begging posture. The approaching bird runs to it silently, and *always* the first action is beak-fencing and cheek-rubbing followed by frenzied snoring and some head bobbing and weaving; this behaviour is identical to that which occurs with the arrival of a feeding adult. Owlets sometimes pull at the hen's bill when she brings in prey and we believe that this action is akin to bill-touching in ritualised feeding. Much weight is lent to our theory of ritualised feeding by some startling observations, two of them made by one of us in Lakeland and the other by E. Soothill and G. Yates in south Lancashire.

Our first observation took place in 1971 at a nest in a derelict house where the owlets were 60, 58, 56 and 52 days old. *Owlets 1* and *3* were outside, snoring loudly for food, with *Owlet 2* standing in the middle of the room which had the nest. The youngest, *Owlet 4*, was a slow developer and was snoring by itself in the nest. Suddenly the hen arrived with a vole and, ignoring the persistent calls of the young outside, fed *Owlet 2*, and quickly left. Then, to the astonishment of the observer, *Owlet 2*, though apparently hungry itself since it had been snoring continuously, ran across the room with the vole in its beak and went to the nest-hole where *Owlet 4* was snoring even more loudly in response to the female's visit: it then fed *Owlet 4*. At the time we regarded this observation as either a case of *Owlet 4* snatching the food from *Owlet 2* after it had returned to the nest to eat the prey, or one of those quirks of nature which occur once in a while without apparent reason. However, we then received a report from Messrs Soothill and Yates concerning a nest they had been working at in the same year. There were five young, one of which was very much smaller than the rest and seemed likely to die, but, to the amazement of the observers, it was fed *regularly* by the eldest two owlets. These would sit in the window awaiting the arrival of the adults with food and, having received an offering, would run to the nest with the prey and drop it at the feet of their backward sibling. Later, when they were spending more time away from the building, to the observers' further astonishment, *Owlets 3* and *4* took over the chore!

Final, conclusive proof that this behaviour is, indeed, innate in young Barn Owls, came in May 1981. Two incubator-hatched owlets were being hand-reared, in A.B.W.'s home, without ever having seen an adult owl. At the remarkably young age of 37 days old, the older owlet began to feed its sibling of 29 days. Two days later its behaviour became even more adult-like, for it began to utter the adult food-offering call (Call 15) whenever it offered the food. Then, if further proof was needed, at 42 days it performed a series of actions which dispelled any lingering doubts that juvenile feeding is a deliberate act. The younger owlet began to snore for food, and its older nest-mate immediately responded by picking up a portion of food and walking directly to, and feeding, the begging youngster, all the while uttering the adult food-offering call. It then picked up another, larger food item, and repeated the process. The younger owlet initially accepted this offering but had evidently been satiated by the first meal and made no attempt to swallow the food, simply dropping it to the floor. Since the smaller owlet had now ceased to snore it was thought that this would be the end of the incident. However, the feeding bird was not so easily deterred and once again it picked up the food and re-offered it. Despite its previous apathy the younger owlet responded by swallowing it on this occasion. Having met with success, the feeding owlet seemed to be stimulated into fresh action and proceeded to pick up an even larger food item – which not surprisingly the small owlet rejected. Undeterred by the lack of response, the older owlet *repeatedly* tried to get its nest-mate to accept the prey – but to no avail. Eventually, after several minutes, it seemed to register that it was wasting its time, and it gave up trying!

The most remarkable aspect of this bird's behaviour was its persistence, even when the stimulus of the younger bird's begging snores had ceased, plus its use of the adult food-offering call at $5\frac{1}{2}$ weeks of age. Perhaps the most significant point is that this bird proved to be a hen, and it would be interesting to discover whether all owlets showing this feeding trait, proved to be females.

Among British birds the Moorhen, House Martin and Swallow are species which rear two or more broods with the earlier broods sometimes helping to feed those of the later. However, we know of no other species except the Barn Owl in which young of the *same brood* have been recorded feeding each other. When looked at circumspectly the behaviour seems completely illogical. It is essential for the survival of any species that some of the year's young are reared to maturity, and with birds, especially birds of prey, this often takes place at the expense of weaker nest-mates. That one owlet should seem to jeopardise its survival by giving food to another seems to be at variance with this principle, unless, perhaps, the donors are not particularly hungry in these instances.

Another feature which further illustrates the good relationships at most nests is the comparative rarity of one owlet stealing prey from another. Should an owlet with prey be approached by one of its nest-mates it will immediately shield the food with its wings, thereby demonstrating the innate behaviour of *mantling*. Young Barn Owls occasionally utter the defensive hiss when an adult arrives with prey – probably because they realise that the other owlets are potential rivals for food even though serious quarrelling is unusual. In the few instances when an owlet *is* successful in stealing prey from a nest-mate it is rare for the deprived bird to become aggressive and it usually appears to accept the situation philosophically.

While in the nest itself the owlets are for the most part inactive, and spend a great deal of time dozing whenever they are not calling for food. We have been amused to find that an owlet will 'fall asleep' without warning in the middle of some activity, though this has sometimes proved frustrating to our enquiring minds! Sleeping – or perhaps, more correctly, dozing – owlets often lie flat out on the floor of the nest in a dog-like manner right up to the time of fledging.

By the time they are ready to fly, the owlets are well grown, somewhat boisterous, and are particularly rough when snatching food from their incoming parents. For this reason some adults, especially cock birds, tend to hesitate for several minutes before coming in to feed the young. They perch at some convenient point a short distance away and at such times are likely to be seen by the owlets. If hunting has been poor and the young are very hungry it sometimes happens that one of them will make its first flight from the nest in order to secure the prey. We have watched carefully for signs that the adults deliberately encourage the owlets to leave in this way, and at first thought this to be so, but we later satisfied ourselves that it was nothing more than an understandable fear of the rough treatment that the parents had come to expect at each feed.

The age at which the owlets begin to fly is remarkably constant. D. Scott and ourselves have each found that they become capable of flight at around 56 days; Baudvin (1975) records 60 days for *T. alba alba* in France, and Pickwell (1948) 62 days for *T. a. pratincola* in America. These first flights mark a great change in the lives of the owlets. This is especially true in the case of nests in boxes and in holes in trees and walls where the owlets have to wait until they can fly before they leave the nest at all. With owlets in buildings every day sees their confidence increasing and they begin to venture farther from the nest until at some time between the eighth and ninth week they start to explore outside. Naturally, owlets from nests in tree-holes will be earlier in their first movements away from the nest site because they do not have any indoor space in which to exercise. Their first flight takes them into the world at large, whereas owlets in buildings are usually content to fly about indoors for a few days before venturing outside. This does not, of course, invalidate the suggestion made earlier, that owlets which are confined in small cavity nest sites are generally less precocious than those at open sites.

One of the principle urges which encourages the young to leave the nest is the urge to indulge in wing-flapping exercises (Photo 11). This occupies much of their time and usually induces frantic snoring from the other owlets, probably because it reminds them of an incoming adult. At enclosed sites, wing-flapping often takes place with the owlet balanced precariously on the edge of the nest hole, and sometimes during high wind this results in an owlet leaving the nest prematurely. A sudden gust lifts the bird off its feet, and several times we have seen one just able to save itself by hanging on with the claws of one foot. On two occasions at different nests we have witnessed owlets actually being dislodged, but in both cases there was a happy outcome. At one site a large crack led up to the nest cavity from ground level, and by using its beak, claws and wings the youngster was able to make its way back to safety. The excited snoring of its nest-mate undoubtedly helped it to orientate itself, and this was one of the first indications we had that the snoring serves more than one purpose. Before the young can fly, the wings are commonly used as an aid in scrambling about the nest area when the occasion demands, but at the other nest site the owlet was able to climb back in a far more sophisticated manner – it used the staircase to reach the nest in the first-floor room!

To watch at a Barn Owl's nest at the stage when the young are in process of becoming independent of the nest site must be one of the most rewarding experiences in an ornithologist's life. We know of no other bird species in which 'play' is so obviously a part of juvenile behaviour, and we could easily fill these pages with fascinating accounts of the many times we have watched such 'play'; owlets have even been seen playing, at three months old, when on the verge of independence.

The play is distinctly mammalian in character and is an unconscious conditioning of the young to help them acquire some of the skills to hunt and capture prey efficiently. They delight in pouncing upon inanimate objects such as dried leaves, pellets and sticks, etc, and will follow each other about from one source of interest to another, keeping up a continuous chorus of excited snores, chirrups and tongue-clicking. A distinctive feature of all this behaviour is the noisy encounters already described, which we consider to be symbolic (or ritualised) feeding. If an adult arrives with prey, the owlets will often endeavour to get back into the nest, for it is still the place they associate with food; and it is this very trait that we utilise in our Breeding and Release Scheme with such success. At first the bouts of activity are short-lived and there are many long periods of lethargy when they doze or indulge in sessions of mutual preening. The latter activity presumably helps to retain a friendly bond amongst them, just as it does with the adults.

When they first leave the nest the owlets are comical in appearance. Their feathers are growing fast, particularly on the head, neck, wings and upper back, and the disk has already taken on its full rounded shape, the pinched features of the young nestling having been replaced by the beautiful open face of the adult; and the dark eyes do much to highlight the pure-white disk. However, the lower half of the body presents a sharp contrast which quickly shatters the illusion of completed development: thick white down still clads the belly and legs, giving the impression that the owlet is wearing a voluminous pair of pantaloons!

The first flights of the young birds are clumsy and reveal none of the silent grace which will typify them at a later stage. Alighting is particularly hazardous for them and they often misjudge distance and crash-land in trees or long vegetation where they lie spread-eagled with a somewhat surprised and helpless expression – or so it seems. Obviously, at this stage they are highly vulnerable and many die.

Almost as soon as they are able to fly with some degree of competence the owlets leave the building, if the nest is indoors, and extend their movements to include the immediate area outside. When this first occurs the youngest members of the brood may still be confined to the nest and it is not unusual for the smallest owlet to be left entirely on its own. At the beginning of this study we found ourselves becoming more and more concerned about the well-being of these seemingly hapless waifs, for they seemed to be faced with overwhelming competition from their noisy, robust and active elders. We felt certain that when met by several begging young the adults would feed those first, with the probable result that the youngest would die from starvation. In other words we were looking no further than the time-worn 'survival of the fittest' concept. We should have known better, for in practice the parents continue to bring most of the prey to the nest and, if anything, those owlets remaining there (invariably the youngest) fare better than those outside. Indeed, a hen owl was once seen to brush roughly past an owlet begging frantically on a window-ledge and go inside to feed a younger owlet that was only snoring quietly in the nest. It is clear, therefore, that the nest provides a strong stimulus *so long as it still contains young* and it is significant that the owlets outside frequently return to it, particularly when they hear the adults approaching with food. They, too, apparently realise that they are more likely to be fed at the nest than away from it.

When all the owlets have fledged they often line up together to await the arrival of an adult with prey, and on these occasions we have taken care to discover what determines which owlet is presented with the food. We have come to the conclusion that the successful owlet is almost always the one which gives the most *active* begging display – and this need not necessarily be the nearest or most noisy bird. The same applies when the young are in the nest, for we have seen a hen lean over an owlet to feed a more active one at the back.

The pattern of the begging display is as follows. When the owlet sees its parent approaching it crouches and spreads its wings, turning its facial disk *upwards* and weaving it from side to side; then, just as the adult approaches, the owlet vibrates its wings. It was mentioned earlier, in the section on nuptial behaviour, that this display is remarkably similar to the threat posture – which of course has the reverse effect on an incoming owl. After a close study of photographs and of owls in the field, we feel that the differences in these two displays are subtle but nevertheless quite clear when analysed in detail. Whereas in the begging display the wings are fluttered and supinated to show the white undersurfaces, in the threat posture they are pronated and held rigid to show the dark uppersides. During threat the face is periodically turned down, so hiding the disk, whereas in begging the face is turned up in order to show it off. In short, the head is the highest part of the body in begging and the lowest part in threatening (see Photos 2 and 12).

As soon as the owlets begin to leave the nest, or even before this, it is usual for the adults to begin roosting away from its close proximity, often in a nearby building, and one sometimes sees them surreptitiously enter a roost as quickly as possible to avoid the attentions of the young. If approached by an owlet, an adult will quickly fly off out of reach, the cock often uttering a series of subdued screeches, the meaning of which – though it sounds aggressive – is difficult to establish. Some adults, particularly hens, will even move well away from the nest site to roosts in another part of the territory, and in such cases they frequently go unseen by the observer for quite lengthy periods. At a nest that was watched very closely, a hen was observed to threaten an owlet on more than one occasion with both hissing (Call 8) and posturing, and this changed to actual aggression when the one remaining owlet was 14 weeks old.

In the evenings owlets which have left the nest become particularly noisy as they wander around in the vicinity of the site. Their loud snoring can often be heard from a considerable distance and they show a remarkable lack of awareness of the dangers which surround them. Also, despite the marvellous powers of the adults, they at first appear to be poor at locating sound sources and this, of course, is to the observer's advantage. One of us has had owlets snoring loudly in a room in a deserted building while he worked noisily in an adjoining room which was linked by an open doorway. The same author has also watched young birds continue to snore and 'play' while their alarmed parents, having caught sight of him, uttered repeated warning screams; others have continued to snore while people talked loudly below the nest hole. At the sight of a human the owlets do go into hiding if they are near to cover, but if caught out in the open they tend to sit staring innocently at the observer and frequently begin to utter the mobbing note. By force of circumstances we have often had to end a watch and leave our hides, walking away in full view of the owlets. Initially, on such occasions, they sometimes uttered the mobbing note and at times even came to circle over our heads. However, within a minute or two of moving away and out of sight the strident snoring would be heard once more. If a single owlet pinpoints a source of danger and utters a warning scream, the other young will follow suit and scream despite the fact that they do not know what that danger is. The warning calls of the owlets may sometimes bring the adults to investigate and they, too, will often scream without knowing what has caused the owlets' unease.

During some watches it was noticed that owlets became apprehensive when Carrion Crows gave their alarm calls nearby, but it is difficult to decide whether this was due to fear of the crows themselves or the possible danger suggested by the crows' warnings. It is possible that an innate fear of corvids might well be justified, for one of us several times witnessed the snoring of one-month-old owlets attract Carrion Crows and Magpies to their nest site, and both of these corvids are important predators of young birds of other species. We have seen owlets threaten cats by giving the mobbing note and in one case an owlet of 87 days also spread its wings and fluffed its feathers in an aggressive display.

Two things which the owlets certainly dislike intensely are strong winds and heavy rain. In these conditions they either remain in buildings or sit dejectedly in sheltered windows. If such weather persists the young birds go through a very hard period until the adults can once again obtain prey with some regularity.

As was mentioned in Chapter 2, the snoring of the owlets serves more than one purpose, for while primarily a begging note it undoubtedly functions also as a contact call. Any increase in volume and frequency will attract other owlets to things and events of interest discovered by the caller, i.e. prey, bushes and patches of ground to explore, roosting sites and incoming adults, etc, and once a new exit hole is found by one bird the rest quickly learn of its existence and begin to use it. Similarly the calling also serves as a guide to newly-fledged owlets as to the whereabouts of the nest, the snores of the young still in the nest aiding their return. Individuals tend to have distinctive voices, and at nests where we have carried out unbroken nightly watches we eventually came to recognise certain birds that were out of sight.

There is some variation in the emergence times of the owlets in the evenings. At most isolated nests they emerged in broad daylight, often about an hour before sunset; at others they only appeared at dusk, and this applied in particular to sites which were near to human habitation, where it was obviously to their advantage to remain hidden. In fact the activity period of a particular brood generally corresponds with that of their parents and is no doubt established at an early stage, depending on the time of day the young come to expect to be fed.

Once they begin to venture outside, the owlets spend a great deal of time on the ground where they show considerable agility. Much of this time is spent in the 'play' already described and one owlet was seen light-heartedly to grab the head of a Foxglove flower *Digitalis purpurea* over which it was flying, while another delighted in jumping on top of its single nest-mate.

They can often be seen making repeated pounces in the same area of grass and this might be an attempt to capture invertebrate prey such as beetles, moths and spiders. One owlet spent considerable time pursuing crane-flies (Tipulidae), meagre morsels indeed but nevertheless useful for learning hunting technique. Two others amused themselves by chasing moths and flies attracted to a light which the author concerned was using for the dual purpose of owl-watching and moth-trapping. Hand-reared owlets have been seen to pursue and consume spiders and moths and it seems likely that invertebrates are important to young birds at this stage, just as Donald Watson (1977) believes they are to young Hen Harriers when they first begin to hunt for themselves.

The earliest recorded serious 'stoop' from a height was at 65 days and the first definite capture at 72 days. The prey was also an invertebrate and it is a long time before the owlets become capable of catching small mammals efficiently. This was proved in a tragic way in the summer of 1980. A four-month-old hand-reared owlet escaped while being shown to an audience at a country fair in the Lake District. The bird was well fed, extremely fit, and wary of humans; the local countryside was ideal for Barn Owls, with a great deal of rough grassland, small copses and woodland edge abounding with small mammals; and there was even a suitable barn for it to roost in. The weather, too, was kind apart from two heavy rainstorms on the fourth and fifth day of its freedom and we were hopeful that the bird would survive, despite the fact that it was untrained on live mice. However, on the sixth day it flew into a barn three miles away, exhausted and emaciated, weighing only half its normal weight. Sadly, the bird died the same day and when examined its stomach was found to be completely empty, suggesting that it had failed to hunt successfully despite everything being in its favour apart from its own inexperience. This, we feel, is a salutary lesson for those people who still insist on releasing untrained birds of prey 'because they have the basic instinct to kill'.

By the seventy-ninth day the owlets no longer snore very often when exploring and hunting, and are therefore more likely to make a capture. Previously it would seem that they must spoil their chances by this constant vocal accompaniment.

Although we have little data on the forcible eviction of the young, we have been surprised to discover that at some nests the hens are much more aggressive than the cocks and take an active part in dispersing them. In this respect it may be significant that the disappearance of the last remaining owlet coincided in certain instances with the return to the nest site of hens that had been roosting away. When they begin to suffer aggression the owlets become extremely nervous while in the presence of the adults, looking around fearfully at even the slightest sound which might herald an attack.

Though D. Scott (pers. comm.) has recorded an owlet being fed at 112 days, all feeding ceased between the twelfth and thirteenth week at our nests, and just before the departure of the young, feeding became very intermittent. At every nest studied by us, either the youngest or next youngest has remained long after the others have become independent. These solitary birds have lagged behind their more robust nest-mates due to their inability to compete for food in the early stages, and they are often noticeably smaller.

TABLE 15: *Fledging success and nestling mortality in the Barn Owl* Tyto alba *on the Côte d'Or, France. (After Baudvin 1975)*

	1972	1974
Total young hatched	652	625
Total young fledged	553	533
% young fledged	84·82	85·28
Total young died in nest	99	92
% young died in nest	15·18	14·72
Total young died from proven cannibalism	4	2
% young died from proven cannibalism	0·61	0·32
Total young dead from probable cannibalism	64	67
% young dead from probable cannibalism	9·81	10·72
Total % young dead from cannibalism	10·42	11·04
Total young dead from other causes (Fell from nest, dislodged from nest, dead in nest, etc)	31	23
Total % young dead from other causes	4·76	3·68
Fallen from nest	11	2
% fallen from nest	1·69	0·32
Dead in nest	41	15
% dead in nest	2·15	2·40

They sit around snoring continually and pathetically, giving the observer every reason to believe that they are slowly starving to death. However, the fact that the youngest of a brood of three continued to do this even when surreptitiously fed with extra food by one of the authors proves that this behaviour is deceptive. We now suspect that rather than expressing extreme hunger the snores serve to allay any aggressive tendencies on the part of the adults until the owlet is of an age and condition to leave safely with a chance of survival. As further proof of this we have noticed that independent owlets of over four months of age frequently snore whenever they return to the vicinity of the nest sites, and this applies even after they have fed to satiation.

In the early days of independence the owlets are highly vulnerable in bad weather, and during heavy rain, gale-force winds or snow they are in serious difficulties. It is by no means unusual to see one sat out in torrential rain, making no attempt to seek shelter or capture prey, and in such conditions they quickly become chilled and lethargic. For this reason many of the dead birds recovered are emaciated owlets which have starved to death, having failed to capture enough prey to sustain themselves. At one nest a fully fledged owlet was found dead, probably due to starvation, only 180 m from the nest-site, and during a period of cold, wind and heavy rain the eldest of a family of five was found at 22 weeks wet and dying only 275 m from the barn in which it was reared.

The unwary youngsters are also frequent victims on roads and railways, for they fail to react quickly enough to oncoming cars and trains. In 1972 one of us studied a nest where two owlets were reared to maturity. The nest site was in a ruined building adjoining a busy road which was used by the author's work colleagues every morning and evening. In the months following fledging it became an almost daily occurrence for someone to report that his car had narrowly missed hitting a Barn Owl hunting alongside the road. Ironically, however, it was the adult cock which finally met its end in this way.

One recently independent owlet was seen hunting ineffectively over the banks of a reservoir where it was repeatedly mobbed by Black-headed Gulls which were nesting on an island in the centre. After a while, demonstrating a complete lack of experience, the owl turned and flew towards the island, whereupon it was immediately surrounded by a veritable cloud of gulls which attacked it from all sides. It eventually extricated itself and returned to the shore where it alighted on a fence-post. On the ground beneath it there was a hen Pheasant, a bird much bigger and heavier than the owl. To the intense amusement of the observer, the latter dropped down and began to approach the Pheasant on foot! The Pheasant showed little sign of fear and merely fluffed up its feathers and slunk off through the long grass.

We have several times drawn attention to the unwariness of the owlets and this trait undoubtedly makes them particularly susceptible to being shot. Irresponsible shooting, especially by youths with air-rifles, is rife, particularly near urban areas, and since much of this shooting takes place in the evenings it coincides with the time when many immature Barn Owls are beginning to emerge. The conspicuous and trusting owlets make easy targets for these 'cowboys' and fall frequent victims. Table 15 shows fledging and nestling mortality in Barn Owls on the Côte d'Or and the picture is very similar in Britain.

CANNIBALISM

Cannibalism occurs fairly frequently amongst the broods of many birds of prey and, indeed, in the Golden Eagle it is actually the rule for the first-hatched to kill its smaller nest-mate. F. N. Gallup (in Henny 1969) noted that in the American Barn Owl *T. a. pratincola*, cannibalism occurred in southern Californian broods in years when the food supply was extremely low, and Baudvin (1975) found it to be the principal cause of owlet mortality – as Table 15 shows. The evidence suggests that this species is more prone to cannibalism than most and Derick Scott has suggested to us that with clutches of four or five it is *usual* for only the first three to be reared, due to the small fourth and fifth owlets being trampled or suffocated by their older nest-mates. Graham Dangerfield, the well-known television naturalist, has theorised that in large broods of eight and nine the eldest owlet may eat the later ones as they emerge from their eggs.

However, both these statements over-simplify the problem. Although it is logical to assume that the smaller owlets will be the first to succumb, in our experience this is not necessarily the case and we have found no evidence to support Dangerfield's theory. Small young certainly do disappear mysteriously from Barn Owl nests, this having been recorded by many observers.

Indeed Baudvin suggests that owlets which 'disappear' without trace may well have been moved to another site by the adults carrying them away after human disturbance – a charming idea which we feel hides a more macabre reason for their disappearance. True, he may be on the right track when he links human disturbance with the owlets' disappearance, but in the light of recent studies it is far more likely that the adults have eaten their young after the disturbance, ultimately ejecting their remains in pellets which are cast elsewhere. Other possibilities are predation by other species or the owlets dying and being dropped away from the nest by the adults (as they do with mammal corpses which have putrefied). We also question the time-worn theory of the survival of the fittest in this context, for it is by no means unusual for the victim of true cannibalism to be other than the youngest of the brood. Furthermore, contrary to Scott's suggestion, it is by no means unusual for four or five young to be reared to maturity in favourable habitats where prey is plentiful.

It is pertinent to reiterate here that some of the cases of supposed cannibalism are reported when an owlet has 'disappeared'. In reality, what has happened in many instances is that the owlet has been dislodged from the nest and has died from neglect, although Baudvin apparently checked that this had not occurred in his examples. Nevertheless, we have noticed that exceptionally hungry or sick owlets become unusually agitated and move around the nest a great deal. Such individuals will be particularly prone to fall from the nest and 'disappear'.

However, there is no doubt that true cannibalism does take place in many Barn Owl nests, though less frequently than one is sometimes led to believe. It is often claimed that in times of food shortage the hen will eat some of her own young in order to alleviate the pressures on the remainder, but we find it difficult to accept this hypothesis because it seems highly unlikely that a hen would deliberately kill some of her own young while continuing to tend the remainder. For this reason we are of the opinion that in the majority of cases the young probably die of starvation or some other cause *before* being eaten, a view shared by Hawbecker (1945) and Pickwell (1948).

When discussing cannibalism it is relevant to point out that Barn Owls, domestic pigeons, and no doubt many other species, even fail to recognise their own mate after it has died, and we have actually known a captive Barn Owl eat its dead partner in these circumstances! We therefore have no difficulty in accepting that adults will eat, or feed to the remaining young, an owlet that has died. Also, since they will readily feed their young on dead day-old chicks if they are provided, it is not hard to concede that to the owl there is little difference between these and a dead and *unresponding* owlet. What did surprise us was an incident of cannibalism experienced in 1972. Four young were hatched in early September and, because of prey shortage and severe weather conditions due to the lateness of breeding, the adults were hard pressed to feed them adequately. The third owlet disappeared in the early days, but as is often the case, the youngest survived this stage. It reached the age of 50 days before suffering a macabre fate – it was killed and eaten by its two nest-mates during a period when they were extremely short of food. This is by far the oldest owlet we have recorded succumbing to cannibalism and the incident is all the more remarkable for the fact that at this stage the youngsters would be virtually identical in size. Considerable violence must have been used to overpower it and it may well have been pure chance that the victim happened to be the youngest of the three. The observer made the following note at the time: 'At 1807 there was a protracted disagreement between the owlets in the nest-hole, with a lot of angry snores and screams of rage or fear from one of them – probably *Owlet 4*, the youngest, being attacked by the other two. The disagreement lasted for four minutes and makes me worried for *Owlet 4*'s safety even at such an advanced stage.' Several more altercations were noted on the same night. Six days later the author concerned climbed up to the nest-hole, as by then both the older owlets had left the nest to roost in another part of the building. Inside the cavity he found the remains of *Owlet 4* which had been dead for several days: only the wings, feet, skull and stripped skeleton remained. In contrast to this record, at another nest two well grown owlets starved to death without molesting each other. The adult hen had been shot and the cock had apparently abandoned the young (or been shot himself).

In 1973 one of us witnessed another incident with a pair of disabled captives and their brood which provides a clue to what might lead to cannibalism in the wild. As he was feeding the owls late one night it soon became apparent that *Owlet 1*, then 16 days old, was extremely hungry: it was snoring loudly and nibbling actively amongst the nest debris. Its eyes were only visible as slits at this stage, although it could probably see to some extent. After a moment it nibbled at the cock's leg and when this was moved transferred its attentions to the wing of *Owlet 5*. This owlet managed to free itself, but then the hungry bird suddenly grasped the tiny *Owlet 6* which was only six days old. It held on to the skin of its neck and retained a firm grip despite the struggles and cries of the little chick. The parents ignored this encounter and it was only when the author concerned hastily put in some food that the attacker released its grip. Fortunately *Owlet 6* was none the worse and survived the night without mishap.

Two points emerge from this observation: (a) the actions of *Owlet 1* would appear to have been governed by hunger; and (b), the owlet showed no discrimination between the leg of an adult, the wing of another owlet and the neck of *Owlet 6*, though only this, the weakest bird, was in danger of being killed. Had food not been immediately forthcoming another case of cannibalism would probably have been recorded.

Similar behaviour can frequently be observed in the nests of wild Barn Owls. Even before their eyes are open the owlets nibble at objects in the nest – and this often includes their nest-mates. Thus, cannibalism may not be a conscious act amongst very young owlets, but in the case of older birds, especially in times of food shortage, it can be deliberate and cold-blooded. It is perhaps only after human interference that the adults are involved, for it is by no means uncommon for captive birds to kill their young after undue disturbance – or sometimes to eat their eggs. The unfortunate victims are invariably decapitated, but are not always eaten. It is important that fieldworkers and photographers bear this danger in mind when contemplating work at a nest, for a perusal of BTO nest-record cards reveals that, regretfully, some of the instances of cannibalism reported by observers are probably a direct result of their own presence.

Before closing this subject, let us list and consider the possible fates of a missing owlet in order to illustrate how easy it is to draw the wrong conclusions:

(1)   An older owlet might have killed and eaten a younger nest mate.
(2)   An owlet might have eaten another which had died.
(3)   An adult might have killed and eaten an owlet.
(4)   An adult might have killed an owlet and thrown it out.
(5)   An adult might have killed an owlet and fed it to the other young.
(6)   An adult might have eaten an already dead owlet.
(7)   An adult might have removed an already dead owlet.

For the reasons already discussed it seems logical that only (1), (2), (6) and (7) are likely in normal circumstances; that (3) and possibly (4) occur on rare occasions when the adults have been placed under stress; and that (5) is most unlikely in any circumstances. In all the years of our study we have never come across a single first-hand observation of (5) taking place. So far as death by trampling and suffocation are concerned, this seems rather unlikely because it is normal behaviour for the smallest owlets to crawl beneath the huddled bodies of their older nest-mates and the fact that they are well able to survive a fair degree of trampling was well illustrated by an incident in which a ten-day-old owlet emerged unscathed after having its neck stood on for a time by an adult.

Because of all these differing facets we find it hard to accept a popular view that asynchronised hatching is purely to facilitate cannibalism when necessary in order to ensure survival. Ingram (1959) stated (referring to the Hen Harrier) that it is better for two or three well nourished progeny to be reared rather than six or seven weaklings, and that without a marked disparity in the age and size of the fledglings, fratricide would be virtually impossible. As we have seen, this is not quite the case and in our opinion cannibalism is just one more by-product of stress — be it prey shortage, severe weather conditions or disturbance at the nest. To say it is an in-built population regulator when food is scarce is to miss the wider implications.

SECOND BROODS

In almost all of the literature relating to Barn Owls one finds such remarks as 'often two broods' (Fitter et al 1969), 'two broods in many cases' (Witherby et al 1943), 'quite often a second brood' (Fisher 1951). In our experience and that of many other present-day workers, however, second broods in the British population are rare. As second broods are triggered by an abundance of prey (Honer 1963), it could be that recent changes in agriculture and/or climatic conditions have affected food supplies sufficiently to change the Barn Owl's breeding biology in Britain. Significantly, the long, exceptionally hot, dry summer of 1976 produced our first Cumbrian record of a genuine second brood in the wild. However, many of the statements regarding double broods are not based on first-hand experience. We suspect that the widespread notion that the British Barn Owl *T. a. alba* is *frequently* double-brooded has originated from a small number of false records by earlier workers — see also Chapter 7. Some observers, e.g. Chislett (in

Dickens 1971), have wrongly assumed that a Barn Owl hunting in daylight is a sure indication of young being fed in the nest and have reported second broods on the basis of this conjecture alone, but, as we have seen, some Barn Owls habitually hunt in daylight whether they are breeding or not. Another possibility is that some writers have failed to separate the behaviour of the East European sub-species *T. a. guttata*, which regularly rears two broods in the cyclic vole irruption years. Nevertheless, that *T. a. alba* is capable of rearing two broods is beyond doubt and this occurs regularly in captive birds where food is available in quantity. In such conditions the owls' experience a simulated vole year and respond by consistently laying a second clutch.

In Britain the weather conditions would seem to preclude the occurrence of successful second broods except in unusually good years. It has already been shown that most eggs are laid in April, May and June; therefore, even allowing for the fact that the hen may lay again before the young from the first brood are all out of the nest, it will be well into autumn before the second brood is fledged – and even then they are by no means independent. At this time of the year the numbers of small mammals are declining, and to a lesser extent the numbers of small birds, so further diminishing the sources of food. It is significant that at one of our nests the young of a first brood hatched in September and the author concerned had to resort to hand-feeding the two surviving owlets in order to keep them alive, the parent birds only putting in sporadic appearances with prey. In the case of a genuine second brood, where young were present in October, one of the three owlets was found dead on the floor and seemed poorly developed. It may also be significant that of the nine eggs laid at this nest, only three hatched.

As with the production of the first clutch the obtaining of a surfeit of food for the hen seems to be essential before a second clutch can result, but in most cases the hen is potentially ready to breed again and behaves as she did in the spring, snoring incessantly. Much depends on the reactions of the cock towards this renewal of breeding behaviour and *his* response is decisive in deciding whether a second brood will be produced. When food is abundant, for example in a 'vole year', his response will be positive and the hen will lay again because the cock is able to cater both for her needs and the needs of the first brood without over-taxing himself. Much also depends on the cock's individual temperament. A minority appear to lose interest in the first brood at around fledging time, while others are extremely slow feeders even when prey is abundant. Such individuals are obviously unlikely to stimulate a second laying. It seems that a cock which feeds continually and well is necessary before a second brood can be produced and it is always possible that an enthusiastic bird might do this without prey being unusually abundant. Another possibility is that an active hen might obtain the surfeit of food for herself. However, we would stress again that renewed breeding is rare in Britain, and even in a vole irruption year in our forest study area, only two of the four breeding pairs produced second broods. Not only that, but one of these failed to achieve fledged young. It is also very significant that by the time the young from a first brood are reared, some cocks look very much the worse for wear and one can scarcely imagine these birds going through the same cycle again without a break. One cock in another habitat gave an apparent indication of his loss of 'masculinity' after the owlets had been reared to independence when he began uttering the begging snore to the hen when she was eating an item of food. He then pursued his mate about the barn, snoring incessantly like a hungry owlet! In our experience this loss of condition coincides with the onset of the annual moult.

The potential for the production of second broods is shown when renewed courtship begins when the first broods are around seven weeks old – in other words, near the time of the first broods' initial flights from the nest. This secondary courtship often seems more excitable than the earlier displays and this is probably linked with the renewed close association of the adults. Even when they have remained together at the same roost, one or both have been busy feeding a brood of lusty owlets and they rarely seem to acknowledge one another if they meet. We have noticed that both cock and hen are more demonstrative after periods of separation, though admittedly at this time of the year our conclusion may in part be due to better observation because of the lighter evenings and more regular watches at the nest site.

Renewed courtship seems to be a regular feature at most nests at this stage, but if one or other of the pair fails to respond adequately a second laying does not result. A revival of screeching in both birds, plus a very obvious tendency for the cock to chase the hen, are the usual first indications. The surest sign of all, the begging snores of the hen, will also be heard frequently again, and point to her willingness to breed if the cock will play his part.

The eggs are frequently laid in the same nest and may even appear while the last owlets of the first brood are still occcupying it (Aplin 1889, Fitter 1959, Baudvin 1975). Other hens choose to lay in a different site, and one studied by us laid a single egg in another part of the barn, but was dissatisfied and only incubated it spasmodically. Three owlets from the first brood, the eldest 70 days old, were still present and had been fed by the hen only two days previous to the laying. This egg was ultimately deserted and five days later the hen was found on yet another new nest containing a single egg. This time she was incubating seriously but she finally gave up her attempt at a second brood when the barn was used for a social event on the following day.

Not content with second broods, some authors have referred to third broods being raised at times (Aplin 1889, Keith 1964 (concerning *T. a. pratincola*)). Although in some years our own captive owls have produced (but not reared) three broods (comprising a successful first brood followed by a failed brood and finally another successful, replacement, brood), this is, of course, wholly linked with a generous and regular food supply plus good weather. Only one ornithologist with whom we have corresponded has ever experienced three broods in the wild in Britain, so there is little comment that we can make. The average total length of the Barn Owl's breeding cycle (including courtship) is about four months which means that, even allowing for the fact that subsequent clutches may follow as soon as the previous broods have vacated the nest, the birds would have to remain in breeding condition for the best part of a year to rear three broods. We feel that such an event would be highly unlikely given British weather and prey availability.

The one recent record of a British third brood, referred to above, was communicated to us by A. Benington, who reported that a pair reared three broods in Lurgan, Co. Armagh, Northern Ireland, in 1966. The nest was in an almost dark attic loft in an old three-storey house with a large garden in the suburbs of a country town. The first brood hatched during the third week in April (so the eggs were laid in late March) and the third flew on December 24th. The second brood's hatching date is unknown because the hen had moved behind a rafter.

Henny (1969) suggests that the production of double broods might be a built-in 'compensating factor' in the more northern areas where mortality is high in years of rodent scarcity and hard winters. However, this seems unlikely in the light of the virtually continuous breeding of Barn Owls in countries such as Rhodesia and Surinam.

POLYGAMY

In one artificial situation at our Cumbrian study area, a cock Barn Owl was able to exploit a daily supply of dead day-old chicks left at the nest-site where his mate was rearing a brood of two owlets. Not only did he take advantage of this to feed himself, his mate and the owlets, but also to court and breed with a second hen who reared her brood successfully with the aid of this enterprising male! Both these broods were reared simultaneously and provided us with our only confirmed record of polygamy in the Barn Owl. Baudvin (1975) suspected that it might have occurred at two of his sites on the Côte d'Or. Two nests were found in one church tower and no less than three at another – all of them in use! Unfortunately the birds were not ringed and the exact pairings were not known. However, it seems most unlikely that three separate pairs were nesting in the same tower without friction, and a shared parentage seems a likely possibility.

Having now traced the progress of the owlets to the point of independence, in the next two chapters we shall describe what happens to them when they disperse, and also investigate to what extent even the adults are inclined to wander in response to adverse climatic conditions and poor food supply.

CHAPTER 6

Movements

In the minds of most birdwatchers the Barn Owl is typically a sedentary species, often remaining faithful to the same roost or nest site all its adult life. Although this may be broadly true of adult birds in Britain, it is much less true if the whole life-cycle is examined, for the juvenile population at least must of necessity move away from the natal area during the post-fledging period, even if only for a very short distance of, say, one or two kilometres. How far such birds do move will be examined in detail in this chapter. It is also necessary to remember that what applies to the typical British race *T. a. alba* may be less (or more) applicable to the continental form *T. a. guttata* which is found chiefly in the northern, central and eastern parts of Europe. Winters are more severe in those areas than in Britain, and in some cases considerably more so, with the result that there is a good deal of cold weather movement by the species. This, also, will be examined later.

The third type of movement to be considered is that which occurs over long distances and is more akin, therefore, to true migration. Although the Barn Owl is not a migratory species in the accepted sense of the word, it would be interesting to show that there was a definite and reliable northward movement in the spring, particularly in those parts of its range where there is a definite southward movement in the autumn. In fact there is some slight evidence of this in North America, the sub-species there being *T. a. pratincola*. This, too, will be examined.

The various aspects of dispersal and migration will now be looked at in greater detail.

OWLET DISPERSAL

This aspect really falls into two parts, although any distinction between them must of necessity be arbitrary. The two parts are (a) immediate post-fledging dispersal and (b) subsequent movement during the year (after ringing).

Immediate post-fledging dispersal

This has been somewhat arbitrarily fixed as the period up to three months after ringing, by which time any association between young birds and the nest site as a place for receiving food from the parents will have ceased in virtually all cases. It is interesting to consider how this comes about.

It is attempts to capture live prey for themselves which mark a significant turning point in the owlets' development. Prior to this they are content to sit around snoring loudly, relying entirely on the adults. Though they make regular short flights they are loath to leave the vicinity of the nest site since it is still the base which they associate with food. At around 66 days, however, they begin to wander farther and also to chase after the adults, presumably for food. These excursions become longer and longer as the days pass and the owlets' confidence increases. They begin to roost elsewhere – in neighbouring buildings and trees such as young conifers and holly which provide thick cover – and gradually they drift away from the home territory, the eldest going first, the remaining ones eventually being forced away by the growing aggression of the adults.

An analysis of the British Trust for Ornithology's ringing records up to 1978 (see Table 16) shows that post-fledging dispersal mostly begins from two months after the young have been ringed and when they will all presumably be about 3½ months old. This assumes that the young are ringed when they are about six weeks old (average age only). As might be expected, those recovered within one month of ringing were near where they were ringed, namely, within 3 km. The tendency towards movement further afield as time progresses is well illustrated in Table 16.

An analysis of Dutch ringing returns up to 1977 shows comparable trends with those in Table 16, the only difference being that the Dutch birds (*T. a.*

TABLE 16: *Recoveries of young British Barn Owls* (T. a. alba) *within three months of ringing. (Source: BTO ringing returns)*

Period elapsed since ringing (months)	Near where ringed (0–3 km)	3–10 km	11–20 km	21–30 km	31–40 km	41–50 km	51–60 km	61–70 km	71–80 km	Total
0–1	7									7
1–2	26	8	4	2						40
2–3	26	14	13	3	6	0	1	0	3	66
										113

TABLE 17: *Recoveries of young Dutch Barn Owls* (T. a. guttata) *within three months of ringing. (Source: Vogeltrekstation, Arnhem)*

Period elapsed since ringing (months)	0–10 km	11–20 km	21–30 km	31–40 km	41–50 km	51–60 km	61–70 km	71–80 km	81–90 km	91–100 km	over 100 km	Totals
0–1	7	2						1				10
1–2	25	12	4	3	1		1	1		1		48
2–3	19	9	10	3	7	1	2	0	1	1	5	58
												116

guttata) tended to move farther (Table 17). The implications of the distances moved will be dealt with later.

Subsequent movement during the year after ringing

A great many dangers face young Barn Owls during their first year or so of life and significant numbers meet with their death near where they were ringed. Had they survived they might well have moved farther and this fact should be borne in mind.

Glue (1973) showed that 39% of ringed pulli recovered in their first winter died through inexperience – in collisions on roads, railways and with overhead wires. An analysis of Dutch ringing recoveries for *T. a. guttata* tells a similar story (Table 18).

How far then, do young Barn Owls travel during the first year after ringing

TABLE 18: *Cause of death in Dutch Barn Owls* (T. a. guttata) *recovered in their first year. (Source: Vogeltrekstation, Arnhem)*

Total recoveries (up to 1977)		640
Pulli recovered dead in first year		289
No details		117
Collisions on roads		103
Dead in buildings		21
Collisions with trains		12
Drowned		9
Hit overhead wires		7
Tangled in wire		4
Shot		3
Poisoned		2
Trapped		2
Collided with window		2
Miscellaneous		7
	Total	289

at the nest? As might be expected from what has been said earlier about movements during the first three months after ringing, a high proportion are recovered near where they are ringed, that is within 3 km. Table 19 shows that this proportion declines from around 60% during the first month to around a quarter during the period one or two years after ringing. The decline is, however, fairly constant, after making allowance for probable errors due to small sample sizes, at 9, 10 and 11 months.

TABLE 19: *Percentage of Barn Owls* (T. a. alba) *ringed in Britain as nestlings recovered locally (i.e. within 3 km) during the first year after ringing. (Source: BTO)*

Period elapsed since ringing (months)	Recovered locally	Total recoveries	%
1	20	32	62·5
2	31	76	40·8
3	21	50	42·0
4	18	52	34·6
5	14	37	37·8
6	11	32	34·4
7	12	38	31·6
8	10	34	29·4
9	11	24	45·8
10	9	21	42·9
11	2	12	16·7
12–24	28	106	26·4

If the whole twelve-month period after ringing of nestling Barn Owls is considered, a fair amount of movement can be seen to take place both with British and Dutch birds as Table 20 illustrates.

TABLE 20: *Nestling Barn Owls recovered within one year of ringing. (Source: Vogeltrekstation, Arnhem, and BTO)*

Distance (km)	Dutch (T. a. guttata)	%	British (T. a. alba)	%
0–10	91	25·6	175	61·5
11–50	150	42·3	88	30·9
51–100	55	15·5	15	5·3
101–200	34	9·6	5	1·7
201–300	9	2·5	1	0·3
over 300	16	4·5	1	0·3
Totals	355	100·0	285	100·0

If the movements of the 16 Dutch birds which travelled over 300 km are analysed, certain interesting facts emerge. Firstly, the predominant direction of movement was SW or SSW (12 of the 16) and this is well depicted in Fig. 7. The farthest distance travelled was that of a bird ringed in Drente (29.6.76) and recovered in western France (30.11.76), a distance of 890 km. It is also worthy of mention that of these 16 birds recovered 13 were ringed in June, but only three in July and none in the months of May or August onwards, although appreciable numbers of young were ringed in July, August and September.

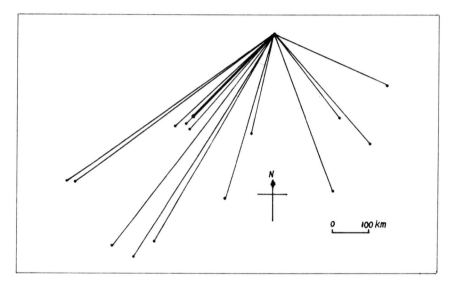

Fig. 7 Direction of movement of Barn Owls ringed as nestlings in the Netherlands and recovered within one year at distances greater than 300 km.

Concerning those Dutch nestlings recovered less than 300 km from the place of ringing, the directions in which they travelled and the distances were quite widespread, the only exception – and this rather on obvious one – being that relatively few birds travelled between west and north (270°–360°), due to the proximity of the North Sea. Table 21 below summarises the direction of movement of Dutch and British recoveries of birds that had moved less than 300 km. The remarkable fact about the British recoveries over 80 km is that most of them lie between N and E or E and S, this contrasting with the long-distance movements of Dutch, German and North American birds. As regards the direction of movement of British birds below distances of 80 km, these show a close uniformity around the points of the compass. So far as recoveries over 80 km are concerned, it should be remembered that, as with the Dutch results at least, the geographical location of ringing must have some bearing on where birds are recovered – after all, if Barn Owls were ringed in Cornwall, then a preponderance of recoveries must surely come from an easterly direction!

TABLE 21: *Direction of movement of Dutch and British Barn Owls recovered within one year less than 300 km from the place of ringing. (Source: Vogeltrekstation, Arnhem, and BTO)*

| | Dutch (T. a. guttata) | British (T. a. alba) | |
		Over 80 km	Below 80 km
No direction (under 10 km)	71		159 (under 3 km)
North to east	95	6	59
East to south	51	8	61
South to west	80	1	63
West to north	42	0	58
	339		
Over 300 km	16		
Total	355	15	400

There was no correlation between the directions and distances travelled by the 339 Dutch birds and the months in which they were ringed. Certain trends are, however, discernible when distances travelled are analysed according to the year of ringing, for in some years more birds travel greater distances (Table 22). The best example is 1934 when three out of only eleven recoveries had travelled distances of over 300 km. The actual distances were 310, 430 and 590 km. There was also considerable movement in 1972 when five birds travelled over 300 km, the actual distances being 380, 390, 410, 810 and 830 km.

In certain years, on the other hand, there was very much less movement than usual, as in 1974 when only two birds travelled distances in excess of

TABLE 22: *Year of ringing of young Dutch Barn Owls* (T. a. guttata) *recovered in their first year more than 300 km from the place of ringing. (Source: Vogeltrekstation, Arnhem)*

Year	Total recoveries	Under 10 km	11–100 km	101–200 km	201–300 km	Over 300 km	Median distance
1934	11	0	5	2	1	3	120
1961	13	2	9	0	1	1	40
1971	32	9	20	2	0	1	10
1972	44	11	24	4	0	5	30
1973	18	4	9	3	0	2	30
1974	39	13	24	2	0	0	10
1975	57	14	31	7	3	2	20
1976	47	7	30	6	2	2	20
1977	20	7	11	2	0	0	10
Totals	281	67	163	28	7	16	

100 km and none over 200 km. The greatest distance travelled in this year was 160 km and one-third (13 recoveries) were from within 10 km. The years 1971 and 1977 were also years when there was comparatively little movement of first-year birds, especially over longer distances.

This variation in Barn Owl movements in Europe from year to year is a well known phenomenon and has been studied closely, for example in Germany (Sauter 1956). Such movements do not occur to any extent in Britain, however, although the dark-breasted form has been noted here on occasions. As early as 1897 the Rev. M. A. Mathew (in Butler et al) commented that 'some of our home-bred owls may leave us for the south in the winter, at which time we also receive an immigration from the continent, as is proved by the dead bodies of Barn Owls having been found hanging frozen in the nets stretched along the sands in the south-eastern counties to capture passing flocks of ducks and waders'. Unfortunately he does not mention the numbers of such corpses or their ages.

The term *wanderjahr* (wander year) has been coined to describe years of mass Barn Owl movement and, broadly speaking, a great deal of this movement is linked to prey availability which fluctuates from year to year. Whereas birds may fail to breed in years when food supplies are low, in years when prey populations are high the Barn Owl may respond with larger clutches or second broods. The second alternative is especially common on the Continent, for example in France, where both *T. a. guttata* and *T. a. alba* are involved. At certain times then, there may be a high owl population, particularly in the late autumn, due to an abundance of prey some months earlier during the breeding season. Prey populations then crash, leading to what Honer (1963) describes as an 'out-of-step' condition. Honer postulates that when this arises there are two main alternatives for the Barn Owl: (a) a change of diet, as with the Tawny Owl in autumn and summer; or (b) an increase in hunting activity (an attempt, that is, to increase hunting efficiency) by, either, more flights over the same hunting territory, or by an expansion of the hunting territory. In extremes this signifies a *wanderjahr*.

Since alternative (a) does not occur in the Barn Owl, this bird must rely upon alternative (b). Very often the increased energy expended to find food can have serious, if not disastrous, effects on populations during severe weather, and indeed this situation has been commented upon by several writers (e.g. Van Ijzendoorn 1948). In fact the physiological ability to withstand severe weather is closely linked with fat reserves and this aspect will be discussed in Chapter 7.

A considerable amount of work on the mass movements of Barn Owls has also been done in West Germany by Ulrike Sauter (1956) and, like Honer, she concluded that *wanderjahren* are brought about by a combination of a high density of Barn Owls and a falling density of 'micro-rodent' populations. When only one of these conditions occurs in a particular year, that year will not necessarily be a dispersal year. Furthermore, since much of the movement occurs during autumn, chiefly up to mid-November, there can be no correlation with weather conditions, since it is unusual for adverse conditions to begin before December.

From Sauter's analysis of the ringing returns of Barn Owls in Württem-

TABLE 23: *Movement of Württemburg Barn Owls* (T. a. guttata) *in their first winter. (From Sauter 1956)*

1/10–31/3	First winter recoveries	Distances Over 25 km	Distances Over 50 km	Distances Over 200 km
1947/48	13	76·9%	69·2%	38·5%
1948/49	5	(20·%)	(—)	(—)
1949/50	29	34·5%	27·9%	17·2%
1950/51	17	41·2%	23·5%	17·6%
1951/52	25	44·0%	20·0%	4·0%
1952/53	41	65·9%	51·2%	39·0%
1953/54	12	66·7%	66·7%	16·7%

burg, southern Germany (Table 23), 1947/48 and 1952/53 can clearly be seen as *wanderjahren*.

Schneider (1937), too, considered that there was little correlation between movement and local weather conditions, and an analysis by Bühler (1964) also supported this view. According to Bühler, of 35 young Barn Owls recovered between 1st October 1961 and 30th September 1962 only three were recovered outside southern Germany, where they were ringed, nor incidentally were any of seven older birds recovered. This was despite the fact that there were several spells of severe weather with varying depths of snow up to 9 cm during the 1961/62 winter, especially during the second half of December, the first week of January and for much of February and March. A number of birds in fact succumbed to these weather conditions, the crucial factor being the depth of snow cover rather than the degree of cold. When snow cover is greater than 7 cm this can significantly reduce catching success but, by contrast, when the cover is between 0·5 cm and 3 cm the Barn Owl may catch more prey than when there is no snow at all, since its prey then tends to move over the snow rather than to tunnel below it and has less cover than usual.

An analysis of Swiss ringing recoveries for the period 1958–63 by Güttinger (1965) also showed that there was little long-distance movement (over 200 km) by first-winter birds. Table 24 illustrates these two points. This was despite several spells of severe weather which were also experienced in southern Germany (see Bühler above).

Unfortunately, available data concerning micro-rodent cycles is often insufficient to determine the validity of Sauter's statement that a *wanderjahr* is triggered by a combination of high owl and low micro-rodent populations, and Honer mentions two difficulties when determining the frequency of micro-rodent peaks and their effect upon Barn Owl populations. Firstly, in some years the population of micro-rodents may be below a recognisable peak, yet may trigger second broods; and secondly, although micro-rodent cycles often have a duration of three years this may not always be the case. There is also a third problem which derives from the fact that micro-rodent cycles may not be synchronised between one country and another, or even between different regions of the same country. In fact, within the United

TABLE 24: *Winter recoveries of Barn Owls in Central Switzerland, 1961/62. (From Güttinger 1965)*

Distances	Months						Totals
	1961 Oct	1961 Nov	1961 Dec	1962 Jan	1962 Feb	1962 Mar	
First year birds							
0–50 kg	4	2	3	9	5	13	36
51–200 km	3	1	0	3	5	4	16
201 km and over	0	4	0	5	2	3	14
Totals	7	7	3	17	12	20	66
Older birds							
0–50 km	0	0	1	3	2	3	9
51–200 km	0	0	0	1	1	1	3
201 km and over	0	1	0	0	0	1	2
Totals	0	1	1	4	3	5	14

Kingdom there are local variations in the levels of micro-rodent populations.

Regarding the distances and directions of movement of first-year ringing recoveries in northern and central Germany analysed by Sauter for selected years between 1934/35 and 1953/54, movement was generally random, but with some concentration between south and west, and west and north (see Table 25).

Sauter also points out that there may be some adjustment due to topographical features, for example the Alps prevent movement of Württemburg birds from southern Germany for more than about 200 km in a southerly direction. It has already been commented upon that the proximity

TABLE 25: *Recoveries of first-year Barn Owls* (T. a. guttata) *in northern and central Germany for selected years from 1934/35 to 1953/54, 1st April to 31st March. (From Sauter 1956)*

Distance (km)	Directions				Totals
	N–E (0°–90°)	E–S (90°–180°)	S–W (180°–270°)	W–N (270°–360°)	
50–100	4	5	12	8	29
100–150	2	1	6	6	15
150–200	4	1	7	1	13
200–400	1	1	9	6	17
400–600	0	1	6	3	10
600–800	0	1	1	2	4
Over 800	0	0	1	0	1
Totals	11	10	42	26	89

TABLE 26: *Movement of young German Barn Owls* (T. a. guttata) *in their first year 1st July to 30th June, 1947–53. (From Sauter 1956)*

Year	Total ringed	Distances (km) 101–200	201–500	501–1000	Over 1000	Totals	% of total ringed
1947	195	1	6	7	1	15	7·7
1948	68		1			1	1·5
1949	536	7	5	3		15	2·8
1950	240	4	4	1	1	10	4·2
1951	242	3				3	1·2
1952	533	20	15	1	2	38	7·1
1953	209	5	4	1		10	4·8

TABLE 27: *Some sibling recoveries of young Barn Owls* (T. a. guttata) *in Württemburg during their first year. (From Sauter 1956)*

Year	Distance (km) and direction	Distance (km) and direction	Distance (km) and direction	Distance (km) and direction
1937/38	50 NNW	50 ESE		
1938/39	18 N	2 W	20 SW	20 NW
1939/40	60 WNW	140 NNW	2 ESE	
1947/48	890 SW	90 SE		
1951/52	25 NW	65 SE	110 SW	
1952/53	402 SW	20 ENE		
1952/53	2 N	185 NE		
1953/54	50 NW	84 NNW	120 NNE	

TABLE 28: *Some sibling recoveries of young Barn Owls* (T. a. alba) *in Britain during their first year. (Source: BTO)*

Year	Distance (km) and direction	Distance (km) and direction	Distance (km) and direction
1969/70	16 NE	13 SW	
1971/72	12 E	6 SW	16 SSW
1971/72	10 SW	8 S	9 SW
1973	20 WNW	40 WNW	
1974/75	local	48 SW	5 SE
1977	local	120 NE	

of the North Sea towards the north and west inhibits the movement of Dutch Barn Owls in those directions.

These figures also show how much further continental Barn Owls travel compared with *T. a. alba* in this country. Table 26 illustrates this point.

Sauter's studies also include many interesting observations concerning the movement of individual Barn Owls. Many examples are given of birds from the same brood being recovered and in most cases from quite different directions. A selection is quoted in Table 27.

The British recoveries also showed a similar disparity of movement between individuals from the same nest, if somewhat less pronounced (Table 28).

Sauter also produced evidence of individual young Barn Owls moving in varying directions during their first year. Three examples follow:

Ringed 18.8.41. Controlled 20.10.41 9 km NE. Found shot 23.11.41 12 km SSE from the above place.

Ringed 24.9.52. Controlled 17.11.52 6 km NNE. Killed by car 18.1.53 50 km SW from the above place.

Ringed 23.9.53. Controlled 2.11.53 97 km NW. Found exhausted 25.11.53 30 km SE.

In some cases movement ended during the first year as the two following examples illustrate:

Ringed 23.7.37. Controlled Nov. 1937 76 km SSE. Controlled 16.2.38 in the same place.

Ringed May 1950. Controlled 23.11.50 54 km SW. Found exhausted 15.2.51 3 km E from the above place.

Some individuals moved away from the place where they were reared, and apparently settled elsewhere:

Ringed 13.8.38. Controlled 4.11.38 16 km SE. Controlled 1.7.39 5 km W from the above place.

Ringed 7.9.51. Controlled 16.2.52 20 km NW. Controlled 20.4.52 5 km W from the above place.

Ringed 8.7.51. Controlled 5.10.51 101 km NE. Controlled 2.3.53 2 km NE from the above place.

Quite clearly the above individuals might have moved away subsequently and in fact Sauter quotes examples of young birds controlled in their first year at some distance from the nest site, which a year or more later had moved on for quite some distance again and, even more interestingly, in completely different directions:

Ringed July 1936. Controlled 2.1.37 90 km WSW. Controlled 10.2.38 41 km NE.

Ringed July 1937. Controlled November 1937. Controlled 16.2.38. On each occasion 76 km SSE. Controlled 15.4.39 117 km NW.

Ringed July 1946. Controlled 13.8.46 70 km N. Controlled 24.7.47 65 km S. The movement of this last individual would have brought it back to about 5 km of the place where it was reared.

Although many young owls move away from the area in which they were reared, there are exceptions, and Sauter lists several individuals which remained in the vicinity of the nest site for a number of years, including one for nearly fifteen years.

Ringed 13.6.28. Found 1.4.43 about 5 km from the nest site.
Ringed 9.9.46. Found 4.1.51 about 3 km from the nest site.
Ringed 17.9.49. Found 14.2.53 and 5 km from the nest site.
Ringed 23.9.49. Found 17.2.53 about 3 km from the nest site (freshly dead).

A number of German Barn Owls (*T. a. guttata*) also travelled remarkably long distances in their first year, as the following examples show:

Ringed July 1937. Found 12.4.38 at a distance of 520 km.
Ringed August 1949. Found 21.5.50 at a distance of 470 km.
Ringed June 1952. Found January 1953 at a distance of 1,380 km (Zaragoza, Spain).
Ringed August 1952. Found April 1953 at a distance of 750 km.

Sauter also produced a paper on German ringing returns in 1955, in which she lists 124 recoveries of ringed Barn Owls. Thirteen of these recoveries (10·5%) were from distances greater than 300 km, 11 of the 13 relating to birds recovered within a year of ringing, most of which will have been young birds. The farthest recovery was in respect of a young bird ringed in Württemburg on 24th July 1947 and recovered in the Gironde district of France on 23rd November 1947, a distance of 890 km WSW.

Little is known about the routes taken by journeying Barn Owls, except that physical barriers such as mountains prevent or deflect movement (Sauter 1956). Movement over water is also rare and such disinclination must have a considerable effect on Barn Owl movement for an island such as Britain. The impact on the movement of Barn Owls in the Netherlands has already been illustrated. Nevertheless, cross-water journeys do take place as Schneider (1937) points out, quoting an observation of a Barn Owl flying WSW at a height of 2 m over the Baltic Sea on 23rd October 1932, 8 km from the shore. Schneider also states that in late autumn small groups of Barn Owls, or single birds, can sometimes be seen coming in from over the Kurischer Nehrung, off the north German coast, and that single birds can be seen at irregular intervals between the island of Heligoland and the German mainland; also that in 1876 a group of 10–11 were observed in this area.

There are also North American records of the movement of Barn Owls over water, for example one ringed in Wisconsin on 11th July 1955 and captured on a ship 360 km due east of Savannah, Georgia, on 11th November 1955, about 1,504 km from the place of ringing (Mueller & Berger 1959). As this bird was an adult and perhaps not on its first migration, it suggests that movement over the sea may not be so isolated as previously supposed.

In recent years a great deal of work on the Barn Owls, *T. a. alba* and *T. a. guttata*, and their hybrids, has been carried out by Hugues Baudvin (1975) in the Côte d'Or region of France where the two sub-species freely interbreeed. One of the most interesting facts to emerge from the study is that not one of the 701 nestling Barn Owls ringed in 1971, 1972 and 1973 was found nesting subsequently, the inference being that a great many must move away altogether from the vicinity of the nest site. Due consideration should, of course, be given to the fact that a high proportion of young Barn Owls die in their first year, but nevertheless the above figures must be of some significance. Furthermore, the few young birds controlled more than a year after ringing were all over 100 km from the nest site. It would appear, therefore, that young birds which are present in a study area are likely to have moved in from elsewhere. Should a breeding bird lose its mate, a young bird (that is, a bird in its first year or thereabouts) will probably replace the lost partner. One of several examples of such an occurrence is given below:

Nest visited 27.4.74: female *guttata* on 5 eggs + 1 chick. Captured and ringed.

Nest visited 1.6.74: 6 dead young (dead for about 3 days) and an unringed *guttata*, probably male, also dead for about 3 days. Another adult near the nest site.

Nest visited 20.7.74: female *guttata* on 3 chicks + 5 eggs. Male *alba* captured and ringed.

As regards movement in general, Baudvin's results are similar to those already mentioned, a high proportion being recovered dead in their first year within 50 km. The more extensive movement in 1972 (a *wanderjahr*) is also apparent from Table 29.

TABLE 29: *Recoveries of nestling French Barn Owls* (T. a. alba, T. a. guttata *and hybrids) within one year of ringing. (From Baudvin 1975)*

Year	Total ringed	Recovered	Distances (km)				
			0–50	51–100	101–500	501–1000	Over 1000
1971	124	11	9	2	0	0	0
1972	623	50	32	4	11	2	1*
1973	27	1	1	0	0	0	0

*This recovery was of a bird which reached Spain (1,120 km).

The North American sub-species of the Barn Owl *T .a. pratincola* has also been extensively studied and a great deal of information is available from ringing returns, earlier ones being analysed by Paul Stewart (1952).

As for the movement of nestling birds, of 236 ringed, 155 (65·7%) were recovered within 80 km of their hatching place. As might be expected, many of the birds which failed to travel were killed near their natal area. The movement of young can take place very soon after they are out of the nest, although a peak is reached when they are about eight months old. Table 30 illustrates these points.

If the above figures are compared with Table 17 it will be seen that *T. a. pratincola* travels farther at a younger age than *T. a. guttata* in Holland, for only one Dutch bird had travelled over 80 km within two months of ringing, compared with seven American birds from a total sample of 336 birds. The Dutch sample was 116.

Table 31 emphasises still further the long-distance movement of North American Barn Owls, much of which is broadly from north or north-east to south or south-west, although there is in fact random movement through all points of the compass, as Table 32 shows.

Interestingly, these figures compare with those in Holland and Germany inasmuch as movements of first-year birds, although random, do show some concentration between west and south. Another point of comparison with the German results is that southward movement is not necessarily related to adverse weather conditions or food shortage, since most movement is in late summer and some birds actually remain in northern areas and succumb to cold or starvation.

TABLE 30: *Recoveries of young Barn Owls* (T. a. pratincola) *in North America during their first year more than 80 km from the place of hatching. (From Stewart 1952)*

Months elapsed since ringing	Number of birds	Months elapsed since ringing	Number of birds
1	3	7	5
2	4	8	10
3	6	9	2
4	7	10	2
5	8	11	4
6	3	12	0

TABLE 31: *Months during which North American Barn Owls* (T. a. pratincola) *were recovered during their first year – and more than 80 km in a southward direction from their natal area. (From Stewart 1952)*

Month	80–160 km	161–320 km	Over 320 km
January	5	5	4
February	8	8	5
March	2	2	2
April	2	1	1
May	2	2	1
June	3	2	0
July	0	0	0
August	0	0	0
September	2	1	1
October	2	2	2
November	8	6	6
December	6	5	5

TABLE 32: *Direction of movement of Barn Owls* (T. a. pratincola) *in North America which travelled more than 80 km during their first year. (From Stewart 1952)*

N, NNE, NE, ENE – 9 birds   S, SSW, SW, WSW – 30 birds

E, ESE, SE, SSE – 7 birds   W, WNW, NW, NNW – 8 birds

Some long-distance records of young North American Barn Owls are of over 1,600 km, and a few of the more interesting records are given below:

Ringed 1.7.53 Milwaukee, Wisconsin. Recovered Palm Beach, Florida 25.11.53 over 1,920 km SSE.
Ringed 1.7.53 Milwaukee, Wisconsin. Recovered Miami, Florida 6.6.54 over 1,920 km SSE.
Ringed 22.5.53 Ohio. Recovered Florida 30.1.34 1,720 km S.
Ringed 11.7.55 Wisconsin. Recovered on board ship 366 km off Georgia coast 1.11.55 1,504 km SE.

From Table 31 above, it is worth noting that there is an absence of recoveries in July and August and none for June over 320 km, which seems to imply that there may well be a return movement in the spring of these northern birds.

Another interesting fact to emerge from Stewart's analysis was that if 35°N is chosen as a line to divide northern and southern birds, all southern birds are relatively sedentary, none having been recovered more than 144 km from its natal area and only eight (or 11·9%) travelling 80 km or more. Of the 119 northern birds, 61·3% travelled at least 80 km, 43·7% travelled at least 160 km and 27·7% at least 320 km. Surprisingly, progressing northwards from the 35°N line, which runs through North Carolina and Tennessee, ringed birds showed a diminishing tendency for dispersal to be restricted to a southerly direction; and at the northern edge of its range in northern Ohio, for example, there was little evidence of birds moving southwards. There is, in fact, some similarity in this respect with British recoveries of young birds beyond 80 km (see Table 21) which showed some bias between north and east, although not between west and north.

Having considered the movement of young Barn Owls within a year of ringing at the nest, what of subsequent movements? This aspect will be examined in two parts: (a) owls ringed as nestlings but recovered more than a year after ringing, in other words, as adult birds; and (b) owls ringed as adult birds.

MOVEMENT OF ADULT BIRDS

Birds ringed as nestlings but recovered more than a year after ringing
Writers such as Sauter and Schneider considered that it was mainly young birds which moved the most, for example, during *wanderjahren*, and this can be substantiated by and large with reference to Dutch, German and American ringing returns. Nevertheless, some interesting facts concerning adult birds are to be derived from the various ringing returns. As regards adult birds recovered more than a year after ringing, it should be remembered that movement may well have occurred during the first year after ringing and not subsequently. Only when a bird has been controlled at least twice in its second year can definite statements be made concerning movement as an adult.

As might be expected, a much lower percentage of birds recovered more than one year after ringing were less than 10 km distant, for they had ample time to move away from the nest site. A greater percentage of birds recovered within a year of ringing was from distances over 100 km, but this was also to

TABLE 33: *Barn Owls recovered more than one year after ringing as nestlings compared with percentage recovered within one year. (Source: Vogeltrekstation, Arnhem, and BTO)*

Distance (km)	Dutch (T. a. guttata)			British (T. a. alba)		
	Recoveries	%	% recovered within 1 yr	Recoveries	%	% recovered within 1 yr
0– 10	26	18·7	25·6	98	53·3	61·5
11– 50	75	53·9	42·3	68	37·0	30·9
51–100	24	17·3	15·5	9	4·9	5·3
101–200	8	5·8	9·6	8	4·3	1·7
201–300	1	0·7	2·5	1	0·5	0·3
Over 300	5	3·6	4·4	0		0·3
Totals	139	100·0		184	100·0	100·0

be expected since there is evidence, already quoted, to show that young birds travel greater distances, for example during *wanderjahren*. Despite this, the farthest recovery was of a bird recovered more than a year after ringing, 1,460 km away in Spain during its second winter, although it may have travelled there in its first year.

As far as direction is concerned, three of the recoveries over 300 km had moved in directions between west and south, which compares with what has been said already on this aspect of movement. In fact the direction of movement was similar to that of first-year birds (see Table 21) with the highest number (39 out of 102) moving in directions between north and east, and the second highest (27 out of 102) moving in directions between east and south and west and north. If, of course, most of the movement of these birds did take place during the first year, then it is hardly surprising that these results should tally fairly closely with those for the first-year birds.

Table 34 also analyses the recoveries of British Barn Owls more than a year after ringing and, again, the figures serve to emphasise how the British owls (*T. a. alba*) are much more sedentary than their Dutch counterparts (*T. a. guttata*). There is, however, no great difference between the movement of

TABLE 34: *Direction of movements over 80 km of Barn Owls* (T. a. alba) *ringed in Britain as nestlings. (Source: BTO)*

Direction	Recovered in first year	Recovered subsequently
North to east (0–90°)	6	4
East to south (90–180°)	8	5
South to west (180°–270°)	1	2
West to north (270–360°)	0	0
Totals	15	11
Numbers ringed in each category	285	184

British owls in their first year and those recovered subsequently. Again, this is to be expected since some, at least, of the birds captured after their first year will have moved during their first twelve months of life. For the same reason the directions of movement are also broadly comparable, both as a whole and for those longer distance ones over 80 km.

Birds from the same brood recovered more than a year after ringing also showed a similar random dispersal to their siblings, regardless of the period of time which had elapsed since ringing.

The wealth of material produced by Sauter tells us something of the movements of Barn Owls after their first year, and it has already been pointed out that some individuals are known to have settled away from their natal area by the following spring. By the second winter others are known to have moved considerable distances from the places where they were controlled in their first winter. Baudvin comments that those birds ringed as young and recovered over a year later were from distances greater than 100 km from the nest site.

Although there must be doubt about the timing of the journeys of young Barn Owls recovered more than a year after ringing, what of those birds which were ringed as adults, in some cases as parents at the nest?

Birds ringed as adults

Only a small number of ringing returns relate to adult birds, so consequently any conclusions that may be drawn must be rather tentative. The most data have come from the Dutch ringing results, but even this only concerns 47 birds, compared with 355 nestlings recovered within one year of ringing and 139 recovered more than one year after the date of ringing. The distances travelled by these 47 birds are given in Table 35.

The fact that nearly half of these birds remained in the neighbourhood of where they were ringed supports the views already commented upon that adult birds are more sedentary than young birds. In fact, several of these birds remained in the neighbourhood for a number of years, the longest time-span being nine years. Only three travelled over 300 km, all into France, following a west-south-west or south-west-south route, the distances covered being 320, 770 and 980 km. As far as the directions followed by birds recovered within 300 km are concerned, little can be said save that the pattern of directions appears to be quite random, but with more returns from the sector between north and east than with the two categories of young birds. The adult British Barn Owls, as might be expected, were even more sedentary, 85% of them being recovered within 10 km of the place of ringing; the farthest distance travelled was 154 km. Since many of the 48 recoveries were within 3 km and no directions are given on the BTO record cards (such information would have little value), no worthwhile comment can be made about the few for which directions were recorded.

Baudvin's work in France makes only a small mention of adult movements, his main comment being about six adults which subsequently were controlled at the places of ringing:

3 females controlled 3 months later on second broods;
2 females and 2 males controlled a year later;
1 female controlled 2 years later.

TABLE 35: *Distances travelled by adult Dutch and British Barn Owls. (Source: Vogeltrekstation, Arnhem; BTO)*

Distance (km)	Dutch (T. a. guttata)		British (T. a. alba)	
	Recoveries	%	Recoveries	%
0– 10	21	44·7	41	85·4
11– 50	16	34·5	4	8·3
51–100	2	4·3	1	2·1
101–200	3	6·1	2	4·2
201–300	2	4·3	0	—
Over 300	3	6·1	0	—
Totals	47	100·0	48	100·0

In Germany, although old birds sometimes move off, it is more usual for them to stay faithful to the nest site or its immediate vicinity. Sauter quotes several instances of adults which did move off, sometimes for quite a considerable distance, as the following examples illustrate:

Ringed 6.7.38 and controlled 26 days later 28 km NNW.
Ringed 15.6.51 on eggs and recovered 22.9.51, 8 km N.
Ringed 22.8.52 on 5 eggs and recovered 22.2.53 129 km W.
Ringed 7.11.53 and recovered 5.2.54 177 km S.
Ringed 1.8.51 and recovered 17.2.54 107 km W.

The above examples are, however, the exceptions; usually the adult birds stay around in the vicinity of the ringing point (often a nest site), sometimes for a number of years.

Concerning *T. a. pratincola* in North America, it seems, according to Stewart, that northern adults travelled further than those ringed south of latitude 35°N, and that they travelled about the same distances as young birds. Stewart gives three examples of adults ringed in the autumn which, within 23 weeks, had moved southward for distances of 360, 960 and 360 km. There also seems to be some evidence for northward movement, this movement being completed in April. Adult southern Barn Owls may, however, move a considerable distance; for example, one was ringed near Sinton, Texas (2.2.67), and recovered near Veracruz, Mexico (November 1974), a distance of 991 km (Bolen 1977).

In conclusion, it can be seen that ringing returns have shed a considerable amount of light on the movements of the Barn Owl, a species which was formerly considered to be essentially sedentary in its habits. We now know much more about distances and about directions of travel and can compare the results between populations in different countries and between different age groups within the same population. More information is also becoming available on such phenomena as *wanderjahren*, enabling us to piece together the underlying controls, whether specific to such phenomena or more general in nature.

CHAPTER 7

Factors controlling population, and possible conservation measures

Generally speaking, Barn Owl population changes can be separated into two distinct categories – short-term fluctuations and long-term trends. Short-term fluctuations are frequent, often spectacular, and therefore more notice-able. They can have many different causes, the first and least complicated being the difficulty of catching food in hard weather, particularly when the ground is covered with snow. Other owls obviously suffer the same hardship, but work done on the continental *T. alba guttata* has disclosed that the Barn Owl has lower fat reserves than other species which, of course, affects its resistance to starvation (Piechocki 1960). Indeed, Piechocki suggested that during unfavourable conditions these reserves may be exhausted in as little as eight days if food is scarce and the bird has to make prolonged hunting forays in order to catch enough food to maintain its body temperature. Consequently, mortality is very high during periods of continuing deep snow cover, especially amongst late-hatched first-winter birds which have even lower fat reserves than the adults.

It is not really known to what extent other seemingly adverse conditions can cause Barn Owl deaths. Extreme cold certainly makes the bird uncom-fortable but does not appear to cause death if no other factors are involved. Stewart (1952) and Henny (1969) reached the same conclusion with respect to *T. alba pratincola* in the USA, snow cover being the decisive factor, cold being only incidental. We have seen Barn Owls repeatedly alighting and fluffing up their feathers in a bitterly cold wind, but we have also noticed that when the vegetation is crisp with frost and conditions windless, the rustlings of small mammals are very much louder than usual and this presumably gives the owls a better chance to make a capture. Heavy rain, on the other hand, *does* prevent Barn Owls from hunting successfully. Not only does it hamper hearing and vision, but the soft, loose plumage soon becomes saturated and most experienced individuals remain at their roosts until the rain abates. However, young birds in their first months of independence often get caught in heavy rain and become waterlogged and chilled; they then turn lethargic and quickly succumb. It should also be borne in mind that freezing weather or heavy rain will reduce vole activity, the animals remaining under dense cover, eating stored food. If an owlet is still sharing the home territory with its parents it may, in the later stages of fledging, be driven out of dry indoor roosts by the adults and forced to roost in the open. We have ample evidence of the disasters that befall these inexperienced birds from the time the cock ceases to provide a regular supply of food.

The first months in the life of a Barn Owl are critical, particularly in areas where winters are normally severe, such as Scandinavia and Central Europe. During Schifferli's study (1957) of Barns Owls in Switzerland, 233 birds were found dead after being ringed as owlets. Of these, no less than 149 (64%) died in their first year, 93% of them between September and March. Frylestam (1972) did a similar study in southern Sweden and Denmark, and in these countries the pattern was one of even higher mortality during the first year, 75% of the birds failing to survive until their second summer. The average length of life was only 4·5–5·3 months and, as might be expected, the greatest losses occurred between November and February, when death was usually associated with a combination of lack of food, low temperature and snow cover. If one extends the period to the first two years of life the known mortality reaches an almost incredible 91% for southern Sweden and 90% in Denmark. As can be seen from these three examples, the further north the population the higher the mortality, and this also applies to other populations, such as *T. a. pratincola* in the USA and *T. a. alba* in the British Isles and south-western Europe.

Since they are usually produced late in the year, the young from second broods have less time than first broods to build up body-fat reserves, and as Piechocki (loc. cit.) has shown, they consequently suffer even higher mortality in their first winter. Additional factors in this respect are a lack of hunting experience and the use of unsuitable roosting sites. Baudvin (1975) confirmed these findings and stated that second broods were three times more likely to die in their first winter than first broods. Of 701 owlets ringed by him, not one was subsequently found nesting! However, one must be cautious when interpreting these figures, for there remains the possibility that most had moved beyond the range of the study area.

Glue (1973) examined the mortality of British Barn Owls from the BTO's ringing records in order to discover when peak numbers of deaths occur of young and old birds. The peak for young birds proved to be September, the time when they cease to be supported by their parents; many more die during the following winter months. Interestingly, the pattern for adults showed two separated peaks: predictably, one in February when food is scarce and the weather adverse, and another in the second half of the summer when they are hard pressed to feed their large young. The highest mortality in this second period of stress occurred in October and Glue suggested this may be due to strife between adults and young.

It is often difficult to find evidence of unusually high mortality in a species that is not numerous at any time, and even when a decrease is observed it is seldom easy to define the cause. For instance, the Barn Owl's scarcity in the mid-1960s, which in 1966 resulted in it being added to the list of rarities in Schedule I of the Protection of Birds Act 1954, was attributed by many to be largely due to the effects of toxic chemicals contained in pesticides; but we believe that a more likely cause was the exceptionally severe winter of 1962/63. A search of the literature reveals little evidence of the Barn Owl suffering from pesticide poisoning to the same extent as the Peregrine and Sparrowhawk, for instance, whereas there is ample proof of previous declines following severe winters.

Baxter & Rintoul (1953) quote excellent documentary evidence of its decline and recovery in Scotland in the late 19th and early 20th centuries, and there is also good evidence that the exceptionally hard winters of 1916/17, 1946/47, 1962/63 and 1978/79 were followed by a dearth of Barn Owls in some areas at least. Jourdain & Witherby (1917 et seq) described the progress of the first of these winters, the results of which are least likely to be confused by the effects of toxic chemicals, as follows (our summary):

First real cold spell occurred late November. January cold with snow. February dry and very cold, especially 2nd–8th; south Cornish coast, parts of west Scotland and Irish coast alone unaffected. March cold and unsettled with frequent snowfalls; no real break in cold which was most severe 6th–10th, especially on east side of Britain. April abnormal and persistent cold and frequent snowfalls; in Scotland cold and inclement weather lasted until 17th or 18th. The coldest April for 30–40 years; heavy snow in Northumberland and Ireland.

Surprisingly, however, these authors reported no record of a decrease in the Barn Owl population. On the other hand, W. J. Williams (1917), in a note entitled 'Mortality among Barn Owls in Ireland', wrote the following highly relevant account: 'Some disease has attacked Barn Owls over a great part of Ireland. During March and the first week in April I examined no less than 160 examples all in the same condition. They were greatly emaciated, the body being so thin and wasted that little more than feathers, skin and bones were left. The stomachs were entirely empty, but the plumage was in excellent condition . . .. I have heard from several correspondents through the country that they have found dead Barn Owls about their farm buildings'.

In the light of what we know about the severity of the winter in question we need hardly doubt that the specimens examined by Williams were simply the victims of 'the most severe climatic conditions of which we have definite records' (Jourdain & Witherby, loc. cit.). It is not only a question of cold and the prey species being hidden by snow. Howard (1951) studied the effect of temperature on the survival of small mammals, particularly when it is associated with inadequate supplies of food and water. Under these conditions small mammals die at temperatures around freezing point, being unable to utilise their fat readily enough to maintain body temperature. He also found that small mammals are unable to withstand sudden changes of temperature such as may occur in severe winters. Therefore, the owls might also have to contend with a reduction in prey numbers and it is small wonder that in these circumstances they become emaciated and die.

Williams' case is not the only occasion on which unusually high numbers of Barn Owl deaths have been attributed to disease, but Honer (1963) discusses the reasons why infectious diseases in particular, are unlikely to be a major cause of mortality. Dealing first with avian tuberculosis, he points out that it would require close contact between individuals to transmit the disease and, since the Barn Owl is in the main solitary, it is impossible to envisage an infection of *Mycobacterium avium* spreading beyond a single pair of owls and their young. However, Honer mentions that another form of tuberculosis caused by *M. muris* has been found in the very species that make up the main prey items of the Barn Owl – the Short-tailed Vole, Bank Vole, Wood Mouse and Common Shrew. When Honer wrote his paper it had not been proved to be communicable to birds, but since then tuberculosis has been found in Barn Owls as well as Kestrels, Golden Eagles, Buzzards and Tawny Owls, and Cooper & Eley (1979) state that any one of the three recognised types of tuberculosis (human, bovine and avian) is capable of producing disease in birds. Quite obviously, therefore, tuberculosis *is* a possible cause of Barn Owl mortality. Moreover, evidence shows that avian tuberculosis appears to be on the increase in wild birds in Britain.

The most often quoted hypothesis that Honer rejects is that coccidiosis (caused by the coccidian *Isopora buteonis*) is responsible for mass mortality. He says that, although the organism does occur in the gut of this and some other birds of prey, the few specimens in which it has been found appeared healthy and unaffected physically. Indeed, Honer remarks, if the birds dealt with by taxidermists had really died from acute coccidiosis, the striking characteristics of this disease would surely not have passed unnoticed. Our most recent evidence of the occurrence of coccidiosis came when Dr Peter Stanley of the Ministry of Agriculture's Pest Infestation Control Laboratory examined thirty dead Barn Owls found during a mass mortality in Cornwall in late 1978. These birds were in an emaciated condition and the disease was present in some cases. However, it is felt that coccidiosis could well be a secondary feature following stress and starvation (S. Davies, pers. comm.). The strongest argument against coccidiosis as a major cause of mortality is that even if a Barn Owl did suffer a fatal infection, it would be unlikely to pass it on beyond its own mate and brood.

It would seem from these remarks and the findings of Greenwood (1977) that, although disease is unlikely to be a major cause of a decline in Barn Owl numbers (or the numbers of any other non-colonial bird species for that matter), this is not to say that such a situation is impossible. In the case of highly infectious diseases such as pasteurellosis, instances have been recorded where Short-eared Owls and Marsh Hawks have become affected in large numbers due to the bacteria being passed on to them through dead waterfowl and rodents on which these predators fed. Similarly, Newcastle Disease (fowl pest) was recorded only sporadically in birds of prey until the outbreak amongst British poultry in 1970–1972. At that time the disease was found for the first time in free-living raptors and the virus conceived was found to be highly virulent and infective. Kestrels and Barn Owls were both susceptible and, although the former was seemingly unaffected on a large scale, the disease may have played a part in the ensuing reduction in Barn Owls (Greenwood, loc. cit.). It should also be noted that as many as 50% of raptorial birds brought in to wild bird hospitals are found to be suffering from one disease or another in addition to the injuries which have incapacitated them.

To return to winter mortality, that of 1946/47 is known to have reduced the populations of many bird species. Warham (1951) says: 'The disastrously severe winter of 1946/47 caused havoc among the Barn Owl population and many corpses were picked up in the woods despite the fact that the birds forsook their nocturnal habits and sallied forth in broad daylight in an attempt to supplement their meagre rations'.

The ravages of the winter of 1962/63 are well-documented, though as we have hinted above, because it coincided with the period when much harm was being done to wildlife by toxic chemicals, it is difficult to establish the relative responsibility of each of these two factors for the low population of the Barn Owl during the remainder of the 1960s. We are sure that the severe winter played a large part, and it is relevant to quote the experiences of two bird-photographer friends who, in their search for a Barn Owl's nest in the West Riding of Yorkshire in 1965, were told by several farmers that there had been owls on their premises until the 1962/63 winter but none since. The data contained in Chapter 8 also provides clear evidence of this and a similar picture emerged after the 1978/79 winter.

However, it is not only severe winters that have an effect on the Barn Owl population. During an average English winter moderately heavy snowfalls can be expected in most inland districts on one or two occasions. If the snow cover lasts for more than a few days, and especially if the temperatures are very low, there are certain to be Barn Owl casualties, particularly among inexperienced first-winter birds. It follows, therefore, that exceptionally mild winters are every bit as important as severe winters in influencing the owl population, though in the opposite direction, of course. The winters experienced in 1970/71, 1971/72, 1975/76 and 1977/78 were all remarkably snow-free in the areas where most of our research has been done and possibly for this reason there was a noticeable increase in Barn Owl numbers during this period. Sadly, the hard weather of 1978/79 brought this welcome recovery to an end and the severe winter of 1981/82, with its deep snow and floods, will have put added pressure on the species.

The second way in which food supply controls the Barn Owl population is much more interesting and complex, and has been mentioned in Chapter 6 as it is inextricably bound up with 'movements'. It will be recalled that a super-abundance of voles results in the birds producing a second brood. The sub-species studied, however, was the dark-breasted Barn Owl *T. a. guttata* and we must be cautious in suggesting that the behaviour of *T. a. alba* in Britain is necessarily the same.

It is well known that on the Continent large numbers of dark-breasted Barn Owls are found dead in some years, and Honer (1963) has attempted to explain these 'mortality bursts'. On collecting together data from various sources, including the literature, ringing records and, rather ingeniously, the number of Barn Owls passing through the hands of taxidermists, a pattern began to emerge which suggested that a mortality burst occurs every three or four years and frequently coincides with the previously mentioned 'wander-years'. These are years in which large numbers of first-winter birds, and sometimes a proportion of adults, spread out across the country and through Europe generally. They are recorded far from their normal haunts, very occasionally arriving on the east coast of Britain in considerable numbers as happened in 1887, 1888, 1891 and 1898. Honer was able to tie in these 'mortality bursts' with the cycles of the 'micro-rodents' on which the owls feed, mainly *Microtus arvalis* but also including *M. agrestis*.

Does anything like this happen with *T. a. alba* in Britain? As mentioned in Chapter 5, in captivity this race is perfectly capable of responding to a generous food supply by laying early and producing a second or, exceptionally, a third brood, and it is significant to record that two wild hens, one in Cumbria and one in Lancashire, were unintentionally induced to lay again in 1972 by artificial feeding. It will also be recalled that the British Barn Owl's potential to rear second broods was nicely demonstrated in our forest study area in 1971 when two of the four pairs laid again in June, no doubt stimulated by the abundance of voles that year.

That second clutches are so uncommon in Britain is probably due to the fact that in the well-managed farmland areas, which provide most of the Barn Owls with territories in this country, the vole population is suppressed and prevented from fluctuating wildly as it does over much of Europe. Frank (1957) found that *Microtus agrestis* only experiences large scale population fluctuations in new or felled plantations, or bare plains that are covered by grass jungles, i.e. in their optimum habitat. Without regular population explosions on the part of British voles there is no stimulus for the owls to produce double broods, and even where there *are* tracts of ungrazed and uncut grass, such as in our young coniferous forest, though second broods may occasionally occur, the areas are far too small to produce anything more than local variations in the populations. This, we believe, is the main reason for the paucity of second broods in Britain, though localised cyclic fluctuations do occur here on rare occasions. Many of the second broods in other types of territory are probably due to local infestations of some kind. Mice and rats on a rubbish tip, or mice, rats and sparrows in a granary, for example, might provide the surfeit of food that is required to trigger off a second laying.

Quite the most remarkable example we have encountered of the effect of weather and food supply on a population of Barn Owls occurred during the exceptionally hot summer of 1976 when the British Isles experienced a long period of severe drought. We have already mentioned the high population of Barn Owls created by our breeding and release scheme in south-west Cumbria, and these were to provide us with a graphic illustration of the problems caused by abnormal conditions.

Initially, the 1976 breeding season appeared to be the best on record, with the aviary birds producing many young from large clutches of eggs and the wild owls also doing well, one pair raising a second brood. Prey populations were high, for the voles, mice and shrews also benefited from the warm, dry weather, and they too raised many young. As a result, Barn Owls were a common sight by July and August and every available territory in the area was occupied by at least one bird. Suddenly, in September, things began to go wrong. First, a two-year-old hen was found dying and emaciated, her weight being only half that of a healthy adult Barn Owl. Within the next two weeks two more individuals were found dead – an old hen and an owlet of the year. Once again both proved to be severely emaciated. At this stage it was suspected that an epidemic disease had hit the owls as a result of the abnormally high population, and fears worsened when three more emaciated owlets were found dead in south-west Cumbria in the next few weeks. It was only when a farmer was noticed feeding his cattle on hay that the truth finally dawned: as a result of the prolonged drought the grass and other vegetation had died off completely, thus denying the voles their staple diet of succulent young shoots; deprived of this, and with a high population needing food due to their successful breeding season, the voles had died in their thousands. With their disappearance the owls in turn lost their staple diet, with fatal results. A close watch on hunting Barn Owls proved the point, for the unfortunate birds could be observed flying for long periods without making a single stoop. A search of the rough grassland revealed an absence of voles and their runs and nests, and the cause of the owl deaths was confirmed – not infection, but starvation! Thus, what had at first promised to be the best breeding season on record proved to be a bigger disaster than all those caused by better-known hazards such as gales, torrential rain, snow and prolonged cold.

Further confirmation that drought could indeed affect the vole, and indirectly the Barn Owl, population adversely came in the autumn of 1978: high Barn Owl mortality was experienced in Cornwall. This south-western county had suffered its worst drought on record and once more the pattern of dead and dying, emaciated Barn Owls emerged. The main mortality occurred in the area between Hayle in the west and Bodmin in the east, where unusually high numbers of victims were found in October and early November. Some of the birds collected survived and were released – apparently confirming that disease was not the main cause of the outbreak. We have already mentioned that some of the victims were found to be suffering from coccidiosis, but Stanley Davies, the RSPB's Regional Officer for South-west England, and Dr Peter Stanley confirmed that the main cause of death was starvation/stress. In this context it is interesting to note that Frank (1957), in his paper on Microtine population cycles, refers to vole crashes being caused by 'shock disease' (i.e. various stress factors), the ultimate trigger being additional stress caused by severe meteorological conditions – the same interpretation could be applied to what happens in the case of the Barn Owl. We should also mention that Dr Stanley was not surprised at the number of birds involved in the Cornish mortality, similar or even larger numbers of Barn Owls having been involved in other incidents elsewhere in previous years.

A search through the literature reveals findings which are of great significance to our observations on this hitherto unrecorded cause of Barn Owl mortality. Bodenheimer (1949) found that the Levant Vole responded to a period of summer drought by having a period of infertility, later adjusting its breeding season to coincide with the time when sufficient water was available to enable it to rear its young. He also found that humidity affected the vole's appearance above ground, fewer appearing on dry nights than in humid conditions. Lindeborg (1952) studied several small rodents and found that, although they could adjust their bodies to a lower than usual water consumption, *Microtus* was the least capable of those he studied to survive drought. Brown (1956) also found overheating and consequent dehydration a serious problem with catches when using Longworth traps in his studies of small mammals at Silwood Park Field Centre, Berkshire. He sums up by saying 'although a great deal of water needed by small mammals comes from their succulent food, additional water requirements of the animal might be even more important over short, but vital, periods of time'.

Thus it can be seen that for those Barn Owl populations which depend on Microtine voles, a period of drought can have as devastating an effect as a severe winter. It may well be argued that the Barn Owl is a species which favours warm, dry climates and should, therefore, be well capable of adjusting to the comparatively short periods of drought normally experienced in Western Europe. However, it must be remembered that in predominantly hot, dry countries such as Africa and the Middle East, non-drought-resistant Microtines are replaced by mammalian species which are specifically adapted to these conditions. Therefore, once again, it can be seen that it is the prey rather than the predator which is the key factor in this situation.

In Chapter 5, Breeding, we have drawn attention to the oft-repeated statements that the British Barn Owl is 'usually' or 'often' double brooded. While it is clear from a perusal of the notes of early writers that most of these ideas were erroneously gained from the asynchronous hatching of the young and from the occasional instances when eggs are laid at intervals of more than two days, it is possible that in the past, when agriculture was less widespread and intense, voles and other small mammals were more numerous and may have provided an easier living for the bird: that is to say that second broods may well have been more common than they are today and a situation might have existed which was nearer to that which still exists on the Continent. If this were the case, it would come as no surprise that Barn Owl numbers have declined in the present century. The warmer summers and colder winters of Central Europe have a great bearing on the endemic vole cycles and, as Frank has shown, the Continental *Microtus arvalis* experiences a fairly regular pattern of population 'crashes' and 'explosions' which are traceable back to the 15th century. Winter mortality is great in this species, particularly in extreme conditions, and this is clearly one of the main reasons why a corresponding rise in Barn Owl mortality invariably follows. Consequently it is reasonable to suppose that Continental Barn Owls *need* to produce second broods to make up their numbers following exceptional mortality, and it has been suggested by Thiollay (1967) that the Barn Owl population is self-regulating. While this might be true of short-term fluctuations, it certainly does not apply to long-term trends.

Several times during the course of this book we have touched on the fact that for various reasons the Barn Owl population in the British Isles has been declining, albeit unsteadily, since the latter part of the 19th century. Sadly, all the evidence points to this being a long-term trend and we must now consider why it is happening and what, if anything, can be done to halt or even reverse the process. We will start by examining the possible causes and will then try to establish which of these are the most important and which can be counteracted by some form of active conservation measures.

'ENEMIES' OF THE BARN OWL

Predators and competitors

The Barn Owl, being a predator itself and high in the food chain, is unlikely to be preyed upon by many other species. The only bird of prey likely to kill Barn Owls in Britain is the Peregrine. Dr D. A. Ratcliffe tells us that he found the feathers of a Barn Owl below an occupied eyrie in 1966, and a Peregrine which one of us saw stoop half-heartedly at a Barn Owl in the forest study area caused the owl to dive under a spruce tree with unusual alacrity – more than the same bird displayed when swooped upon by Hen Harriers, for instance, a species which must also command respect on account of its size and speed. Lockley (1970) describes a remarkable incident involving another large bird of prey, the Buzzard. He once saw one fly from a tree and seize a Barn Owl which had alighted on a post. The Buzzard flew away low with the owl in its talons, but dropped it after a few moments, whereupon the owl flew off to the cover of a nearby wood. The Buzzard followed and the writer subsequently found the feet of a Barn Owl in the same wood. He had no direct proof the Buzzard had killed it, but Mikkola (1976) recorded two Barn Owls being taken by this normally non-aggressive species.

It can safely be assumed that neither the Peregrine nor the Buzzard exert any control on the Barn Owl population in Britain, either directly or by competition. On the other hand, the Tawny Owl has been placed under suspicion on a number of occasions, for both species frequently use the same sort of situations for roosting and nesting. The latter's greater size and bolder disposition towards humans have led some workers to suppose that the decrease of the Barn Owl may in some measure be due to the increase of the Tawny Owl (e.g. Blaker 1933, Bowman, pers. comm.). To anyone who has not made a special study of Barn Owl behaviour such a theory seems quite tenable, especially when, as happened to Blaker and a friend of ours, Harry Shorrock, there is circumstantial evidence to indicate this. Blaker had reported to him the case of a 'dead and torn' Barn Owl being found beneath a tree usually occupied by a Tawny Owl, and Shorrock had an almost identical experience when he discovered a Tawny Owl occupying a Holly bush where a Barn Owl had previously been roosting. Below was the body of the Barn Owl surrounded by feathers stripped from its breast. It is perhaps significant that this last incident occurred in April 1947, the end of a particularly severe winter, so the Barn Owl could have died from starvation before being stripped of its feathers – Barn Owls often die at their roosts when in a weak condition.

In the forest study area, however, where Tawny Owls were numerous and undoubtedly short of nest sites, it is noteworthy that Barn Owls occupied all those derelict farmhouses which had nest sites suitable for either species. On the other hand, Neil Bowman (pers. comm.) found that, in 1978, Tawny Owls had taken over at least two known Barn Owl sites in mid-Wales, and a total of nine suitable sites had evidence of Tawny Owl usage. In one of these there was every indication of a fight between a Tawny and Barn Owl and one observer reported an instance of a young Barn Owl being chased off by an adult Tawny Owl.

However, it should not be thought from all this that Tawny Owls and Barn Owls regularly fight when they meet. In Cumbria both species inhabit the garden of one of the authors and to date not a single altercation has been observed. Similarly, a Tawny Owl has been seen to enter a building where a Barn Owl was roosting and to emerge a few minutes later quite casually, thus indicating that no friction had taken place between them. A much more positive incident was witnessed while one of us was watching a building favoured by both Barn and Tawny Owls. The hen Barn Owl was resting in the window when a Tawny Owl swooped straight at her from outside, knocking her into the building and following through itself. A terrific screaming ensued and then silence. The observer feared that the Barn Owl had been killed, for five minutes later the Tawny reappeared and flew away. However, all was well, for shortly afterwards the Barn Owl returned to the window, apparently none the worse, and flew off with a screech. It is impossible to say which, if any, of these birds was the winner, but there could be no doubt about the outcome of another scuffle one of us observed. D.S.B. was just about to leave a building where a Barn Owl was nesting, when the cock entered. He remained still and a moment later a Tawny Owl entered through a small ventilation hole at the back of the building. Without hesitation the cock Barn Owl flew straight at it, screeching loudly, and knocked the bigger bird backwards off the beam on which it had alighted. The Tawny immediately dashed out via the same ventilation hole, leaving the Barn Owl still screeching in anger, the harsh tone of the screech plainly revealing his feelings.

Further observations of the same Barn Owl during the following winter (1971/72) produced evidence of continued animosity between the two species. On two occasions when the Barn Owl emerged at dusk it was attacked by a Tawny Owl, believed to be a hen. In both cases the Barn Owl responded by dashing back into the barn and here it appeared to be able to hold its own, as was demonstrated by a further observation that winter. D.S.B. had entered his hide outside the building while the cock was away hunting. During the bird's absence two Tawny Owls must have gained entrance to the barn through the ventilation holes at the rear, for when the Barn Owl returned, screeching, one Tawny flew out immediately and another followed after the rightful owner had screeched for a minute or two in the main entrance hole. The Barn Owl again bred successfully in the building the following season, thus demonstrating this species' ability to withstand efforts by Tawny Owls to oust it.

The Barn Owl's generous endowment of bizarre threat and defensive displays may place it at a considerable advantage in its encounters with other species. In captivity the Barn and Tawny Owls kept by one of the authors live together remarkably peaceably, but there is no doubt whatsoever that the Barn Owl is the dominant species – if any mild friction does occur it is always the Tawnies which back down.

Regarding predation by mammals, we know of two cases involving Stoats.

D. Scott told us of an instance where one of these animals destroyed a Barn Owl's nest and carried away the owlets, while another Stoat killed two newly fledged owlets at a Cumbrian nest. We can readily accept the danger this versatile animal represents, for one of us was once treated to an excellent demonstration of the climbing prowess of this little predator. Whilst watching outside an old house in which an owl was nesting, a Stoat came by carrying some small prey and, finding the building in its way, it ran straight up the side of the house, over the top of the roof and down the other side, seemingly without effort; thus demonstrating that few Barn Owl's nests would be inaccessible to so agile a creature. On the other hand, it may be that the hen owl is a fair match for a Stoat and, if this is so, her habit of staying continually with the eggs and small young must give this predator and its smaller relative, the Weasel, very little opportunity to destroy the nest in its early stages. Irrespective of this, a more important reason for dismissing predation by these mammals as a possible cause of the decline is the fact that they themselves, particularly the Stoat, have suffered a similar decrease in many areas.

Surprisingly, we have no records of domestic cats predating Barn Owl nests, although we feel sure that this must occur at times. We know of several instances in which cats and owls shared the same barn quite amicably, the cats being normally ignored unless they began 'caterwauling'. If that happened the owls would fly to a convenient vantage point from where they would watch them with mild interest. Again, we are confident that cats have played no part in the decline.

Parasites

We have already discussed disease, but what of internal and external parasites as a contributory factor towards the decrease? Like all other birds the Barn Owl harbours its share of parasites: feather-lice and feather-mites denude the feathers of their barbules, while fleas, flies and ticks gorge themselves on the bird's blood. As is so often the case, the Barn Owl has species of feather-lice that are found on no other bird. These are *Kurodaia subpachygaster* and *Strigiphilus rostratus*. Dr Clay of the British Museum (Natural History) tells us that the *Strigiphilus* species on the Barn Owl are of particular interest because while *S. rostratus* parasitises the bird in Europe, the Middle East and Africa, it is replaced by another species, *S. aitkeni*, in the New World, Far East and India. *Kramerella humulata* is probably the only species of feather-mite recorded from the Barn Owl while *Ixodes arboricola* is probably the only species of tick. Fleas are much more temporary in their associations with their host and are apparently seldom found on the Barn Owl in Britain. The Common Bird Flea *Ceratophyllus gallinae* will parasitise almost any species that happens by. Indeed, one of us well remembers an occasion when, noticing several fleas around the opening of a nest-box recently vacated by a family of Blue-tits, he leaned forward for a closer look, whereupon they launched themselves into the air and landed all over his face! Possessing this behaviour it is not surprising that fleas of several species have been recorded on a wide variety of strange hosts. Thus *C. rossitensis*, normally found on crows, and *Monopsyllus sciurum*, the Red Squirrel Flea, have also been recorded from the Barn Owl in Britain. Another, rather uncommon, blood feeder is the Louse Fly *Ornithomyia avicularia*, an unpleasant but wonderfully adapted Dipteran that is flattened like a crab and just about as difficult to crush! Our own experience with this fly leaves us with mixed feelings of revulsion and admiration. The insect seeks to avoid capture by slipping easily between the feathers and, when caught and given a squeeze that would pulverise a blue-bottle, flies off quite unharmed!

When assessing the harm caused by these ecto-parasites one is confronted with the age-old riddle of which came first, the chicken or the egg, but it is generally believed that healthy birds succeed in keeping in check the numbers of lice, etc, and that it is only when the host is weakened from some other cause that they begin to multiply and seriously affect the bird. Endo-parasites, however, are probably much more damaging and there would seem to be nothing that the bird can do to control them. Parasitic worms usually have complicated and indeed fascinating life-histories, involving two or more very different hosts. Understandably, some of these life-histories have not yet been fully worked out and, in any case, it would be exceeding the scope of this book to make more than brief mention of those species that we know to have been recorded in the Barn Owl*. These, then, are:

TREMATODA (flukes)
   Strigea strigis – found in the intestine.
CESTODA (tape-worms)
   Paruternia candelabraria – found in the intestine.
NEMATODA (thread-worms – comprising a huge number of parasitic and non-parasitic species).
   Porrocaecum depressum – found in the intestine, the larval stage existing in the body cavity of shrews.
   P. spirale – found in the intestine; the larval stage is probably similar to *P. depressum*.
   Spiroptera perihamata – found between the tunics (ridges) of the gizzard (ventriculus).
   Synhimantus affinis – found in the oesophagus.
   S. laticeps – also found in the oesophagus.
   Capillaria tenuissima – found in the intestine.
ACANTHOCEPHALA (spiny-headed worms – parasites possessing a spiny proboscis used to cling to the tissues of the host).
   Centrorhynchus aluconis – found in the intestine, the larval stage occurring in amphibians, snakes and shrews.
   C. globocandatus – no details known.
   C. tumidulus – no details known.

Despite the debilitating effect of infestation by such parasites it must not be assumed that in the ordinary way the host is greatly inconvenienced. On the contrary it is in the parasite's own interests that the host should survive. Neither is there any reason to suspect that Barn Owls are more heavily parasitised now than formerly so we need not ponder on whether to include them as a cause of the decline.

*For further information on parasites, etc, the reader is referred to *Fleas, Flukes and Cuckoos* by M. Rothschild & T. Clay (see References).

PESTICIDES

In the mid 1960s J. H. Lawton and M. Crompton of the University of Durham undertook a study of the Barn Owl's status on the Lancashire mosslands, where Oakes (1953) had stated it was common, nesting on almost every farmstead. We are grateful to these two workers for allowing us to quote from their findings. In 1965, thirty-five farms were visited and interviews with the farmers revealed the following:

(a)   Birds present and nesting successfully.... 2 farms
(b)   Birds present but no attempt to nest.... 6 farms
(c)   Birds present in the past but no longer present, even though buildings where they had nested were still apparently suitable.... 5 farms
(d)   Owls never present to farmer's knowledge, though buildings probably suitable.... 21 farms
(e)   Owls never present and buildings not suitable.... 1 farm

Group (b) could be separated further into:
1.   Only single unmated birds, not regular in appearance.... 3 farms
2.   Pair of birds but no eggs laid. (Of these one pair had nested unsuccessfully in 1964, one pair had last nested 6–8 years before, and the remaining pair had not nested 'for some time'.).... 3 farms

Group (c) could be separated further into:
1.   Last nested 11 years ago.... 1 farm
2.   Last nested 'a few years ago'.... 3 farms
3.   Last nested 1963.... 1 farm

Even allowing for the fact that the farmers' statements suggested that the species was never as common in that part of the mossland as Oakes had indicated, it was evident that the occupied and successful nesting sites had shown a marked decrease during the previous six years or so. In 1964 two pairs on nearby farms had both attempted to breed: one pair failed while the other pair reared seven young, a most unusual degree of success. In the following year the first pair made no attempt at nesting while the second pair reared four young. In view of the success of one pair and the numbers of non-breeding birds, it was concluded that the habitat and food supply must have been adequate and that the failure to breed, apparent infertility and decline in numbers was strongly indicative of toxic chemicals being responsible.

In 1969, R.D.S.W. undertook a similar survey in Cheshire, visiting and circulating a total of about 60 farms. Usable data was obtained for 48 of these and the results were as follows:

(a)   Birds present and nesting successfully.... 4 farms
(b)   Birds present but not attempting to nest.... 13 farms
(c)   Birds present in the past but no longer present, though former nesting buildings still suitable.... 4 farms
(d)   Birds present in the past, but no longer present. Never nested though buildings apparently suitable.... 11 farms
(e)   Birds present in the past, but no longer present. Buildings unsuitable for nesting.... 1 farm

(f)   Owls never present, though buildings apparently suitable.... 10 farms

(g)   Owls never present and buildings unsuitable.... 5 farms

The picture which emerged was remarkably similar to the findings of Lawton and Crompton four years previously in Lancashire, i.e. a fair number of birds present but very few nesting. Additionally, however, the enquiry showed that there had also been a considerable reduction in the number of non-breeding birds. Of some interest is the fact that if the survey had been conducted in 1964 there would have been eight pairs successfully breeding, but the numbers had dropped by one pair in each of the years that followed, suggesting that the decline had not yet been arrested. That there *had* been a decline was made abundantly clear by the remarks of some of the farmers, for example: 'Not seen for several years'; 'Not seen in recent years, but regular at one time'; 'Last seen about seven years ago'.

Questionnaires sent out by Prestt (1965) also produced some very interesting statistics. The contributors were presented with a list of possible factors and asked to award one point for each that they felt played a part in the change in status, except for the first, second and third in importance which were to be given a score of four, three and two points respectively. The results for the Barn Owl are given in Table 36.

It can be seen that the effects of toxic chemicals were considered to be by far the most important factor, though it must be pointed out that the survey was made at a time when the contributors would be acutely aware of the potential threat to wildlife from this source. The importance attached to this factor in East Anglia and the counties of Lincolnshire, Nottinghamshire and Kent is of course consistent with the fact that the greatest quantities of the most dangerous pesticides were used in those areas. Despite the strong emphasis placed on toxic chemicals as the main reason for the decline we must re-affirm that, so far as we are aware, these assumptions were not confirmed by positive laboratory analyses of large numbers of dead specimens in the case of the Barn Owl (Parslow (1973) also noted that there was little proof that chemical poisoning was a key factor in the decline).

TABLE 36: *Factors thought to be contributing towards the change in breeding status of the Barn Owl* Tyto alba *in Britain during the period 1953–1963. (After Prestt 1965)*

Factors	Score	Factors	Score
Increase of toxic chemicals	153	Increase in game preservation	27
Loss of suitable habitat	87	Destruction of hedges	23
Changes in agriculture	49	Hard winter	20
Decreased breeding success	49	Less enlightened gamekeeping	14
Decrease in food supply	47	Decrease in conservation activity	9
More disturbance	39	Deaths on railways	3
Increase in unorganised shooting	34	More disease	2
More road deaths	27	Change in bird habits	1

In order to put into proper perspective the amount of damage caused by pesticides it is important to know a few facts about them. Firstly, the most dangerous pesticides, the chlorinated hydrocarbons, principally dieldrin, aldrin, endrin and heptachlor, which combine high toxicity with persistence, are supposedly no longer used – although at the time of writing (1982) the suspicion is growing that some of them are now being used illegally. (It is to be hoped that this is not the case for the situation has improved considerably since they were replaced by less persistent and less toxic substances.) The susceptibility of a species to accumulate a lethal level of chemicals in its body depends largely on its position in the food chain, *and* on its actual diet. Each species forming a link in the chain feeds upon many other individuals containing smaller amounts of chemicals, so the higher its position in the chain, the greater the concentration of residues becomes. However, it is not quite so simple as that because different species have varying abilities to excrete these poisonous substances. Most significantly, mammals are more efficient in this than birds, which fact was no more strikingly illustrated than by the way in which the Sparrowhawk, a bird-eater, declined catastrophically over almost the whole of England while the Kestrel, primarily a mammal-eater, showed little or no decrease except in the most contaminated areas. Similarly, the Peregrine, another bird-eater, had been almost exterminated before the dangers were realised, while the mammal-eating Buzzard was hardly affected in many parts and even increased in some localities.

Where, then, does this leave the Barn Owl? Basing one's theories on the above, the species should have been even less affected than the Kestrel, for it certainly eats fewer birds. And yet the majority opinion was that pesticides were largely responsible for its decrease in the late 1950s. The more one investigates the subject, the more one comes to appreciate its complexity, since so many factors are involved. Where high levels of chemicals are demonstrated by autopsy there can be no doubt as to the cause of death, but what of smaller levels discovered in birds that have died from other overt causes? One might well ask such questions as 'Could it have bred successfully?'; or 'Did it starve to death because of a lowering of its hunting efficiency due to toxic chemicals?'; 'Did it hit the telegraph wires, or fail to react to the car due to an error of judgement caused by toxic chemicals?'; or 'Did it succumb to some disease as a direct result of chemical poisoning – and, if so, why did the Tawny Owl show scarcely any decline at all?' These are but some of the questions to which the Nature Conservancy Council in Britain and its counterparts in other countries are still trying to find the answers.

At all events, with the phasing out of the most harmful chemicals the situation has been considerably, though as we have hinted, not entirely, relieved for the time being at least. We can now perhaps be more hopeful that, since the dangers of persistent toxic chemicals are now fully appreciated, a recurrence of the dreadful mortality which struck down some of our finest bird species will be avoided in the future.

Before leaving the subject of chemical poisons, we must sadly mention the growing concern of the conservation bodies regarding the vast upsurge in the use of poisoned bait in the open countryside. Some of the poisons being used are highly toxic, i.e. strychnine, mevinphos and, to a lesser degree, alphachlorose; and of course they kill indiscriminately. Victims have so far included some of our rarest birds of prey, dogs and other wild and domestic animals including the now protected Badger. Fortunately the Barn Owl does not take carrion so will presumably not suffer as badly as species such as the Red Kite, Buzzard and Golden Eagle. However, as we have mentioned in Chapter 4, Warfarin has been implicated in some Barn Owl declines, such as in the Isle of Man, so it too can be vulnerable to some poisons.

LOSS OF HABITAT AND NEST SITES

The reason for the decline that has been awarded the second highest score in Table 36 is 'loss of suitable habitat'. This may be interpreted in two ways: firstly, lack of suitable hunting territory and, secondly, lack of breeding sites. As is pointed out at the beginning of Chapter 8, it is likely that in the past the Barn Owl has benefited greatly from Man's alteration of the landscape and it is possible to cite instances of how changes, even in modern times, have favoured the species. The removal of hedgerows in arable areas *may* affect the habitat adversely, but if the vast fields of corn, thereby created, harbour inflated numbers of prey species the practice may ultimately be to this owl's advantage. As is also mentioned in Chapter 8, the establishment of commercial forests in previously wind-swept and inhospitable areas can create ideal short-term habitats for Barn Owls, especially when the farmsteads are vacated and furnish attractive nest sites. Even our ever-growing unsightly rubbish tips may provide the Barn Owl with additional food sources. There can be no doubt, however, that the progressive urbanisation of the country is gradually reducing the Barn Owl's living space.

The second interpretation of 'loss of habitat', i.e. loss of nest sites, is, we feel, the most important factor of all, for it is generally agreed that it is the replacement of old stone farm buildings by modern, prefabricated structures that has decimated the Barn Owl population in most counties. Just a few decades ago the situation was temporarily alleviated in upland areas by a reduction in farming activities in these relatively unproductive places: the numerous deserted farmhouses provided a Barn Owl paradise, especially since they were seldom visited due to their remoteness. Unfortunately, this state of affairs no longer obtains, for the ruins have reached such a state of dilapidation that they are either being demolished in the interests of public safety or the upper floors, ceilings and roofs, without which the owls have no nesting sites, are falling in. By and large the vacation of farms has ceased, so further deserted buildings are not becoming available to the owls, especially in view of the current tendency for such places to be renovated as country abodes for wealthy townsfolk. An important additional point is that few places are sufficiently remote today to escape disturbance by human agency. The above conclusions were arrived at by Neil Bowman (pers. comm.) in his study of the recent decline in mid-Wales, and the same remarks clearly apply equally to the upland areas of the north-west of England where much of our own work has taken place.

A factor which, on the contrary, has not applied to the north-west is the reduction of nest sites due to Dutch Elm Disease caused by the fungus *Ceratocystis ulmi*, for not only have our Wych Elms *Ulmus glabra* remained

relatively unaffected until recently, but they never have provided a significant percentage of nest sites – few trees of any species in this region reach
sufficient stature to develop the roomy hollows required by large hole-nesting
birds. In southern England the English Elm *U. procera*, by virtue of its
abundance in the tree population, is – or more accurately was – of considerable importance, and its almost total destruction could have far-reaching
effects on the populations of all birds that need large cavities in trees. It is
ironical that many dead elms are being needlessly felled although they are
not in a situation where they are likely to be a hazard – trees which would
otherwise be a haven for a whole spectrum of animal life for many years to
come. This seems to be a lesson still to be learnt by even some enthusiastic
conservationists!

It will have been appreciated that persistent highly toxic chemicals,
besides directly reducing the population by killing the birds, act more
insidiously by lowering breeding success, a factor which the contributors for
the enquiry rated highly as a separate cause of the decline. Similarly, 'loss of
habitat' also really embraces 'changes in agriculture', 'decreased breeding
success', 'decreased food supply' (which we would not have thought to be
more than a local factor) and 'destruction of hedges', all of which we have
now mentioned.

DISTURBANCE

Though we have no figures for comparison, it seems inevitable that a
species whose nest is as easily accessible as that of most Barn Owls must
suffer more disturbance nowadays than it did formerly. Today, when so
many families own a car, enormous numbers of people converge on the
countryside at weekends and public holidays, a practice which must
jeopardise the nests of many 'normal' species with nesting periods (i.e. time
taken to build the nest, hatch the eggs and rear the young) of around a
month. How much more vulnerable, then, must be the nest of the Barn Owl
which needs over three months to complete its cycle! Linked with the
popularity of these country trips is the complete disregard for private
property by some sections of the public. Barns and old buildings seem to
form a centre of attraction for many people, with the result that owls nesting
in them are frequently discovered and interfered with. A good example of this
was demonstrated to us by two well-meaning but ill-informed country
walkers who innocently told one of the authors they had been paying weekly
visits to some of the barns in the forest study area simply to see the owls fly
out! This was in the pre-nesting season at the critical stage when the owls
would be deciding whether to adopt the buildings for nesting.

It is national policy nowadays actively to encourage the public into many
areas of outstanding natural beauty such as nature reserves, National,
Country and Forest Parks, etc. While this, together with the setting up of
nature trails, no doubt helps to foster a benevolent attitude towards natural
history, a lack of supervision in a minority of cases can lead to disastrous acts
of vandalism that only serve to strengthen the hostile feelings of many field
naturalists and conservationists. Sadly, this minority will always be with us,
so would it perhaps not have been better if we had retained the old tradition

of keeping parts, at least, of our state forests and reservoir catchment areas strictly private? In Grizedale Forest in the Lake District, for instance, as many as fifty-five nest-boxes were vandalised in a single weekend, despite the efforts of the Forestry Commission to foster a caring attitude amongst its visitors (S. Craig, pers. comm.). In such circumstances the erection of nest-boxes, intended to help the birds, might instead turn out to be a dis-service to them by encouraging them to breed in unsafe places. This is a factor to be reckoned with when nest-box schemes are being contemplated.

UNORGANISED SHOOTING AND GAMEKEEPING

There can be no doubt that shooting by irresponsible people, who will kill almost anything that moves, is rife at the present time, particularly in suburban areas. Unfortunately the law seems to be relatively ineffective and we can only console ourselves with the knowledge that persecution by gamekeepers has apparently decreased. We say 'apparently' because it is sad to relate that by no means all gamekeepers show this welcome change in attitude. The Royal Society for the Protection of Birds still receives many reports of the destruction of birds of prey from widely scattered areas throughout England, Wales and Scotland, and methods used include pole-trapping (long since outlawed in Britain), shooting and, increasingly, poisoning. Despite the outraged protestations of the game-rearing fraternity, it remains indisputable that many of these incidents occur on keepered estates. Indeed one of us first became interested in Barn Owls through having to hand-rear some orphaned owlets whose parents had been shot by a gamekeeper. Individual reports frequently concern the deaths of several birds and one hardly dares to think of the total numbers that must be killed every year. The current worry is that, as a result of the RSPB's re-doubled efforts to enforce the law, poison is being substituted as a less easily detectable method of eradicating 'vermin'. We ourselves may have been unfortunate, but our own experiences in the north-west of England give us no reason to believe that a more enlightened attitude has now superseded the old prejudices regarding birds of prey – a feeling apparently shared by the late Leslie Brown (1976) in his New Naturalist book on British diurnal birds of prey. Photo 29 illustrates the point only too well.

DEATHS ON ROADS AND RAILWAYS

Glue (1971) examined the causes of death and other recovery circumstances of 320 ringed Barn Owls recovered during the period, 1910–1969. Thirty-eight (12%) of these were found dead on roads and 35 (11%) were found dead on railways or on railway engines. A comparison was made between the circumstances during the periods 1910–1954 and 1955–1969 and it was noted that while the railway deaths had risen by just 2% – probably as a result of electric and diesel trains superseding the noisier steam trains – the road deaths had risen by 9%. This is hardly surprising when one considers the increased speed and density of present-day traffic, and unfortunately such a trend seems certain to continue as roads become wider, straighter and faster. Motorways are a particular problem and many of the reports received during our population surveys (see Chapter 8) refer to this major cause of death. The nearest motorway to our own homes, the M6, is no exception, and we know of two examples where it has had a noticeable effect on known Barn Owl populations. During a twelve week period in 1974, eight individuals were found dead on the section just north of Penrith, while in 1976 six were killed in a few weeks immediately north of the Carnforth intersection. Everett (1977) also mentions finding five dead Barn Owls on a 50 km (30 mile) stretch of main road in England (in what period of time is not stated). Incidentally, a study of Barn Owl road victims (Ratcliffe 1977) showed that broken right wings outnumber broken left wings by more than two to one, due, perhaps, to cars driven on the left-hand-side of the road in Britain tending to strike the birds as they fly from the nearby left-hand verge.

COLLISIONS WITH WIRES AND POWER CABLES

In Glue's sample 11 Barn Owls (3%) are described as having been found dead beneath telegraph wires and power cables.

From one cause or another, Barn Owls do seem particularly prone to suffer wing injuries, a fact which is very evident from the number of permanently disabled birds maintained in 'bird hospitals' and elsewhere. Fortunately, such individuals take very well to confinement and will often breed successfully if paired up. As will be seen later, the release of healthy young birds bred from these crippled parents, provided it is done properly, can be a rewarding project.

DROWNING

The number of Barn Owls found dead, having drowned in water butts, drinking troughs and garden pools, etc, is quite extraordinary. Glue found that 3% had died in this way. He suggested that such accidents occur when inexperienced owls come to steep-sided containers to drink or bathe, misjudge the depth and are unable to rise from the surface. Our own observations suggest an additional possible explanation: we have seen some young birds mistake their own reflections in the water for another owl and jump down to join or attack it. Two captive owlets appeared to be fascinated by their reflections in water and we reproduce the original notes of one observation: 'One of the owlets flew down to the side of the water container and stood looking down. I thought I was going to see an owlet drink or bathe for the first time but it soon became clear that the youngster was attracted by its own reflection. It bobbed and weaved its head at the water. Suddenly it jumped into the water and stood there, appearing surprised at the sensation. It made no attempt to bathe or drink and quickly came out, looking very bedraggled with drooping wings. If it had been a deep container it would certainly have drowned.'

It is also relevant that an adult Barn Owl kept by us struck viciously at its reflection in a mirror. There is no doubt that owlets share the curious and playful nature exhibited by many mammalian predators and it seems quite likely that this trait, combined with their susceptibility to mistake their reflections for another owl, is responsible for this peculiar type of mortality. Two reports by A. Robinson and S. Wilson (1973) of Barn Owls striking window panes may, perhaps, be similarly explained.

TAXIDERMY

In Victorian times the popularity of stuffed birds may have resulted in Barn Owls being killed specifically for this purpose, although persecution was such then that it was perhaps more a case of owls that had been killed as vermin being passed on to taxidermists rather than consigned to the gibbet and wasted. Thankfully, lack of demand for stuffed birds in Britain nowadays has removed any incentive to kill owls for this purpose. Nevertheless, there has been a local re-awakening of the interest in taxidermy of late and the number of legally protected birds in the possession of a Lancashire taxidermist who was prosecuted was both astonishing and horrifying. J. A. Benington (pers. comm.), the well-known Ulster ornithologist, gives taxidermy as one of the causes of the decline of the Barn Owl in Northern Ireland.

LONGEVITY

In the absence of the many hazards described above, the Barn Owl appears to be quite long-lived. One of the authors has a captive cock and hen, still breeding successfully each year, which are 9 and 11 years old respectively. The oldest Barn Owl we have heard about was a male at the London Zoo which died at the age of 20 years; the oldest female at the Zoo was 14 years old (P. J. Olney, pers. comm.). The oldest wild birds we have seen mentioned in the literature (whose ages were discovered from ringing records) were 17 years, 10 months, 29 days (L. Barriety 1965), 8 years (Schneider 1937) and $11\frac{1}{2}$ years (Stewart 1952). On the other hand, the average age of 220 Barn Owls ringed as nestlings in the USA by Stewart was only 1 year, 5 months and 25 days. Similarly, Verheyen's (1968) oldest owl was 4 years, 11 months, but the average age was only 1·7 years. According to Glue (in the March 1980 edition of *BTO News*), the oldest ringed Barn Owl in Britain was eight years old.

In the foregoing we have tried to assess which factors are the most significant in bringing about the long-term decline of the Barn Owl population and it is now time to consider what, if anything, can be done to alleviate or counteract them.

THE PROTECTION OF BIRDS ACTS, 1954–1976

In Britain, The Wild Birds (Various Species) Order 1966 added the Barn Owl to Part I of the First Schedule of the Protection of Birds Act 1954. Any person guilty of an offence against the species on this list in England and Wales is subject to 'special penalties'. Originally the maximum penalties in the case of Schedule I species was a fine of £25 for each egg, nest, skin or bird and, additionally, a term of imprisonment not exceeding one month for a first offence or three months for a subsequent offence. The Protection of

Birds Act 1967 brought in an important addition, namely that anyone 'wilfully disturbing' a Schedule I species while it is on or near a nest containing eggs or unflown young shall also be liable to the above special penalties. The Protection of Birds (Amendment) Act 1976 raised the fine of £25 to £100 and the Criminal Law Act 1977 further raised the fine to £500 in view of the high prices being obtained for rare birds of prey, especially young Peregrines for falconry. The Barn Owl is also included in Schedule IV of the Act, which renders it an offence, subject to a fine of £50, to sell, exchange, or have for such purpose, any egg, skin or live bird, unless it is close-ringed and bred in captivity.

Stern measures, one would think, especially since the taking of each egg, nest, bird or skin constitutes separate offences and thus renders the longer term of imprisonment applicable in most cases. However, the practicalities of enforcing the Act are often very difficult and it is seldom that a caring person actually witnesses at first-hand an offence against a Barn Owl, or any other Schedule I bird. When nests are robbed it is, usually, almost impossible to trace the culprit and furthermore to prove his guilt. More often than not children are involved and most naturalists feel disinclined to bring them into the courts.

Our own experiences have borne out the difficulties of conserving the bird by legal action. We know of one assistant gamekeeper who was threatened with dismissal unless he carried out his orders to shoot a pair of nesting Barn Owls, and a futile attempt to bring about justice when the deed was done only resulted in the person concerned being excluded from the estate where he was deeply involved in the BTO's Common Bird Census. A bird-photographer we know was wiser: even though he was told that a nest of young Sparrowhawks was to be destroyed, valuing his permit to enter the estate, he took no action.

One of us had a close study ruined when a nest of eggs was taken by children at the point of hatch. It was deemed best to merely admonish the children in the presence of their parents, but the latter took the stance that the act was 'all part of growing up' and even suggested that the author involved was simply trying to recover the eggs for himself! Yet another incident concerning wilful disturbance ended a valued friendship, not only with the photographer creating the problem, but with the occupants of the farm where the study was being carried out. The resulting correspondence and trouble which ensued made the author regret that he had ever intervened. Perhaps the most amazing example of the weakness of the law came when one of us attempted to enlist the aid of his local police over a case involving a Schedule I bird. 'What Protection of Birds Act?' said the sergeant behind the desk, 'I've never heard of it'! What is even worse, is the reluctance of most magistrates to impose the maximum fines (as the RSPB's own magazine, *Birds*, regularly illustrates) when the culprits are brought to justice. To date (1982) we know of only a single case in which this has happened. For all that, the Protection of Birds Acts state a principle and enable the conservationist to speak and act with the backing of the law when the need arises. It remains to be seen whether the Wildlife and Countryside Act, taking effect in 1982, will further aid the conservation of the Barn Owl.

NEST-BOXES FOR BARN OWLS

The provision of nest-boxes can be a most rewarding and effective means of boosting the Barn Owl population. The type of box is largely a matter of common sense based on a knowledge of existing nest sites, and in view of this we feel quite unable to recommend the roofless, two-compartment tray-type illustrated in the BTO's booklet on the subject. As some desperate Barn Owls will use almost anything, in the absence of other more suitable sites, specifically sites which are 'roofed in' and dark, we do not doubt that such boxes have been adopted now and again, but they would certainly not seem to be ideal.

Almost any *closed* box with a suitable hole in the front will suffice and will be used not only during the breeding season, but often throughout the year for roosting. The original boxes used in our forest scheme were designed by a bird-photographer friend, the late Herbert Brigg, and were approximately 43 cm square, having a retaining lip to prevent the eggs and young from falling out. A similar though slightly larger box is illustrated in Fig. 8a. A layer of old pellets, etc, from the floor of the barns was put in the boxes to give the birds a start in forming a soft bed for the eggs. After those buildings without nesting sites had been provided for, a few extra boxes were put up in large deciduous trees. These were slightly deeper from front to back, the roof continuing forward and being covered with felt, with the entrance narrowed to keep out the rain as well as giving the birds more privacy. With hindsight we would now recommend this type of box for indoor (minus the roofing felt) and outdoor use, for it is the design most favoured both by our aviary and wild Barn Owls (see Fig. 8b). The forest scheme was a small one and was commenced in 1966, well before the breeding season. Few Barn Owls were present at that time, but many buildings were available as roosts, though lacking nest sites. The scheme was enlarged and monitored until 1971; the results are summarised in Table 37.

TABLE 37: *Results of a nest-box scheme in a young coniferous forest in the north-west of England during the period, 1966–1971*

	1966	1967	1968	1969	1970	1971
No. of nest-boxes	6	7	8	11	11	13
Barn Owls nesting in boxes	—	—	2	2	2	2*
Tawny Owls nesting in boxes	1	2	1	—	—	3
Kestrels nesting in boxes	2	2	1	1	1	3
Stock Doves nesting in boxes	1	—	—	—	—	—
Totals	4	4	4	3	3	8

* 1971 was a 'vole year', hence the high occupancy rate. Both pairs of Barn Owls had double broods.

N.B. There were a number of orthodox nest sites in the forest; some birds used these, others apparently preferred the boxes.

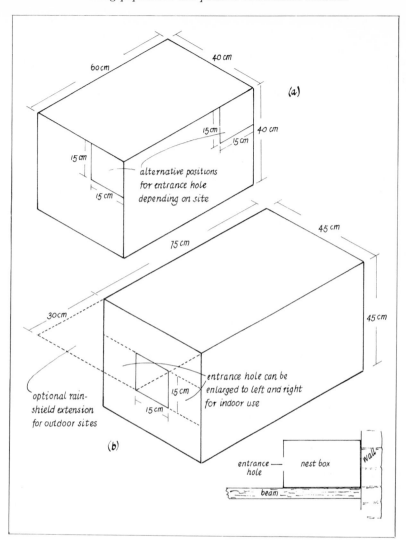

Fig. 8 Nest-box designs suitable for the Barn Owl.

The lessons learned from this project were that, on the one hand, adding to the basic number of boxes within a given area does not necessarily produce better results, as it is fruitless to provide for more birds than the territories can support; and on the other hand, since a variety of species will use the boxes, enough must be erected to cater for all of them in order to avoid inter-specific competition. Additionally, in view of the possibility of double broods, or even the desire of Kestrels to nest in the same buildings (which they do quite readily), it might be prudent to provide two boxes per building.

We would also suggest that if cost of materials is no problem, larger boxes than the ones in the forest should be used so as to allow the owlets to exercise their wings and run about, which they certainly do in more open sites. We *have* had instances of owlets falling out of our boxes, but since they seem to fall often enough from spacious nesting sites, such as the floors of haylofts, we are not sure that the small size of our boxes was responsible. Unfortunately, if they are unable to climb back, or at least reach some reasonably high perch, such owlets are usually ignored by the parents and allowed to die of neglect. A box which is considerably longer than wide, so that the owls can retire far back inside, would undoubtedly be an improvement, both in attracting the adults to breed in them and in giving the young more room; but one must bear in mind that large boxes can be heavy and rather difficult to fasten up in the roofs of buildings, especially when one is poised precariously on top of a ladder!

A final point is that we have found it advisable to empty our small boxes every two or three years, as the debris soon becomes level with the retaining lip which then ceases to function.

Lamentably, in 1973 this particular nest-box scheme came to a premature end. Not only were the boxes systematically robbed, but the buildings have since been subjected to continual disturbance, and there seems to be no practical way of preventing this. Not a single breeding pair remains.

In recent years similar schemes have been tried in a few other areas of north-west England, usually as a result of the interest taken by local ringing groups. The most comprehensive and successful of these is still in operation and was begun in 1972 in an area of 44 km² covered by the South-west Lancashire Ringing Group. The primary aim of the scheme was to provide better nesting facilities for the local Barn Owl population which, at that time, was inclined to nest in unsuitable sites such as hayricks, etc. Ultimately, it was hoped to attain the maximum breeding density for the area by placing boxes in every barn, the population theoretically reaching a level where it would be governed by food requirements and territorial behaviour rather than a lack of nest sites. As a side benefit, it was hoped that the boxes would enable the owlets of the year to have access to warm, dry roosting sites in winter, thus reducing mortality at this critical stage of their lives. It was planned to extend the project in a network of selected sites spreading outwards from the original area.

In 1972, nine pairs of Barn Owls were known to be nesting at traditional sites in the area (i.e. almost one pair per 5 km²) and 16 owlets were ringed from these nests. Forty boxes were erected, and these were increased to 73 in 1973, 75 in 1974 and to a phenomenal 105 by the breeding season of 1975. The reward for all this effort came when 37 owlets were ringed in the 1975 season, 14 active box-sites being recorded (nine of them new), with seven other pairs using natural sites. By this time the scheme area had extended to 200 km², giving a breeding density of around one pair per 10 km². As can be seen, breeding density had in fact lessened, suggesting that the original area had already held the maximum number possible. Ringing returns have shown that most young birds leave the area covered by the scheme, so although the home territory has not acquired all these birds it is more than likely that, because of the sterling work of the South-west Lancashire

TABLE 38: *Usage of nest-boxes provided for Barn Owls in SW Lancashire. (After Kennedy 1979)*

Year	No. of boxes checked	Birds roosting in boxes	Birds nesting in boxes
1972	35	8·5%	—
1973	65	29%	3%
1974	73	19%	8%
1975	75	35%	19%
1976	42	25%	19%

Other species using boxes: Pigeons (breeding), Tawny Owl (roosting and breeding), Kestrel (roosting).

Ringing Group, other depleted Barn Owl populations have benefited by the arrival of new blood. Table 38 gives a good indication of the impact and usefulness of this type of conservation work.

It is obvious from these figures that nest-box schemes *can* help the Barn Owl to maintain and increase its numbers in some areas. Sadly, some of the problems facing Barn Owl populations generally, were highlighted during the 1975 census. Of the 75 box-sites visited, two barns had been demolished, one burned down and one box had been destroyed by stone-throwing. Another box had been removed during re-roofing of the barn, and at one of the natural sites a brood was stolen by youths. All these are typical of the pressures which have contributed to the present decline of the species. Recoveries of dead birds ringed during the scheme give a good idea of the mortality pattern of British Barn Owls (Table 39).

TABLE 39(a): *Months of death of Barn Owls ringed in SW Lancashire, 1968–1976. (After Kennedy 1979)*

January	10	April	2	July	2	October	3
February	6	May	2	August	0	November	4
March	6	June	1	September	1	December	3

TABLE 39(b): *Causes of death 1971–1976. (After Kennedy 1979)*

Unknown	27	Drowned	1
Car	11	Pullus stolen	1
Emaciation	5	Overhead wires	1
Trapped in building	4	Killed by catapult	1
Train	2	Broken wing	1
Shot	2	Caught by ring on wire	1
Pesticides	2		

In view of the success of the South-west Lancashire scheme it is strange that a pioneer project carried out by the Leigh Ringing Group in Greater Manchester, was not successful in the long-term. Although initially enjoying enormous success, with 52 owlets being ringed in 1971, the following years were very disappointing and the population has noticeably decreased since 1973, for reasons largely unknown (G. Yates, pers. comm.).

BREEDING AND RELEASE SCHEMES

A more involved method of building up wild populations is the practice of captive breeding from permanently disabled adults and the release, in suitable areas, of the owlets which result from these pairings. We ourselves are engaged in such a scheme in Cumbria and a slightly different technique is employed by author and naturalist Jane Ratcliffe, who is well known for her rehabilitation work with Badgers and birds of prey. Her method is to place single birds or pairs of Barn Owls (young birds or birds which have been treated successfully for minor injuries) in the barns of co-operative farmers and landowners. All exits are closed and food provided daily. With single birds, the exits may be opened after two weeks, food continuing to be provided. With pairs, nest-boxes are erected and the barns kept closed until the owls breed and hatch out their young. When the owlets are approximately one month old, the doors and windows are opened up and the adult birds allowed out to hunt for natural food in the surrounding countryside. This they achieve without any undue problems since they are trained to catch and kill live mice before being introduced to the barns where, probably, they will be able to catch the mice which usually infest such places and thus keep their hand (or foot!) in, so to speak. The theory behind this method is that the presence of the young will draw the adults back to the barn, and either they or some of the young will subsequently claim the building as their permanent base. However, the information given above is only intended to outline Mrs Ratcliffe's methods and we would emphasise that many additional details need to be known if success is to be achieved: we would not wish to encourage any readers to embark on such a scheme after reading only the brief account we have just given.

Our own method has the same basic theme with the important difference that the young birds are removed from the parents and hand-reared up to the stage where they can swallow whole mice and voles, and pull food to pieces; that is, at five to six weeks old. They are then placed in a nest-box in an open outbuilding (or barn if one is offered by a local farmer) and fed at dusk with enough food to last them 24 hours. In effect we act out the role of the parent owls and the owlets are reared in exactly the same way as at a wild nest. Despite the fact that they have been hand-reared, they quickly react to human presence as would wild owlets – within 48 hours in fact – and their fledging behaviour follows the normal pattern. When the owlets have become adept at catching their own prey, they eventually leave the home territory of their own accord. Nest-boxes are placed strategically in the local countryside and many of these are taken over by the young birds of the year. Other individuals leave the area completely, as they do normally (see Chapter 6), and we are hopeful that ringing returns will provide us with data showing how far these birds travel.

There are many advantages in this method: (1) the adult pairs usually produce a second brood when the first brood is removed, thus doubling the normal output; (2) hand-rearing ensures that all the owlets can normally be raised, whereas leaving them with the adults frequently results in some mortality; (3) the provision of abundant food *every* night, no matter what the weather conditions, means that the owlets fare better at the fledging stage than at most wild nests; and (4) the absence of an adult pair means that the inexperienced owlets do not have to suffer from their parents' aggression during the later stages of their nest-cycle. They can thus remain in the home territory (where food continues to be provided) as long as they wish. They will then leave only when they are fully ready to do so.

We started this work in 1973 and to date a total of 103 'scheme' owlets have helped to swell the ranks of the wild population. At the time we started there were no wild Barn Owls remaining in the area, and yet by 1977 we had three pairs breeding within 800 m of the scheme aviaries, and four other pairs in territories inside a 10 km circle. Of the 98 young ringed, 14 have subsequently been found dead from the following causes:

Emaciation	5 (3 in 1976 drought)
Stoat predation	2
Car victim	2
Drowned	1 (in cattle trough)
Train victim	1
Electrocution	1 (on 'live' wire)
Natural causes	1
Trapped in long grass	1 (waterlogged owlet on first flight)

The longest distance travelled by a ringed 'scheme' owlet to date is only 21 km south. A 1977 owlet recovered in 1980 had only travelled 1·5 km in three years, and a 1976 owlet was recovered alive but emaciated (in snow), 16 km south in December 1981.

We hope the examples quoted here will be of some help to other enthusiasts or groups who, by organising a worthwhile conservation scheme, will provide themselves with a population of Barn Owls (and often of other interesting species) that, so long as the necessary authorisation is first obtained from the Nature Conservancy Council, will furnish ideal subjects for photography and research, especially the ringing of nestlings. More to the point, they will be helping to ensure the continued presence in the British countryside of a species which undoubtedly, in the years ahead, is going to need all the help it can get if it is to remain a viable member of our fauna.

One final plea. Every week a perusal of the advertisements in avicultural periodicals reveals aviary-bred Barn Owls for sale. In the cause of this beautiful bird's future, can we not persuade the breeders to think again about how they dispose of these birds? As we have shown, with careful training and a little forethought such individuals can be put into the wild to augment the dwindling population. How much more satisfying it is to see them flying free – as happens nightly in our Cumbrian area – than to see them merely as a means to monetary gain.

18 This owlet at 75 days is on the verge of independence (photo: D. Malpus).

19 'Post-hopping' is a hunting technique used by some Barn Owls. Since fence posts tend to be close to rough verges containing good numbers of prey their use is energy-saving and is often very effective (photo: E. W. & E. J. Ratcliffe).

20 Barn Owl about to pounce from a hunting post, having located prey. Note the concentration by the owl with sight and hearing in full play (photo: E. W. & E. J. Ratcliffe).

21   The alert expression of this bird is typical of a hunting Barn Owl (photo: E. W. & E. J. Ratcliffe).

22   The white underparts of the Barn Owl in flight, coupled with its unearthly screech, are undoubtedly the origin of many 'ghost' tales, haunted churchyards and houses (photo: E. W. & E. J. Ratcliffe).

23 A Barn Owl rising steeply to its perch on a beam is caught in a perfect 'heraldic' posture (photo: E. W. & E. J. Ratcliffe).

24 A departing Barn Owl reveals the long wings and beautiful plumage of the species (photo: E. W. & E. J. Ratcliffe).

25 The threat display of the Barn Owl can be an effective deterrent to any would-be attacker (photo: E. W. & E. J. Ratcliffe).

26 A Barn Owl poses in its nest box opening, revealing the characteristic heart-shaped facial disk (photo: E. W. & E. J. Ratcliffe).

27   The loss of stone-built farm buildings such as this, in Cumbria, is the main cause of the Barn Owl's decline in Britain. Note the ventilation holes which allow the birds free access (photo: A. Lumley & A. Gate).

28   Isolated buildings such as this typical stone barn in open countryside are ideal sites for nest-box schemes (photo: E. W. & E. J. Ratcliffe).

29 Sadly, some Barn Owls still die in the jaws of illegally set pole traps (photo: J. Storey).

30   The dark-breasted Barn Owl *T. a. guttata* inhabits Eastern Europe. Apart from its much darker coloration, it is very similar to *T. a. alba* and where their ranges overlap the two races interbreed, producing many intermediate forms. However, as can be seen, the dark facial disk and breast of the true *guttata* are quite distinctive (photo from a transparency: W. Walter/Aquila).

31 The African Barn Owl *T. a. affinis* was introduced to the Seychelle Islands in 1949 with disastrous results to the endemic fauna. It is larger and more powerful then *T. a. alba*, and is more heavily spotted on the underparts (photo from a transparency: Eric Hosking).

CAUSES OF MORTALITY OUTSIDE BRITAIN

Before closing this chapter, as this book has throughout attempted to include information on the Barn Owl in other countries, it is appropriate to say a few words about the chief causes of mortality outside the British Isles. From the literature it seems that the species is faced with much the same hazards in many parts of its range. Hard weather, in particular snow cover, exerts the greatest depressing effect on numbers wherever such conditions occur. Stewart (1952) found that the average age of southern birds in the United States was 2 years, 2 months and 26 days, whereas in the north this was reduced to 1 year, 1 month and 4 days. The climate was presumed to be responsible for this. Similarly, Henny (1969) demonstrated a relationship between mortality rates and latitude: his mortality estimate for the southern United States was 34·3% as against 55·8% in Switzerland. Pesticides, rodenticides and (undefined) pollution are considered important in Spain, Italy and Belgium (Chancellor 1977). Collisions with vehicles, so important in Britain nowadays, are also listed for Spain, where they are said to die by the hundred from this cause (Garzon in Chancellor, loc. cit.), Holland (Braaksma & de Bruijn 1976), Belgium (Verheyen 1968) and the USA – Smith & Marti (1976) cite a record of 35 dead Barn Owls being picked up in a single day along the interstate highway between Pocatello and Jerome, Idaho. Taxidermy still remains a widespread cause of decline in many countries according to Chancellor in the Report on the Proceedings of the World Conference on Birds of Prey which took place in 1975, and Braaksma & de Bruijn (loc. cit.) quote a figure of over 10,000 Barn Owls being stuffed since World War II. Loss of nest sites is another familiar cause: Heintzelman (1966) comments upon the number of church towers wired off in Northampton and Lehigh Counties, Pennsylvania; and competition with Jackdaws is given as one cause of a 'marked regression' in Spain by Garzon (in Chancellor). In Malta, it seems that as many birds are shot annually as the total number of breeding individuals (Sultana & Gauci in Chancellor); shooting is also mentioned by Heintzelman (loc. cit.) and Smith & Marti (loc. cit.) for the United States, and by Verheyen (loc. cit.) for Belgium. In Belgium and Holland changes in biotype, i.e. changes in agricultural practices, were mentioned by Kesteloot (in Chancellor) and Braaksma & Bruijn respectively. Kesteloot also considered the activities of bird watchers and photographers to be a major threat to the species in Belgium, and Verheyen found cases of drowning in wells. In southern Sweden, where the Barn Owl seems to be approaching extinction, egg-collecting has become a problem.

Finally, there is one cause of mortality which, though probably not figuring very prominently, is worthy of mention if only because of its special interest. This is predation by other birds of prey, European records having been analysed by Mikkola (1976). The most notorious killer of other birds of prey is the Eagle Owl, the percentage taken exceeding their proportion in the bird population available to it. The explanation would seem to be that predatory species are more conspicuous and less wary than most birds. Five Barn Owls succumbed to the Eagle Owl in Mikkola's study. The other dangerous predator is the Goshawk, seven Barn Owls having fallen victim.

As the Goshawk is at present recolonising Britain remarkably successfully, one may speculate on its effect on the Barn Owl population in some areas. The only other predator was the Buzzard which took two. However, Mikkola found that the Barn Owl figured less than other medium-sized owls. A further record, of a Ural Owl killing a Barn Owl, was considered to be the result of a fight over a nest site. In the USA the Golden Eagle has been recorded eating a Barn Owl (Gordon 1955), and Luttringer (1930) and Wayne (1934) recorded the Great Horned Owl predating the Barn Owl.

CHAPTER 8

Distribution in the British Isles

HABITAT

The artificial environment created by Man in the British countryside during the last two thousand years or so would appear to suit the Barn Owl very well indeed. It can never have been a woodland bird, since its method of hunting requires the existence of open spaces with a thick ground layer of vegetation to provide a suitable habitat for its small-mammal prey. Therefore, although we may lament that the species is much less common than a hundred years ago, there must have been a time, before Man began his devastation of the forests, when Britain was a very uncongenial place for a Barn Owl and we may ponder on exactly where it could have found the required habitat in those days.

As we have said in Chapter 5, we believe that it was a cliff-haunting bird, breeding and roosting in the natural crevices and caves that are simulated to all intents and purposes by the old buildings the owl now inhabits. A large percentage of rocky terrain in Britain consists of chalk and limestone and we may have here an explanation for the Barn Owl's predominantly light coloration, i.e. camouflage at its roosts and nesting sites. There may well have been suitable hunting territories on the more open rocky areas that often exist where cliffs are found, for even today it is by no means averse to frequenting such places if the climate is mild enough. However, since in Britain one commonly associates this sort of terrain with high ground and severe weather, it is difficult to imagine a Barn Owl being able to occupy many of these areas for more than a short period of time. Nevertheless, as we have seen, some individuals *are* occasionally encountered at heights up to 500 m, particularly in Wales and Scotland. Neil Bowman (pers. comm.) suggests that birds occupying these upland areas are an excess population forced to live on high ground when all the lowland territories are occupied after years of high productivity. He feels that when the population is low, either through poor productivity or high mortality, surviving upland birds move into lowland territories which have become vacant.

The Barn Owl's habits are well suited to the present British countryside with its predominance of fields and hedgerows for hunting and numerous old buildings (and, in some parts, roomy hollow trees) for breeding. Unlike the Tawny Owl, which will be found in any municipal park with a trace of woodland, it shuns the towns; but provided it is within reach of suitable hunting territory, it will establish itself in suburban areas wherever it is unmolested. It can become remarkably accustomed to the daily routine of human activity and will sometimes take up permanent residence in farm buildings that are used a great deal. When it does this, it usually prefers the quieter retreats such as a hayloft or outbarn where it can hide from view.

In retrospect it is easier to describe where a Barn Owl will *not* be found than to mention all the habitats it frequents. Despite this, there are certain areas in which it appears to do better than elsewhere. One of these is the low-lying arable land near the coast, where the supply of rodents and small birds ensures an abundance of prey in territories which usually have a mild winter climate. Another type of habitat which encourages inflated populations of Barn Owls in that provided by young forestry plantations. Where these are not at too great an altitude – below 300 m in Britain – the bird can survive most winters and finds an easy living preying on the vast numbers of Short-tailed Voles whose populations tend to build up in the long grass that develops when the pressure of grazing by domestic animals is removed. As an additional attraction, the existing farms are vacated when land is taken over by forestry and they then become available to the owls, which quickly adopt them for roosting and breeding. Indeed, without such buildings it seems unlikely that they would be able to exploit this rich habitat, despite the abundance of voles. Coniferous plantations have a peak of suitability which is reached soon after their establishment, but unfortunately this declines rapidly when the trees become impenetrable and smother the long grass which provides the vole habitat.

Areas which are definitely shunned by the bird are those with a paucity of vegetation and of shelter from the elements, for as already mentioned the Barn Owl has difficulty in surviving severe weather, especially snow.

STATUS

When considering the distribution of the Barn Owl in Britain it must be realised that, as the population is noted for its instability, any account of its status at a given time, however accurate, can at best be no more than temporarily correct. It only requires a 'vole year' or a prolonged period of extreme weather to bring about radical changes, and there are constant references to such happenings throughout this chapter. To try and trace all the small, short-term fluctuations which have taken place in different parts of the country during the present century would be pointless and is, in any case, scarcely possible. We have therefore concentrated on dramatic changes in population wherever these have occurred, and in particular have attempted to show where the long-term decline is having the greatest effect.

A glance through the 18th century literature leaves one in no doubt that the Barn Owl was once a good deal more common than it is now. It is significant that most of the references to owls clearly apply to this species, for its white plumage is frequently mentioned. The Tawny Owl, on the other hand, is seldom referred to and we must assume that this reflects the relative numbers of the two species at the time. The use of the adjective 'familiar' to describe the Barn Owl is, in itself, an indication of its healthy status at that period and E. Donovan, in his *Natural History of British Birds* (1794–1819), confirms this when he states: 'It need scarcely be said that the white owl is common in every part of England . . .'. Furthermore, the bird appears to have been well known in both town and country.

By the beginning of the present century, however, it was clear that the species had already begun to falter, though the reports of some observers show that the degree of decline varied from county to county. In Scotland it was even said to be increasing in the south. Blame for the decrease in England was repeatedly laid at the hands of gamekeepers and we need hardly doubt that this was largely justified, though other factors were no doubt involved as well. R. B. Lodge (1903), for instance, quotes the famous Lincolnshire naturalist, John Cordeaux, as follows: 'The useful Barn Owl, too, has been ruthlessly destroyed whenever opportunities offered in this same cruel fashion [by the use of the pole-trap]. Noiselessly across the waste in the twilight, like a flitting phantom, comes the soft-winged owl, and seeing, as if placed ready for his use, a post of vantage from which he may mark each stealthy movement of the mischievous Field Vole, stays his flight to settle on the treacherous perch; and then during all the long sad night – and often, we fear, through the succeeding day – with splintered bone protruding through smashed flesh and torn tendon, hangs suspended in supreme agony, gibbeted head downwards till death puts an end to his suffering.'

It is lamentable that even today such is the fate of the Barn Owl in certain areas, though not sufficiently often as to reduce the general population.

In 1932, by which time many ornithologists had expressed their concern at the rapid decline of the Barn Owl, G. B. Blaker of the RSPB organised a remarkably ambitious enquiry into the status of the Barn Owl in England and Wales. In view of the immensity of the task with which Blaker was faced and the enthusiasm with which the survey was undertaken, we are reluctant to offer criticism in any form, but in the interests of scientific accuracy we feel bound to express the opinion that, if our own experiences are anything to go by, Blaker seems to have been extraordinarily over-confident about the accuracy of his results. In this respect it is relevant to note that the British Trust for Ornithology in their recent *Atlas of Breeding Birds in Britain and Ireland* considered the Barn Owl to be the third hardest species to locate, and Neil Bowman, conducting an enquiry into Barn Owl numbers in mid-Wales, makes the comment: 'the degree of awareness of the farmers varied

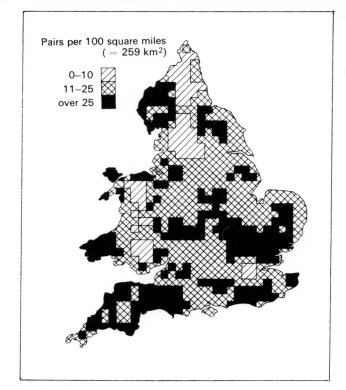

Fig. 9 Breeding distribution and density of the Barn Owl in England and Wales in 1932 (after Blaker 1934).

considerably; some knew every site in their local area while at the other end of the scale a farmer slap in the middle of an occupied territory "had not seen one for years".' Blaker's claim to have accounted for every breeding pair, or to within one nest, in many squares really does seem unduly optimistic in the light of these difficulties.

Nevertheless, despite any shortcomings, the census served its purpose in confirming the suspicions of so many ornithologists that the Barn Owl population had indeed been diminishing over most of the country during the previous thirty to forty years, and it was calculated that the annual rate of decrease had been around 4% during the previous ten years. Blaker stated: 'In parts of Essex and Suffolk the decline was less marked, while in Devon and parts of Somerset and Cornwall the Barn Owl seems to be holding its own. Cumberland, Westmorland [both now Cumbria] and Northumberland are the only counties to record an increase.' Fig. 9 shows the status of the bird at the time of Blaker's survey.

We have no reason to suspect that the causes of the decline in the Barn Owl population in the early part of the present century were substantially different from those operating today; discussion of these and the steps which can be taken to counteract them have been included in Chapter 7. Suffice it to say here that Blaker estimated a population of 25,000 Barn Owls in England and Wales in 1932 and a rate of decrease that had risen over the preceding three years. (It is noteworthy that Blaker did not appear to be aware of the short-term fluctuations that are so characteristic of the species.)

In the late 1950s the sudden disappearance of the birds from their regular

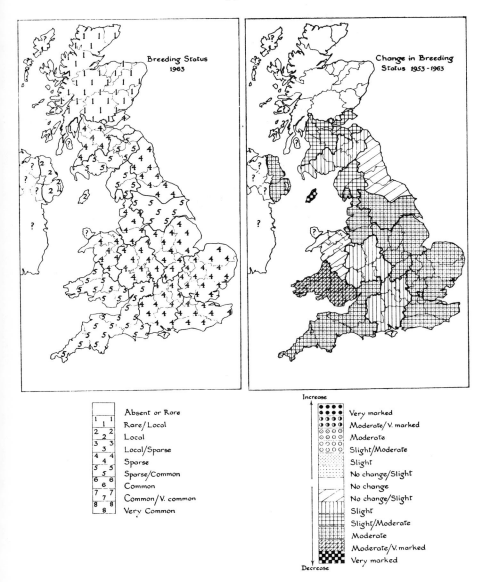

Fig. 10 Breeding status of the Barn Owl in Britain in 1963, and changes in status during the period 1953–63 (after Prestt 1965).

haunts once again attracted the attention of many ornithologists. On this occasion, however, it was not just Barn Owls that were affected but almost all predators. This marked the beginning of the 'toxic chemicals' scare which has featured prominently in the mass media ever since. Because of the serious implications of the decline, which it was realised might only be the forerunner of a catastrophe affecting Man himself, the then Nature Conservancy and the BTO organised a survey (Prestt 1965) of the breeding status of 'some smaller birds of prey', among which the Barn Owl was included, during the period 1953–1963. The information acquired is highly relevant to this chapter.

Questionnaires were sent to all the BTO regional representatives and to as many officials of natural history societies and other interested organisations and individuals as possible. Ireland, and more than half of Wales and Scotland, were virtually uncovered, but some information was obtained for every English county except Middlesex. The survey revealed that the Barn Owl had undergone a recent decrease in just under three-quarters of the counties for which information was received and that it had been subject to a fairly widespread long-term decline in about half the counties. Furthermore, the recent decrease had begun in the late 1950s and was most evident in 1959–60. Fig. 10 summarises in map-form the breeding status in 1963 and the changes in breeding status that were thought to have taken place in the opinions of the contributors. Though the drop in numbers had been very marked in a few *counties*, in each of the larger *regions* into which Britain had been conveniently divided for the census, the decline was not so drastic and was more in the nature of a gradual overall decrease, except in the north of Scotland where the bird was very local or rare anyway.

Indications were that the bird was commonest in South-west England, South Wales, South Yorkshire, North-west England and southern Scotland. (This was also confirmed by the findings of the BTO *Atlas of Breeding Birds in Britain and Ireland* in 1976.)

A year later an attempt was made to record the breeding status of the Kestrel, Tawny Owl and Barn Owl in greater detail (Prestt & Bell 1966), but so far as the latter bird was concerned this was something of a failure, and perhaps for the first time the difficulties in locating the species began to be appreciated. The method used in this follow-up survey was to try to establish breeding in as many 10 km squares in Britain as possible and it is perhaps hardly necessary to add that this was the same method by which information was obtained for the BTO *Atlas of Breeding Birds in Britain and Ireland* project. This monumental work provides a valuable insight into the very recent distribution of the bird and the map depicting confirmed breeding records (see Fig. 11) shows a marked similarity to the earlier findings of Prestt.

At first glance the picture given in *The Atlas of Breeding Birds in Britain and Ireland* appears to be a remarkably healthy one for a bird placed on the First Schedule of the Protection of Birds Act. However, care should be taken when using these maps in an attempt to assess population densities. Although it is evident that between 1968 and 1972 the species was widely distributed throughout most of England and Wales (a more healthy situation, perhaps, than if it were commoner but only locally distributed), it will be seen that the maps give no indication of the number of Barn Owl nests in each square.

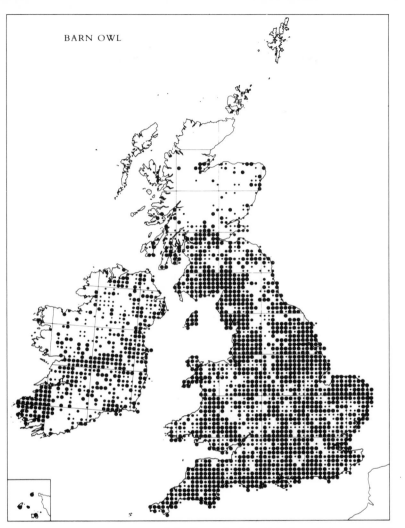

Fig. 11 Breeding distribution of the Barn Owl in Britain and Ireland in the period 1968–72 (from The Atlas of Breeding Birds in Britain and Ireland*).*

As we have said, the task of assessing actual numbers of Barn Owls is a difficult one, but in 1969 D. Scott began an enquiry into the population density and recent changes in status of the Barn Owl in Britain and subsequently passed on the results to us. We in turn made further requests for information from local naturalists and Regional Representatives of the BTO in 1972/73, and again in 1978/79 when RSPB Regional Officers and County Naturalists' Trusts were also brought into the survey. The amount of information given was extremely variable and depended to a large degree on the numbers and interest of the observers concerned; it was frequently rather vague due to a lack of field-workers in some areas. However, taken as a whole the enquiry was very worthwhile and provides the most accurate and up-to-date overall assessment of its status in Britain for some time.

The picture seems to be one of a widely distributed bird in non-urban areas throughout England, Wales, southern Scotland and Ireland. Generally it is rather sparse in numbers but locally it can be almost common, and it is rare for it to be absent where the habitat is suitable. Many observers recorded the decrease in the late 1950s, and the dramatic decline after the severe winter of 1962/63 is a recurrent theme. Several reports mentioned a recovery around 1972–73 but sadly the 1978/79 survey showed that another decline had occurred in many counties in the years 1976–78. The prolonged snow and cold of the 1978/79 winter was the latest disaster for an already depleted population and the appalling summer of 1979 resulted in a very poor breeding season which did nothing to remedy the situation. The 1979 decline is probably short-term in most counties but we fear that the factors which brought about the less obvious decrease between 1976–78 are long-term and insidious and bode ill for the future of the bird in Britain.

In central and northern Scotland it is much more thinly distributed than in the milder, maritime south-west, becoming rarer the further north one progresses. However, isolated breeding records do exist even in the extreme north. Despite this, it is reasonable to suppose that neither the climate nor the terrain are suitable for the species in the north of Scotland and *The Atlas of Breeding Birds in Britain and Ireland* remarks that those Barn Owls nesting in Ross and Cromarty (and also south-east Sutherland immediately before *The Atlas* period) probably represent the most northerly breeding Barn Owls in the world.

Using a conservative estimate of 2–4 pairs per occupied 10 km square *The Atlas of Breeding Birds in Britain and Ireland* puts the total population of the species, for the period 1968–72, at between 4,500–9,000 pairs, compared with Blaker's figures of 12,000 pairs in 1932. As our survey has shown, numbers have declined further since *The Atlas* days and, in our opinion, are likely to continue to do so in the future.

We now pass on to a county-by-county assessment of the bird's distribution in Britain as it stood in 1980. The county names used are the new ones applicable from 1974. Where changes in county boundaries have occurred these are mentioned in the text. For convenience and easy reference the old Welsh counties are listed separately within the present large county surveys. The same applies to Scotland which is now separated into Regions, which are too large for accurate survey purposes. The counties are listed in a roughly south–north, west–east arrangement. Contributors' names are shown at the end of each county report.

SOUTH-WEST ENGLAND

Cornwall

This is a very good county for the bird due to the nature of the farming methods, i.e. small, non-intensive farms with little use of chemicals. The continued use of old stone barns is also an undoubted factor in its success. Like many other counties there was a decline around the mid 1950s and early

1960s but fortunately a good population survived around Liskeard and to the north of Bodmin on relatively high, open ground at about 260 m. Here the numerous farmsteads provide suitable nest sites and on one 2000 ha estate in mid-Cornwall the gamekeeper estimated a population of 15 pairs. In the south-east of the county an estimate was made of at least one pair per parish. The bird did remarkably well between 1972 and 1978 and records from the Cornwall Bird Watching and Preservation Society show the following picture:

1973   Recorded during the breeding season in 13 localities, ranging from Penzance in the west, Lostwithiel in mid-county, and from North to South Cornwall.

1974   Recorded from 21 localities and widespread in winter.

1975   Recorded from 30 localities in the breeding season.

1976   Recorded from 30+ localities and bred in most of its known sites. Now regarded as common on Bodmin Moor and widespread throughout the county in winter.

1977   Another good year with records from all over the county. The stronghold still Bodmin Moor and one recorder reported 38 sightings on the new Bodmin by-pass, between 21st September and 31st December, of at least 10 different birds.

The picture changed dramatically in 1978, however. Between October and early November heavy mortality occurred in the area between Hayle in the west, to Bodmin in the east, with up to 30 birds being found dead or dying. This mortality was discussed in the previous chapter, but it is too soon to say what the long-term effect has been on the Cornish Barn Owl population. (R. D. Penhallurick, S. L. Powell)

Devon

A slight decrease occurred from 1957 but it was still widespread in 1969 in very small numbers, mainly on lowland farmland. *The Atlas of Breeding Birds in Britain and Ireland* estimated 2–4 pairs per occupied square, but a breeding bird survey by the Devon Bird Watching Society in 1977 suggested a figure of 10–12 pairs per occupied square in the agricultural hill country. There seems more than a possibility that the species has been under-recorded in the past, for where two observers made special efforts to find Barn Owls they were found in considerable numbers, i.e. in SY 09 (Whimple) it was present in 15 out of 25 tetrads, and in SS 53 (Barnstaple) 20 out of 25. Some of these records might refer to the same bird crossing tetrad boundaries, but certain tetrads were known to contain more than one pair. The feeling is that the population is fairly high at the moment. (H. P. Sitters)

Dorset

This is another county where the familiar pattern of a decline in the early 1960s took place. Little improvement was noted until 1970 when *The Atlas of Breeding Birds in Britain and Ireland* workers found *proved* and *probable* breeding in many squares. The question must be asked whether this apparent improvement was a true picture or whether it simply reflected improved coverage by observers, as happened in many counties during *The Atlas* project. A handful of breeding records is received from many parts of the county in most years and individual sightings in winter are quite numerous and widespread. These always include some road casualties. There is a steady increase in reports of Barn Owls nesting in trees rather than buildings, including at least one in a dead Elm. After the 1978/79 winter a worrying shortage of Barn Owls was reported by the Dorset Naturalists' Trust and J. V. Boys reported 'few breeding reports' in 1979. However, there were four pairs with young at Purbeck, a pair with young at Maiden Newton and a pair with two young at Povington Heath. Many individual sightings were made by 37 observers in all parts of the county and at all seasons, but two people suggested a decline and one observer registered a specific *nil* return from his area. (J. V. Boys, Miss H. J. Brotherton)

Somerset
The general opinion amongst local birdwatchers in 1972 was that the bird was undergoing a marked recovery after the usual story of a decline around 1954–65. The number of new records increased annually during the course of *The Atlas of Breeding Birds in Britain and Ireland* survey and the final figures showed *proved* breeding in 17 out of the 41 squares, with *possible* breeding in a further 16. The Somerset Ornithological Society records for the years 1975–78 are as follows:

1975   Five birds found dead on M5 between St. Georges, Bristol, and Dunball. One breeding record (4 young); many reports of single birds from all parts of the county.

1976   Autumn/winter reports from 32 sites in all parts of the county. 4 fledged owlets killed when tree blown down in a September gale.

1977   An excellent year with autumn/winter records from 54 sites in all parts of the county, 2–3 birds sometimes seen together. 8 breeding records.

1978   Another good year. Non-breeding season records from 36 sites from all parts of the county. 3 road victims found in different places. 17 breeding season reports and at least 5 nests recorded. A breeding season pair reported from alongside the M5 at Brent Knoll. (G. H. E. Young, D. Ladhams)

Avon
The northern half of this completely new county consists of part of old Gloucestershire, while the southern half used to be the northern third of Somerset. Distribution of the Barn Owl in the new county in 1979 was very sparse with most being found on the southern boundary with Somerset.

SOUTH-EAST ENGLAND

Hampshire and Isle of Wight
In 1972 the Barn Owl was reported to be well distributed, though hardly common, throughout the county and Isle of Wight. Up to 1957 there had been little evidence of a change in status since 1905, but from 1957 there were persistent reports of a marked decline in some south-eastern parts of the county. In 1961 it was said to be widespread and not uncommon on the Isle of Wight, but in 1964 a decrease was noted in the Basingstoke area of Hampshire, possibly due to toxic chemicals. This can still be detected on *The Atlas of Breeding Birds in Britain and Ireland* map. However, some areas

maintained their numbers and *The Atlas* survey revealed that a recovery was under way by 1968. It was still well distributed throughout the county, though still not common, in 1979. (J. H. Tavener)

West Sussex

Since 1968 there has been much evidence of a steady increase from the decline of the late 1950s and early 1960s and the high mortality on the roads seems to suggest a healthy population. In 1972 it was reported as 'well distributed and breeding throughout the county, but nowhere very numerous'. Large areas of permanent grassland supported the largest populations and a survey of about 80 km² in the Pulborough district disclosed five pairs and three single birds in 1970, while another survey in the same year found seven occupied territories in a 52 km² area of the Selsey Peninsula. (M. Shrubb)

East Sussex

The same applied in 1972 as in West Sussex but no detailed surveys were made in this county, making comparisons impossible. *The Atlas of Breeding Birds in Britain and Ireland* shows that fewer pairs breed in East Sussex than West Sussex, and the population is particularly sparse in the northern parts of the county.

Recent *Sussex Bird Reports* suggest that in 1978 the bird might have declined in both West and East Sussex, for in 1976 single birds or pairs were reported during the breeding season from 26 localities, whereas in 1977 pairs were located in 10 localities and single birds in a further 31. However, in 1978 the number of single bird sightings dropped to 16 with breeding pairs remaining fairly constant at nine (eight of these coming from West Sussex). First-winter birds were reported from a further eight localities. (M. Rogers, M. Shrubb)

Surrey

The Atlas of Breeding Birds in Britain and Ireland project provided records of *proved* breeding in 14 of the 23 squares, *probable* breeding in two and *possible* breeding in four squares. The population appeared to be sparse in the west of the county. Records from the Surrey Bird Club between 1967 and 1977 provide the following figures:

Year	Occupied areas	Proved breeding	Probable breeding
1967	16	5	Nil
1968	10	2	Nil
1969	14	1	3
1970	16	2	Nil
1971	16	3	Nil
1972	11	3	3
1973	22	1	2
1974	14	2	2
1975	7	2	1
1976	11	Nil	2
1977	7	1	Nil

The contributor felt that it was possible that Bird Reports only reveal around one quarter of the actual numbers of Barn Owls present in an area, and suggests that an actual decline from 22 records in 1973 to only seven in 1977 (a decline of 68%) is unlikely. However, he believes that there may well have been a slight though not very serious drop in numbers in recent years up to 1979. (R. H. B. Foster)

Kent

In Kent the 1950s' decrease was regarded as slight, but by 1970 the bird's status was precarious with only ten pairs known to have bred. The Kent Ornithological Society's Breeding Bird Survey 1967–72 indicated *possible* breeding in 50 tetrads (5·0%), *probable* breeding in 19 tetrads (1·9%) and *confirmed* breeding in 39 tetrads (3·9%). The total number of tetrads in which Barn Owls were recorded was 108 (10·8%). In 1973 seven pairs were reported breeding, but in 1974 and 1975, although it was reported from numerous localities, there were few confirmed reports of successful breeding. In 1976 three pairs were reported breeding and this apparent steady decline has continued in recent years. Many birds are killed on the roads and most fatalities can be ascribed to this cause, 34 birds being reported dead in the six years 1971–76. No data has been received for the years since 1976. (C. Hindle)

THAMES VALLEY AND THE CHILTERNS

Wiltshire

In 1969 the Barn Owl was much decreased and rare in the majority of its former haunts, though isolated pockets still held breeding pairs. There has been little change in status since then and a survey by the Wiltshire Ornithological Society during the winter of 1977/78, in which members of the public were invited to take part, resulted in *sightings* from nineteen 10 km squares, *confirmed* breeding in five squares and *possible* breeding in several more. The majority of sightings were in south- and mid-county, with only a few in the north and none at all in the area north of Marlborough and east of Malmesbury. Most of the sightings were in or adjacent to river valleys, especially those that run into the Hampshire Avon. Of those records which mentioned breeding or roosts, Elms were the commonest site, and in view of the large number of these trees being felled as a result of Dutch Elm Disease, it appears certain that the Barn Owl population will be affected adversely in the future. (J. Taylor, C. L. Webber)

Berkshire

In 1972 the Barn Owl was generally, but fairly thinly distributed, breeding regularly in a number of localities and being regularly reported from all parts of the county outside the breeding season. Nowhere was it considered common. During the five years of *The Atlas of Breeding Birds in Britain and Ireland* survey, breeding was *proved* in 19 out of 21 squares, with *possible* breeding in the remaining two. Since then there has been a remarkable paucity of breeding records, with only one or two between 1972 and 1975, and none whatsoever in 1976 and 1977. This suggests a decline in detailed observations rather than a true assessment of the present breeding status, for individual birds have been recorded from all over the county as follows:

1972–25 sightings; 1973–19; 1974–15; 1975–14; 1976–23; 1977–9. On the basis of these sightings, favoured areas appear to be Hungerford, south-west Reading, Bradfield and Theale.

The *Birds of Berkshire, Annual Report* 1976–77, records Barn Owls from 22 widely scattered localities in 1976 and 14 in 1977, no breeding being recorded in either year. The frequency of records increases from east to west. A factor which might limit the Barn Owl population in the future is the widespread practice of buying up old houses and barns as second homes. There has been little recent information in the years following 1977. (P. Hanson, P. E. Standley, G. W. Wilson)

Oxfordshire

A partial survey in 1967 disclosed 13 pairs and *The Atlas of Breeding Birds in Britain and Ireland* found *proved* breeding in 13 out of 18 squares, *probable* breeding in two and *sightings* in the remaining three; however, they probably bred in very small numbers in all squares. Little further information was available until 1979 when it was found to be scattered fairly evenly, but thinly, over the county. A survey conducted by the Banbury Ornithological Society and the Oxford Ornithological Society suggests that the status given in *The Atlas* (i.e. 'breeding in most 10 km squares') is about right today. The county does not have a great deal of rough ground and the species has to rely on the headlands around arable fields for its hunting. (R. Knight, C. M. Reynolds)

Buckinghamshire

In this county the bird is generally believed to have decreased from the early 1950s. This is most apparent on the chalk in the south of the county, where several long-established sites are no longer occupied. The decrease coincides with the spread of urbanisation and the introduction of modern farming methods. Despite this assessment it is still widespread, though continuing to decrease at the present time. The population is far sparser here than in the adjacent counties of Oxfordshire and Hertfordshire. (J. Devan, R. S. Youngman)

Greater London

The Barn Owl was once evenly distributed in the rural areas around London, but declined markedly in the 1920s and 1930s. A second, severe decline occurred in the late 1950s and early 1960s, and the only definite breeding records for the whole London area in 1962 and 1963 were of single nests at different sites in each year. Recovery was slow, with confirmed breeding at only two sites in 1964 and in 1965, and three in 1966. In 1967 the London Natural History Society carried out a survey of the 158 squares within 32 km of St. Paul's and this showed *proved* breeding pairs at seven sites and 15 further tetrads in which birds were *present* without breeding being proved. *The Atlas of Breeding Birds in Britain and Ireland* project showed *proved* breeding in 28 tetrads, *probable* breeding in 20 and birds *present* in 61. It is considered that a genuine increase occurred during this period. As is to be expected the bird still favours rural areas and it has never been found breeding in Inner London, unlike the Tawny Owl. However, it does breed in suburban areas such as Richmond Park, Osterley Park, Waltham Abbey, Chigwell and Romford, and its status seems to be static at the present time, a few pairs breeding in favoured sites and disappearing in others, while individual birds are seen at other sites during the breeding season without breeding being proved. It appears to be commonest in the north-east, west and south-west of London and, despite the pressures of urbanisation, it seems to be holding its own, though it must be said that any further increase seems unlikely. Even those pairs which do survive suffer from egg collectors and vandalism. (D. Montier)

Hertfordshire

The species is extremely scarce in this county, with most breeding taking place in the east. The certain situation in 1977 and 1978 was as follows: 2–3 pairs in the north-east of the county (Ashwell, Barley and near Reed), perhaps 10–12 pairs in mid and east Herts (Branfield, Ware and east to Bishop's Stortford, Standon and Much Hadham). Only one pair known in west Herts – at Chipperfield. It is considered doubtful if more than two pairs have gone unrecorded. There was a massive decline between 1962–67, but since 1973 the situation has remained fairly stable. (T. W. Gladwin, C. J. Mead)

Bedfordshire

Recent work shows that the species is far more common than was formerly realised, but it also indicates the difficulty in locating the birds. For instance in 1968 only two nests were found and in 1969 it was thought to be very scarce and extremely local throughout. However, it is now considered to be well distributed but under-recorded. A concentrated effort by B. D. Harding in contacting farmers in square TL 06 (the most northerly square) between 1968 and 1978 resulted in confirmed breeding records in six tetrads out of 25, a far higher number than elsewhere. Yet not a single Barn Owl was recorded by casual observers in this square, outside the breeding season, between 1972–77. In the 21 Bedfordshire 10 km squares (some being part squares) Harding *proved* breeding in 19 tetrads, *probable* breeding in 12 and *possible* breeding in 50 tetrads. (B. D. Harding, A. J. Livett, B. J. Nightingale, A. Smith)

EAST ANGLIA

Essex

A census in 1932 produced an estimate of 500 pairs in the county, but by 1968 it was thought that only one third of that number existed. Following that, *The Atlas of Breeding Birds in Britain and Ireland* survey suggested a further decrease, with the north of the county supporting the highest population. The number of breeding pairs during *The Atlas* period was as follows: 1968–18, 1969–26, 1970–18, 1971–19 and 1972–22. In the years following, the figures were: 1973–13 *proved* breeding pairs and five other pairs reported during the season; 1974–15 *proved* breeding pairs and nine other pairs, single birds noted at 16 sites during the breeding season and six single birds outside the breeding season; 1975–13 breeding pairs, single birds at six sites and 23 outside the season; 1977 – reported from 20 localities in the breeding season and 29 sightings at other times. Of the twenty 1977 records, nine were in the Colchester/north-east Essex area, six in the Dengie Hundred (the eastern part of the county), four in central Essex, and the remaining record was of four birds at Ilford. Of the 29 sightings outside the breeding season 15 came from the north-east, seven from central, five from south-east and two from the Metropolitan area. The species appears to be holding its own at the present time, though in much reduced numbers. (G. Smith, Mrs. P. V. Upton)

Cambridgeshire
This county now includes the old county of Huntingdonshire where the species was a common breeder prior to the advent of toxic chemicals. It had decreased by 1969 but was still widely distributed at that time. In 1932 there were 96 occupied territories recorded in Cambridgeshire, these being densest in the south of the county where they averaged one pair per 10·4 km². By 1972 the situation had changed, with the numbers in the Fenland in the north of the county being not very much lower than in 1932, despite the heavy use of pesticides in that area and in contrast to the relative scarcity of other birds of prey. However, numbers in the south of the county were much reduced despite the fact that *The Atlas of Breeding Birds in Britain and Ireland* map does not reveal this. Out of a total of 26 squares *proved* breeding was recorded in nine, *probable* breeding in two and *possible* breeding in 12 squares. The present position seems to be unchanged and there is evidence that the Barn Owl still has not returned to its former haunts in anything like its previous numbers in the south of the county. Lack of wide observer coverage in the north continues to hinder an accurate assessment of numbers in that area. (M. J. Allen, B. Milne, A. E. Vine)

Suffolk
As elsewhere, there was a sharp decline in the 1960s and it was thought that numbers were still declining steadily around 1969, due to poisons and pesticides and the destruction of old farm buildings and hollow trees. Since then there appears to have been little change and the Barn Owl remains local and scarce. It is apparently absent from a large part of south-west and south Suffolk, but around Lowestoft in the extreme north there has been an increase after the 1960s' decline. Birds are seen regularly in the breeding season in many areas of the triangle formed by Bungay, Saxmundham and Lowestoft, and numbers hold steady throughout the coastal belt and in parts of the Breckland. (D. Moore, W. H. Payn)

Norfolk
Having declined noticeably in the west during the 1960s it appeared to have recovered slightly during the 1971 and 1972 seasons, breeding being *proved* in almost all suitable squares. Since 1972 there has been a slow but steady increase in numbers in the area of Downham Market, though these are still fairly low. It was widely distributed in the east in 1973, concentrations occurring in permanent grassland areas, mainly along the river valleys. Taking the county as a whole, the population remains virtually unchanged

since the early 1970s. This is a species for which all records are asked for by the *Norfolk Bird Report* each year, and apart from two freak years (1971 with 91 localities and 1974 with 105) each year's returns fall within the bracket 69–75 localities where the bird has been recorded. These figures include winter and summer sightings and the breeding population is probably somewhat lower. A rather rapid disappearance of meadowland is currently taking place and it remains to be seen how long this owl will remain common. Mortality on the roads is heavy and in January 1971 eleven dead Barn Owls were found on a 16 km stretch of road through marshland near Great Yarmouth. (A. Bull, J. G. Goldsmith, A. Hale, M. Seago)

WEST MIDLANDS

Gloucestershire

Like many others this county suffered a decrease in Barn Owls after the 1962/63 winter when 16 were found dead on one estate alone. The bird was widespread but not common in the Severn Vale and the Cotswolds. It was also found around the perimeter of the Forest of Dean and very locally within the Forest area, though breeding was not proved. The population has apparently remained stable up to 1979 but, as *The Atlas of Breeding Birds in Britain and Ireland* map shows, this is a rather poor county for the species. (C. Swaine, P. Dymott)

Hereford & Worcester

In 1969 the Barn Owl was reported to be very thinly scattered over most of the old county of Herefordshire, while the West Midlands Bird Club pilot survey of 1966–68 showed a very patchy distribution in Worcestershire. However, J. Lord found it 'not scarce' and received reports of a steady increase in many areas. *The Atlas of Breeding Birds in Britain and Ireland* showed a strong breeding population in the centre of the county, most being in the Worcestershire section, with the Herefordshire population being more scattered. G. R. Harrison feels that the difference between these surveys reflects better observer coverage during *The Atlas* survey rather than a real improvement in Barn Owl numbers. His summary in 1979 was 'widely, but thinly distributed with noticeable short-term fluctuations masking long-term population trends'. A typical example of this is shown in the following figures: 1974 – reported from 40 sites; 1975–53; 1976–62; 1977–31. An apparent steady increase was therefore followed by a marked decline in 1977 and this has continued in 1978 and 1979. (Mrs J. Bromley, G. R. Harrison, J. Lord, R. Owen, A. J. Smith)

Warwickshire

In 1947, Norris described the Barn Owl as 'local and scarce' – a similar picture to the West Midland Bird Club pilot survey for its *Atlas of Breeding Birds of the West Midlands*, conducted in 1966–68. This showed a very patchy distribution but the final *Atlas* map suggests a more widespread distribution with breeding birds being present in most squares apart from the southern tip. A large part of the old north-west section of the county is now part of the West Midlands county and, since many of the squares concerned held breeding Barn Owls, this has automatically resulted in a drop in numbers for this county. There is also evidence of a decrease in the last few years. (G. R. Harrison, J. Lord)

West Midlands

This entirely new county takes in part of the old counties of Staffordshire, Worcestershire and Warwickshire, and is dominated by the urban sprawl of Wolverhampton, Birmingham and Coventry. There is little recent information on the status of the Barn Owl in the West Midlands Metropolitan county, but since 1973 the annual reports of the West Midlands Bird Club have included records from Bartley Green, Hockley Heath, Kings Winford, Selly Oak, Solihull and Wolverhampton. Most of these records only involved 'sightings', and only at Bartley was breeding reported, in 1976. The species almost certainly suffers from under-recording and a West Midland Bird Club survey during 1966–68 and the BTO *The Atlas of Breeding Birds in Britain and Ireland* survey of 1968–72 revealed *proved* breeding or *probable* breeding in 10 squares, including those containing the major urban areas. This probably reflects the more detailed observer coverage rather than a real increase in the species. However, it appears that the bird is widespread and not uncommon throughout the county at present. (A. R. Dean, J. Lord)

Shropshire

There is a shortage of observers in Shropshire but it is felt that there was little change in status between 1959 and 1969, the bird being present in very small numbers in nearly all parts. It is still under-recorded but is sufficiently common for observers to record unusual sightings only, such as daylight hunting, road casualties and occasional nest records. Between 1973 and 1978, there were 285 records submitted to the Shropshire Ornithological Society, and these indicate that the bird is apparently absent from the high moorland over 300 m in the south and south-west of the county, but is fairly well distributed elsewhere. Assuming that observer coverage has remained constant there appeared to be a steady increase in records from 39 in 1973, to 68 in 1975, followed by a decline to 35 in 1976, and 32 up to November 1978. Of all records, 5% related to birds found dead (all were road casualties apart from one on a gamekeeper's gibbet). (Lt-Col. H. R. Perkins, C. Wright)

Staffordshire

The Barn Owl has seemingly had a chequered history in this county, the south-east tip of which is now part of the West Midlands county. Smith (1938), in his *Birds of Staffordshire*, stated that it was almost, if not quite, extinct in many areas of Staffordshire, while Lord & Blakes (1962) said there were very few in the northern moorlands, the Black Country and the south-east part of the county, and rather more, but still few, in the west and south-west and in parts of the north-west and Trent Valley areas. Norris (1951) showed it as breeding in all areas of the county, and Fincher (1955) suggested that the previous decline had stopped and numbers were perhaps increasing. Around this period Lord & Manns stated in *The Atlas of Breeding Birds of the West Midlands*, 'recent reports suggest a steady increase in many areas'; and F. Gribble, who gathered much of this information (and also for the BTO *Atlas of Breeding Birds in Britain and Ireland* for Staffs.), feels that the bird has become more common. He believes that *The Atlas of Breeding Birds in Britain and Ireland* probably showed the present status of the species in this county, i.e. 'widely spread throughout the county in small numbers'. The West Midlands Bird Club reports show it recorded as follows for Staffs: 1972 – recorded from 31 localities, seven breeding records; 1973 – 21 localities; 1974 – six localities; 1975 – 17 localities, four breeding records; 1976 – 15 localities; 1977 – twelve localities.

F. Gribble believes that the increase in 1972 and 1973 reflects the increased efforts of observers in the first years of *The Atlas of Breeding Birds in Britain and Ireland* rather than a true increase in owl numbers. By 1979/80, it was certainly scarce in the north-eastern moorlands and the Black Country (now part of the West Midlands county). Quite a large part of the county is not watched over regularly, but most records of the species are sent in to the Report – many being of single birds seen at dusk while people are motoring. (F. Gribble, J. Lord)

Cheshire

It is a story of steady decline in Cheshire and, although in 1972 the Barn Owl was still widely distributed, it was much less common than formerly. *The Atlas of Breeding Birds in Britain and Ireland* showed *proved* breeding in 18 out of the 32 squares, but some of these squares have now been lost to the new county of Merseyside. *Probable* breeding was shown in two squares and *possible* breeding in nine. The general opinion at present is that the species is even less common than at the time of *The Atlas*. Known breeding sites have been lost to demolition and this is one of the causes of the decline. (J. Dawson, J. R. Mullins)

EAST MIDLANDS

Northamptonshire

The Barn Owl is a species for which 'all sightings' are asked for in Northamptonshire, and as observer coverage is fairly uniform the following information is a reasonably accurate year to year comparison of its status. It shows the number of localities that the species was reported from each year, with numbers of breeding pairs in parentheses: 1973 – 38 (4); 1974 – 46 (1); 1975 – 43 (2); 1976 – 42 (3); 1977 – 33 (2); 1978 – 29 (0). As can be seen, the years 1974–76 are fairly constant, but there was a disturbing drop in 1977 and 1978, though the 1969 assessment of 'thinly but widely distributed' still appears to be accurate. No specific request for breeding information has been made and the actual number of breeding pairs must be greater than is shown. *The Atlas of Breeding Birds in Britain and Ireland* indicates that there are fewer breeding birds to the west of the county in the area between Rugby and Northampton. (C. J. Coe)

Leicestershire

Leicestershire now includes the old county of Rutland, but this has not really altered the status of the bird to any extent, for in each former county the position was basically the same. It was widespread, though a scarce breeder in 1969, and was thought to be declining. Although recent information is difficult to obtain, there is nothing to suggest that the position is any different at the present time, and the bird can be found breeding in most of the county with the exception of the area immediately surrounding the city of Leicester. (Mrs K. Allsopp)

Derbyshire

In Whitlock's day almost every Derbyshire village had its resident Barn Owls, but by the 1950s they had become scarce. There was a further slight decrease from 1957–69, and the present picture is that of a thinly, but widely scattered population with strongholds at Chatsworth, Culland and the Rother Valley. *The Atlas of Breeding Birds in Britain and Ireland* found them to be absent from many parts of the west and this is probably linked with the predominance of high moorland in that region. Ringing recoveries indicate a sedentary population, deaths being due mainly to cars and trains. When quiet diesel trains were introduced, several Barn Owls were killed on the Derbyshire railway network. (G. Mawson, P. B. Wassell)

Nottinghamshire

The Atlas of Breeding Birds in Britain and Ireland showed the bird to be not scarce, and present in all squares, with breeding being *proved* in all but two. Its main stronghold was in the north and north-east. Ten pairs bred in eight parishes in 1972. The bird is still not scarce, but the apparent stronghold in the north and north-east might be due to observer bias caused by a specialised study of owls by one observer in that area. It is well represented in other parts of Nottinghamshire, such as the Trent Valley (cattle pasture and rough grazing associated with gravel workings provide good feeding areas). Elsewhere in central and southern Nottinghamshire it is present in those areas not affected by highly intensive arable farming. Road victims are a good indication of presence, and numbers and mortality increased with the coming of the M1 motorway through Nottinghamshire. The urban spread of Nottingham is now forcing it further away from the city centre, although it is still found fairly close, where habitat allows. There has been no detectable change in status in recent years and it is now classed as a fairly common resident, bearing in mind its territorial requirements. (A. Dobbs, D. Scott)

Lincolnshire

This is another county where boundary changes have taken place, the northern part of the old county now being south Humberside. The bird was not scarce in 1972, though it was rather locally distributed. *The Atlas of Breeding Birds* shows it as breeding in almost all squares, though fewer were *proved* breeding in the south of the county. Suitable buildings for nesting are now becoming scarce and this might well affect the general population in due course. At the present time it is not uncommon, being frequently seen by motorists at night over most of the county. An exception to this is the Fenland area, where the statement 'not scarce, though locally distributed' would apply. One group of ringers made a special effort on owls in 1977 and 1978, and reported that the Barn Owl did very well in 1978 despite the bad weather which resulted in the failure of every Little Owl nest found. (D. Scott, P. J. Wilson)

NORTH-WEST ENGLAND

Merseyside

This new county (once part of Lancashire and the Cheshire part of the Wirral Peninsula) has had a Barn Owl nest-box scheme operating in the southern part of the county for the past ten years or so. Despite this, there are only three regular sites occupied in south Merseyside and one other site which has been used occasionally since 1968. There is also at least one site on the Wirral and possibly a second. Two Barn Owls have been shot in the last year or so in the Speke/Halewood area and nest predation by schoolchildren still takes place. It is uncommon in the northern coastal dunes strip, very few being recorded on the Ainsdale National Nature Reserve. There are no recent breeding records for the dunes and it is much commoner on the mosses around the Ribble Estuary. There are, therefore, more frequent records around the northern and eastern boundaries of Merseyside. (R. Cockbain, K. Payne)

Greater Manchester

This is yet another new county, comprising the south-east of old Lancashire and the extreme north-eastern tip of old Cheshire and a small part of Derbyshire. The Lancashire section includes the city of Manchester and its suburbs, and not surprisingly *The Atlas of Breeding Birds in Britain and Ireland* fails to show any records of the species in this largely industrial area. One of the authors spent 19 years of his life here and in all that time he failed to see a single Barn Owl! The species is just about holding its own in many parts, has disappeared from others and has a few traditional strongholds. It is probable that the species will decline in this county as urbanisation inevitably spreads from the large towns and cities. If it has any future at all it must surely be on the agricultural land on the periphery, particularly in the south. (A. Meakin)

Lancashire

By 1972 the population was greatly depleted compared with the previous 20–30 years, numbers having reached a particularly low ebb in the early 1960s. Despite this the species remained well distributed and an increase was noted in the early 1970s when, after a succession of mild winters, it was not uncommon in some parts. The county is smaller since the boundary changes and some areas now form parts of Merseyside and Greater Manchester, while the Furness area has been added to Cumbria. All the lost sections held breeding populations and the present situation in the new county is as follows. In north Lancashire any slight improvement apparent around 1970 has now been lost and the species has markedly declined. It is still fairly widely scattered and appears to become commoner as one moves north. Instances of *proved* breeding are now hard to find, only one being known in 1978, and for the first time there were no records of the species on the RSPB's Leighton Moss Reserve, though one returned in early 1979.

In mid and east Lancashire it is now more numerous than is generally realised, breeding pairs being thinly distributed but very widespread from town centres to the edges of lonely moors. Any comparison with past years is probably unreliable due to varying observer coverage. From casual observations it is evident that it was a common breeder on the Fylde between 1966 and 1972, and in the same period it was regularly observed in south Lancashire, particularly in the area between Leyland and Ormskirk. In 1976, the *Fylde Bird Report* produced ten records of the species with three of the birds being found dead on the M55 motorway. There were eight records in 1977, and once again one of the birds was killed on the M55. In 1978, the *Lancashire Bird Report* included records from the Fylde, and six for south Lancashire (including two in the Chorley area which are the first for a few years). On the Fylde it is now no longer a common breeder but is widely, though thinly, spread. A poor breeding season was reported in south-west Lancashire in 1978. (C. Clapham, A. Duckels, M. Jones, K. G. Spencer)

Cumbria

As elsewhere the population showed a marked decrease during the 1960s, but a steady revival began in 1971 and was maintained until 1976. By then it was widely distributed and only absent from the high central fells at over 500 m. After an outstanding breeding season in 1976, the prolonged drought brought a 'crash' in the Short-tailed Vole population, with subsequent Barn Owl mortality. Successive dry summers in 1977 and 1978 kept vole numbers low and a noticeable decline in Barn Owl numbers was apparent. The severe winter of 1978/79 has aggravated the situation and Barn Owl numbers are now at their lowest level since the early 1960s. A poor breeding season in 1979 has done nothing to help matters, but breeding pairs are still to be found in the farmland and coastal mosses of the western plain. Old stone farm buildings are being replaced by modern structures in many areas and this is causing a noticeable reduction in viable Barn Owl nest sites. Several former breeding sites in young conifer plantations have also been deserted as the trees have matured, and the overall decline may well continue as a result of these factors. Although Cumbria has lost some of its breeding pairs it has gained the entire area of old Westmorland in the county boundary changes and this has added many breeding pairs to its population. (J. A. G. Barnes, A. B. Warburton)

NORTH-EAST ENGLAND

Yorkshire

This vast county has been split into three sections in the new county restructuring and these will be treated separately for convenience. In addition, a large part of old south-east Yorkshire is now north Humberside and this has affected the picture considerably. *The Atlas of Breeding Birds in Britain and Ireland* shows that this area held an exceptionally strong breeding population of Barn Owls at the time of the survey and this has now obviously been lost.

1. South Yorkshire. This county is dominated by the four large towns of Doncaster, Sheffield, Barnsley and Rotherham. Around 1972, a few Barn Owl pairs bred annually in farm buildings around Doncaster, where Rhodes in his *Birds of the Doncaster District* (1967) reported it as 'fairly common but thinly distributed', having declined since the 1940s. In this area the position seems to have changed little in recent years. Around Sheffield it is a resident breeder on farmland, rough pasture and wasteland, but only in very small numbers. Breeding pairs recorded are as follows: 1968 and 1969 – breeding recorded at one site in each year; 1970, 1971, 1972 and 1973 – nil; 1974 – bred at two sites; 1975 – nil; 1976 – bred at three sites (including one double brood at one site); 1977 – *probable* breeding at one site; 1978 – bred at three sites. At least eight pairs are thought to be breeding within a 15 km radius of Barnsley and, although only two pairs were reported breeding in 1977 and 1978, it is thought that this was entirely due to incomplete coverage by observers. In the four 10 km squares around Rotherham it is estimated that 8–10 pairs probably breed, though actual *proved* records only totalled three in 1977 with *sightings* in seven other areas.

2. *West Yorkshire*. Again large towns dominate the county – in this case Leeds, Bradford and Huddersfield. The Barn Owl was generally distributed in small numbers and currently increasing in 1972, but the bird became rare in the Leeds area in the ensuing years. The Leeds Bird Watchers' Club covers the area within 16 km of the city centre but breeding only occurs regularly at one site. Occasional birds turn up elsewhere, but it is distinctly rare and there does not seem to be any sign of an increase at the present time. The same picture applies to the Bradford Naturalists' area, where only a single pair seems to be breeding. In the Huddersfield area up to three pairs were *proved* to have bred since 1972 with five different sites being used. It is considered certain that more pairs actually breed, but the whole area is under-surveyed for the species.

2. *North Yorkshire*. In this county the population became greatly reduced after the 1962/63 winter, no doubt due to the amount of high ground in the area. However, a recovery took place in the years following, though the bird remained locally distributed and avoided the large expanses of open moorland. This is clearly shown on *The Atlas of Breeding Birds in Britain and Ireland* map. In the Scarborough area the bird has undergone fluctuations of population for the past 80 years, but its status in 1975 was as healthy as at any time. An owl survey carried out by the Scarborough Field Naturalists' Society in 1975 produced 45 records from 36 localities. These showed the population to be centred on the Wolds, the Carrs and the farmland immediately north and west of Scarborough. The Carrs is an undoubted stronghold as 20 of the 36 sites reported were situated here. Even allowing for a large hunting range the records indicate that 10–15 pairs are present in the Carrs. An estimate is harder for the Wolds due to less frequent observer coverage. However, there appears to be not fewer than five pairs. The bird appears to have spread into new areas north of Scarborough and for the general area of the town the total population appears to be in the order of 20 pairs at the present time. (Recorders for all Yorkshire: D. S. Bunn, M. Densley, I. Proctor, D. Scott, A. Wallis)

Humberside

As we have mentioned earlier, *The Atlas of Breeding Birds in Britain and Ireland* shows that this new county held a strong population of Barn Owls with breeding being *proved* or *suspected* in almost all squares. Unfortunately, the north of the county (the old East Riding) has not been adopted by the Yorkshire Naturalists' Union, nor many other field-workers, and consequently there has been little work done on the species since *The Atlas*. However, casual observations suggest that its status remains unchanged in the north and there is no evidence of a decline after the 1978/79 winter. Along the coastal area just south of Hornsea, Barn Owls are frequently seen in the early evening – at least four pairs breeding between Hornsea and Mappleton. We have no recent evidence of any change in status in the southern half of the county, but regrettably there is again a lack of observer coverage. (H. O. Bunce, W. Curtis, D. B. Cutts, P. Dene, I. Forsyth, R. G. Hawley, B. S. Pashby)

Cleveland

This is another new county, formed by the south-east tip of old Durham and the north-east tip of North Yorkshire, and is basically the area surrounding Teeside. Until about 1950, two to three pairs of Barn Owls bred along the southern edge of the coastal plain, but had ceased to do so by 1964. A general decline occurred in the early 1960s, and, even as a casual visitor to the marshes in the Cowpen/Saltholme region, the Barn Owl decreased from 1956. In 1967 it was reported to be recovering a little, with breeding taking place in a few areas from 1966. In 1977 the Teesmouth Bird Club made a special effort to determine the bird's status in the new county and this resulted in 30 records from 22 observers. The records came from 12–15 different localities, mainly in urbanised areas and the North Tees marshes, with some from the Graythorpe–Greenabella area. One or two pairs are thought to have bred around Hartburn. From the reports it is difficult to make an accurate assessment of the bird's status in Cleveland, though it is apparently patchily distributed and breeding in very small numbers – probably less than 10 pairs. (P. J. Stead, Dr D. Summers-Smith)

Durham

A decrease occurred from 1957 and very little is known about the bird's status in the 1960s, although it was certainly rather scarce throughout. In 1973 the county bird report described it as 'undoubtedly scarcer than in the past, though the position is perhaps not so bad as the scanty records have suggested in recent years. During 1973 it was recorded in a number of areas apparently not covered before and a detailed survey of the county would probably produce a much healthier picture'. Since 1973 the pattern has been of quite a few reports from perhaps 10–20 localities each year, often with reports from new localities but also including negative results from previously known sites. This suggests unsystematic recording of an under-observed species and there appears to be no scientific evidence for or against the suggested decline. Since *The Atlas of Breeding Birds* survey the county has lost its south-eastern tip to Cleveland and its north-eastern tip to Tyne & Wear. Both these areas contained breeding Barn Owls and Durham's population has fallen accordingly. (D. G. Bell, D. Sowerbutts)

Tyne & Wear

This small new county comprises parts of old Durham and Northumberland, and is literally the area of Tyneside and its immediate surroundings. Much of the area is urbanised and unsuitable for Barn Owls. However, *The*

Atlas of Breeding Birds in Britain and Ireland shows that the entire boundary of the county contained breeding pairs of Barn Owls at that time and the species still continues to live and breed in the low-lying agricultural regions at the present time. (I. Armstrong, L. C. Macfarlane)

Northumberland

Northumberland has lost the breeding population of Barn Owls in its south-eastern corner to the new county of Tyne & Wear. However, the area involved is too small to effect the overall population to any great extent and the Barn Owl was, in any case, considered to be the scarcest and most irregular of all the breeding owls in the county. It is estimated that nearly 20 pairs, or probable pairs, existed in 1967–68, but only five pairs were *proved* to have bred. It is believed that the bird has increased as a breeding species since then, although it was still rated as 'very local' in 1979. (I. Armstrong, L. C. Macfarlane)

WALES

Like the rest of Britain, Wales has been much altered by county restructuring and has been split into five large counties which incorporate the old counties as shown in brackets after each heading. Wales is a diverse country and, although almost half of it consists of high ground over 250 m, the distribution of the Barn Owl does not seem affected by this to the same extent as in England and Scotland. Possibly the long, lush valleys which intersect many of the Welsh mountains offer a habitat which is lacking in the other two countries.

South Glamorgan, Mid Glamorgan, West Glamorgan (Glamorgan)

Glamorgan's restructuring has been different from that of the other Welsh counties which have, in almost every case, been amalgamated with their nearest neighbours. Glamorgan on the other hand has been divided into three – South, Mid and West. The county is highly populated and, with towns like Swansea, Bridgend and Cardiff within its confines, this obviously affects the Barn Owl population in many areas, for it is estimated that one-fifth of the county is urbanised or industrialised. In *The Birds of Glamorgan* (1967), Salmon, Heathcote & Griffin state that the species has fluctuated in numbers over the years. During the 1920s and 1930s it maintained itself at a moderate level but became very scarce during and after the Second World War, probably due to successive hard winters. In 1949, however, there occurred an extraordinary influx into the county and during the next few years breeding was noted in a number of places where the species had long been absent. By 1967 there was a thinly scattered breeding population throughout the county, including Gower, except for the higher valleys of the coalfields. *The Atlas of Breeding Birds in Britain and Ireland* shows the bird to be still thinly scattered throughout, with breeding being *proved* in 14 squares, most being in the southern half of the county. It evidently still did not breed in the higher valleys of the coalfields but eight to ten pairs were believed to be attempting to breed on the Gower Peninsula (now in West Glamorgan). The population everywhere in Glamorgan seemed to be stable at that time. No reports of any change in status have been received by the Cardiff Naturalists' Society since then, and records of individual birds usually average seven or eight a year. The paucity of breeding records is probably due to poor observer coverage of inland areas rather than a genuine lack of breeding pairs. (M. Chown, H. Grenfell)

Gwent (Monmouthshire)

There are many areas of farmland and low-lying water-meadows in this county and *The Atlas of Breeding Birds in Britain and Ireland* showed *proved* breeding in many squares. In 1969 the bird was considered to be declining though widespread, but having remained stable between 1969–77 the population declined again in 1978. Breeding was *proved* in most years, generally one or two pairs, but four in 1972. In 1978 breeding was not proved anywhere, though it was suspected at two sites. The only regular birds apart from these were at Skenfrith and Mardy. There were seven records of solitary birds in widely scattered areas throughout the county. Several birds were found dead on the A449 in 1977, but the fact that only one road casualty – on the A40 – was recorded in 1978 might be a further indication of an overall decline. *The Birds of Gwent* (1977) and the *Gwent Bird Report*, 1977 and 1978, show that it is still a breeding resident though nowhere common. It is mostly found in the agricultural areas, including the coast, but is not so frequent in the coalfield valleys. (P. Martin, W. Price)

Dyfed (Pembrokeshire, Carmarthenshire, Cardiganshire)

This is a very large and varied county and *The Atlas of Breeding Birds in Britain and Ireland* showed the main breeding population to be in central and eastern Dyfed, with fewer by far in the old county of Pembrokeshire. In the latter county it was resident throughout in 1969 but was not common anywhere. Rather surprisingly, breeding has been recorded on the small islands of Skomer, St Margaret's and Caldy in the past, but not in recent years. Many former breeding sites in old disused cottages are no longer occupied as these are being rebuilt for human habitation. Other sites are still available, however, and the bird has perhaps been a little more frequent in recent years. A few are killed on roads, but unlike 1962/63, there was no evidence of deaths due to the hard winter of 1978/79.

In Carmarthen it was breeding regularly, though somewhat sparsely, in 1969. In the coastal and northern upland areas it was more widely distributed, but it was rarely seen in the south-east of the county and a general decrease was noted everywhere around that time.

The *Dyfed Bird Report* and *The Atlas of Breeding Birds in Britain and Ireland* also noted its scarcity· in the south. Its present status in Carmarthen is 'resident throughout, but not common and certainly decreasing'.

In 1969 it was considered to be widespread throughout Cardigan and certainly not scarce. Breeding mostly occurred on the high, open hill ground in the north and east, and one nest in an old building in 1968 was at 442 m. Evidence of roosting birds could be found in most isolated buildings, even in the remoter areas, but some pairs have lost nest sites in recent years due to the collapse or restoration of derelict houses. Although a slight decrease might have occurred since 1969, its status has not really changed to any extent apart from the usual short-term fluctuations that occur in upland areas. These are often connected with the Short-tailed Vole cycles and in 1980 the upland population was reported to have had a poor breeding season every year since the last vole peak in 1975. (P. Davis, J. Donovan, D. H. V. Roberts)

Powys (Montgomeryshire, Radnorshire, Breconshire)

Powys is a large county, taking up much of the central and eastern parts of Wales. It is a sparsely populated and mountainous region with varied habitats such as moorland, river valleys, woodland and wetlands interspersed throughout. Farmsteads are few and far between and this factor and the mountains probably account for the sparseness of breeding pairs in the central and eastern parts of old Radnorshire and Montgomeryshire.

The Montgomeryshire population suffered badly in the 1962/63 winter and since then it has certainly decreased further in the east of the county. In the spring of 1978, Neil Bowman carried out a breeding survey, using local ornithologists and requests for information in the county press. Poor returns, combined with the opinion of local ornithologists and farmers, suggested that there were fewer Barn Owls than in previous years. Although six occupied territories were found, only one of these contained a *proved* breeding pair. In October 1978 a search was made of the southern half of a 10 km square near Newtown, every barn and derelict building being examined and every farmer spoken to. Evidence of occupation was found at 18 sites, probably representing three territories. One territory was occupied and had been for some considerable time; one had not been occupied for at least one, probably two, years; the third had not been occupied for a long time, no evidence being found apart from the knowledge of local farmers. Many of the once ideal derelict farms in the uplands have decayed beyond the point where they are suitable for Barn Owls and this has now become a major factor in the reduction of the upland population.

In Radnorshire the Barn Owl declined steadily from the 1920s and by the early 1950s it had become a scarce breeding species with very few pairs in the county. A positive increase was noted between 1971 and 1973 with breeding being *proved* in four of the squares during *The Atlas of Breeding Birds in Britain and Ireland* survey. Neil Bowman's survey found five occupied territories in 1978, three of which contained *proved* breeding pairs. Against this, nine former sites were unoccupied.

The Breconshire population was badly affected by the 1962/63 winter, but a definite increase began again after 1966 and there were six successful breeding records in 1968. In 1969 it was resident in fairly good numbers and was often found nesting on the bedroom floors of deserted cottages in upland valleys. There has been no evidence of a change in status in recent years. (N. Bowman, V. J. Macnair, M. Preece, A. J. Smith)

Gwynedd (Merionethshire, Anglesey, Caernarvonshire)

As might be expected, the Snowdonia National Park dominates central and southern Gwynedd, and only the Lleyn Peninsula, the western coast and Anglesey lie outside the park. It boasts some of the highest mountains in England and Wales and not surprisingly no Barn Owls are to be found in the four 10 km squares containing the Snowdon and Carneddau Mountains, Tal-y-bont and Betws-y-Coed. The Lleyn Peninsula and western Caernarvon is ideal Barn Owl habitat and *The Atlas of Breeding Birds in Britain and Ireland* showed that a good breeding population exists here (12 out of 14 squares). The same applies to the flat countryside of Anglesey where it breeds from Newborough in the south-west to the forested area of the north-east.

A paucity of observers in Merioneth makes an assessment of its population in this county difficult. In 1972 it was thought to be well distributed, though nowhere common, in the lowlands and into the uplands, especially along the valleys. It was absent from the high mountain land and from 1978 a general decline has taken place elsewhere from a line north of Dolgellau.

In some areas of Caernarvonshire, such as the lower Conway Valley, it was actually described as 'numerous' up to the mid-1950s, but by 1970 it was better described as a regular and widespread breeder, the amount of high ground limiting its distribution. In their *Birds of Caernarvonshire* (1976), Jones & Dare stated that it was 'a widely but thinly distributed species, present throughout the year in the lowlands (below 150 m), most plentiful in Lleyn (though nowhere common) and breeding as far west as Aberdaron; rather scarce in the north and east, including the Conway Valley, and especially so in upland areas'. Since 1976 the few records submitted each year to the *Cambrian Bird Report* suggest that there might have been a decline, but once again the elusiveness of the species is noted as a possible reason for this. Most birds are sighted along roads, particularly in winter. There were no records of dead birds being found during the 1978/79 cold winter. (N. Bowman, Dr P. J. Dare, E. Hardy, P. Hope-Jones)

Clwyd (Denbighshire, Flintshire)

Clwyd is another county holding a wide variety of habitats ranging from flat agricultural land to large moors and industrial areas. The latter are mainly in the east and north-east, from the Dee Estuary to Wrexham and Ruabon, and the coastal belt is also under immense pressure from the vast numbers of holidaymakers who use the popular resorts in summer. Both these factors may seriously affect the Barn Owl population in the future.

In Denbighshire the bird was frequent in the lowlands and many upland areas in the early 1950s, but like so many other counties there was a drastic decline after the 1962/63 winter, only odd birds being reported from the coast and heavily populated east in 1963. By 1972 it was again locally frequent, especially in the valleys of the Rivers Dee and Clwyd and the coastal area, though, probably owing to building and improved farming methods, it has never reached the 1950 level. The recovery continued until it had achieved a wide if somewhat local distribution, but sadly the 1978/79 winter brought very heavy snow which lay for a prolonged spell in North Wales, and above 150 m the owl either moved out or suffered heavy losses. The lower regions fared better, but there are now definitely fewer Barn Owls there than in 1978, and Neil Bowman's survey suggests a more general decline apart from the north coast.

The picture is virtually the same for Flintshire and *The Atlas of Breeding Birds in Britain and Ireland* showed *proved* breeding to be even rarer in this county. (N. Bowman, E. Hardy, J. M. Harrop)

SCOTLAND

Dumfries and Galloway Region (Dumfriesshire, Kirkcudbrightshire, Wigtownshire)
There seems to be a great deal of evidence to suggest that Kirkcudbrightshire might well be one of the main strongholds of the Barn Owl in Britain.
Daylight sightings are common around the Castle Douglas area and one
report mentions six being seen in a day between Southerness and Isel Steps
in January 1978, a distance of only 10 km. Donald Watson regards it as
unusual *not* to see one or two hunting by day, mainly in the afternoons,
between Dalry and Castle Douglas – a pleasant change from the gloomy
picture in most other counties. Numbers appear to have remained stable in
this region for the past twenty to thirty years or so, and breeding has
probably been helped by the afforestation of much of the area; G. Shaw
reports six pairs breeding in Glentrool Forest in 1977, with 19 young being
reared from four sites, and 6–7 pairs rearing 14 young from four sites in 1978.

An extension of forest planting in east and central Wigtownshire has also
helped the species in that county, but it is not as common here as in
Kirkcudbright. It is plentiful in the eastern parts but less so in the west.
Breeding numbers fluctuate and have done so since 1969. Although numbers
appear to increase in winter this may be due to the birds being more readily
seen hunting in daylight at this time of the year.

It is found throughout Dumfriesshire and numbers are now stable after a
decline in the 1950s. However, they have not yet reached their old level.
(R. Dicksen, J. Maxwell, D. Watson)

*Borders Region (Berwickshire, Midlothian (South), Peeblesshire, Roxburghshire,
Selkirkshire)*
The Barn Owl seems to have suffered mixed fortunes in this region and
nowhere can it be regarded as common. Numbers have definitely decreased
in Berwickshire, particularly after the 1978/79 winter, and although populations traditionally fluctuate in Selkirkshire and Peeblesshire it always
remains a scarce bird. Fortunately it still breeds in these counties in several
regularly used nest sites. Sometimes it almost disappears entirely and many
known nest sites are no longer available. It is also thought that the 1978/79
winter may well have reduced the population once more.

In the Borders Region it appears to fare best in Roxburghshire, where
its population has stabilised itself after a decrease in the late 1960s, and
it is frequently seen hunting in most areas during the breeding season.
(A. W. Brown, Dr J. I. Meikle, R. J. Robertson, A. J. Smith)

*Strathclyde Region (Ayrshire, Renfrewshire, Argyllshire, Dumbartonshire,
Buteshire, Lanarkshire)*
This is a huge and very varied region, ranging from the urban sprawl of
Glasgow and its surrounding towns, to the unspoiled peninsula of Kintyre
and the remote islands of the Inner Hebrides. In some areas, such as the
northern parts of Ayrshire and Argyll, a shortage of observers makes an
accurate assessment of the Barn Owl population difficult. For example,
M. E. Castle found it slightly more numerous in the northern half of

Ayrshire in 1969, while R. H. Hogg, the county recorder in 1979, had most observations sent in from central and southern Ayrshire!

In 1972, J. Mitchell found it 'not uncommon' on the good agricultural ground below 150 m, to the south of Loch Lomond. Just the odd pair occurred elsewhere below the Highland Line and it was only seen occasionally in the extensive built-up southern part of the area. It was apparently absent north of the Highland Line, with the exception of a pair associated with farmland at the very head of Loch Lomond. Its status remained the same here in 1979, and throughout the entire region it appears to be holding its own, though the population is very small in south Lanarkshire and central and northern Argyll. *The Atlas of Breeding Birds in Britain and Ireland* showed that it bred on some of the off-shore islands such as Arran, Islay, Jura, Mull and Bute, while Dr. J. A. Gibson (pers. comm. 1973) gave us breeding records for Inchmarnock, Great Cumbrae and Little Cumbrae. Breeding also once occurred on one of the islands of Loch Lomond in 1974.

H. J. P. Gregory, the local recorder for Argyll and the Inner Hebrides, reported in 1979 that he received very few records of Barn Owls and *none* of breeding. He feels that the species is under-recorded and this is borne out by the fact that in 1978 Miss M. MacMillan sent us breeding records from the south of Kintyre (2) and the small islands of Clachan Seil (2) and Scarba (1). (M. E. Castle, Dr J. A. Gibson, H. J. P. Gregory, R. H. Hogg, Miss M. MacMillan, J. Mitchell)

Lothian Region (West Lothian, Midlothian, East Lothian)

There is no doubt that the main population of Barn Owls in this region is now to be found in central and eastern Midlothian, where it definitely increased in the years following 1974. The population declined sharply in the 1950s and none were seen until 1970. By 1972 there were three breeding records, but even in 1973 it was by no means common, so the present continued increase is especially welcome.

In West and East Lothian the present breeding status is rather vague and much of the information relates to sightings of individual birds rather than of breeding pairs. There can be little doubt that the Barn Owl is very scarce in both of these counties, for the local recorder for West Lothian did not even receive a *sight* record for the species between 1974 and 1976. The few pairs which do breed show a fondness for deserted shale mine workings as nest sites.

The only breeding records in East Lothian occur on the western side bordering Midlothian, and the bird is virtually absent from the North Sea coast. The contributor for this county has been birdwatching in the area since the war and in all that time he has only seen one nest and about three individuals. A bird seen in Aberlady Bay in February 1977 was the first there for three years. There are no records of it ever occurring on the Forth Islands. (A. W. Brown, K. S. Macgregor, R. W. J. Smith, Dr T. C. Smout)

Central Region (Stirlingshire, Clackmannanshire)

The Barn Owl is a regular but very scarce breeder in the Central Region, with concentrations on the rich agricultural ground of the carse-land from

Cartmore to Stirling, and in the Endrick and Blane Valleys. It is absent elsewhere on land over 150 m. There does not seem to have been any change in status since *The Atlas of Breeding Birds in Britain and Ireland* survey, one or two new pairs having turned up and one or two old pairs having disappeared. Odd pairs are sometimes reported in the more urbanised and industrial parts of the region. (C. J. Henty, D. Merrie, J. Mitchell, H. Robb)

Fife Region (Fifeshire)

The Barn Owl is regarded as uncommon and very local in this small region and, although a slight increase was reported in the coastal area of the north-east in 1969, this has not been maintained and in 1979 its status remained basically unchanged. (K. Brockie, P. K. Kinnear, D. W. Oliver)

Tayside Region (Perthshire, Kinross, Angus)

It is in the south of the Tayside Region that the main Barn Owl population begins to die out in Britain, leaving only scattered outliers any further north. It is no coincidence that the Scottish Highlands begin here, with little land below 750 m. This is more than double the height at which Barn Owls normally breed in Britain and is obviously a limiting factor on their numbers.

A few breeding pairs were found in Perthshire during *The Atlas of Breeding Birds in Britain and Ireland* project and there has been no evidence of any change in status since then, the bird remaining scarce and local. Most of the recent records have been of road casualties, four in 1974, eight in 1975, one in 1976, two in 1977 and one in 1978. The 1975 figure is probably biased as one of the county's most active ornithologists, the late Mike Marsland, was commuting daily between Perth and Stirling University. It is noteworthy that *all* these road casualties came from the low-lying area between Perth and Dunblane, or the area east of Perth, towards Dundee. This probably indicates that these areas hold the main concentrations of Barn Owls in Tayside. Occasionally, Barn Owls do occur at higher levels as is shown by the presence of a bird in the Rannoch area in June 1975, which R. L. McMillan disturbed from Ivy growing on a crag at 400 m.

The few recorded in Kinross are mainly from the eastern section of the county, but no breeding pairs have been recorded in recent years and there were no records whatsoever during *The Atlas* period.

The picture is similar in Angus, where most records are of winter birds. However, *The Atlas* produced two *proved* breeding pairs and seven *possibles*, none of these being in the north of the county which is dominated by the Braes of Angus. (E. C. Cameron, G. M. Crighton, J. H. Swan, Miss V. M. Thom)

Grampian Region (Aberdeenshire, Kincardineshire, Morayshire, Banffshire)

Most records for the Grampian Region come from Aberdeenshire and *The Atlas of Breeding Birds in Britain and Ireland* project revealed that it was more widespread than had previously been thought. The fact that most records come from the area around Aberdeen itself might well reflect the fact that most observers are based there and that Aberdeen University has an active Ornithological Society. Nick Picozzi reported the species to be 'not uncommon' in 1972, and in *The Atlas* period breeding was *proved* in six squares, *probable* breeding in two and *possible* breeding in nine. The *1975 North-East Scotland Bird Report* states that the species is under-recorded with two pairs at Dyce-Persley (on the northern boundary of the City of Aberdeen) being the only birds reported in the breeding season. Singles were noted outside the breeding season at Strathbeg and Loriston (inside the City boundary). 1976 was another poor year, with only two records of single birds – one at Old Aberdeen and a dead bird at Loriston. No breeding was reported in 1977 but singles were seen at Newburgh, Turiff, Aberdeen (2) and Cruden Bay. The present status is that the bird is uncommon, though a resident breeder in *very* small numbers. There has been little change in recent years.

The bird is even scarcer in Kincardineshire and little data is available for this county. Only two cases of *possible* breeding were found by *The Atlas* workers and between 1975 and 1977 only one record occurred – that of a breeding pair at St Cyrus in 1977 which reared two young.

There are no records for the inland hilly area of Banffshire, and what sightings there are occur in the lower part of the county. *The Atlas* survey showed *proved* breeding in three squares and *possibles* in two more. There have been numerous sightings since then, almost entirely from the Spey Valley, with a few on the lowland coastal strip. However, there have been no definite breeding records since *The Atlas of Breeding Birds* and all of the sites occupied at that time were deserted by 1978. The present status in Banff appears to be that of a very scarce breeder, though the lack of serious ornithologists in the area and the large number of disused crofts and farm buildings make an accurate assessment of actual numbers impracticable.

In Morayshire it is scarce and elusive, *The Atlas* project revealing the bird's presence in five out of 20 squares, none of these being breeding records. The present status remains unchanged and is likely to remain so. (M. J. H. Cook, A. Dunthorn, J. Edelsten, A. G. Knox, N. Picozzi)

Highland Region (Invernesshire, Ross & Cromarty, Nairnshire, Sutherland, Caithness, Skye)

This region is vast and varied, and of course contains some of the wildest and highest land in Britain. A glance at *The Atlas of Breeding Birds in Britain and Ireland* map clearly reveals that Barn Owls find it impossible to breed in the Highlands, and what records there are come mainly from land lower than 300 m in Ross & Cromarty. Nowhere is this better illustrated than in the one solitary record of *proved* breeding in Wester Ross. This came from the only square in a block of Highland squares (land over 750 m) which contained some lower-lying terrain – around Kinlochewe. All other mainland records – apart from a *probable* record on the shores of Loch Ewe – came from the eastern part of the county around the low-lying parts of the Cromarty Firth and the Moray Basin. These sheltered areas have rich ground and mild winters in contrast with the rest of the county and provide a northern limit for the species. C. G. Headlam feels that the few very sheltered areas and nest locations at this latitude are the only reasons this northern outpost remains viable. Though mild winters are usual, severe frost and heavy snow can sometimes occur and, if these persist for any length of time (as it did in the winter of 1978/79), this factor, plus occasional predation by Man, is quite sufficient to kill off any young birds and some of the old. It would therefore appear that the Barn Owl's status in the county is precarious – as one would expect, for this population is the most northerly in the world.

There are no recent records for Nairnshire and Caithness, but it is interesting to note that the species has bred in Sutherland in recent times. This occurred in a small cave in a sea-cliff between Golspie and Brora in 1961 and 1962. The site was not visited in 1963 but breeding was again confirmed in 1964. An interesting sequel to this record is that a Barn Owl was hit by a car near Laing on 19th September 1977 – just 32 km west of this site. These birds were probably outliers from the Moray Basin population, as no doubt are a few birds which breed near Inverness and a passage bird recorded at Dornoch in November 1954.

There are no confirmed records of the bird breeding on Skye but *The Atlas* revealed that it was present and *probably* breeding in very small numbers. There are no records for the other islands. (Mrs P. Collett, C. G. Headlam, D. MacDonald, Dr I. Pennie, Dr R. Richter, Dr M. Rusk, D. H. Stark, Hon. D. Weir)

Islands Region (Western Isles)
There have been no records for many years and any Barn Owls which did arrive there would be unlikely to stay due to the rough conditions and absence of voles on these islands. (W. A. J. Cunningham)

NORTHERN IRELAND

There is a lack of observers in remote areas of this country and a reluctance to explore old ruins. The bird is, therefore, probably under-recorded but was considered to be widespread but nowhere common in 1972, having held its own since the early 1960s. From 1972 onwards there has been an alarming decline and some farmers who were familiar with this owl in the past now report that none have been seen for three or four years or more. D. Clarke carried out intensive local enquiries in Co. Down between 1975 and 1978, but although he found pellets in some old haunts, not a single owl was seen. He found the same picture in the counties of Armagh, Fermanagh, Tyrone and Antrim. One farmer near Enniskillen, Co. Fermanagh, saw a Barn Owl in his yard in November 1978, the first for a few years. One found dead at Seskinore, Co. Tyrone, in the winter of 1977/78 was the only one seen there for several years. The RSPB Northern Ireland Office is taking the decline very seriously and has requested birdwatchers to erect Barn Owl nest-boxes. A cause of decline not recorded elsewhere was a renewed increase in demand by taxidermists around 1972. (R. W. Bailey, A. Bennington, D. Clarke, J. S. Furphy)

THE REPUBLIC OF IRELAND

D. Scott feels that *The Atlas of Breeding Birds in Britain and Ireland* results reflect observer coverage to a large extent, but considers that one or two pairs occur in almost all squares except in west Galway, west Mayo and west Donegal, all desolate areas with few suitable territories for Barn Owls. Though no comparative data are available, in 1973 the general opinion amongst observers throughout the country was that there˙had been a substantial reduction in numbers from the 1950s onwards. The bird's status does not seem to have changed materially since then. Four owls found roosting at a site in Galway in 1970 were feeding almost entirely on Wood Mice – there being no voles in Ireland. (F. L. Clark, J. S. Fawley, D. Scott)

MAJOR ISLANDS

Isle of Man
The Barn Owl was apparently very rare at the beginning of the present century but increased up to the mid-1940s. The population probably never exceeded 30 pairs and was normally around 20 pairs. Since the early 1960s the status of the bird has been causing much anxiety amongst Manx naturalists and a number of known nest sites have been deserted during the ensuing period. An accurate assessment is difficult as the birds are hardly ever seen, but it is suspected that the poisoning of rats on the Island is affecting the population, both by reducing the food supply (there are no voles and only Pygmy Shrews on the Isle of Man) and by killing the owls directly. Approximately one-third of all records in recent years have been of corpses and, apart from Warfarin poisoning, Dieldrin has also been implicated. Although 10–12 pairs were thought to be present in 1971/72, it now seems that the population is even lower, only nine individuals being seen in 1977, of which three were dead or dying, and nine in 1978 (three of which could have been the same bird), with two former nest sites being unused. The sad conclusion is that the situation is still deteriorating and one fears for the future of this species on the Island. (Dr L. S. Garrad)

Scilly Isles
The Barn Owl is only a very rare vagrant to the Scilly Islands and is usually associated with cold weather movement of other birds in late autumn and winter. Records are as follows: 1975 – one at St Agnes, 25th October; 1976 – one found injured at St Mary's, January; 1977 – one found dead on Tresco, 19th October. This bird was considered by Dr I. M. Wallace to be of the race *T. a. guttata* (after examination of the body). Continental origin is suspected for most of the birds reported on the Scilly Isles. (D. Hunt, Mrs H. M. Quick)

Channel Islands (Jersey, Guernsey, Sark, Alderney)
Jersey C. G. Pile (1958) estimated a density of very approximately one pair to every 2·6 km^2 of suitable territory, town areas being occupied more sparsely. A similar picture still appears to exist today. (C. G. Pile, Mrs A. Le Sueur)

Guernsey A population of around 6–12 pairs is estimated. (A. J. Bisson)

Sark and Alderney The *Atlas of Breeding Birds in Britain and Ireland* survey provided no breeding records though odd birds were seen occasionally at that time. Since then the species has begun to breed on Alderney.

Of considerable interest is the fact that a small proportion of the Channel Island Barn Owls are almost as dark as *T. a. guttata*. Others are intermediate, but the typical race *T. a. alba* predominates. It seems likely that interbreeding takes place on these islands, as it does where the two races overlap in Europe.

Orkney Islands
There is no record of the bird ever having bred on Orkney and there have been no sightings in the past ten years. (E. Balfour, C. Booth)

Fair Isle
There are no breeding records and the few birds seen on Fair Isle have been on passage. These are single individuals recorded in 1926, 1940, 1943, 1944 and 1958. The 1943 bird was thought to be of the *T. a. guttata* race, while the 1958 bird was confirmed as *T. a. alba*. (R. Dennis, Dr B. Marshall, K. Williamson)

Shetland Islands
The Barn Owl is a vagrant to Shetland. Old records exist of *T. a. guttata* being found on the islands but there are very few recent records of either this race or *T. a. alba*. One shot at Sumburgh in October 1951, one (of the white-breasted race) on the Out Skerries on 3rd–5th June 1973, and one seen in a hangar at Sumburgh Airport in either 1961 or 1962 are the only instances we have been able to find. (Dr B. Marshall, R. J. Tulloch)

CHAPTER 9

Folk-lore

Owls are better documented in folk-lore, legend and historical accounts than most other species. More than most species, however, they have suffered from the ignorance and superstition of mankind and this has led to a great many misconceptions about them, often resulting in persecution. With the more scientific approach to natural history, which first began to achieve real momentum, albeit slowly, during the early part of the nineteenth century, the true facts began to emerge and to some degree owls began to lose their often dubious reputation. It is rather interesting to note that owls were also attributed with quite different characteristics from those associated with death, disaster and the like, for example they were supposed to be endowed with wisdom. These other traits will also be examined in due course. The main purpose of this chapter is to show how owls have been commonly regarded in the past and to illustrate the way these views have undergone a process of change. Generally speaking, references have only been included which apply specifically to the Barn Owl, but in some cases important references have been quoted which concern owls in general.

Even in the earliest times opinions about owls were remarkably consistent with those still held in the nineteenth century. Over two thousand years ago Ovid was extremely harsh against the owl in his *Metamorphoses*:

> *Ill-omen'd in his form, the unlucky fowl,*
> *Abhorr'd by men, and called a screeching owl.*

In his *Fasti* Ovid makes an early mention of the owl in connection with witchcraft. He tells how, in ancient times at Rome, it was believed that witches were able by their magic arts to transform themselves into screech owls, or screech owls to transform themselves into witches, and that, entering the window of the nursery in which young children were sleeping, they sucked their blood as they lay in their cradles. With such an evil reputation it is not surprising that it was the custom for any unfortunate owl which blundered into a Roman house to be nailed alive to the house door to avert the evil that it would supposedly have caused. Similar practices were carried on in Europe, for example Germany, at a much later date.

Vergil also mentions the owl in his *Twelfth Book of the Aeneid* prior to the end of the conflict between Aeneas and Turnus. At this point Juturna hears its boding cry, sees its flapping wings and despairingly utters:

> *Alarum, verbera nosco*
> *Letalamque sonum.*
>
> *(I recognise the beating of wings*
> *Dreadful sound.)*

Also, according to Vergil, it was an owl which, perching upon the house-top at Carthage, predicted the desertion, the desolation and death of Dido. The owl is also said to have predicted the death of Caesar.

There are also early references to owls in the Bible. The Hebrew prophet, Isaiah, pictures Babylon given over to be inhabited by owls and by what he regards as their proper associates:

> . . . their houses shall be full of doleful creatures; and owls shall dwell there, and satyrs shall dance there . . . the owl also and the raven shall dwell in it . . . and it shall be an habitation of dragons, *and* a court for owls . . . and the satyr shall cry to his fellow; the screech owl also shall rest there, and find for herself a place of rest. *Isaiah XIII, 21 and XXXIV, 11, 13 & 14.*

When Herod Agrippa entered the Theatre of Caesaraea, clad in a robe of silver tissue, it was an owl which suddenly perched upon a rope above his head to warn him of his coming end. Again, when the Roman army was about to give battle at Carrhea in the plains of the Euphrates and Tigris, in what is now south-eastern Turkey, an owl appeared in the ranks of the soldiers and warned them of what was to prove one of the greatest blows ever inflicted upon Roman imperial might, the death and mutilation of Crassus, the richest of men, the annihilation of the Roman army by the Parthians and the loss of the Roman eagles.

An examination of the earliest references to owls in English literature soon tells us that the bird was still regarded with serious misgivings. In many ways it is not too difficult to appreciate why such a bird should have acquired a sinister reputation. The main reason is probably that it is a bird of the night, a bird of the darkness, and since night and darkness were associated with death, magic and the like, it is not surprising that the owl itself became associated with such phenomena. A second important factor is the screech of the Barn Owl. Even during the daylight hours such a call would have been viewed with uncertainty, to say the least, but being normally heard only at dusk or during darkness, it might well have been considered blood-curdling and sinister – a probability that is not at all difficult to appreciate for anyone who has heard its eldritch screech pierce the stillness of the night. The colour of the Barn Owl would hardly need to have been added as further proof of its association with denizens of the night, particularly ghosts.

One of the earliest English references to owls is contained in *The Legend of Good Women* (a. 1385) by Chaucer:

> *The owle al night about the balkes word*
> *That prophete is of wo and mischaunce.*

A similar theme continues throughout much of English literature and a selection of verse has been made to illustrate poetical ideas about the Barn Owl from the fourteenth century down to the present time.

Edmund Spenser speaks eloquently against the screech owl in several of his poems, for example, in *The Faerie Queen*:

> *A greedy grave*
> *That still for carrion carcases doth crave,*
> *On top whereof ay dwelt the ghostly owle,*
> *Shrieking his balefull note, which ever drove,*
> *Far from that haunt all other cheerfull fowle;*
> *And all about it wandering ghosts did wayle and howle.*

And again in *The Teares*:

> *Foule goblins and shriek owles,*
> *With fearful howling do all places fill.*

There are many references by sixteenth and seventeenth century poets, first and foremost amongst which must be mentioned Shakespeare. One of the less well-known references occurs in one of his poems:

> *But thou, shrieking harbinger,*
> *Foul precursor of the fiend,*
> *Augur of the fever's end,*
> *To this troop come thou not near.*

A well-known reference occurs in *Macbeth* (ii, 2) when its weird shriek pierces the ear of Lady Macbeth:

> *Hark! – Peace!*
> *It was the owl that shrieked, the fatal bellman,*
> *Which gave the stern'st good night.*

And when the murderer rushes in exclaiming: 'I have done the deed. Dids't thou not hear a noise?,' she answers: 'I heard the owl scream.'

The appearance of an owl at birth as an omen of ill-luck is also mentioned by Shakespeare and is referred to by King Henry in 3, Henry VI (v. 6), when addressing Gloucester:

> *The owl shriek'd at thy birth, an evil sign.*

In *A Midsummer Night's Dream* (v. 1) we are informed how:

> *The screech-owl, screeching loud,*
> *Puts the wretch that lies in woe*
> *In remembrance of a shroud.*

Again, when *Richard III* (iv 4) is exasperated by bad news, he interrupts the third messenger by saying:

> *Out on you, owls! Nothing but songs of death?*

In *Comedy of Errors* (ii, 2), the owl is represented as a comparison of the fairies in their moonlight gambols, when Dromio of Syracuse says:

> *This is the fairy lord: O, spite of spites!*
> *We talk with goblins, owls and elvish sprites,*
> *If we obey them not, this will ensue,*
> *They'll suck our breath, and pinch us black and blue!*

References from other poets during this period include Michael Drayton who says in his *Third Song from Polyolbion* (1613):

> *The deadlie Screech-owle sits, in gloomie covert hid.*

In similar tone, John Webster (1580?–1625?) comments:

> *Hearke, now everything is still –*
> *The Screech-owle, and the whistler shrill,*
> *Call upon our Dame, aloud,*
> *And bid her quickly don her shroud.*

During the eighteenth and nineteenth centuries the Barn Owl is still the poet's favourite bird of doom; for example Robert Blair (1699–1746) says of it in his *Church and Church-yard at night*:

> *Again! The Screech-owl shrieks, Ungracious sound!*
> *I'll hear no more, it makes one's blood run chill.*

Likewise William Wordsworth in his poem *The Waggoner* (1805):

> *Yon owl! – pray God that all will be well!*
> *Tis worse than any funeral bell;*
> *As sure as I've the gift of sight,*
> *We shall be meeting ghosts tonight!*

Other references at this time include: 'Birds of omen, dark and foul' (Scott – *Gaelic Legend*); 'The bird of darkness' (Byron – *Childe Harold's Pilgrimage*); 'Sad companion of the night' (Abraham Cowley – *Sylva*); 'Gloom bird's hated screech' (John Keats – *Eve of St Agnes*); 'the screaming owl's accursed song' (Mark Akenside – *Pleasures of Imagination*); 'night's foul bird' (Robert Blair – *Grave*); 'The screech-owl dire!' (Charles Churchill – *The Duellist*); 'Foule Bird of Hate' (John Milton – *Sonnet*).

By the nineteenth century, poetry was beginning to reflect a more rational, less hostile attitude towards owls. This is particularly true of that fine poet-naturalist, John Clare. He says this of the Barn Owl in his poem, *Evening*:

> *Now the owl on wheaten wing,*
> *And white hood scowling o'er his eyes,*
> *Jerking with a sudden spring,*
> *Through three-cornered barn-hole flies.*

One frequently mentioned supposed characteristic of the owl is its wisdom, and poetical sources make many references to this. Such an attribute is quite contrary to what has been said so far in this chapter and it can be traced back to Greek times when the owl was held sacred to Athene, goddess of wisdom. Although it is not certain why the owl should be attributed with wisdom, there are three possibilities. The first of these is its power to see in the dark, an ability possessed by few other species. Alternatively, the appearance of the owl itself, with its large, round, but above all, front-facing eyes, may have helped to place it apart from other species of birds. The third possibility is that its supposed wisdom is an anthropomorphic feature, in other words it has the appearance of looking wise. It may have been for similar reasons that the owl was thought to be a solemn bird. An early reference in English literature to the owl's wisdom is contained in *A remedy for Love* (a. 1586) by Sir Philip Sidney:

> *O you virtuous owl,*
> *The wise Minerva's only fowl.*

Probably the best known poetical reference to the owl's wisdom is to be found in *The White Owl* by Alfred Lord Tennyson:

> *Alone and warming his five wits,*
> *The white owl in the belfry sits.*

Elizabeth Carter (1717–1806) makes a reference in her poem, *Ode to Wisdom*:

> *In philosophick gloom he lay,*
> *Beneath his ivy bow'r.*

Proverbs and folk-lore also provide an interesting and valuable insight into popular ideas about owls. Most of these reflect the characteristics mentioned by poets and which have already been dealt with in full. One of the earliest proverbs is quoted by J. Ray in his book, *English Proverbs:* 'He's in great want of a bird that will give a groat for an owl'.

In *Folk-lore and Stories of Wales*, 1909, Marie Trevelyan quotes that: 'The flight of an owl across a person's path was considered very baleful', and according to *The Folk-lore of Suffolk*, 1893, by Lady Eveline Gordon, the screech of an owl flying past the window of a sick room signifies that death is near. In similar vein it was considered by some to be unlucky to look into an owl's nest. Elizabeth Mary Wright tells of how, once upon a time, a foolhardy person ventured to do so and in consequence he became melancholy and destroyed himself.

Numerous proverbs relate to the wisdom and the gravity of the owl. One of these is quoted by T. Fuller in his *Gnomologie* (1732) – 'The owl is not accounted the wiser for living retiredly' – and another by Allan Ramsey in his *Scottish Proverbs* (1737) – 'The gravest bird's an owl'. In his fable, *The Shepherd and the Philosopher* (1727), John Gary asks:

> *Can grave and formal pass for wise,*
> *When men the solemn owl despise?*

Finally, the screech of the owl was considered useful in forecasting weather. Thus, a screeching owl was supposed to indicate cold or storm, or, if owls screamed during bad weather, there would be a change. A third idea was that the owl's calling foretold hailstorms.

There are also many interesting legends concerning owls in general which are worth quoting at this stage. Although the actual species may not be apparent, there is no reason why they should not apply to the Barn Owl.

Various legends exist as to the pedigree of the owl. Dafydd of Guylim, the idyllic poet of Wales in the fourteenth century and a contemporary of

Chaucer, renders in verse the ancient tradition with reference to the owl in his poem, *The Owl's Pedigree*. The poem consists of a dialogue between owl and poet, during which the owl explains that she was the daughter of a chief, but was changed into an owl by a certain Gwydion, son of Don, as an act of revenge. Shakespeare also refers to the pedigree of the owl in *Hamlet*, when Ophelia exclaims:

> *They say the Owl was a baker's daughter.*

One version of the legend, according to Douce, is as follows:

> Our Saviour went into a baker's shop where they were baking and asked for some bread to eat; the mistress of the shop immediately put a piece of dough into the oven to bake for Him, but was reprimanded by her daughter, who, insisting that it was too large, reduced it to a very small size; the dough, however, immediately began to swell and presently became a most enormous size, whereupon the baker's daughter cried out, 'Heugh, heugh, heugh', which owl-like noise probably induced our Saviour to transform her into that bird for her wickedness.

There are also legends explaining why the owl is a night bird and these are mentioned by J. Sparks and T. Soper (1970) in their book, *Owls – their Natural and Unnatural History*.

Other interesting legends, the origins of which are lost in antiquity and which are consequently open to some conjecture, concern the hunters of owls. The owl was formerly hunted in Suffolk at Christmas, whilst on St Valentine's Day in the West Country three single young men had to go out and catch an owl and two sparrows which they carried round the village. These annual hunts of owls (and squirrels) in various parts of England are reminiscent of wren-hunting, but differ from it in certain respects. The species of creature hunted is not held specially sacred at other times, the dead body of the victim is not the subject of any subsequent rite, and the pursuit is apparently normally carried on in some particular spot, not visited or accessible at other times of the year. The likeness to the wren-hunt is in fact only the superficial one of its annual occurrence. It has been suggested that this invasion of private enclosures was made for the purpose of testing or asserting a customary right of common.

Another interesting custom relating to owls took place during the Whitsuntide Ales held at Woodstock, in Oxfordshire. During this festival a Maypole was set up on the green and a dancing booth called 'My Lady's Bower' was erected there, built of green boughs, which would hold a large number of people. A refreshment booth was erected in a garden where the police station now stands and over the door was fixed a cage containing a pair of owls, which were referred to as 'My Lady's parrots'. Over the cage a pair of flails were placed, which were called 'My Lord's nut-crackers', and there was also a wooden horse which was called 'My Lady's palfrey'. Anyone who miscalled the owls, the flail or the horse was fined a quart of ale. The last Queen of the Revels, and a few of the Morris dancers, were still living just before the end of the nineteenth century. The receipts from the Whitsun Ale went for very many years to defray church expenses.

There are also various references from many parts of the world to owls in folk medicine and magic. Swan in his *Speculum Mundi* recommended owls' eggs to be broken and put into the cups of a drunkard, or of one who wished to follow drinking. The eggs would so work with him that he would suddenly detest drink and refrain from the habit. Another reference is mentioned in a book called *The Long Hidden Friend* which was published in Pennsylvania in 1863 and is referred to by E. A. Armstrong (1958). The reference is as follows: 'If you lay the heart and right foot of a barn owl on one who is asleep, he will answer whatever you ask him and tell what he has done.' This can be traced back to Albertus Magnus who almost certainly obtained the information from Pliny, who says that an owl's heart placed on the left breast of a sleeping woman will cause her to disclose secrets.

Finally, in the North Riding of Yorkshire, owl broth was once prescribed occasionally for whooping cough, although in this case the Tawny Owl was probably the species involved; and in the Orkneys and Shetlands old wives used to say that a cow would give bloody milk if it were frightened by an owl, and would fall sick and die if touched by one. Horace, Ovid and Shakespeare all refer to the use of owls in concocting magical potions.

Having discussed the Barn Owl in poetry, legend and folk-lore, it is time now to review some historical accounts. These are of considerable interest as they emphasise many of the distorted and erroneous views once held about the bird, and at the same time help to illustrate how opinions began to change, so that this species came to be regarded finally as a friend of mankind, by all but the most ignorant, and in no way deserving of the evil reputation with which it was once accorded. We shall begin by examining those references which concern the supposedly dubious side of the Barn Owl and then show how certain writers, such as Waterton and Gurney, began to defend it by invoking the use of scientific fact. One of the grimmest contemporary pictures is painted in *A Natural History of Birds* by the Count de Buffon, who says this of the species:

> When it flies or alights, it utters also different sharp notes which are all so disagreeable that, joined to the awfulness of the scene, re-echoed from the tombs and the churches in the stillness and darkness of night, inspire dread and terror in the minds of women and children, and even of men who are under the influence of the same prejudices, and who believe in omens and witches, in ghosts and apparitions. They regard the White Owl as a funeral bird and the messenger of death; and they are impressed with an idea that, if it perches upon a house and utters cries a little different from ordinary, it then summons the inhabitants to the tomb.

He also accused these owls, perhaps unjustly, at least with regard to Woodcock, of taking birds from traps and eating them:

> In autumn they often pay a nightly visit to the places where the springs are laid for the woodcocks and thrushes; they kill the woodcocks which they find hanging and eat them on the spot; but they sometimes carry off the thrushes and other small birds that are caught, often swallowing them entire with the feathers, but generally when they are larger, plucking them previously.

It seems likely that such misdemeanours were only of rare occurrence, but were conveniently described or implied as being commonplace in order to blacken the reputation of the Barn Owl so as to justify its extermination.

The Gentleman's Magazine of 1822 makes an interesting reference to the evil which could supposedly be done to human beings by the Barn Owl. This is contained in a letter dated 1st July 1684, and I quote the extract:

> Near St Dunstan's Church, Fleet Street, I stepped into a Stone Cutter's and, casting my eyes up and down, I spied a huge marble with a large inscription upon it, which was this:
>
>> Here lies John Oxenham, a goodly young man, in whose chamber as he was struggling with the pangs of death, a bird with a white breast was seen fluttering about his bed, and so vanished!
>>
>> Here lies also Mary Oxenham, sister of the above John, who died the next day, and the same apparition was in the room.
>
> Another sister is spoken of thirdly and then the fourth inscription is as follows:
>
>> Here lies, hard by, James Oxenham, son of the said John, who died a child in his cradle, a little after, and such a bird was seen fluttering about his head a little before he expired, which vanished afterwards.

Another interesting comment occurs in W. H. Hudson's *Birds and Men*, 1901, which, although it refers to the Tawny Owl, gives us a valuable insight into local superstitions. It is not unexpected that such superstitions were stronger in rural areas than in the towns, and the remarks quoted below were made to the author during a visit to the Midland village of Willersey, one mile from Saintbury. A villager said to him:

> Have you heard about the young woman who had dropped down dead a week or two ago, after hearing an owl hooting near her cottage in the daytime? Well, the owl had been hooting again in the same tree, and no-one knew who it was for and what to expect next. The village was in an excited state about it and all the children had gathered near the tree and threw stones into it, but the owl had stubbornly refused to come out.

A little later the author comments:

> One of the villagers, who was engaged in repairing the thatch of a cottage close to the tree, informed us that the owl's hooting had not troubled him in the least. Owls, he truly said, often hoot during the daytime during the autumn months, and he did not believe that it meant death for someone. The sceptical fellow, it is hardly necessary to say, was a young man who had spent a good deal of time away from the village.

In view of what has been said so far in this chapter, it is not surprising that there is excellent evidence available of the persecution suffered by the Barn Owl – it is hardly necessary to add that because the species is unlucky enough to possess a hooked beak and sharp talons, it has suffered at the hands of game-preservers and the like in the same way as the diurnal birds of prey. A stuffed pair of Barn Owls, shown to the writer by a Cheshire farmer, which were killed in the early part of the twentieth century, provides just one of the countless examples. It should also be remembered that birds' feathers were of commercial value and those of the Barn Owl were no exception. Thus, Butler, Mathew and Forbes (1897) observe:

> There is no bird more commonly found stuffed and distorted in a case in cottages and farmhouses throughout the land than this poor Owl . . ... Then, too, there is the wretched fashion of turning the *masks*, wings and tails of these birds into fire-screens, and the still more senseless decoration of ladies' hats with their soft and downy feathers. There is hardly any season of the year when specimens of the four common English Owls, and chiefly of the Barn Owl, may

not be noticed hanging up for sale in Leadenhall market in London, and on enquiring for what purpose they are bought, the answer has been given to the writer, 'These, Sir, are fancy birds, people buy them to have them stuffed'.

There is a similar observation by R. B. Smith in his book, *Bird Life and Bird Lore*, referring to an advertisement seen by a Mr Ward Fowler in a public house:

> Wanted at once by a London Firm: 1,000 Owls.

The same author is one of a number who criticise the attitude of many game-preservers towards the owl, especially in the use of the vicious pole-trap:

> I heard from a friend on the borders of the county of Dorset, that a gamekeeper finding, I presume, that he could no longer, with impunity to himself, put up pole-traps on his master's ground, had induced the gardener of a large garden which adjoined one of his owl-haunted covers, to plant the forbidden instrument of torture there, and that, in the few weeks it was allowed to remain, it had caught and lacerated to death seven owls of various kinds – for every week, in fact, an owl.

Further references will be made to the pole-trap when something is said later about the efforts to put the reputation of the Barn Owl into its true perspective.

The Barn Owl also suffered persecution on account of its being considered a nuisance. The earliest examples of this are to be found in churchwardens' accounts, since efforts were sometimes made to exclude the owl from church buildings. Two examples are quoted below:

> 1711 (Redenhall, Norfolk) For worke and stuffe and nailes in stopping out ye owles at ye church ....3s. 6d.
> 1759 (St John's, Chester) Paid for bird-lime to catch Owles in the Church   2d.

Two interesting records are quoted by the Rev M. A. Mathew in *Birds of Pembrokeshire*, 1894, when Barn Owls were persecuted primarily because of the nuisance they were causing. In both cases an unusual number of Barn Owls was involved:

> Although the Barn Owl is generally a solitary recluse, we have, in our experience, met with two instances of it living in society in such numbers that the association might fairly be termed an 'Owlery'. One of these had its location in some old cottages, just below a beautiful Henry VII church tower. The roofs of the cottages all communicated, and were tenanted by such a number of barn owls that at last the cottagers rose up against them, being annoyed by the smell and noises proceeding from the birds, and we were informed that between forty and fifty were either driven out or destroyed.

Mathew quotes a second similar example, but in this case the owls, about a dozen in all, in addition to owlets, were only killed after they had supposedly carried off some young pheasants. There are, no doubt, many less spectacular examples when Barn Owls were killed merely because they were considered vermin and a nuisance, as would have been rats or mice.

During the nineteenth century we saw the first real attempts to be more scientific in determining the usefulness or otherwise of the Barn Owl. One of its first champions was Charles Waterton and his paper entitled *The habits of the Barn-owl and the benefits it confers on Man*, published in 1832, was the first real defence of the species and is certainly worth quoting at length:

> I own I have a great liking for the bird; and I have offered it hospitality and protection on account of its persecutions and for its many services to me – I say services, as you will see in the sequel I wish that any little thing I could write or say might cause it to stand better in the world at large than it has hitherto done; but I have slender hopes on this score; because old and deep-rooted prejudices are seldom overcome; and when I look back into the annals of remote antiquity, I see too clearly that defamation has done its worst to ruin the whole family, in all its branches, of this poor, harmless, useful friend of mine.

He then goes on to describe how times are changing:

> Indeed, human wretches in the shape of body-snatchers seem here in England to have usurped the office of the owl in our churchyards . . . .. Up to the year 1813, the barn-owl had a sad time of it at Walton Hall. Its supposed mournful notes alarmed the aged housekeeper. She knew full well what sorrow it had brought into other houses when she was a young woman; and there was enough of mischief in the midnight wintry blast, without having it increased by the dismal screaming of something which people knew very little about, and which everybody said was far too busy in the churchyard at night-time. Nay it was a well-known fact that if any person were sick in the neighbourhood, it would be for ever looking in at the window, and holding a conversation outside with somebody, they did not know whom. The gamekeeper agreed with her in everything she said on this important subject; and he always stood better in her books when he had managed to shoot a bird of this bad and mischievous family.

He then tells of how he erected a nest-place for the Barn Owls:

> On the ruin of the old gate-way . . . .. I made a place with stone and mortar, about four feet square.

He continues by commenting that the housekeeper was not happy about this:

> I do not think that up to the day of the old lady's death, which took place in her eighty-fourth year, she ever looked with pleasure, or contentment on the barn-owl, as it flew round the large sycamore trees which grew near the old ruined gate-way.
>
> When I found that this first settlement on the gate-way had succeeded so well, I set about forming other establishments. This year I have had four broods, and I trust that next season I can calculate on having more . . . .
>
> If this useful bird had caught its food by day, instead of hunting for it by night, mankind would have ocular demonstration of its utility in thinning the country of mice, and it would be protected and encouraged everywhere . . . . I am amply repaid for the pains I have taken to protect and encourage the barn-owl, it pays me a hundred fold by the enormous quantity of mice which it destroys throughout the year. The servants now no longer wish to destroy it. Often, on a fine summer's evening, with delight I see the villagers loitering under the sycamore trees longer than they would otherwise do, to have a peep at the barn-owl as it leaves the ivy-mantled tower.

By the end of the nineteenth century and the beginning of the twentieth century there were still many reports about the persecution of the Barn Owl and sometimes comments were made about its scarcity. Persecution must, indeed, have had some effect on the bird's status, probably quite a serious one in some areas. J. H. Gurney made some significant remarks in *The Norfolk and Norwich Naturalists' Society's Transactions* for 1886/7:

> There is one bird now rapidly becoming scarce with us, owing to constant persecution, for which we would especially plead, we refer to the Barn Owl, than which the farmers and game-preservers do not possess a greater friend and yet there is scarcely a game-keeper's gibbet on which it is not found, and very many are annually brought to the Norwich bird-stuffers.

Indeed, even as early as 1866, H. Stevenson had commented in *Birds of Norfolk* that:

> The Barn-Owl is resident with us throughout the year, but I wish I could add that the term 'common' is as applicable now as in former times.

Despite Gurney's comments in 1886, persecution was still apparently rife in 1917, and we quote again from this author:

> On April 5th, 1917, a Barn Owl brought into Norwich to be stuffed proved to contain six shrew mice . . .. Who can deny the beneficial nature of this species, which is of such service to man? Yet I once counted the skins of forty-six Barn Owls in a bird-stuffer's shop in Norfolk, but am thankful to think that the efforts of the Norwich Naturalists' Society have done much to check such senseless persecution.

Similar stories of the persecution of owls also came from other parts of the country. J. R. B. Masefield reports from North Staffordshire around 1910 that:

> The lamentable increase of the brown rat, the long-tailed field-mouse and the field and bank voles in recent years, and the consequent and serious damage done to our crops, have to a great extent been caused by the destruction of the Owls, which are Nature's remedy for keeping these destructive rodents in check.

At this point the reader should be reminded that the relative importance of the controls which affect the populations of birds and mammals are extremely complex and a statement such as that by Masefield might be difficult to substantiate in full. The real point, however, is that persecution was widespread and must have had at least some effect on mammal populations.

Similar remarks to those just cited came from Glamorgan, the *Cardiff Naturalists' Society's Report* for 1900 commenting that:

> This bird is rapidly decreasing and will soon become rare owing to its wanton destruction by gamekeepers and others by guns and pole-traps.

The *Transactions of the Worcestershire Naturalists' Club* for 1911–13 makes the same point:

> This beautiful white owl is most unfortunately a frequent victim of the stupidity of the man with a gun, and all too often one will find its corpse among the keeper's gruesome collection, or even fastened to a post in a field to scare the crows.

The same article observes, however, that:

> The Barn-owl is not so uncommon as many people think, and may be heard calling in most country districts at dusk.

It is essential to remember that because the Barn Owl is a fairly nocturnal bird, it is all too easy to overlook and, as was mentioned in Chapter 7, this was a problem for the devisers of the BTO's *The Atlas of Breeding Birds* project.

One further aspect of its persecution remains, and that is the notion that it raided pigeon-lofts, taking adult pigeons and young and thus providing an excuse for its slaughter. Once again such actions were usually quite unjustifiable, as E. Stanley remarked as long ago as 1838 in *A Familiar History of Birds*:

> Many, however, condemn them on account of the ravages they commit in pigeon-houses, by carrying off the young ones; but this seems to be an unfair charge; their real reason for entering pigeon houses being rather for the purpose of picking up the vermin that are constantly harbouring there, ignoring the inmates.

Mr Waterton observes that when farmers complain that the Barn Owl destroys the eggs of their pigeons they put the saddle on the wrong horse. It ought, he says, to be put upon the rat, stating from his own experience that his increase of pigeons was 'inconsiderable till the rats were effectively excluded from the dove-cot, since which time they have increased abundantly, though the Barn Owls frequent it, and are encouraged all about it'.

Finally, a very good plea for the Barn Owl is made by P. Robinson in *Birds of the Wave and Woodland*, 1894. He advocates the erection of nesting-barrels, pointing out the benefits which they confer on Man and that pigeon-keepers need not be alarmed. He comments that gamekeepers should be forbidden to destroy the birds, adding that they had a bad name given to them in the beginning which still clings to them because of the persistence of popular prejudices and superstition.

Space does not permit us to say anything about the persecution, legends and folk-lore of the Barn Owl in foreign countries, although there are quite a number of references to this in English writings.

Despite the supposedly evil reputation of the Barn Owl, and of owls in general, their names were used as an element in place-names as well as in heraldry. Interesting place-names include:

Olcoates (Nottinghamshire), which means cottage (cot) inhabited by owls (ule), can be traced back to 1199.

Outchester (Northumberland) means a Roman fort (chester) inhabited by owls and is traceable back to 1206.

Ulcombe (Kent) means the valley (combe) of the owl (also Alecumbe, Derbyshire) and dates back to 946.

Ulgham (Northumberland) means valley or nook (ham) of the owl and dates back to 1139.

Ullenhall (Warwickshire) means nook (hall) of the owl and is first mentioned in 1200.

Similarly, Ullswater and Uldale, both in Cumbria, refer to the owl.

Various other pseudonyms are sometimes encountered in the names of streets (e.g. Ullett Road, Liverpool), woods (e.g. Owlet Wood, near Blackburn, Lancashire, farms (e.g. Ullardhall Farm in Cheshire) and even personal names (one of the cast of ITV's series 'Please Sir' was called Howlett).

A brief mention must be made of the use of the owl as a heraldic device. It appears in the Coats-of-Arms of three north of England towns: Leeds, Dewsbury and Oldham. The Leeds Coat-of-Arms was adopted in 1626 and the owls were part of the Arms of Sir John Savile, the first alderman, and were adopted by Leeds Corporation as a compliment to him. The owls which appear on the Dewsbury Coat-of-Arms are also taken from the Crest of the Savile family, the principal land-owners in the district for nearly six centuries; the Coat-of-Arms was adopted in 1893. The Coat-of-Arms of the Borough of Oldham was granted in 1894.

The owl also appears on the Crest of some schools, for example Manchester Grammar School, the obvious inference being that it is a symbol of wisdom and learning and, as mentioned above, it was used occasionally on family Crests.

Finally, there have been many local names for the Barn Owl, although most of them have long been extinct. Some of the names signify its predilection for buildings and others refer to its plumage or to its call – see the list at the end of this chapter.

Having traced some of the facts and fallacies about the Barn Owl, including the occasional reference to owls in general where appropriate, it will be all too obvious that the species can justly be described as 'unfortunate'. Prior to the nineteenth century it was the object of a considerable amount of superstition which earned for it a very wide range of dismal epithets, e.g. deadly, dreadful, wicked, hateful, fearful, fatal, dire, accursed, unhallowed, obscure, and resulted in its being called every kind of name, e.g. 'bird of hate', 'harbinger of doom', 'herald of disaster', 'foul bird of omen' and many more. Although it was subjected to much less superstitious belief in the nineteenth century, it was still the object of persecution, since the possession of a hooked beak and talons provided all the proof that was needed to condemn it for preying upon a variety of game. Such persecution was probably quite common until at least 1914, after which the reduction in the number of keepered estates and the advent of bird protection laws finally began to give it a degree of the protection it so richly deserves.

Other names of the Barn Owl – based largely on *British Names of Birds* by Christine E. Jackson and *A Dictionary of English and Folk-names of British Birds* by the Rev H. K. Swann and H. Kirk.

Berthwan – Cornwall
Billy Owl, Billy Wise, Billy Wix – Norfolk
Cherubim, Church Owl – northern England (Craven)
Cream-coloured Owl, Deviling – Surrey
Gil-hooter – Cheshire
Gill Houter – Staffordshire
Gill-howter – Norfolk
Gillihowlet, Gilly-howlet – Scotland
Gilly White (immature) – Shropshire
Hissing Owl – Yorkshire
Hobby Owl – Northamptonshire
Hoolet – Scottish lowlands
Hullart, Hullot, Ullet – Cheshire
Jenny Howlet – northern England (variations are Jinny Hullut, Jinny Oolert, Jinny Yewlatt)

Jenny Owl, Jenny Owlen – Northumberland
Madge Howlet – Norfolk (a name found in Janson's *Every Man*, 1598)
Moggy – Sussex
Ooler, Oolert (corruption of Howlet), Owlen, Owlerd – Shropshire
Padge – Leicestershire
Povey – Gloucestershire
Pudge, Pudge Owl – Leicestershire
Roarer – northern England and southern Scotland
Screaming Owl – Yorkshire
Screeaghag Oie – Isle of Man
Screecher – Surrey
Screech Owl – widespread
Scrich-owle, Scritch-owl, Silver Owl – Scotland
Stix – Cornwall
Ullot – Yorkshire
White-breasted Barn Owl, White Hoolet – Surrey, Sussex, Worcestershire
White Owl – widespread
Willow Owl – Surrey
Woolert – Shropshire
Yellow Owl
European Screech Owl

Vertebrate species in the text

MAMMALS
American Pine Vole *Pitymys pinetorum*
Badger *Meles meles*
Bank Vole *Clethrionomys glareolus*
Brown Hare *Lepus europaeus*
Brown Rat *Rattus norvegicus*
Common Shrew *Sorex araneus*
Common Vole *Microtus arvalis*
Domestic Cat *Felis catus*
Dog *Canis familiaris*
Dormouse *Muscardinus avellanarius*
Eastern Chipmunk *Tamias striatus*
European Pine Vole *Pitymys savii*
Fox *Vulpes vulpes*
Greater Horseshoe Bat *Rhinolophus ferrum-equinum*
Ground squirrel *Citellus beecheyi* (full vernacular name unknown)
Guinea-pig *Cavia porcellus*
Harvest Mouse *Micromys minutus*
House Mouse *Mus musculus*
Kitten (young Domestic Cat)
Levant Vole *Microtus guentheri*
Long-eared Bat *Plecotus auritus*
Meadow Mouse *Microtus pennsylvanicus*
Mediterranean Pine Vole *Pitymys duodecimeostatus*
Microtus mustersi (vernacular name unknown)
Mole *Talpa europaea*
Mouse-eared Bat *Myotis myotis*
Multimammate Mouse *Praomys natalensis*
Natterer's Bat *Myotis nattereri*
Noctule Bat *Nyctalus noctula*
Otter *Lutra lutra*
Pipistrelle Bat *Pipistrellus pipistrellus*
Pocket Gopher *Thomomys bottae*
Pocket Mouse *Perognathus inornatus*
Pygmy Shrew *Sorex minutus*
Rabbit *Oryctolagus cuniculus*
Rat Kangaroo *Potorous tridactylus*
Red Squirrel *Sciurus vulgaris*
Ring-tailed Opossum *Pseudochirus peregrinus*
Roe Deer *Capreolus capreolus*

Sheep *Ovis aries*
Short-tailed Shrew *Blarina brevicauda kirklandi*
Short-tailed Vole *Microtus agrestis*
Skomer Vole *Clethrionomys glareolus skomerensis*
Stoat *Mustela erminea*
Water Shrew *Neomys fodiens*
Water Vole *Arvicola amphibius*
Weasel *Mustela nivalis*
Western (or Least) Chipmunk *Eutomias minimus*
Whiskered Bat *Myotis mystacinus*
White-toothed Shrew *Crocidura russula*
Wood Mouse *Apodemus sylvaticus*

BIRDS
African Bay Owl *Phodilus prigoginei*
Blackbird *Turdus merula*
Black-headed Gull *Larus ridibundus*
Black-tailed Godwit *Limosa limosa*
Blue-tit *Parus caeruleus*
Buzzard *Buteo buteo*
Carrion Crow *Corvus corone corone*
Celebes Barn Owl *Tyto rosenbergii*
Chaffinch *Fringilla coelebs*
Common Barn Owl *Tyto alba*
Common Bay Owl *Phodilus badius*
Common Grass Owl *Tyto capensis*
Common Snipe *Gallinago gallinago*
Cormorant *Phalacrocorax carbo*
Corncrake *Crex crex*
Cuckoo *Cuculus canorus*
Curlew *Numenius arquata*
Domestic Fowl *Gallus domesticus*
Domestic Pigeon *Columba livia*
Dunlin *Calidris alpina*
Eagle Owl *Bubo bubo*
Fairy Tern *Gygis alba*
Fantail Pigeon *Columba livia*
Feral Pigeon *Columba livia*
Golden Eagle *Aquila chrysaëtos*
Goldfinch *Carduelis carduelis*

Goshawk *Accipiter gentilis*
Great Horned Owl *Bubo virginianus*
Hammerhead Stork *Scopus umbretta bannermanii*
Hawfinch *Coccothraustes coccothraustes*
Hen Harrier *Circus cyaneus cyaneus*
Heron *Ardea cinerea*
House Martin *Delichon urbica*
House Sparrow *Passer domesticus*
Jackdaw *Corvus monedula*
Kestrel *Falco tinnunculus*
Lapwing *Vanellus vanellus*
Linnet *Carduelis cannabina*
Little Owl *Athene noctua*
Long-eared Owl *Asio otus*
Madagascar Grass Owl *Tyto soumagnei*
Magpie *Pica pica*
Marsh Hawk *Circus cyaneus hudsonius*
Masked Owl *Tyto novaehollandiae*
Meadow Pipit *Anthus pratensis*
Merlin *Falco columbarius*
Minahassa Barn Owl *Tyto inexpectata*
Moorhen *Gallinula chloropus*
New Britain Barn Owl *Tyto aurantia*
Nightjar *Caprimulgus europaeus*
Peregrine *Falco peregrinus*
Pheasant *Phasianus colchicus*
Pied Flycatcher *Ficedula hypoleuca*
Raven *Corvus corax*
Razo Short-toed Lark *Calandrella razae*
Red Kite *Milvus milvus*
Redstart *Phoenicurus phoenicurus*
Red-winged Blackbird *Agelaius phoenicus*
Robin *Erithacus rubecula*
Rook *Corvus frugilegus*
Scops Owl *Otus scops*

Serin *Serinus serinus*
Short-eared Owl *Asio flammeus*
Skylark *Alauda arvensis*
Snowy Owl *Nyctea scandiaca*
Sooty Owl *Tyto tenebricosa*
Sparrowhawk *Accipiter nisus*
Spotless Starling *Sturnus unicolor*
Starling *Sturnus vulgaris*
Swallow *Hirundo rustica*
Swift *Apus apus*
Tawny Owl *Strix aluco*
Tengmalm's Owl *Aegolius funereus*
Ural Owl *Strix uralensis*
Woodcock *Scolopax rusticola*
Wood Pigeon *Columba palumbus*
Wren *Troglodytes troglodytes*

REPTILES
Gopher Snake *Pituophis catenifer*
Green Lizard *Lacerta viridis*
Spanish Sand Lizard *Lacerta hispanica*
Wall Lizard *Podarcis muralis*

AMPHIBIANS
Common Frog *Rana temporaria*
Common Toad *Bufo bufo*

FISH
Brown Trout *Salmo trutta*
Carp *Cyprinus carpio*
Perch *Perca fluviatilis*
Roach *Rutilis rutilis*
Rudd *Scardinius erythrophthalmus*

Development of young Barn Owl

This brief summary is based on the eldest owlet, which is normally more precocious than the rest. It is biased towards fast development because we have used the earliest age at which we have noted the acquirement of each characteristic of appearance and behaviour. It is therefore only accurate for those broods that are well supplied with food.

Eggs Laid at 2–3 day intervals, or sometimes greater. Eliptical, dull white, average size 39·74 × 31·57 mm. Incubation period 30–31 days.

Owlets on hatching Approx. 50·0 mm. (2 in) long, markedly 'pot-bellied' and large headed, the closed eyes making bulbous lumps on the sides of the head. Legs ill-developed. Skin pink; bill ivory with pinkish suffusion at base, bearing an egg-tooth. Covered with short, fairly plentiful greyish-white down on upperparts, but with bare patches on sides of neck and sparse on belly; front of tarsus and toes covered to claws but back of tarsus bare. Voice mostly chittering, especially when left by hen; snores faintly. Owlets still in eggs will answer calls of hatched young one or even two days before hatching. Defaecation occurs in nest, faeces being quickly eaten by hen.

Day 1 Can move about nest but normally stays amongst eggs.

Day 2 Already noticeably larger and can carry head better. When left by hen calls loudly with chittering note and occasional snores.

Day 3 Legs much stronger and thicker; is much more capable of moving around nest. First prey noted at nest.

Day 4 Noticeably bigger and heavier.

Day 5 Snores lustily. Head may get bloody during feeds by hen.

Day 6 Huddles against other owlets. Seen to nibble at nest debris and younger nest-mates. Calls loudly if left and during feeds. Increase in snoring and prey offerings point to increasing appetite.

Day 7 Still rests sprawled out. Unable to lift head for long. Chittering becomes faster in tempo.

Day 8 Remains quiet while being brooded, chitters when left uncovered. Responds to hen's food-offering call with begging snores. At 'enclosed' nests entire brood will move from centre of nest as soon as last owlet hatches, and transfer to darkest part of cavity.

Day 9 Is far bigger than nest-mates. Still defaecates in nest and hen still eats droppings. Snores repeatedly and voice getting stronger.

Day 10 No longer looks fragile. Chittering still main note when disturbed. Seen to flap stumpy wings and uses them in moving about nest.

Day 12 Very ugly, as down no longer adequate to cover much larger body. Able to hold up head indefinitely and eyes open for short periods. Pupil has blue, blind-looking appearance (as in young Tawny Owl). Moves about nest, looking for food and nibbling at nest debris and prey items. Chitters almost constantly while doing this. Hisses when disturbed, giving feeble tongue-clicks.

Day 13 Tiny quills present which will give rise to second down. Markedly 'pot-bellied'. Still chitters readily.

Day 14   Second (white) down begins to make its appearance. Egg-tooth shed about this time. Moves around freely in nest and begins to preen. Still keeps eyes shut for long periods. Nest still cleaned of faeces by hen. Answers adult with chitters. Snores develop an occasional rasping quality. Gives loud sustained defensive hisses when disturbed by noise or movement of observer. Increased supply of prey at nest.

Day 15   Too large for hen to cover and size accentuated by thickening second down. Stands upright in nest and, in absence of hen, other owlets gather round it for warmth. Still keeps eyes shut for long periods. (Recorded as rolling over and striking with feet but this not seen by us until much later).

Day 16   Second down continues to thicken. Still chitters when restless. Responds to arrival of adults with food by snoring excitedly and can swallow small voles whole. Change in nest sanitation – now backs out of nest area with raised wings and tail wagging from side to side to defaecate. Hen may leave nest to hunt a little, but much variation depending on age of youngest owlet.

Day 17   Second down almost fully developed – 'a ball of clean white fluff'. Facial disk feathers beginning to grow. Pupils still have blue appearance. 'Nest' covers much larger area due to accumulation of fragmented pellets. Still hisses loudly when nest approached, thus advertising presence to possible predator. When handled will hiss and tongue-click. Number of prey items around nest continues to increase. Cock either increases supply in excess of demand, or this is due to some help by hen.

Day 18   May still be helped by hen with feeding where difficulty is experienced.

Day 19   Second down covers all body except protruberant stomach. Lower half of tarsus and toes sparsely covered with short tufts. Primary quills almost 2·5 cm long, not yet unfurling, with tuft of down at their tips. Eyes fully open when awake but still spends most of time dozing. Will move head from side to side in beginning of a defensive display, opening bill as if to give brief hisses, but no sound noticed.

Day 20   Snatches food from feeding adult.

Day 21   Facial disk just beginning to show. Pupils still blue.

Day 22   Second down very long and thick. Hen's brooding drive weakening further. Attempts to cover owlets at this stage fail – may crouch down by side of them so that small members of brood can creep under her. Prey items normally strewn around nest. An owlet at this stage attempted a warning scream or mobbing note.

Day 24   Facial disk more pronounced but not fully developed. Pupils losing blue appearance.

Day 25   Primary quills c. 2·5 cm long and beginning to unfurl. Tail feathers also unfurling. Claws beginning to lengthen and sharpen. Hen merely stands by young, feathers fluffed and wings drooping a little. Youngest of brood of six might well be only 13 days old but presumably warmth from other owlets suffices. Prey items normally present at nest.

Day 26   Will roll on back when threatened, but in authors' experience, fails to strike or grip with feet when given opportunity.

Day 27   Facial disk well defined. Eyes turning brown as in adults. Thick accumulation of droppings around edge of nest.

Day 29   Begins to come to edge of nest to look around. Flaps wings when receiving prey from adult. Hen no longer stays at nest, youngest now being able to feed itself.

Day 31   Primaries about 7·5 cm long, last 2·5 cm of which is unfurling. Only 1–2 prey items around nest now, probably because appetites of brood is such that they eat prey as soon as it is brought in. Snores loudly when hungry. Begins to stretch and flap wings.

Day 33   Facial disk quite well developed.

Day 34   Much wing-flapping.

Day 35   Facial disk well developed and body feathers growing rapidly. Can pull prey to pieces. Peers about with exaggerated head movements typical of young owls. If nest site permits, some owlets may leave nest between feeds and wander about, running, jumping and flapping wings. When such an owlet returns to nest it is greeted with much excitement and snoring. When examined will roll over, striking with feet. Pellets in nest getting larger.

Day 36   Feathers appearing on back of head. Primaries unfurled for almost full length, secondaries for half their length; end of tail feathers unfurled. Tarsus beginning to feather at back.

Day 37   Droppings copious. An owlet at an 'enclosed' nest site left nest for first time.

Day 40   Nest smelly; droppings very thick around perimeter. Preens thoroughly. Still much time spent dozing, resting on tarsi. If site permits will run from nest when examined. Snores incessantly when awake. Sometimes tongue-clicks when fed, perhaps in excitement or to threaten other owlets.

Day 42   Facial disk becoming more rounded. Nest debris now very thick, forming dense mat.

Day 43   When examined some owlets will give defensive display with loud sustained hisses and when pressed will roll on back, striking viciously and effectively with talons; others are passive and lie prostrate with eyes closed.

Day 44   Primaries about 12·5 cm long.

Day 45   Appearance now changing rapidly due to white, rounded facial disk. Flapping of wings causes much down to fly and when owlets are handled it comes away freely. Still sleeps flat out on stomach with head on bottom of nest. Slight disputes over prey.

Day 47   Tail extends *beyond* primaries. Losing down especially from head. Mutual preening observed for first time. Still roosts at nest.

Day 49   Does not utter defensive hissing unless handled, tending to remain silent and immobile in hope of remaining undetected.

Day 50   Some owlets have lost quite a lot of down.

Day 51   Mutual preening increasing. Snoring continues and when hungry these calls become louder. First 'play pounces' noted and first short flight.

Day 52   Still flaps wings, tongue-clicks and snores excitedly when fed.

Day 55   Still has down on top of legs and on belly but amounts vary and some birds have considerably more, particularly on breast. Begins to fly more, though very clumsy especially on alighting. Begins to roost in places away from nest but still in nest area, i.e. in same part of building, visiting actual nest site regularly. Snores more loudly and raucously than ever.

Day 56   May leave building for first time.

Day 57   Adults, particularly hen, very much inclined to roost elsewhere and stay away from young except to feed. Owlet still calls from nest area a good deal, especially just before dusk. Sits around waiting to be fed.

Day 60   Still bears traces of down on lower body but now very similar to adult. 'Plays', making pounces, rushes, etc, at inanimate objects. Still greets other owlets at nest, and any which join it outside, with loud snores, reaching up to other's beak as though for food.

Day 63   Still spends much time snoring loudly as it waits for food, and stays by nest area. Flies perfectly.

Day 65   Hen may lay again at about this time. Owlet very adult in appearance, but exaggerated head movements distinguish it in poor light. First serious pounce recorded – outcome unknown. Begins to roam farther afield, often in company with another owlet. Distinctly sociable and owlets follow one another about. Still pursues adults for food sometimes and still snores loudly.

Day 66 Sometimes chases adults determinedly for food but turns back after short distance.

Day 68 Less tied to nest-mates and spends lengthy periods alone away from nest-site.

Day 70 Still 'plays'.

Day 72 One owlet observed to make capture. Still roosts near nest site, often with other owlets from nest, but often ignored by adult when bringing in food, perhaps because it now snores less persistently.

Day 76 May leave parental territory.

Day 79 When exploring and hunting owlet no longer snores very often so more likely to make capture.

Day 82 Owlet remains away from building a good deal, perhaps even roosting elsewhere.

Day 85 Aggression increasing among owlets and there is a strong suspicion that they are also aggressive towards the adults – hissing, using defensive display and advancing.

Day 86 Last record of several prey items being brought in. By this time, however, an owlet of this age should be independent and be spending little time at the parental barn, so food would be given to the younger owlets.

Day 93 Last feed recorded. Only one or two prey items brought in.

Day 102 Record of aggression by adult. This finally disperses any remaining owlets.

Day 105 Owlet heard to give almost perfect screech.

Watching the Barn Owl

It is the hope of the authors that this monograph will stimulate other workers to advance the study of the Barn Owl. Although the book is the result of many years field work there are still questions that remain unanswered and an enthusiastic field-worker could do much to further our knowledge of this fascinating species. For that reason a few words from us may prove helpful to those who feel inclined to undertake such work, while the less enthusiastic reader may be interested to gain some insight into the techniques we used while carrying out these studies.

It should be made clear at the outset that if the aspiring worker lacks the essential qualities of limitless patience and the ability to sit perfectly still for long periods he should forget all about the Barn Owl and find a less exacting species to study; for, interesting as this bird is, outside the breeding season there will be occasions when the observer will spend hours without seeing or hearing anything of an owl; and if he is prone to fidget he will inevitably be detected, for a Barn Owl's superb hearing enables it to pinpoint the slightest sound-source immediately. Since much of the owl's activity takes place at night, it follows that another attribute of the successful owl watcher is the ability to forego sleep! A typical watch begins an hour before dusk and, particularly during the nesting period, the observer will have to remain into the early hours if he wishes to record an adequate portion of the bird's nocturnal behaviour. It will also be desirable to carry out all-night watches at times in order to record the complete cycle of activity.

One of the difficulties inherent with watching a nocturnal species is the problem of how to see one's subject. We have found, however, that this is not usually the insurmountable handicap it at first appears. After struggling along with a torch bearing a red filter – which resulted in somewhat restricted viewing – we learned that white light had been used successfully both with Badgers and Barn Owls without apparently affecting their behaviour, and since then we have used ordinary torches of the spotlight type, both inside buildings and out in the open. Provided that some common sense is used we have found that white light does not inhibit the birds in the slightest. Similarly, the brilliance of electronic flash does not affect them unduly, though contrary to the experiences of Hosking & Newberry (1945) we found that the sound of a camera shutter reduced them to panic whenever they were photographed indoors. Before long such disturbance affects their natural behaviour and for this reason we have never regarded photography and observation as compatible. For the same reason it is a great advantage to have a torch that will switch on and off silently.

For general observation away from the nest site, a good vantage point is needed, but before this can be selected some preliminary work will be necessary. This involves determining the extent of the bird's territory, favoured roosts, flight-lines and hunting grounds. Once these are known the observer should endeavour to find some high ground which affords as wide a field of view as possible, preferably including the bird's most regular roost. In flat areas, where high points are scarce or non-existent, use can sometimes be made of such features as railway embankments, roadside banks and climbable trees, etc. We would also suggest that the observer endeavours to establish the direction of the prevailing wind and should then try to find a vantage point which offers at least some shelter from the elements. This can often mean the difference between success and failure, as he will be operating during the coldest hours. The most essential requirement for general observation is, of course, that a bird can be located that is active in reasonably good light.

For watching early courtship and post-fledging behaviour it will be necessary for the observer to take up a position outside the nest site, and of course at natural sites such as tree holes he will spend all his time outdoors. At this comparatively close range he will require a hide, but in these circumstances the conventional type is at a disadvantage due to its limited field of view. As an alternative we have found nothing to better a hide made out of camouflage netting such as is used by pigeon shooters. This gives unrestricted vision all round and, surprisingly, owls seem unable to recognise the human form within even though, to our eyes, he is clearly visible. A.B.W., who has used this type of hide a great deal, was intrigued to note the differing reactions of various species to this method of concealment. Sheep invariably spotted him immediately, yet on other occasions when the wind was right he has had Roe Deer grazing unconcernedly a few metres away and Foxes trotting past obliviously. Bird species which seemed able to detect him behind the netting included Jackdaw, Carrion Crow, Starling and Robin, while normally sharp-eyed species such as Pheasant, Cuckoo, Tawny Owl, Woodpigeon and Wren seemed incapable. The Barn Owls themselves frequently perched on these net hides when the observer was inside at a distance of no more than 45 cm!

While still on the subject of outdoor vigils we have one last but important word of warning. If the observer is working in the vicinity of damp woods or water around dusk and after dark, one item of equipment is essential: *an insect repellent.* One of the crosses the owl watcher frequently has to bear during the summer months is to suffer the agonies of being the target of countless hordes of midges, flies and mosquitoes. If he goes unprotected he does so at his peril. He will arrive home demented, with face and other areas of bare skin blotched and swollen from their attentions. Not only this, but he will probably be minus any notes, having been obliged to leave – or having driven the owls away by his frantic swatting – before anything useful could be observed.

Before passing on to describe the methods of studying the Barn Owl at really close quarters we wish to emphasise that the first concern of the field-worker or photographer should be the welfare of the bird itself. In any case where doubt arises as to how an owl will react, the worker should rule in favour of the bird. This will ensure that the minimum of stress is imposed and will not only increase the likelihood of the bird behaving normally on that occasion but will also increase the chances of its remaining in its favoured haunt and being available for further study. In addition, the reader must be reminded that, in order to safeguard the welfare of the species, it has been placed on the First Schedule of the Protection of Birds Act 1967, and this means that it is an offence even to visit its nesting site without first obtaining a special licence from the Nature Conservancy Council.

We have mentioned elsewhere that the Barn Owl is prone to desert its roost if disturbed, and the observer must make every effort to ensure that this does not happen. Knowledge of the individual bird's habits will help in this respect; for instance, once he learns the usual hunting times of a particular owl the observer can try to arrive and enter his hide while the bird is away. Great care should be taken during the period of egg-laying and during the week following, for this is possibly the most critical time of all. Unless disturbance is absolutely essential in order to obtain exact data, the birds should be left severely alone at this stage. Once the young are over the early stages more liberties may be taken, but even so the birds should not be exposed to undue interference, otherwise not only may their welfare be in jeopardy but unnatural behaviour may distort the information acquired.

When working at nest sites or roosts a hide will usually be necessary, for the beginner should not expect to encounter such obliging owls as those watched by D.S.B. from the comfort of an unconcealed chair! For watches inside buildings the standard canvas hide incorporating peep-holes on each side cannot be bettered, although we would recommend that only part of the peephole is used because of the need for maximum cover. As with most species, care must be taken in positioning and erecting the hide, and 3 m would seem to be the minimum working distance at a nest. Though many pairs will tolerate immediate erection of the hide, it is our policy to leave it in a collapsed state initially; on subsequent visits it can be heightened until ready for use. Even when this final stage is reached, if time permits it is a good idea to leave it unused for several days to give the birds chance to become accustomed to its presence. This minimises the possibility of accidental noises making the birds associate the hide with danger, for this might conceivably cause desertion. In our opinion the best time to begin hide erection is the week following the hatching of the last owlet, and if an observer wishes to carry out studies of the earlier stages of nesting it is essential that it is erected long before courtship starts. This means beginning in the winter months, because any attempt to erect a hide during the period of courtship will almost certainly result in the site being forsaken for another. The best policy by far, if this is possible, is to leave the hide in position from year to year. Needless to say, a hide should never be erected at a site where it might draw attention to the nest.

An aspect that is likely to be overlooked by the uninitiated is the necessity for as much comfort as the observer can arrange. Faced with late-night and all-night watches, an old blanket and comfortable seat with a back-rest will time and again prove blessings which will amply repay the trouble of transporting them to the hide. It is also worth remembering that as note-making will be in the dark and in the close presence of one of the world's best sound-detectors, note-books should be of the type which make little sound when the pages are turned. This very definitely rules out those with coiled spring spines as these make an infernal din in the hush of night.

If possible it should be arranged that the observer can emerge from the hide unseen by the owls, though they will inevitably be aware of the noise of his departure. It should be remembered that it is the natural instinct of the hen to sit tight in the face of disturbance, and so if the observer can leave unseen she may well stay on the nest. If a hidden exit is not possible, some device must be fixed which enables him to cause some noise *away from the hide* so that the hen may be flushed without drawing her attention to the hide and its occupant. This need only be a simple affair and A.B.W. used one such method successfully for several seasons. This consisted of a long rope stretching from the interior of the hide to a room below in which it was attached to a board upon which large stones were placed. By pulling gently on the rope it was easy to simulate the sound of a person moving about downstairs and after a few minutes of this the hen would slip quietly off her nest and leave the building without being unduly alarmed. The observer could then sneak away himself.

If, after all this, we still have a few devotees who are determined to study this species, let us cheer them up by asserting that they will never regret their decision. The hardships are real enough at times but the rewards are greater for any who are prepared to put up with a little discomfort. They will find themselves fortified not only by the knowledge that some of what they see is new, but also by experiencing indescribable excitement at the magical world of Nature when other people are asleep and the shy, secretive creatures of the night emerge. The quiet observer will share their lives and see aspects of behaviour which only the privileged few have seen before, and we are certain that once he has experienced the moments of expectancy before an adult owl returns to its nest, or the owlets emerge to play, that observer will remain – like us – an owl addict for the rest of his life.

References

Many books and papers have been consulted during the preparation of this book. Those quoted in the text are listed below, with the exception of those appertaining to folklore which are more appropriately mentioned within the chapter.

Aplin, O. V. 1889. *The Birds of Oxfordshire*. Oxford.
Armitage, J. S. 1968. A study of a Long-eared Owl roost. *Naturalist*, 905: 37–46.
Amstrong, E. A. 1958. *The folklore of Birds*. London.
Ash, J. 1954. Barn Owls roosting on stumps in a reed-bed. *Brit. Birds*, 47: 84.
Bannerman, D. A. & Bannerman, M. 1966. *Birds of the Atlantic Islands*, vol. 3. London and Edinburgh.
Barriety, L. 1965. Longévité des Oiseaux Bagúes. *Bull. Cert. Étud Rech. Scientr. Biarritz*.
Baudvin, H. 1975. Biologie de reproduction de la chouette effraie (*Tyto alba*) en Côte d'Or: Premiers Resultats. *Le Jean le Blanc*, 14: 1–51.
Bauer, K. 1956. Schleiereule (*Tyto alba* Scop.) als Fledermausjäger. *J. Ornith.*, 97: 335–340.
Baxter, E. V. & Rintoul, L. J. 1953. *The Birds of Scotland*. London and Edinburgh.
Behle, W. H. 1941. Barn Owls nesting at Kanab. *Condor*, 43: 160.
Bent, A. C. 1938. Life histories of North American birds of prey. Part II. *U.S. Nat. Mus. Bull.*, 1–482.
Bentham, H. 1962. Barn Owl sunbathing. *Brit. Birds*, 55: 482.
Blackman, R. 1965. Bristol University Seychelles Expedition. Part 7: Biological Control. *Animals*, vol. 8, No. 3. London.
Blaker, G. B. 1933. The Barn Owl in England. *Bird Notes and News*, vol. 15, Nos. 7 and 8: 169–172, 207–211.
Bodenheimer, F. S. 1949. Problems of vole populations in the Middle East. Report on the population dynamics of the Levant Vole (*Microtus guentheri*). *Res. Council Israel*. Jerusalem.
Bolen, E. G. 1977. Long-distance displacement of Two Southern Barn Owls. *Bird Banding*, 49: 78–79.
Boyd, E. & Shriner, J. 1954. Nesting and food of the Barn Owl (*Tyto alba*) in Hampshire County, Massachusetts. *Auk*, 71: 199–210.
Braaksma, S. & de Bruijn, O. 1976. Der kerkuilstand in Nederland. *Limosa*, 49: 135–87.
Brodkorb, P. 1971. Catalogue of Fossil Birds, vol. 4. *Bulletin of the Florida State Museum. Biological Sciences*, vol. 15. USA.
Brosset, A. 1956. Le regimen alimentaire de L'Effraye *Tyto alba*, an Maroc. Oriental. *Alauda*, 24: 161–205.
Brown, J. C. & Twigg, G. I. 1971. Mammalian prey of the Barn Owl (*Tyto alba*) on Skomer Island, Pembrokeshire. *Notes from the Mammal Society*, No. 23.
Brown, L. 1976. *British Birds of Prey*. London.
Brown, L. E. 1956. Field experiments on the activity of the small mammals *Apodemus, Clethrionomys* and *Microtus*. *Proc. Zool. Soc. London*, 126: 549–564.
Buckley, J. 1976. Barn Owl (*Tyto alba alba*) pellets from Portugal. *Bolm. Soc. Port. Cienc. nat.* 16: 133–136.

Bühler, P. 1964. Brutausfall bei der Schleiereule und die Frage nach dem Zeitgeber für das reproduktive System von *Tyto alba. Vogelwarte*, 22: 153–158.

Bühler, P. 1970. Schlupfhilfe-Verhalten bei der Schleiereule (*Tyto alba*). *Vogelwarte*, 91: 121–130.

Bühler, P. 1977. Zur Brutbiologie der Schleiereule. *Vogelwarte*, 1: 8–11.

Bühler, P. & Epple, W. 1980. Die Lautauferungen der Scleiereule (*Tyto alba*). *Journal fur Ornithologie*, 121: 36–70.

Bunn, D. S. 1972. Regular daylight hunting by Barn Owls. *Brit. Birds*, 65: 26–30

Bunn, D. S. 1974. The voice of the Barn Owl. *Brit. Birds*, 67: 493–501

Bunn, D. S. 1976. Eyesight of Barn Owl. *Brit. Birds*, 69: 120

Bunn, D. S. 1977. Voice of Barn Owl. *Brit. Birds*, 70: 171

Bunn, D. S. & Warburton, A. B. 1977. Observations on breeding Barn Owls. *Brit. Birds*, 70: 246–256

Burton, J. A. *et al.* 1973. *Owls of the World – their evolution, structure and ecology.* London.

Butler, A. E., Mathew, M. A. & Forbes, H. O. 1897. *British Birds with their Nests and Eggs.* London.

Buxton, J. & Lockley, R. M. 1950. *Island of Skomer.* London.

Cahn, A. R. & Kemp, J. T. 1930. On the food of certain owls in east central Illinois. *Auk*, 47: 323–324.

Callion, J. 1973. Barn Owls nesting close together. *Scottish Birds*, 7: 260.

Carpenter, M. L. & Fall, W. M. 1967. The Barn Owl as a Red-winged Blackbird predator in North-western Ohio. *Ohio J. Sci.*, 67: 317–318.

Chancellor, R. D. 1977. Report of the Proceedings of the World Conference on Birds of Prey, Vienna, 1–3 October 1975. *International Council for Bird Preservation.*

Chitty, D. 1938. A laboratory study of pellet formation in the Short-eared Owl *Asio flammeus. Proc. Zool. Soc. London*, 108: 267–287.

Coetzee, C. G. 1963. The prey of owls in the Kruger National Park as indicated by owl pellets collected during 1960–61. *Koedoe*, 6: 115–125.

Contoli, L. 1975. Micro-mammals and environment in central Italy. Data from *Tyto alba* pellets. *Bull. Zool.*, 42: 223–229.

Coombes, R. A. F. 1933. Barn Owls nesting in crags high up in Westmorland. *Brit. Birds*, 26: 309.

Cooper, J. E. & Eley, J. T. 1979. *First Aid and Care of Wild Birds.* Newton Abbot.

Coward, T. A. 1920. *The Birds of the British Isles and their Eggs*, series I. London.

Curtis, W. E. 1952. Quantitive Studies of Vision in Owls (*Tyto alba pratincola*). Unpublished Ph.D. dissertation. Cornell University, USA.

Davis, D. H. S. 1933. Rhythmic activity in the Short-tailed Vole *Microtus. J. Anim. Ecol.*, 2: 232–238.

Dickens, R. F. 1971. Late breeding of Barn Owl. *Leeds Naturalist*, 917: 71.

Dickson, R. C. 1972. Daylight hunting by Barn Owls. *Brit. Birds*, 65: 222–223.

Doersken, J. P. 1969. An analysis of Barn Owl pellets from Pitt Meadows, British Columbia. *Murrelet*, 50: 4–8.

Donovan, E. 1794–1819. *Natural History of British Birds.* London.

Dunn, P. J. 1979. Kestrel robbing Barn Owl. *Brit. Birds*, 72: 337.

Emeis, W. 1935. Massensterben von Schleiereulen in Schleswig-Holstein. *Orn. Monatsber.*, 43: 93–94.

Errington, P. L. 1932. Food habits of Southern Wisconsin raptors. *Condor*, 34: 176–186.

Evans, F. C. & Emlen, J. T. 1947. Ecological notes on the prey selected by a Barn Owl. *Condor*, 49: 3–9.

Everett, M. 1977. *A Natural History of Owls.* London.

Everett, M. J. 1968. Kestrel taking prey from Barn Owl. *Brit. Birds*, 61: 264.

Fairley, J. S. 1966. Analysis of Barn Owl pellets from an Irish roost. *Brit. Birds*, 59: 338–340.

Fellowes, E. C. 1967. Kestrel and Barn Owl sharing entrance to nest-sites. *Brit. Birds*, 60: 522.

Fernandez Cruz, M. & Garcia, M. P. 1971. *Tyto alba* alimentandose principalmente de *Sturnus unicolor*. *Ardeola*, 15: 146.

Fisher, A. K. 1893. Hawks and Owls of the United States in their relation to agriculture. *Dept. of Agriculture, Division of Ornithology and Mammology*, Bulletin No. 3. Washington, USA.

Fisher, J. 1951. *Bird Recognition*, vol. 2. Harmondsworth.

Fisher, J., Simon, N. & Vincent, J. 1969. *The Red Book*. London.

Fitch, H. S. 1947. Predation by Owls in the Sierran foothills of California. *Condor*, 49: 137–151.

Fitter, R. S. R. 1949. *London's Birds*. London.

Fitter, R. S. R. 1959. *Collin's Pocket Guide to Nests and Eggs*. London.

Fitter, R. S. R. *et al.* 1969. *Book of British Birds*. London.

Ford, N. L. 1967. A systematic study of the owls based on comparative osteology. Dissertation abstr., University of Michigan.

Frank, F. 1957. The causality of Microtine cycles in Germany. *Journal of Wildlife Management*, 21: 113–121.

Frylestam, B. 1972. Über Wanderungen und Sterblichkeit beringter Skandinavischer Schleiereulen *Tyto alba*. *Ornis. Scand.*, 3: 45–54.

Glue, D. E. 1967. Prey taken by the Barn Owl in England and Wales. *Bird Study*, 18: 137–146.

Glue, D. E. 1970a. Prey taken by Short-eared Owls at British breeding sites and winter quarters. *Bird Study*, 17: 39–42.

Glue, D. E. 1970b. Avian predator pellet analyses and the mammologist. *Mammal Review*, 1: 53–62.

Glue, D. E. 1971. Ringing recovery circumstances of small birds of prey. *Bird Study*, 18: 137–146.

Glue, D. E. 1972. Bird prey taken by British owls. *Bird Study*, 19: 91–95.

Glue, D. E. 1973. Seasonal mortality in four small birds of prey. *Ornis. Scand.*, 4: 97–102.

Glue, D. E. 1974. Food of the Barn Owl in Britain and Ireland. *Bird Study*, 21: 200–210.

Glue, D. E. 1977. Feeding ecology of the Short-eared Owl in Britain and Ireland. *Bird Study*, 24: 70–78.

Glue, D. E. (in prep.) Breeding Biology of the Barn Owl in Britain.

Glue, D. E. & Morgan, R. 1977. Recovery of bird rings in pellets and other prey traces of owls, hawks and falcons. *Bird Study*, 24: 111–113.

Gordon, S. 1955. *The Golden Eagle*. London.

Gooders, J. et al. 1970. Introduction to Fossil Birds (et seq.) by C. J. O. Harrison & C. Walker in *Birds of the World*. 9: 2857–2871. I.P.C., London.

Greenwood, A. 1977. The role of disease in the ecology of British raptors. *Bird Study*, 24: 259–265.

Grossman, M. L. & Hamlet, J. 1965. *Birds of Prey of the World*. London.

Guérin, G. 1928. *La vie des chouettes. Régime et croissance de l'effraye commune* (Tyto alba alba L) *en Vendée. Encyclopedie Ornithologique*. Paris.

Güttinger, H. 1965. Zur Wintersterblichkeit schweizerischer Schleiereulen *Tyto alba* mit besonokrer Berücksichtigung des Winters 1962/63. *Orn. Beob.*, 62: 14–23.

Hanney, P. 1962. Observations on the food of the Barn Owl (*Tyto alba*) in Southern Nyasaland, with a method of ascertaining population dynamics of rodent prey. *Ann. Mag. Nat. Hist.*, Ser. 13. 6: 305–313.

Haverschmidt, F. von 1962. Beobachtungen an der Schleiereule *Tyto alba* in Surinam. *Journal fur Ornithologie*, 103: 236–242.

Hawbecker, A. C. 1945. Food habits of the Barn Owl. *Condor*, 47: 161–166.

Heim de Balsac, H. & Maysaud, M. 1962. *Les Oiseaux du Nord-Ouest de l'Afrique*. Paris.

Heim de Balsac, H. 1965. Quelques enseignements d'ordre faunistique. Tirés de l'étude du régime alimentaire de *Tyto alba* dans l'ouest de L'Afrique. *Alauda*, 33(4): 309–322.

Heim de Balsac, H. & de Beaufort, F. 1966. Régime alimentaire de l'Effraye dans le Bas Dauphine. *Alauda*, 34: 309–324.

Heinroth, O. & Heinroth, K. 1958. *The Birds*. Ann Arbor, USA.

Heintzelman, D. S. 1966. Distribution and population density of Barn Owls in Lehigh and Northampton Counties, Pennsylvania. *Cassinia*, 49: 2–19.

Henny, C. J. 1969. Geographical variation in mortality rates and production requirements of the Barn Owl (*Tyto alba* ssp.). *Bird Banding*, 40: 277–290.

Henwood, P. 1954. Barn Owl: Breeding records. *Brit. Birds*, 47: 31.

Herrera, C. M. 1973. Regimen alimenticio de *Tyto alba* en España Sudo occidental. *Ardeola*, 19: 359–394.

Herrera, C. M. 1974. Trophic diversity of the Barn Owl *Tyto alba* in continental western Europe. *Ornis. Scand.*, 5: 181–191.

Hibbert-Ware, A. 1936. Report of an investigation of the food of captive Little Owls. *Brit. Birds*, 29: 302–305.

Honer, M. R. 1963. Observations on the Barn Owl (*Tyto alba guttata*) in the Netherlands in relation to its ecology and population fluctuations. *Ardea*, 51: 158–195.

Hosking, E. J. 1970. *An Eye for a Bird*. London.

Hosking, E. J. & Smith, S. 1943. Display in the Barn Owl. *Brit. Birds*, 37: 55–56.

Hosking, E. J. & Newberry, C. W. 1945. *Birds of the Night*. London.

Howard, W. E. 1951. Relation between low temperature and available food to survival of small rodents. *J. Mammal.*, 32: 300.

Ingram, C. 1959. The importance of juvenile cannibalism in the breeding of certain birds of prey. *Auk*, 76: 218–226.

Ijzendoorn, A. L. J. van. 1948. Sterfte onder Kerkuilen, *Tyto alba* (Scopoli). *Limosa*, 21: 135–138.

Jourdain, F. C. R. & Witherby, H. F. 1917. The effects of the winter of 1916/17 on our resident birds – part I. *Brit. Birds* 11: 266–271.

Jourdain, F. C. R. & Witherby, H. F. 1918. The effects of the winter of 1916/17 on our resident birds – Part II. *Brit. Birds*, 12: 26–35.

Kaufman, D. W. 1973. Captive Barn Owls stockpile prey. *Bird Banding*, 44: 225.

Keith, A. R. 1964. A thirty year summary of the nesting of the Barn Owl in Martha's Vineyard, Massachusetts. *Bird Banding*, 35: 22–31.

Kennedy, R. J. 1979. A nest-box study of Barn Owls (*Tyto alba*). *Bird Ringing in SW Lancashire*, 9: 18–53.

Kingsley, J. S. ed. 1885. *Natural History of Birds*. Boston, USA.

Kirkman, F. B. & Jourdain, F. C. R. 1938. *British Birds*. London.

Knight, M. 1956. *Animals after Dark*. London.

Kolbe, F. F. 1946. The case for the Barn Owl. *African Wildlife*, 1: 69–73.

Konishi, M. 1973. How the owl tracks his prey. *Amer. Sci.*, 61: 414–424.

Lack, D. 1947. The significance of clutch size. Part I: Intra-specific variations. *Ibis*, 89: 302–352.

Lack, D. 1956. *Swifts in a Tower*. London.

Lack, D. 1966. *Population Studies of Birds*. Oxford.

Lack, D. 1968. *Ecological Adaptations for Breeding in Birds*. London.

Laurie, W. A. 1971. The food of the Barn Owl in the Serengeti National Park, Tanzania. *J. E. Afr. Natur. Hist. Soc. and Natur. Museum*, 28: 1–4.

Lindeborg, R. G. 1952. Water requirements of certain rodents from Xeric and Mesic habitats. *Contrib. Lab. Vert. Biol.*, *Univ. Michigan*, 58: 1.

Lockley, R. M. 1970. *The Naturalist in Wales*. Newton Abbot.

Lodge, R. B. 1903. *Pictures of Bird Life on Woodland, Meadow Mountain and Marsh.* London.

Lovari, S. 1974. The feeding habits of four raptors in Central Italy. *Raptor Research*, 8: 45–57.

Lovari, S., Renzoni, A. & Fondi, R. 1976. The predatory habits of the Barn Owl (*Tyto alba*) in relation to the vegetation cover. *Bull. Zool.*, 43: 173–191.

Luttringer, L. A. 1930. Great Horned Owl vs. Barn Owl. *Auk*, 47: 84.

MacNally, L. 1970. *Highland Deer Forest.* London.

MacPherson, H. A. 1892. *A Vertebrate Fauna of Lakeland.* Edinburgh.

MacWorth-Praed, C. W. & Grant, C. H. B. 1970. *Handbook of African Birds.* London.

Marti, C. D. 1969. Re-nesting of Barn and Great Horned Owls. *Wilson Bulletin*, 81: 467–468.

Marti, C. D. 1969. Some comparisons of the feeding ecology of four owls in North Central Colorado. *Southwest Natur.*, 14(2): 163–170.

Marti, C. D. 1973. Food consumption and pellet formation rates in four owl species. *Wilson Bulletin*, 85: 178–181.

Marti, C. D. 1974. Feeding ecology of four sympatric owls. *Condor*, 76: 45–61.

Martin, D. J. 1973. Burrow digging by Barn Owls. *Bird Banding*, 44: 59–60.

Massey, C. I. 1971. Prey taken by a Barn Owl. *Leeds Naturalist*, 920: 11–13.

Medway, L. & Yong, G. 1970. Barn Owl pellets from Kulai, Johore. *Malay Nat. J.*, 23: 171–172.

Merriam, F. A. 1896. Some birds of Southern California. *Auk*, 13: 117.

Mikkola, H. 1976. Owls killing and killed by other owls and raptors in Europe. *Brit. Birds*, 69: 144–154.

Mitchell, J., Placido, C. & Rose, R. 1974. Notes on a Short-tailed Vole plague at Eskdalemuir, Dumfriesshire. *Trans. Dumf. and Gall. Nat. H. and Antiq. Soc.* II: 11–13.

Moffatt, C. B. 1940. The notes of the Barn Owl. *Irish Naturalists' Journal*, 7: 289–292.

Moltoni, E. 1937. Observations on the food of Italian birds of prey. *Riv. Ital. Ornitol.*, 15: 13–33, 61–109.

Montgomery, T. H. (Jnr.) 1899. Observations on owls, with particular reference to their feeding habits. *Amer. Nat.*, 33: 563–576.

Moon, E. L. 1940. Notes on hawk and owl pellet formation and identification. *Trans. Kansas Academy Science*, 43: 437–461.

Moore, N. W. 1965. Pesticides and birds – a review of the situation in Great Britain in 1965. *Bird Study*, 12: 222–252.

Mountfort, G. 1957. *The Hawfinch.* London.

Mueller, H. C. & Berger, D. D. 1959. Some long-distance Barn Owl recoveries. *Bird Banding*, 30: 182.

Nader, I. A. 1969. Animal remains in pellets of the Barn Owl (*Tyto alba*) from the vicinity of An-Najaf, Iraq. *Bull. Iraq Natur. Hist. Mus.*, 5(1): 1–7.

Nice, M. M. 1954. Problems of incubation periods in North American birds. *Condor*, 54(4): 173–197.

Norberg, R. A. 1973. Ear asymmetry and owl taxonomy. *Phil. Trans. R. Soc. London*, 375–408.

Oakes, C. 1953. *The Birds of Lancashire.* London and Edinburgh.

Otteni, L. C., Bolen, E. G. & Cottam, C. 1972. Predator-prey relationship and reproduction of the Barn Owl in southern Texas. *Wilson Bull.*, 48: 434–448.

Parslow, J. 1973. *Breeding Birds of Britain and Ireland.* Berkhamsted.

Payne, R. 1971. Acoustic location of prey by Barn Owls (*Tyto alba*). *J. Exp. Biol.*, 54: 535–573.

Peters, J. L. 1940. *Checklist of the Birds of the World*, vol. IV. Cambridge, Mass., USA.

Phillips, R. S. 1951. Food of the Barn Owl (*Tyto alba pratincola*) in Hancock County, Ohio. *Auk*, 68: 239–241.

Pickwell, G. 1948. Barn Owl growth and behaviourisms. *Auk*, 65: 339–373.

Piechocki, R. 1960. Über die Winterverluste bei Schleiereulen (*Tyto alba*). *Vogelwarte*, 20: 274–280.

Piechocki, R. 1961. Über die Grossgefieder – Mauser von Schleiereule und Waldkauz. *J. Orn. Lpz.*, 102: 220–225.

Pile, C. G. 1958. The Barn Owl. *Bulletin of the Societe Jersiaise*, 17: 187–190.

Potter, J. K. & Gillespie, J. A. 1925. Observations on the domestic behaviour of the Barn Owl *Tyto alba pratincola*. *Auk*, 42: 177–192.

Prestt, I. 1965. An enquiry into the recent breeding status of some smaller birds of prey and crows in Britain. *Bird Study*, 12: 196–221.

Prestt, I. & Bell, A. A. 1966. An objective method of recording breeding distribution of common birds of prey in Britain. *Bird Study*, 13: 277–283.

Pycraft, W. P. 1910. *A History of Birds*. London.

Ratcliffe, E. J. 1977. Traffic casualties, Barn Owls on the decline. *Wildlife*, 19, No. 8: 362–363.

Ratcliffe, E. J. 1979. *Fly High, Run Free*. London.

Reed, J. H. 1897. Notes on the American Barn Owl in eastern Pennsylvania. *Auk*, 14: 374–383.

Robinson, A. & Wilton, S. 1973. Owl imprints on window panes. *Bird Study*, 20: 143–144.

Rogers Brambell, E. W. 1970. *Voles and Field Mice*. Forestry Commission leaflet No. 44. HMSO.

Rothschild, M. & Clay, T. 1952. *Fleas, Flukes and Cuckoos*. London.

Ruprecht, A. L. 1979. Bats (*Chiroptera*) as constituents of the food of Barn Owls *Tyto alba* in Poland. *Ibis*, 121: 489–494.

Sage, B. L. 1962. Barn Owls catching sparrows at roost. *Brit. Birds*, 55: 237–238.

Saint Girons, M. C. & Martin, C. 1973. Adaptations du régime de quelques rapaces nocturnes au paysage rural. Les proies de l'effraye et du Moyen-Duc dans le department de la Somme. *Bull. Ecol.*, 4: 95–120.

Sauter, U. 1955. Beringungsergebnisse an den Schleiereulen *Tyto alba* des Neckarraumes. *Jh. Ver. vaterl. Naturk. Württemb.*, 109: 153–165.

Sauter, U. 1956. Beiträge zur Ökologie der Schleiereule (*Tyto alba*) nach den Ringfunden. *Vogelwarte*, 18: 109–151.

Schifferli, A. 1957. Alter und Sterblichkeit bei Waldkauz (*Strix aluco*) und Schleiereule (*Tyto alba*) in der Schweiz. *Orn. Beob.*, 54: 50–56.

Schneider, W. 1937. Beringungs-Ergebnisse an der Mitteleuropaeischen Schleiereule (*Tyto alba guttata* Brehm). *Vogelzug.*, 8: 159–170.

Scott, D. 1979. Long-eared and other owls taking Moorhens. *Brit. Birds*, 72: 436.

Sharrock, J. T. R. 1976. *The Atlas of Breeding Birds in Britain and Ireland*. Berkhamsted.

Sibley, C. G. 1960. The electrophoretic patterns of avian egg-white proteins as taxonomic characters. *Ibis*, 102: 215–284.

Smith, D. G. & Marti, C. D. 1976. Distributional status and ecology of Barn Owls in Utah. *Raptor Research*, 10: 33–44.

Smith, C. R. & Richmond, M. E. 1972. Factors influencing pellet egestion and gastric pH in the Barn Owl. *Wilson Bulletin*, 84: 179–186.

Snow, D. W. 1967. A Guide to Moult in British Birds. *British Trust for Ornithology, Field Guide No. 11*.

Southern, H. N. 1954. Tawny Owls and their prey. *Ibis*, 99: 384–410.

Sparks, J. & Soper, T. 1970. *Owls – their Natural and Unnatural History*. Newton Abbot.

Stanley, E. 1838. *A Familiar History of Birds*, vol. I. London.

Stellbogen, E. 1930. Über das Äussere und Mittlere Ohr des Waldkauzes (*Syrnium aluco* l). *Zeitschrift Morphologie und Ökologie Tiene*, 19: 686–731.

Stewart, P. A. 1952. Dispersal, breeding behaviour and longevity of banded Barn Owls in North America. *Auk*, 69: 227–245.

Stone, W. 1937. Bird studies at Old Cape May. *Del. Valley Ornith. Club, Phila.*, 2: 521–541.

Stokoe, R. 1962. *Birds of the Lake Counties*. Carlisle Natural History Society.

Straton, R. A. 1967. Barn Owl perching on man. *Brit. Birds*, 60: 253.

Stresemann, E. & Stresemann, V. 1966. Die Mauser der Vögel. *J. Orn.*, *107*, *Supplement 1*.

Tegetmeier, W. B. 1890. *The Field*. LXXV, 1956: 906.

Thiollay, J. M. 1968. Le régime alimentaire de nos rapaces: quelques analyses francais. No. 3. *Oiseaux*, 319: 249–269.

Thorpe, W. H. & Griffin, D. R. 1962. The lack of ultrasonic components in the flight noise of owls compared with other birds. *Ibis*, 104: 256–257.

Ticehurst, C. B. 1935. On the food of the Barn Owl and its bearing on Barn Owl populations. *Ibis*, 2: 329–335.

Trollope, J. 1971. Some aspects of behaviour and reproduction in captive Barn Owls. *Aviculture Magazine*, 77: 117–125.

Uttendorfer, O. 1952. *Neue Ergebnisse liber die Ernährung der Greifvogel und Eulen*. Stuttgart.

Valverde, J. A. 1967. Estructura de una comunidad de vertebrados terrestres. *Cons. Sup. Invest. Cient. Madrid*.

Vaurie, C. 1960 Systematic Notes on *Strigidae*. *Amer. Mus. Novitates*, No. 2021: 17–19.

Vaurie, C. 1965. *The Birds of the Palearctic Fauna*. London.

Verheyen, R. F. 1968. La Mortalité de la Chouette effraie en Belgique. *Bull. Res. Nat. et Orn., Belg.*, 49–58.

Vernon, C. J. 1972. An analysis of owl pellets collected in South Africa. *Ostrich*, 43: 109–124.

Voous, K. H. 1960. *Atlas of European Birds*. London.

Wallace, G. J. 1948. The Barn Owl in Michigan. *Tech. Bulletin 208. Michigan State College*.

Warham, J. 1951. *Birdwatcher's Delight*. London.

Waterton, C. 1838. *Essays on Natural History*. London.

Watson, D. 1977. *The Hen Harrier*. Berkhamstead.

Wayne, A. T. 1934. A death trap to the American Barn Owl (*Tyto pratincola*). *Auk*, 41: 342.

Webster, J. A. 1973. Seasonal variation in mammal contents of Barn Owl castings. *Bird Study*, 20: 185–196.

Williams, W. J. 1917. Mortality among Barn Owls in Ireland. *Brit. Birds*, 11: 21–22.

Williamson, K. 1965. *Fair Isle and its Birds*. London and Edinburgh.

Wilson, V. J. 1970. Notes on the breeding and feeding habits of a pair of Barn Owls *Tyto alba* (Scopoli) in Rhodesia. *Arnoldia*, 4: 1–7.

Witherby, H. F., Jourdain, F. C. R. Ticehurst, N. F. & Tucker, B. W. 1940. *The Handbook of British Birds*, Vol II, 1943 revision. London.

Yalden, D. W. 1977. The identification of remains in owl pellets. *Mammal Society, Reading*.

Yalden, D. W. & Warburton, A. B. 1979. The diet of the Kestrel in the Lake District. *Bird Study*, 26: 163–170.

Zelenka, G. & Pricam, R. 1974. Variations d'effectifs des populations de petits mammifères revelées par le régime alimentaire d'un rapace nocturne. *Terre et Vie* III: 178–184.

Index

Where known, only the English names of the vertebrates have been included here. Their scientific names may be found in Appendix 1.